Catholic Perspectives on Crime and Criminal Justice

Catholic Perspectives on Crime and Criminal Justice

WILLARD M. OLIVER

LEXINGTON BOOKS

A division of
ROWMAN & LITTLEFIELD PUBLISHERS, INC.
Lanham • Boulder • New York • Toronto • Plymouth, UK

LEXINGTON BOOKS

A division of Rowman & Littlefield Publishers, Inc.
A wholly owned subsidiary of The Rowman & Littlefield Publishing Group, Inc.
4501 Forbes Boulevard, Suite 200
Lanham, MD 20706

Estover Road
Plymouth PL6 7PY
United Kingdom

British Library Cataloguing in Publication Information Available

Library of Congress Cataloging-in-Publication Data

Oliver, Willard M.
   Catholic perspectives on crime and criminal justice / Willard M. Oliver.
      p. cm.
   ISBN-13: 978-0-7391-1747-7 (cloth : alk. paper)
   ISBN-10: 0-7391-1747-5 (cloth : alk. paper)
   1. Christianity and justice—Catholic Church. 2. Criminology—Religious aspects—
Christianity. 3. Crime—Religious aspects—Christianity. 4. Criminal justice,
Administration of—United States. I. Title.
   BX1795.J87O45 2008
   261.8'33088282—dc22   2008000630

Printed in the United States of America

♾™ The paper used in this publication meets the minimum requirements of American
National Standard for Information Sciences—Permanence of Paper for Printed Library
Materials, ANSI/NISO Z39.48–1992.

Dedication

To Donald P. Fellers.

A good man, a good Catholic, and a good friend.

Requiescat in Pace.

Prayer

Saint Michael, the Archangel, defend us in battle.
Be our defense against the wickedness and snares of the devil.
May God rebuke him, we humbly pray;
and do Thou, O Prince of the Heavenly Host, by the Power of God,
thrust into hell Satan, and all the evil spirits,
who prowl about the world, seeking the ruin of souls.
Amen.

Table of Contents

Preface

We are still a long way from the time when our conscience can be certain of having done everything to prevent crime and to control it effectively so that it no longer does harm and, at the same time, to offer to those who commit crimes a way of redeeming themselves and making a positive return to society. If all those in some way involved in the problem tried to . . . develop this line of thought, perhaps humanity as a whole could take a great step forward in creating a more serene and peaceful society.

-Pope John Paul II, July 9, 2000-

In the Spring of 1995, after a long intellectual journey, I was Baptized and Confirmed into the Roman Catholic Church. A year earlier I had switched careers, from that of police officer to college professor, giving me much time to think and reflect on my life. As I grew both in my faith and in my role as a professor of criminal justice, I was influenced by a number of individuals who were strong in their Catholic faith. One most can readily identify is Pope John Paul II. I remember him on numerous occasions speaking to the faithful to not separate their work from their faith. Pope John Paul II made a passionate assertion that we must always be Catholic in all that we do, including the numerous hours we spend in the workplace.

I pondered how that would apply to me, when my profession seemed so far removed from my faith. In some of the gospel readings, I noticed a lot of discussion of the concepts of justice and the law. Over time I paid more attention to the teachings of Jesus as they related to crime and justice, ranging from his dealings with the death penalty (e.g., the prostitute who the Pharisees and Scribes wanted stoned to death) and with those sentenced to prison (e.g., "I was in prison, and you visited me."). I then began contemplating what a criminal justice system, based on the faith of God, Christ, and the Church, would look like. When working on my book on community policing, I came across numerous references to the concepts of restorative and community justice, and felt that they might somehow reflect a Catholic perspective of justice. Looking to community policing for the police, victim-offender mediation programs for the courts, and community-based corrections for corrections solidified my belief that this might be the answer to how the criminal justice based system could adhere to Catholic teachings.

Although these thoughts stayed with me, completing the Ph.D. in political science at West Virginia University, writing books and journal articles, and raising a young family gave me little time to develop this concept more fully. Then in 2000, two things happened. One, I completed my Ph.D. which freed up an amazing amount of time. Second, the United States Conference of Catholic Bishops published a short statement titled *Responsibility, Rehabilitation, and Restoration: A Catholic Perspective on Crime and Criminal Justice*. It fit exactly into what I had been thinking the previous five years, so much so that I was at once elated and depressed. Elated to see that my thinking was in line with the Bishops. Depressed to learn that the Bishops had beat me to the publication. However, then I began considering the Bishops' statement and not so much what was there, but rather, what was missing. It was, in my impression, a skeletal structure of a call for reform in the criminal justice system, but it had no depth. Expanding the Bishops' statement into a more complete understanding of a Catholic perspective of crime and justice became the impetus for this book.

Acknowledgments

The author would first like to acknowledge and thank all of those people who were instrumental in bringing him into the Catholic faith, not by word but by deed. The first is Pope John Paul II, clearly a role model whose Catholic faith, as exemplified in his actions, travels, and engagement of public policy on the world stage, influenced this author. The second is my wife, and Godmother, who never pressured me on the Catholic faith, but simply tried hard to live her faith. Her actions spoke to me stronger than any words she could have ever delivered. Third, I must acknowledge my wife's parents, Donald and Ilaria Fellers, for demonstrating to me the beauty of a strong and lasting Catholic marriage. Don died during the writing of this book, June 30, 2006, and with his death I lost a good role model and friend; that is why I have dedicated this book in his memory. Finally, I want to thank some friends who also had a great influence on me, again solely by deed, showing me the beauty of a good, happy, and strong Catholic family, and they are Michael and Stephanie Caulfield. And I would be remiss if I did not acknowledge their children: Maria, Joseph, Catherine, Stephen, Teresa, Timothy, Peter, Thomas, and Clare.

There have also been a number of people that have proven instrumental in helping me work out the technical aspects of writing this book. I am gratefully indebted to Diane Dowdey, the Director of the Sam Houston State University Writing Center, as well as all the staff, for proofing my work. The resources provided by the Writing Center have been invaluable, and I truly appreciate your assistance. I also would like to thank Harriet Brewster and Chris Fisher of the publication office of the College of Criminal Justice at Sam Houston State University for helping me with the further editing and formatting of the book. Their work and dedication greatly improved the final product. However, while I am indebted to all of the assistance I have received, I readily acknowledge that any mistakes are mine and mine alone.

Finally, I am greatly indebted to those at Lexington Books that made my thoughts and ideals become a reality. I appreciate the kind words and encouragement provided to me by the acquisitions editor, Jim Langford. During the writing of this book I learned that Jim retired from Lexington Books. I wish you all the best in your retirement. In addition, the publisher at Lexington Books has proven both kind and helpful, and so I must acknowledge Jon Sisk. Finally, I would like to thank Julie Kirsch and Tricia Knight for their kind assistance in helping me finalize the final manuscript. Their kindness highlights the quality and professionalism of all those who work at Lexington Books, and for this, I am most grateful.

Introduction

This book does not try to emulate the Bishop's publication *Responsibility, Rehabilitation, and Restoration: A Catholic Perspective on Crime and Criminal Justice.* Rather it incorporates many of their thoughts and reflections into the book, but organizes itself in a vastly different way. The book is divided into three sections: Justice, Criminal Justice, and Criminal Justice Issues. In the first section, the book will deal with those issues that underlie our contemporary criminal justice system and what should be the underlying tenets based on the Catholic faith. To this end, the first chapter deals with the concepts of justice, both as implied throughout the scholarly field of philosophy and within the Catholic Church. It then discusses how the basis of justice from the Catholic perspective would influence the criminal justice system.

In the second chapter, criminal justice is first defined as consisting of police, courts, and corrections, and how it works to address the problem of crime and disorder in modern society. A discussion of how criminal justice functions today in America is presented, and the suggestion that from a Catholic perspective, criminal justice should emphasize the tenets of restorative and community justice is presented. These two concepts are then explored with more depth in the third chapter and their concepts tied to the Catholic teachings.

The second section on criminal justice is divided into three chapters with each chapter discussing one component of the criminal justice system and how it would reform to reflect Catholic teaching. Chapter four relates how the police would organize under the philosophy and strategies of community policing. The fifth chapter, related to the courts, advocates a more community justice orientation for the courts through various community outreach programs. In addition, non-governmental community mediation programs would be established that would allow for neighborhood justice to be the first course of action, avoiding the more formal criminal justice altogether. Finally, chapter six, on community-based corrections, advocates for moving the corrections system from the traditional punishment orientation that relies heavily on imprisonment, to alternative methods that work to keep the offender closer to the community in order to make an easier transition back to society when the offender's sentence is completed.

The third and final section looks to various criminal justice issues and how a Catholic perspective to crime and justice would deal with these particular issues. The seventh chapter discusses the death penalty, which is clearly a criminal justice issue of great debate, and in this chapter, the Catholic doctrine as it relates to the death penalty is applied to modern American application of executions. The eighth chapter looks at two divisive public policy issues in America, abortion and euthanasia, both of which are generally considered largely outside of the criminal justice system, and discusses how these two issues would be handled from a Catholic perspective on justice. Finally, the last chapter, chapter nine, presents a collection of what are often referred to as "victimless crimes," such as prostitution, pornography, and drugs, and discusses why from a Catholic perspective, these behaviors, even among consenting adults, would be illegal.

Part One

Justice

Chapter 1

Justice

"I, the Lord, have called you for the victory of justice, I have grasped you by the hand; I formed you, and set you as a covenant of the people, a light for the nations."

- Isaiah 42:6 -

Introduction

In order to have a deeper understanding regarding Catholic perspectives of crime and criminal justice, it is imperative that one has an understanding of the central concept that lies at the root of our legal and criminal justice system: Justice. Every person has a desire for and cares about justice. Those that are young seek justice when they play games and urge their friends to "play fair." Those who are old may seek justice if they feel that they are being treated differently because of their age. Those that are religious seek justice in the world so that God's will is done on earth. And those that profess no religion still seek justice through the court system based on the rule of law. Even those who profess to be moral relativists, claiming that one cannot be judgmental of others, find themselves demanding that justice be served in the wake of the attacks on the World Trade Center or when a child has been raped and murdered. Yet, while nearly everyone seeks justice, not everyone understands the concept of justice in the same way.

When a person commits a crime, most people will argue that justice must be served, but they may differ on what they mean. One may argue that anyone who steals should be arrested and prosecuted, even those that are poor, starving, and steal food to live. Likewise, they may also argue that it should not matter if you are famous or rich, such as Martha Stewart, who used her powerful position to conduct insider trading, because, regardless, it still amounts to stealing. In this case, stealing from those who were not privy to the insider information. In both cases, the person is arguing that it is only fair when justice is served regardless

3

of stature or circumstances. Another, however, may argue that justice is served in both of these cases only if the criminal justice system is impartial and that politics do not enter into the prosecution. Many have argued that Martha Stewart should have been found not guilty, but because the system was not impartial toward her, she was convicted and sentenced to prison. Yet, still others may argue that in order for justice to be served, there has to exist a sense of equality in that both the starving thief and Martha Stewart should be afforded the same protections, the same level of legal representation, and the same deference to their cases, and only then, can it be said that justice was served, regardless of the outcomes. In both cases, justice was sought, but in both cases, justice is perceived, and achieved, very differently.

Justice, in the Catholic faith, brings in yet another perspective. From the Catholic viewpoint, justice is based on the Word of God, the teaching of Jesus Christ, and the Traditions of the Roman Catholic Church. Catholic faith is concerned with justice, and in many ways, it is a central theme throughout scripture and found most decisively in the Ten Commandments and the Beatitudes. In fact, when Micah the prophet spoke to his people, he told them very succinctly what they were required by the Lord to do when he stated:

You have been told, O man, what is good, and what the Lord requires of you: Only to do right and to love goodness, and to walk humbly with your God (Micah 6:8).

In this passage, Micah is saying we are to do good, to do what is right, and what is just in our daily lives, for as Saint Augustine drawing from the discussion in Plato's *Republic* once said, "how like kindgoms without justice are to robberies."[1] Micah further states we must love goodness, not what is bad, evil, or wrong. Thus, in order to do what is right and just, we must do what is good, for this is what God wants of His people. Finally, Micah tells us we are to walk humbly with the Lord, which means that we are to follow God, and in doing so, we will do what is right, good, and just. Therefore, justice is the key to righteous living, and it is justice, from a Catholic perspective, which we must understand first in order to understand what criminal justice from a Catholic perspective portends.

Thus, in order to understand justice, and particularly criminal justice, from a Catholic perspective, one must take a broader and more holistic view of how justice is perceived in both the secular and non-secular worlds. The concept of "justice" is largely derived from an understanding of ethics, morals, and virtues. From this, we come to understand how the many definitions and perspectives of the word "justice" are thus derived. Once we have a more holistic view of the term "justice," we can then explore the Catholic perspective of justice, and explore more fully what is meant by "criminal *justice*." It is, therefore, the intent of this chapter to walk the reader through these various concepts with the final goal being the development of an understanding for how criminal justice under the Catholic perspective of justice would begin to differ, if at all, from the more contemporary and secular understanding.

Ethics

When someone discusses ethics, they often use the word "moral" and "ethics" interchangeably, as if they had the same meaning. The word ethics is derived from the Greek word "ethikos," which can be defined as "character." In this sense, the term deals with a person's moral character and whether they exhibit good or bad conduct. The related term "moral" comes from a Latin root with a similar meaning that has become much more defined over time. Ethics, today, can be more readily defined as the study and analysis of what constitutes good and bad behavior.[2] It is essentially the attempt to study behavior and determine what is right and what is wrong. At its core, as Professor Sam Souryal explains, it is the search for truth.[3] Turning back to the term "moral," this is then defined as having the capacity to know right from wrong, but more on this later. For now, let it suffice that ethics is the study of right and wrong.

The study of ethics has expanded greatly over time and has created a variety of "schools" of ethics. These have developed based on various theories of ethics. Ethical theory is essentially the attempt to develop a view of how the world works from an ethical perspective. It does this to introduce general principles that reduce the complexity of the world and help us more easily understand the study of ethics. It also does this to allow those who study ethics to constantly test theories, determining their validity and, ultimately, their truth. In addition, these world views also help us understand the world we live in by providing the principles which we can draw from when faced with a new and difficult ethical situation. For instance, thirty years ago, the ability to clone an animal was the work of science fiction. Today it has become a reality, and there is great trepidation that tomorrow it will be a human that is cloned. Ethical theory and its principles allow us to process a new ethical dilemma by drawing upon general principles that apply in all situations. Moreover, ethical theory also gives us a means by which to educate the next generation in order that they may continue the study of what constitutes good and bad behavior.

Ethical theories tend to have certain characteristics about them. These include, first, that they are prescriptive, as certain behaviors are demanded or proscribed. They are not just abstract principles of good and bad, but rather have substantial impact on what people do. Second, they are authoritative, as they are not ordinarily subject to debate. Once an ethical framework has been developed, it is usually beyond question. Third, moral considerations arising from ethical systems are logically impartial and universal. If something is considered wrong, it is wrong for everyone. Relativism has no place in an ethical framework. Finally, they are not self-serving. They are directed toward others by detailing that

5

what is good is good for everyone, not just the individual.[4] Despite ethical theories tending to share these characteristics, they do not all share the same beliefs or perspectives on what is right and wrong behavior. Because people have varying views of how the world works, ethical theory has many views on how ethics should be studied, giving us a number of branches or categories of ethics.

Ethical theories have traditionally been divided into two major categories: meta-ethics and normative ethics.[5] Meta-ethics has been defined as "the highly technical discipline investigating the meaning of ethical terms including a critical study of how ethical statements can be verified."[6] Meta-ethics will often analyze the specific words being used in an argument, and the meaning behind the terms as related to field of ethics. In a sense, it is the ethical version of English Semiotics which looks to understand how meaning is made and understood. Further, meta-ethics also delve into the logical arguments made in ethics in order to understand the reasoning and justifications used in various moral judgments. While there are benefits from this approach, it is a highly cognitive and abstract approach to the study of ethics, thus most perspectives of ethics and ethical theory tend to fall into the category of normative ethics.

Normative ethics deals with the formulation of moral standards of behavior and articulates the principles that govern such conduct. While ethics as a whole is concerned with right and wrong behavior, normative ethics is concerned with right and wrong behavior as it applies in certain situations. It does this by establishing moral norms as guidelines for good moral behavior, by proposing and evaluating moral conduct, and by establishing moral duties.[7] More specifically, normative ethics is concerned with what people *ought* to do, and, conversely, what they ought *not* do. It also looks at the type of relations people ought to pursue in order to lead a moral life and what behaviors, when exhibited, are considered worthy behaviors. Thus, normative ethics looks to terms such as "good" and "bad" or "right" and "wrong" in order to state when behaviors are considered ethical or unethical. To this end, normative ethics asks a series of questions in order to address these types of issues: "(1) What should I do?; (2) What characteristics of people are morally good or bad?; (3) How should society be organized and what specific policies should various agencies pursue?; (4) What is a good life and what experiences are considered worthwhile or desirable?; (5) How can people choose among a hierarchy of values, especially conflicting ones?; and (6) What is the profile of the ethical person?"[8] These questions are typically what is explored within the category of normative ethics.

Within normative ethics, however, there is another division: the subcategories of deontological and teleological theory.[9] This major division analyzes right and wrong behavior by either looking specifically at the behavior itself (deontological) or at the consequences this behavior brings (teleological). For instance, in the case of an abortion, a person who explores ethics from a deontological perspective would analyze whether or not the action of having an abortion is good or bad behavior, whereas the teleological theorist would look at the consequences of having had the abortion in order to determine if an abortion is right or wrong behavior. Another way of looking at this division is that deontology explores that which leads to an ethical situation, while teleology explores the outcomes of an ethical choice. With this in mind, it can also be said that if an act is considered good, but results in bad consequences, the behavior is still considered right behavior (deontological); if an act is bad, but results in good consequences, the behavior can be said to be good (teleological). Because this is a very important distinction in understanding normative ethics, these two perspectives will be explored more deeply.

Deontological is based on the Greek root *deontos* meaning duty or obligation, thus deontology has also been termed obligation theory. Because it is based on duty and obligation, deontological theorists judge behavior to be right and wrong based on the act itself, hence motivation, intent, and the consequences of the act do not matter. What matters is that the act itself was right or wrong. Returning to the characteristics of ethical theories described earlier, deontological theories are prescriptive. They describe right and wrong behaviors. They are also authoritative in that these behaviors are always right or always wrong. Moreover, they are universal in that they are right or wrong anywhere, everywhere, and at all times. Finally, they should never be self-serving.

These characteristics are what help determine right and wrong behavior and they are often based on a specific moral principle, sometimes several, that guides the deontological theorists to arrive at their understanding of ethical behavior. Because some deontological theorists believe there is only one singular moral principle or value, while others believe it may be more than one, there is yet another sub-categorization and that is monistic and dualistic/pluralistic categories. Monistic theorists believe that there is one, and only one principle that guides all ethical behavior. At one extreme you may have the hedonist who believes that pleasure is the one and only good, while at another extreme there is Kant who believed that the one and only obligation in life is duty. In the case of the dualist, they believe that there can be more than one guiding principle that determines right and wrong behavior and that these must be balanced. Combining the two extremes could result in a dualist who believes that one must adhere to the principle of hedonism, thus seeking pleasure, but not at the expense of duty. Hence, they seek a balance between these two principles. A pluralist simply has more than two principles that they see as determining moral behavior and may include, for instance: duty, honor, and self-control.

Looking at the other sub-category of normative ethics, the teleological, this term comes from the Greek word *teleios* which means "consequence," thus teleological theory is concerned with the consequences of one's actions. The consequences of the act, not the act itself, are what determine whether or not the behavior was right. If the consequences are good, then the behavior was good. If the consequences were bad, then the behavior was bad. For instance, in choosing to go to war, if the peace is restored, then the decision was morally acceptable. If executing a murderer both prevents that murderer from committing further murders and deters others from committing murder (both hard to determine), then the death penalty would be considered morally acceptable. Again, returning to the characteristics of ethical theories described earlier, teleological theories are prescriptive, authoritative, universal, and they are not self-serving.

Like the deontological theories, teleological theories can also be divided into two sub-categories: the quality of goodness and the locus of goodness. In the first category, the teleological theorists would essentially rank the various principles upon which they determine if the behavior is good or bad. For instance, in the case of holding individuals at the military facility in Guantanamo Bay, Cuba, who are suspected of plotting terrorist acts against the United States, the principles of security and justice are at play. Holding these individuals may make America more secure, or as some would argue, it may not. Additionally, holding them there without being afforded due process may violate the concept of justice, but if given a trial, they may be released only to attack America in the future. Hence, these two principles would be rank-ordered to determine the quality of goodness and the consequences of these various courses of action in order to determine what is right in this situation.

In the second sub-category of teleological theory, the locus of goodness, teleologists make their determination of right behavior by looking at the locus of goodness. Here the concern is with the location of the goodness of action in order to determine what benefits the most. Perhaps the easiest understanding is to look at the two extremes of the egoist and the utilitarian. The egoist is solely concerned with his or herself, hence the location or locus of goodness is with that individual. According to the egoist, consequences that are good for them are considered good behavior. To the utilitarian, who is concerned with achieving the greatest benefit for all, the locus of goodness is with the masses, so consequences that are good for the many are considered right behaviors.

Sources of Ethics

Recognizing the various ethical theories and their various categorizations, the next natural question that follows is how one decides which category they fall in. What determines if one is a deontological or teleological theorist? Still further, how does one know which sub-category they fall into? How does one know what principle or principles they adhere to and how does one know if they are a monoist, a dualist, or a pluralist? It is generally agreed upon that people tend to learn these principles as children from their parents, friends, and teachers. Even in the most simplistic principles, people often find themselves forming their ethical theory and system for how they see the world and how they determine what is right and wrong. A best-selling book by Robert Fulghum is a perfect example of this; his book was titled: *All I Really Need to Know I Learned in Kindergarten.*[10] In this book he mentions those basic moral premises that we still often cite: "share

8

everything," "play fair," "clean up your own mess," and "say you're sorry when you hurt somebody." These simple things we learned at an early age contribute to the building of our ethical system.

Religion also plays a major role in the formation of our ethical system. The benefit of religion, especially organized religion, is that it has an established belief system upon which individuals can unite and share in the same moral community. If people were left to their own interpretations and beliefs regarding religion, there could not be a shared sense of morality. Taken further, O'Dea and Aviada have identified six essential functions of religion in society: (1) providing society with a point of reference that transcends the everyday world; (2) promoting among believers a feeling of security and a sense of worth; (3) giving an added emphasis to the norms and values of society; (4) presenting the believers with a sense of prophecy; (5) assisting the individual in establishing a group identity; and (6) facilitating the growth and maturation of members of the church group.[11] While this is a very secular understanding of the benefits of religion, central to any religion is the teaching of its ethical system.

There are a number of other sources from which people's ethical systems are developed, and they include the more formalized methods of conveying right and wrong behavior. In a sense, this is working backward. It is from an ethical theory and system that we derive our constitution, laws, and professional ethics, but often it is these very things that drives a person's ethics. Constitutions establish the relationship between government and citizens creating the framework in which people live ethical lives. Often derived from constitutions is the establishment of a codified body of laws that further tells us what is and is not acceptable behavior. Laws typically establish what is considered by the people to be wrong behavior. They also determine what is appropriate punishment for committing such behaviors. In a sense, they establish what one must do to lead an ethical life (Laws will be discussed in the next chapter). Further, in many professions, including police, lawyers, and correctional officers, there is often an established set of professional ethical standards or codes of conduct that members of that profession are required to work by. All of these communicate what is considered ethical behavior and often help to form and shape a person's ethical school of thought.

One other concept of law that shapes a person's perspective on ethics is natural law. The term natural law has come to have many definitions as its meaning has shifted over time. The early definition of natural law was simply stated as being God's law. These were the laws that God established for all mankind, and they were the laws necessary for society to exist. These laws were recognized as immutable and were no different from the physical laws that govern the earth. Over time the concept came to mean those laws that regulate behaviors that are universal in nature, such as the law against murder. It is universally accepted that murder is wrong and that if it were not, society could not form. Thus, murder, regardless of culture or time, is always wrong. Taken further, natural law infers rights on people, these being the "undisputed entitlements that people possess by virtue of being human beings,"[12] and include life and liberty. Thus, it can be said that these laws supersede all other laws, including those set forth by constitutions, laws, or professional codes of ethics.

Recognizing that there are many things that help to build one's ethical system over one's life-time, it is important to explore the various schools of thought regarding ethical theory to understand how these different schools of thought have developed over time. Each of these schools consists of many philosophers who have attempted to advance the truth and ascertain what is right and wrong behavior. In most cases they have put forth an extensive ethical system that addresses many of the ethical issues previously reviewed, such as whether ethics is best focused on the actions (deontological) or the consequences (teleological). It should also be noted that these philosophers did not always agree on the details of the philosophical school of thought, but on the whole they did adhere to the specific school and its tenets. Professor Souryal, a professor of criminal justice ethics, categorizes the philosophers into ten schools of thought: Stoicism, Hedonistic, Virtue, Religious, Naturalistic, Utilitarian, Duty, and Social Justice; it is to these ten schools we now turn.[13]

Schools of Ethics

Stoicism is the oldest of the philosophical schools of thought and was founded on the teachings of Zeno of Citium, a Greek, who wrote in late 300 and early 200 B.C.[14] His teachings were widely known throughout Greece and would spread throughout the Roman Empire. Stoicism was advanced by the later writings of Cicero, Epictetus, and Marcus Aurelius, who himself was a Roman Emperor from A.D. 121 to 180 Stoicism was based on the precepts of natural law, arguing that there were universal laws and a "rational will" that must be followed. In addition, Stoics recognized the various gods and believed that one must always remain pious to them. While Stoicism argued for enhancing all forms of knowledge, for by doing so one could lead a virtuous life, it was ultimately the outcomes, or end values, that were key. As reason, courage, justice, and self-discipline were the consequences of leading the virtuous life, and the greatest value was one's ultimate moral worth, Stoicism was primarily a teleological school of thought.

The second school of thought is the Hedonistic school. Much like its name, which is based upon the Greek word *hedone* meaning sweet, the ultimate value of this school is the desire of pleasure and the minimization of pain. This school of thought originated with the Ancient Greeks Aristippus and Epicurus and also includes such well known philosophers as Hobbes, Hume, Locke, and Bentham. The philosophy is that when those behaviors which are sought by an individual induce pleasure, these behaviors are considered to be good. Because the focus is on the actions of seeking pleasure, Hedonism is a philosophy that aligns itself with the deontological category of normative ethics.

Perhaps the most renowned of the philosophers, Socrates, Plato and Aristotle, are proponents and founders of the ethical school of Virtue. While Socrates was the primary founder of this school of thought, Plato was the noted disciple and the author of those books that have been preserved regarding this school of ethics. Aristotle was Plato's disciple. Aristotle, however, had some disagreements with his mentor. The primary premise of this philosophical school was that man must live a virtuous life and that in order to do so, one must be moral. As Plato argued, "if you want justice, you must be moral."[15] Thus, justice was the key to living a virtuous life. In order to achieve this life, one must be able to distinguish right from wrong, and Plato argued that moral absolutes do exist in the world. In addition, because one's moral behavior determines whether one is just or not, the school of Virtue is a deontological school of philosophy. Argued as being the primary means of achieving the good life by all three of these masters of philosophy, was the pursuit of knowledge, for it is knowledge that allows people to understand what is moral and immoral, and to conduct their behaviors accordingly.

The next school of thought is categorized as the Religious school and is based on the Catholic teachings of Saints Augustine and Aquinas. The premise of the religious school of philosophy is the love of God. The Religious school of thought has also been noted as the Scholastic school of thought, for most of the arguments were written by scholars in universities who utilized both logical and linguistic defenses of the Church's teachings. Reason and deductive logic were employed in order to explain the tenets of Christianity. Augustine and Aquinas became Saints because of both their extensive arguments in defense of the Roman Catholic Church and those elements of the creed (Apostle's and Nicene). Augustine, however, adhered more closely to the Stoical philosophy of ethics, while Saint Thomas Aquinas was more an adherent to the tenets of Aristotle. As Thomistic ethics, the common referent to Saint Thomas Aquinas' teachings, moved Aristotle's ethics forward and explained it more fully under a Christian understanding, it was Pope Leo XIII who named Aquinas as the official philosopher of the Roman Catholic Church. In either case, Augustine or Aquinas, because their ethical theories are focused on right and good behaviors, what is right and good in the eyes of God, it is a deontological theory. As Aquinas explains, in order to judge what is moral, one must look at the intentions behind the behavior, for this is what makes something good or evil, not the outcomes (consequences).

In deep contrast to the Religious school, the Naturalistic school is based on the ethics of ego and power. While the Religious school holds a strong belief in God, the Naturalistic school ignores God (Hobbes) or outright rejects God's existence (Nietzche), hence human behavior is more animal-like and, therefore, naturalistic. Because human behavior was based on power much akin to Charles Darwin's theory of "survival of the fittest," the Naturalistic school of thought rejects any concept of good and evil and adheres to the belief that the key to ethical living is to dominate and control one's environment to be superior. As there is no good or evil, right or wrong, in the Naturalistic school of philosophy, this school is only considered with the outcomes and consequences of one's actions, hence it subscribes to the teleological category of ethics.

The ethical theory of choice during the enlightenment was that of Utilitarianism. This school of thought, popularized by the writings of Jeremy Bentham and John Stuart Mill, argues that utility is the only intrinsic good. Moral judgment is determined by the extent that an action has the capability of creating the greatest pleasure for the greatest number of people. Thus, all judgments of morality are based on the outcomes of one's behaviors, making Utilitarianism a teleological theory. In a sense, this is the Hedonistic school writ large in that it is no longer what brings "me" the most pleasure, but rather, what brings "everyone" the most pleasure.

The Duty school of ethics is primarily centered on the writings of Immanuel Kant. Kant argues for a monistic moral foundation, that being the duty that each individual has to their fellow man. Only those behaviors that are conducted in accordance with one's duty can have any moral worth. Lacking any moral worth the behavior is then said to be immoral or wrong. Taken further, if the behavior, the duty, is wrong for one person, it can never be right for another, hence it is universally wrong. Because Kant is focused solely on the moral virtue of duty and one's behavior, it is a deontological theory.

The final, and most recent, school of philosophy is the ethical school of Social Justice. In the latter half of the twentieth century there have been many authors espousing the tenets of Social Justice; however, the seminal writings of John Rawls are generally seen as being the foundation for understanding this particular school of philosophy.[16] Because Rawls evokes the concept of justice, and we already know that there are many definitions and interpretations of justice, it is important to understand how he defines this concept. To Rawls, justice is the equal distribution of society's good and services among all members of a society. His definition of "social" is the participation of individuals and government institutions in social agreements. Thus, for Rawls, social justice is the application of justice (equality) to all social agreements. Everyone should be given their "fair share" of society's benefits, and, when they are not, justice has not been served. This then raises a question as to whether or not Rawls' Social Justice is deontological or teleological. Because it is focused on equality for all as the desired outcome, one would logically argue it is a teleological theory. However, Rawls argued it was a deontological theory because the equal liberty for all is a form of justice and behavior that is sought after, thus equality is a right behavior that will result in a right consequence.

Very clearly the Religious school of ethics is the one embraced by the Catholic Church. The rich heritage of Saints Augustine and Aquinas provide the Church with a deep understanding of the faith and the ethical system by which all Catholics should live. Perhaps what is most important is to recognize what sets the Religious school of ethics apart from the other schools of thought. While each of the ten ethical systems seek to know truth, the Religious school, and particularly the Catholic faith, recognizes that truth is derived from the holy trinity, the Father, Son and Holy Spirit. All of the other schools of ethics attempt to find truth either within oneself (e.g., What pleases me?) or within the context of their relation to the city-state (e.g., What is my social relation with the government? What is my duty to government? Etc.). Catholics seek truth through God. Still further, it should be noted that unlike many Protestant denominations that only find truth in the written word of God, the Bible, Catholics base their ethical system on a much broader scale, thus it can incorporate such teachings as those provided by Augustine and Aquinas into its school of ethics.

The comparison of the ten schools of ethics also demonstrated that all fall into the category of normative ethics, but they are then divided between deontological and teleological theories. A Catholic ethical system must always adhere to the deontological school of thought and reject all teleological theories. The *Catechism of the Catholic Church* explains that "a morally good act requires goodness of the object, of the end, and of the circumstances together," but that "an evil end corrupts the action, even if the object is good in itself."[17] Moreover, "the object of the choice can by itself vitiate an act in its entirety," for some concrete acts are always wrong to choose "because choosing them entails a disorder of the will, that is, a moral evil."[18] The Catholic Church thus concludes that "it is therefore an error to judge the morality of human acts by considering only the intention that inspires them or the circumstances which supply their context" for "there are acts which, in and of themselves, independently of circumstances and intentions, are always gravely illicit by reason of their object; such as blasphemy and perjury, murder and adultery."[19] The concluding key statement that sums up the Catholic Church's understanding of ethics then is encapsulated in the avowal that "one may not do evil so that good may result from it."[20] St. Thomas Aquinas has further explained that, "an evil action cannot be justified by reference to a good intention,"[21] or as we typically say in modern lingo, "the end does not justify the means." So, while the Church argues that one must judge the intentions, act, and outcome because no good can come from an evil act, this excludes teleological theory from the Religious school of ethics. Therefore, a Catholic system of ethics must subscribe to deontological theory, always judging the act first. The consequences of the act thus become a secondary element of the moral act.

In terms of the various deontological subcategories, such as monism and pluralism, the Church could be said to be monistic in the sense that the fundamental belief adheres to faith in God and only faith in God. However, the Catholic faith also leaves room for the recognition of other principles that guide ethical behavior, such as the Cardinal Virtues, thus a Catholic ethical system is, in fact, a pluralist system. It is important to recognize this, for in order to understand Catholic teaching on morality and virtues, one must understand the ethical system that underlies its teachings. Still further, in order to understand the laws, explanations for criminal behavior, and how criminal justice ought to be ordered from a Catholic perspective, one must first recognize that the ordering is based first and foremost on serving God, and second, on a deontological and pluralist ethical system.

Morals

As it has been said that ethics is the philosophy that examines the principles of what is right and wrong or good and bad, morality is then the "practice of these principles on a regular basis."[22] Morality is the application of our ethical system. We utilize our ethical system in order to help us determine what is acceptable and unacceptable behavior. In order to do this, there must be the recognition of several factors regarding our ability to determine morality. First, we must have free will in order to make this decision.[23] If we are forced to identify something as being right or wrong, against our will, then there is inherently no determination of what is moral. This particularly includes those that are mentally ill, mentally retarded, or under the age of reason. As they do not have the mental capacity to judge something as being right or wrong, moral determination cannot be made. In addition, when considering the determination of moral behavior we are considering only human acts, for the capacity of free will and moral judgment is reserved to humans. Finally, it is generally considered that there must be an act in order for something to be judged.[24] However, in terms of Catholic teaching, this is not necessarily the case. Matthew writes in his Gospel that Jesus taught, "you have heard that it was said, 'You shall not commit adultery.' But I say to you, everyone who looks at a woman with lust has already committed adultery with her in his heart."[25] While this is clearly not a behavioral act, but rather a thought or emotion, the secular understanding of morality leads one to state definitively that this is not an act, while in Catholic teaching it is an act that can be judged as right or wrong.

Another aspect of moral behavior extends to the question of whether or not a universal morality exists. If behavior is judged to be right or wrong, then not only must it always be right or wrong, it must be right or wrong in all cultures and all societies. This is often difficult to ascertain because many people cannot distinguish moral principles from cultural and societal differences. There is such a diversity of political, social, and economic systems in the world that it is difficult to understand how a universal morality could apply to everyone everywhere, thus many are unwilling to accept the notion of a universal morality. Moreover, there is also the problem that many people want to believe they have no moral problems or that one cannot judge other cultures, societies, or individuals for what they do. It is at this point that they begin to tread toward being moral relativists and no longer absolutists.

Moral relativism is the belief that one cannot judge a behavior as being right or wrong because what may be unacceptable and immoral behavior to one may be acceptable and moral to another. Those proponents of moral relativism argue that there are too many moral standards for our behavior. As a result, various moral standards may conflict with one another or, if we search hard enough, we may be able to find a moral standard for every act. Moral relativists also make the argument that in order to follow moral absolutes, someone must determine what is always right and what is always wrong. The natural question is: who gets to make this determination?

As previously mentioned, one of the reasons that many people lean toward moral relativism is because they cannot separate moral principles from cultural. As the world has become smaller, we have become far more aware of the many cultures that exist in the world and that each culture has its own norms and values. As a result, we have also become more aware of the concept of cultural relativism, which states cultures often define what is good for the survival of their culture, and we cannot judge other cultures for doing what may seem strange and odd to us. For instance, some cultures have arranged marriages as a normal part of their institution of marriage. While this concept is foreign to Americans, to those living in a caste system dominated by cultural norms and values, this is a perfectly normal and practical part of life. To say that in one society arranged marriages are acceptable behavior, whereas in another society they are not, is cultural relativism. This does not negate, however, the moral principles that underlie this behavior. We must look to moral principles to determine if this behavior is right or wrong, not to cultural ones.

Socrates, Plato, and Aristotle all recognized this dilemma over two thousand years ago, but they still believed that there were in fact universal truths. Plato believed that through a process of rational thought a universal code of conduct could be identified that carries across all cultures and in all situations. While the cultural window-dressings may change and new issues will come along that society perceives as new, at the root of all of these variations are certain core behaviors that can be judged as being right or wrong by our moral principles.

This perspective, absolutism, is also adhered to by the Catholic Church, which argues that moral absolutes do exist. The Church teaches that these moral absolutes come from God and that they can be known by all mankind, as long as they listen and open their hearts to God. In the Vatican II document, *Gaudium et Spes,* the Church explains:

> In the depths of his conscience, man detects a law which he does not impose upon himself, but which holds him to obedience. Always summoning him to love good and avoid evil, the voice of conscience when necessary speaks to his heart: do this, shun that. For man has in his heart a law written by God; to obey

it is the very dignity of man; according to it he will be. Conscience is the most secret core and sanctuary of a man.[26]

It is this moral conscience that is at the heart of Catholic discernment regarding what is good and what is evil. As the *Catechism of the Catholic Church* explains, "conscience is a judgment of reason whereby the human person recognizes the moral quality of a concrete act that he is going to perform, is in the process of performing, or has already completed."[27] Thus, according to the Church, "in all he says and does, man is obliged to follow faithfully what he knows to be just and right."[28] This means that God provides the law, Catholics are obliged to listen to the law of God, and through their moral conscience discern right from wrong.

To this point we have discussed the underlying foundation of ethics that helps us discern moral truths: the determination of what is right and wrong. What we have not clarified is the proper choice. It is one thing to know what is right and what is wrong, but this does not necessarily mean people will always choose what is right. As a police officer, I often asked suspects when they committed their crime if they knew that it was wrong. Invariably, they answered "yes." People commit evil and violate laws all the time, despite the fact they were able to apply their ethical system to the behavior and determine the morality of the behavior. Just because someone knows right from wrong does not mean they will always choose what is right. Therefore, it is simply not enough to know what is moral; rather, it is hoped that people will use prudent judgment and choose what is right. Discerning what is morally good and evil and choosing what is right is known as a virtue.

Virtues

Aristotle defined virtues as "excellences."[29] These are the chosen moral beliefs, which move us toward human perfection. Aristotle divided these into both moral virtues, such as self-control and generosity, and intellectual virtues, such as understanding and wisdom. Aristotle argued that it is not good enough to only adhere to the moral virtues, but one must apply both in order to live the good life. In addition, one must always choose what is good and what is right in order to develop the habit of moral virtue. Aristotle explained that these moral virtues were always based on the principle of the mean. Virtue always lies at the mean of the two extremes of human character and behavior. A simple conceptual understanding of the mean can be found in eating. If one does not eat at all (e.g., they suffer from anorexia) or one eats too much (gluttony), they are on the extremes of human behavior and are not leading a virtuous life. In the case of pride, one may be on the extreme of empty vanity, while on the other end is undue humility; hence they are not leading the virtuous life. One other example is fear. On one extreme is cowardice; while on the other extreme is recklessness. But, if one were to live the virtuous life, they would adhere to the mean, that being the exhibition of courage.

This concept of virtues is reflected in the teachings of the Catholic Church. The *Catechism* defines a virtue as "an habitual and firm disposition to do the good,"[30] by not only allowing the person to perform good acts, but to also give the best of themselves. The Catholic Church breaks down the concept of virtues into two related parts: the human virtues and the moral virtues. Human virtues are defined as "firm attitudes, stable dispositions, habitual perfections of intellect and will that govern our actions, order our passions, and guide our conduct according to reason and faith."[31] Moral virtues are defined as those "acquired by human effort" for "they are the fruit and seed of morally good acts; they dispose all the powers of the human being for communion with divine love."[32] It is the combination of these two virtues, human and moral, through a process of learning and education, and guided by God, that we come to live the virtuous life. The Catholic Church further identifies the specific virtues which we should adhere to, and these are divided into two categories themselves: theological virtues and cardinal virtues.[33]

The theological virtues—faith, hope, and charity—are the root of Christian moral activity. Faith is a theological virtue because it is through faith that a person commits their entire self to God. Because the moral law is written by God, if faith in God is not present, then the virtuous life is lost. As Paul explains in the Bible, "the one who is righteous by faith will live."[34] The second theological virtue is hope, for it is the affirmation of faith. Hope ensures that one does not lose faith in God, and it gives a sense of purpose for making prudent judgments in moral decisions. Charity is the third and final theological virtue, which explains that in order for us to love God above all things, we must love our neighbor as ourselves and do good works on earth. Of the three theological virtues, charity is considered to be the superior virtue, for as Paul explains, "so faith, hope, charity abide, these three, but the greatest of these is charity."[35]

The cardinal virtues also play a pivotal role in doing morally good acts and living the virtuous life. In the book of Wisdom it is said that "If anyone loves righteousness, the fruits of [Wisdom's] works are virtues; for she teaches temperance and prudence, justice, and courage."[36] Temperance is the moral virtue that, like Aristotle's mean, moderates the attraction of pleasures and provides a balance in the use of created goods.[37] Prudence is the virtue that disposes us to practical reason and helps us discern the good of every act and choose that good. As St. Thomas Aquinas explained, prudence is "right reason in action."[38] Courage, or fortitude, "is the moral virtue that ensures firmness in difficulties and constancy in the pursuit of the good."[39] This is the virtue that allows us to overcome fear and to face the trials and tribulations that come our way. Finally, justice is the moral virtue "that consists in the constant and firm will to give their due to God and neighbor."[40] Justice toward God is the virtue of religion, while justice toward one's neighbor is right thinking and upright conduct, and it is to this virtue we now turn, for justice is the root of our criminal justice system.

Justice

The term "justice" is said to originate from the Greek word "dikaiosunel" or "dike," meaning that everything should be properly ordered and should stay in its proper place. This reflects one of the earliest discourses on the topic of justice, coming from Plato's *Republic,* in which Plato presents a Socratic dialogue on the very nature of justice. Plato's understanding is that justice is "giving to each what is owed," and that this contributes to the maintenance of the societal status quo.[41] In fact, many philosophers still subscribe to this definition of justice today as one modern day author, James Feibleman, explains justice to be "the demand for order: everything in its proper place or relation."[42] Yet, as discussed in the opening of this chapter, many people have a tendency to define justice more simply as being about fairness, equality, and impartiality. While rooted in the concepts of justice and most assuredly aspects of justice, these are gross oversimplifications for people who have not contemplated why fairness, equality, and impartiality represent our notions of what is just. In order to more fully understand the term "justice," as well as the concept within a Catholic context, it is important to analyze the many perspectives and categorizations of the term.

In general, justice can be divided into four separate and distinct categories: distributive, corrective, commutative, and restitutive. Distributive justice is centered on ensuring that both the goods and burdens of a society are distributed equitably to the members of society. In this case, the term equitably should not be confused with the term equally. While distributive justice is concerned with the distribution for what each person in society deserves, that does not mean that in order for it to be just, all members must receive an equal distribution. In the distribution of benefits, such as health care, welfare, education, etc., some people may argue that an unequal share may be just (e.g., welfare), while at the same time arguing that other distributions that are unequal are not just (e.g., education). The same holds for the burdens of society as well, such as who must pay for the elderly, who must fight in wars, and who will pay taxes. An equal distribution of the burdens, such as the requirement that everyone pay $10,000 in taxes annually, would burden the less fortunate and merely be a slight nuisance to the wealthy. Thus, distributive justice is concerned with ensuring that all benefits and burdens are shared equitably, but not necessarily equally.

Corrective justice, also called retributive and punitive justice, is comprised of how we determine who should be punished and the method we ultimately use to punish. In corrective justice we often hear about giving people their "just deserts" to ensure they get what they deserve. We also hear statements that the "punishment should fit the crime." Both of these statements reflect a component of corrective justice known as substantive justice. Substantive justice is determining the proper methods to judge someone and the proper punishment for one convicted of a crime. Corrective justice is also concerned with the system we use to determine who should be punished and how we determine the type of punishment. In this case we want to ensure that the individual gets a "fair trial" and is given the opportunity for "due process." Both of these statements reflect the other component of corrective justice known as procedural justice. Procedural justice is concerned with the policies and procedures used to determine guilt and punishment. Taken together, substantive and procedural justice reinforce the larger goal of corrective justice and that is to acknowledge wrong behavior and then punish the individual for his or her behavior in order to prevent the individual from making the same wrong choice in the future.

While corrective justice is often associated with the terms retributive and punitive, word usage is important here. Corrective paints the image of seeking rehabilitation, while retribution and punitiveness paint the picture of seeking "just deserts." It is the ordering that is important here for Hall who explains that retributive justice seeks out just deserts first and then considers the good of society second, primarily because it is looking backwards toward the wrong behavior.[43] Utilitarian justice, another extension of corrective justice, looks forward by placing the good of society first and the "just deserts" of the criminal second. The recognition that the offender must be brought back into the folds of society, means that the rehabilitation of the offender is the more important aspect of determining punishment.

The third category of justice, commutative justice, which Aristotle termed contractarian justice, is focused on those transactions and exchanges in society where one person feels that they were wronged or unfairly treated. Commutative justice is attempting to balance the rights of two or more parties, along with the interests of these parties. These types of issues are represented daily by our civil law system which is focused on rectifying some transaction where someone feels they have been cheated. Landlord/tenant disputes are a good example of the contractual nature of the exchange, for landlords are often accused of taking advantage of tenants, while tenants are often accused of abusing the property of the landlord. In the area of criminal law, however, these types of wrongs are not relegated to individuals, but society as a whole is said to be wronged as well. Thus, commutative justice seeks a resolution to the wrong in order to come to a fair and just settlement between individuals, individuals and society, and between two or more societies as a whole.

The final category of justice is known as restitutive justice and is encapsulated in a number of other justice concepts that have developed in the latter half of the twentieth century, namely social justice, restorative justice, and community justice. Restitutive justice, like retributive justice, looks backwards toward the offending act, but not to the offender and the call for his "just deserts." Rather, restitutive justice looks back to the victim and his or her loss or injury.[44] The goal then, is to have the offender make restitution for his or her crime, thus restoring the natural order of things, which is reminiscent of Plato's definition of justice. It is the concept of restoration through reciprocity that Rawls calls for in his theory of Social Justice. While Rawls speaks of social justice meaning that everyone has equal liberty, that every person should have equal opportunity, and that our social and economic institutions should provide maximum benefits to those worst off, it is the concept that when inequalities do occur, a civilized society and its citizenry must be tolerant, compassionate, and merciful. Thus, when a wrong has occurred, people and society as a whole must be willing to forgive and allow the wrong to be righted.

The concept of social justice has greatly expanded into many other areas since Rawls' publication, and it has been adopted by a number of varying theoretical perspectives.[45] One particular perspective arose out of the prison ministry of Charles Colson and his colleague Daniel Van Ness, for they have argued that it is imperative that justice affirm personal responsibility. In addition, they call for a focus on the rights and needs of the victim, as well as the humanity of the offender, and that restitution is the primary means by which personal responsibility can be assumed.[46] Another extension of social justice has come to be known as "Restorative Justice," which is believed to have been coined by Albert Eglash. Eglash argues that there are three types of justice: retributive, distributive, and restorative.[47] He explains that Restorative Justice is focused on the harmful impact of offenders' actions and that in order to restore justice, victims and offenders must come together and participate in the process of reparation and rehabilitation.[48]

What has come to be known as one of the most important works in the area of restorative justice, however, was a 1990 publication by Howard Zehr titled, *Changing Lenses: A New Focus for Crime and Justice.*[49] Zehr makes the argument that there are really only two types of justice: retributive and restorative. He describes restorative justice by explaining that "crime is a violation of people and relationships" and "it creates obligations to make things right."[50] Zehr explains further that "justice involves the victim, the offender, and the community in a search for solutions which promote repair, reconciliation, and reassurance."[51] This concept has been greatly advanced since Zehr's publication, as there has been a great interest, both in and out of the criminal justice field, regarding the concepts and tenets of restorative justice. More specifically, in the criminal justice field, we have seen a strong focus on Zehr's statement that justice involves the community for the development of "community justice."[52] This more modern concept has drawn heavily on the tenets of social and restorative justice to create a reconceptualization of what the criminal justice system ought to look like if this theory of justice were applied.

Recognizing there are four broad categories of justice—distributive, corrective, commutative, and restitutive—it is important to understand which of these the Catholic Church would subscribe to in order to understand more fully a Catholic perspective of criminal justice. Drawing upon the previous discussion of ethics, morals, values, and virtues, it is to the Catholic understanding of justice that we now turn.

Catholic Justice

Beginning with the book of Genesis, through the Gospels, and into the Acts of the Apostles, the concept of justice is a prominent theme in scripture. The Bible articulates God's justice, justice among humanity, and justice as it relates to the adjudication of the law. It raises the issue of justice as equity, integrity, and it explores what is meant by the inverse of justice: injustice. The primary emphasis tends to be humanity giving their due to God and neighbor. The Ten Commandments assert this when it states, "You shall worship the Lord your God and Him only shall you serve," and the Fourth Commandment to "Honor your father and your mother, as the Lord, your God, has commanded you."[53] Jesus takes this further, for when asked by one of the scribes which was the greatest commandment, he explains:

> The first is this, 'Hear, O Israel! The Lord our God is Lord alone! You shall love the Lord your God with all your heart, with all your soul, with all your mind, and with all your strength. The second is this: 'You shall love your neighbor as yourself.' There is no other commandment greater than these.[54]

St. Paul, writing in his letter to the Romans, succinctly states that we should "owe nothing to anyone, except to love one another; for the one who loves another has fulfilled the law."[55] According to St. Paul, when one bases all moral decisions on these greatest Commandments, then all of the other Commandments are secured and justice will always be served.

Scripture gives us many examples of how we should live through "habitual right thinking" and through an uprightness of conduct toward our neighbors. A passage from the Old Testament in Leviticus states, "You shall not be partial to the poor or defer to the great, but in righteousness shall you judge your neighbor."[56] And in the New Testament, St. Paul's letter to the Colossians expresses a similar sentiment about justice when he writes, "Masters, treat your slaves justly and fairly, realizing that you too have a Master in heaven."[57] So, the Bible is very clear that when each of us "loves our neighbor as ourselves," we thereby respect the rights of others and "establish in human relationships the harmony that promotes equity with regard to persons to the common good."[58] We establish justice.

While scripture does present the basis for our understanding of justice, it does not present a comprehensive approach to justice, nor does it directly define

21

it. As a result, we must look further to the many Church scholars who have written on the subject. As most writings on justice that reach beyond the Bible begin with St. Thomas' articulation of justice, this is a natural place to begin. St. Thomas explains in his *Summa Theologica* that "justice is a habit whereby a man renders to each one his due by constant and perpetual will."[59] He further states that "just as love of God includes love of neighbor, so too the service of God includes rendering to each one his due."[60] This is clearly a reflection of Jesus' response to the scribe who inquired as to which was the greatest commandment. While St. Thomas acknowledges this as the basis of justice, he elaborates further by dealing more fully with relationships among humanity.

St. Thomas continues his discourse on justice by discussing the concepts of general justice, which he describes as adherence to the law (i.e., legal justice), and social justice, which he describes as justice that concerns the community as a whole. The relationship of justice, from both perspectives, is between the governed and the governing. Government has a responsibility to ensure justice for all of society, but those in society have the responsibility of abiding by the law. As people come together in society to find the means to live and to enjoy the good life, it is the government's duty to ensure that the common good is secure for everyone. St. Thomas argues that this is achieved through the regulation of possessions (property), for "the regulation of possessions conduces much to the preservation of the state or nation."[61] Thus, people must have access and be granted the necessities of life, and should not have to live in fear of losing their possessions, in order for justice to be served. Without these assurances, social disorder will reign. What St. Thomas described here, within his explanations of general and social justice, is the basic concept of economic justice.

St. Thomas also raises the previously discussed issues of commutative and distributive justice in his writings, offering us some of the earliest writings on these concepts of justice. He defines commutative justice as being concerned "with the mutual dealings between two people," while distributive justice "distributes common goods proportionately."[62] St. Thomas further elaborates by comparing these two forms of justice when he states that commutative justice is the equal exchange of something for something (i.e., buying and selling), while distributive justice takes a person's station in life in consideration and is based more on equity than equality. Governments must take this into consideration when it establishes its systems and structures in order for justice to be achieved.

Unfortunately, as is all too often the case, governments become corrupt, and they create unjust structures. St. Thomas acknowledges these, but argues that Christians must work peacefully for change and that unless the hearts and minds of the leaders are changed, injustice will continue to reappear in society. Justice must be had at all levels in order for a healthy society to exist. Yet, justice itself cannot be the unifying and changing factor, for it is a product of both love and charity. St. Thomas explains:

Peace is the work of justice indirectly insofar as justice removes the obstacles to peace; but it is the work of charity directly because charity, according to its very nature, causes peace. For love is a unitive force and peace is the union of the appetite's inclinations.[63]

So, while corrupt governments do exist, justice cannot be served through violence against the government. It is, rather, the work of charity and doing good works that must be made in order to achieve true justice.[64]

The relationship discussed so far is first giving God his due and second living within the boundaries of the law in order to exist in a just society. Both government and man have a duty to God, first and foremost.[65] But government also has a duty to man, and man has a duty to government: to abide by the law and to resolve disputes through peaceful means. This, however, does not override the rights given to man. If people live in solidarity with one another, all striving for the love of God, then the rights of man will not be trampled. For the premise of "do unto others as you would have done to you," ensures the rightful order among men. However, no man or government has the right to violate those fundamental rights of man, given to him by his Creator.

The rights of all humanity in a society are premised on the acceptance of one fundamental principle, and that is "each individual man is truly a person."[66] God has given each individual his or her own identity, endowed them with their own intelligence, and has formed them in his own image. Each person has free will. And it is strongly noted that "these rights . . . are universal and inviolable."[67] The first right is that man has the right to live. From conception to death, man has the right to bodily integrity and to the means necessary for the proper development of life, particularly food, clothing, shelter, medical care, rest, and finally, the necessary social services. Second, he has the right to be respected, to have a good name, to have freedom in investigating the truth and—within the limits of the moral order and the common good—to have freedom of speech, publication, and to pursue whatever profession he may choose. Third, he has the right to the benefits of culture, a good general education, technical or professional training consistent with the degree of educational development in his own country, to engage in advanced studies, and to attain (as far as possible) positions of responsibility commensurate with his talent and skill. Fourth, he has the right to be able to worship God according to his conscience and profess his religion in private and in public. Fifth, he has the right to choose the life which appeals to him, to marry and found a family, in which men and women have equal rights. Sixth, he has the right to the opportunity to work and to take personal initiative in it. Seventh, he has the right to engage in economic activities suited to his degree of responsibility. Eighth, men have a right to form associations with their fellows, to confer on such associations the type of organization best calculated to achieve their aims. Ninth, every human being has the right to freedom of movement and residence in his own state and, where just reason favors it, to emigrate to other countries. Tenth, man has a right to take an active part in public life to make his own contribution to the common welfare. And finally, every human is entitled to the legal protection of his rights, effective, unbiased, and just.

Along with these rights, however, come the duties of man. Just as the rights are "universal and inviolable," so too are the duties.[68] These rights and duties derive their origin, their sustenance, and their indestructibility from the natural law, which in conferring the one imposes the other. For instance, the right to live imposes the duty to preserve one's life. The right to be free to seek out the truth imposes the duty that one devotes himself to a deeper and wider search. In addition, none of these duties may violate natural law, God's law, as previously discussed, for this would be a violation of the first premise of giving God his due. Once all of this is admitted, it follows that in human society one man's natural right gives rise to a corresponding duty in other men; the duty, that is, of recognizing and respecting that right. Every basic human right draws its authoritative force from the natural law, which confers it and attaches to it its respective duty. Hence, to claim one's right and ignore one's duty, or only half fulfill them, is like building a house with one hand and tearing it down with the other.[69]

Before a society can be considered well-ordered, creative, and consonant with human dignity, it must be based on truth.[70] Human society demands that men be guided by justice, respect the rights of others, and do their duty. It demands, too, that they be animated by such love as will make them feel the needs of others as their own, and induce them to share their goods with others, and to strive in the world to make all men alike heirs to the noblest of intellectual and spiritual values. It is these spiritual values which exert a guiding influence on culture, economics, social institutions, political movements and forms, laws, and all the other components which go to make up the external community of men and its continual development.

Thus, it can be said, that each person brings into society an understanding of these rights and duties, based on their being made in the image and likeness of God, having been given both intelligence and free will, and knowing the difference between right and wrong through natural law (right reason) and God's revelation of the law (Ten Commandments, scripture, Church teachings, etc.). While the state must respect these rights and freedoms, each person must adhere to their duties and respect the rule of law. In fact, this becomes the very purpose of government emerging in societies. Its primary function is to secure the common good for every member of society. In order to achieve this, society establishes laws to ensure that justice is served. And remembering that justice is derived from the moral law of God, when the eternal law is followed by all, we know that the common good for all has been achieved. As St. Thomas explained, "the very idea of the government of things in God, the rule of the universe, has the nature of a law, and since the Divine Reason's conception of it is eternal, that law is eternal."[71] And, as St. Thomas further expounds, "the light of natural reason, by which we discern what is good and what is evil, is nothing else than an imprint of the divine reason, the sharing in the eternal law by intelligent creatures."[72] Thus, our law should be a reflection of natural law and God's law, adhering to the rights and duties of man as previously set forth, in order that justice in society and the regulation of society may be achieved.

Conclusion

The term "justice" is a term that has a broad array of meanings and contains numerous philosophical perspectives in the world today. Justice, however, in Catholic doctrine, has a very specific definition that is based on scripture and tradition. As the *Catechism of the Catholic Church* states, "justice is the moral virtue that consists in the constant and firm will to give their due to God and neighbor."[73] The reader must first recognize that a Catholic perspective of justice is based upon love and honor to God. It is from both the word of God, as given to us in scripture, and through God's imprint of the natural law upon each of us, that we derive our ethical system. Our Catholic ethical system drives our understanding of morality, the determination of what is right and what is wrong. From this we develop our understanding of how to live the virtuous life, with one of the most important of those virtues being justice.

Justice is then based on giving God his due and giving unto others as we would have them give to us. Understanding that a just society is premised on this also means that when governments form, they form to give God his due and to secure the common good, the good of society's people. While human beings have universal and inviolable rights, they also have duties by which they must adhere, duty to themselves, family, and community. In order to achieve justice within society, laws are created to ensure that each receives what is his due. When someone violates this law, to ensure justice, laws are enforced by the criminal justice system. Thus, in order to understand more fully criminal justice from a Catholic perspective, one must understand the concept of justice as related in this chapter, as well as how the law establishes justice and how the criminal justice system enforces the law. From this we can derive a better understanding of what criminal justice, from a Catholic perspective, ought to look like. It is to these subjects that the next chapter turns.

Notes

1. Saint Augustine, *The City of God,* trans. Marcus Dods (New York: The Modern Library, 2000), 112.
2. Joycelyn M. Pollock, *Ethics in Crime and Justice: Dilemmas and Decisions,* 3rd ed. (Belmont, CA: International Thompson Publishing Company, 1998); Sam S. Souryal, *Ethics in Criminal Justice: In Search of the Truth,* 2nd ed. (Cincinnati: Anderson Pub-

lishing Company, 1998).

3. Sam S. Souryal, *Ethics in Criminal Justice: In Search of the Truth*, 2nd ed. (Cincinnati: Anderson Publishing Company, 1998).

4. Peter Baelz, *Ethics and Beliefs* (New York: Seabury Press, 1977), 19.

5. Richard A. S. Hall, *The Ethical Foundations of Criminal Justice* (Boca Raton, FL: CRC Press, 2000).

6. Vincent Barry, *Applying Ethics: A Text with Readings* (Belmont, CA: Wadsworth, 1985), 11.

7. Sam S. Souryal, *Ethics in Criminal Justice: In Search of the Truth*, 2nd ed. (Cincinnati: Anderson Publishing Company, 1998), 64.

8. Sam S. Souryal, *Ethics in Criminal Justice: In Search of the Truth*, 2nd ed. (Cincinnati: Anderson Publishing Company, 1998), 65.

9. Richard A. S. Hall, *The Ethical Foundations of Criminal Justice* (Boca Raton, FL: CRC Press, 2000).

10. Robert Fulghum, *All I Really Need to Know I Learned in Kindergarten* (New York: Villard Books, 1986).

11. T. O'Dea and J.O. Aviada, *Sociology of Religion* (Englewood Cliffs, NJ: Prentice Hall, 1983).

12. Sam S. Souryal, *Ethics in Criminal Justice: In Search of the Truth*, 2nd ed. (Cincinnati: Anderson Publishing Company, 1998), 83.

13. Sam Souryal, *Ethics in Criminal Justice: In Search of the Truth*, 2nd ed. (Cincinnati, OH: Anderson Publishing Company, 1998).

14. Sam Souryal, *Ethics in Criminal Justice: In Search of the Truth*, 2nd ed. (Cincinnati, OH: Anderson Publishing Company, 1998).

15. Sam Souryal, *Ethics in Criminal Justice: In Search of the Truth*, 2nd ed. (Cincinnati, OH: Anderson Publishing Company, 1998), 137.

16. John Rawls, *A Theory of Justice* (Cambridge, MA: Harvard University Press, 1971).

17. Catholic Church, *Catechism of the Catholic Church*, 2nd ed. (Washington, D.C.: United States Catholic Conference, Inc., 1997), 435.

18. Catholic Church, *Catechism of the Catholic Church*, 2nd ed. (Washington, D.C.: United States Catholic Conference, Inc., 1997), 435.

19. Catholic Church, *Catechism of the Catholic Church*, 2nd ed. (Washington, D.C.: United States Catholic Conference, Inc., 1997), 435..

20. Catholic Church, *Catechism of the Catholic Church*, 2nd ed. (Washington, D.C.: United States Catholic Conference, Inc., 1997), 435.

21. Thomas Aquinas, *Collationes in Decem Praeceptis*, 6: 1759.

22. Sam Souryal, *Ethics in Criminal Justice: In Search of the Truth*, 2nd ed. (Cincinnati, OH: Anderson Publishing Company, 1998), 17.

23. Catholic Church, *Catechism of the Catholic Church*, 2nd ed. (Washington, D.C.: United States Catholic Conference, Inc., 1997); Joycelyn M. Pollock, *Ethics in Crime and Justice: Dilemmas and Decisions*, 3rd ed. (Belmont, CA: International Thompson Publishing Company, 1998).

24. Joycelyn M. Pollock, *Ethics in Crime and Justice: Dilemmas and Decisions*, 3rd ed. (Belmont, CA: International Thompson Publishing Company, 1998), 8.

25. Matthew 5:27-28 (*The New American Bible*).

26. Catholic Church, *Gaudium et Spes*, http://www.vatican.va/archive/hist_councils/

ii_vatican_council/documents/vat-ii_cons_19651207_gaudium-et-spes_en.html (See paragraph 16).

27. Catholic Church, *Catechism of the Catholic Church*, 2nd ed. (Washington, D.C.: United States Catholic Conference, Inc., 1997), 438.

28. Catholic Church, *Catechism of the Catholic Church*, 2nd ed. (Washington, D.C.: United States Catholic Conference, Inc., 1997), 438.

29. Sam Souryal, *Ethics in Criminal Justice: In Search of the Truth*, 2nd ed. (Cincinnati, OH: Anderson Publishing Company, 1998).

30. Catholic Church, *Catechism of the Catholic Church*, 2nd ed. (Washington, D.C.: United States Catholic Conference, Inc., 1997), 443.

31. Catholic Church, *Catechism of the Catholic Church*, 2nd ed. (Washington, D.C.: United States Catholic Conference, Inc., 1997), 443.

32. Catholic Church, *Catechism of the Catholic Church*, 2nd ed. (Washington, D.C.: United States Catholic Conference, Inc., 1997), 443.

33. Catholic Church, *Catechism of the Catholic Church*, 2nd ed. (Washington, D.C.: United States Catholic Conference, Inc., 1997), 446.

34. Romans 1:17 (*The New American Bible*).

35. 1 Corinthians 13:13 (*The New American Bible*).

36. Wisdom 8:7. (*The New American Bible*).

37. Catholic Church, *Catechism of the Catholic Church*, 2nd ed. (Washington, D.C.: United States Catholic Conference, Inc., 1997), 445.

38. St. Thomas Aquinas, *Summa Theologiae. Latin text and English translation, introductions, notes, appendices, and glossaries Thomas, Aquinas, Saint, 1225?-1274* (New York: McGraw Hill, 1964), II-II, 47, 2.

39. Catholic Church, *Catechism of the Catholic Church*, 2nd ed. (Washington, D.C.: United States Catholic Conference, Inc., 1997), 444.

40. Catholic Church, *Catechism of the Catholic Church*, 2nd ed. (Washington, D.C.: United States Catholic Conference, Inc., 1997), 444.

41. Tom Campbell, *Justice*, 2nd ed. (New York: St. Martin's Press, 2001).

42. James Feibleman, *Justice, Law, and Culture* (Boston: Martinus Nijhoff, 1985), 23.

43. Richard A. S. Hall, *The Ethical Foundations of Criminal Justice* (Boca Raton, FL: CRC Press, 2000), 209.

44. Richard A. S. Hall, *The Ethical Foundations of Criminal Justice* (Boca Raton, FL: CRC Press, 2000).

45. Bruce A. Arrigo, *Social Justice; Criminal Justice: The Maturation of Critical Theory in Law, Crime, and Deviance* (Belmont, CA: West/Wadsworth, 1999).

46. Charles W. Colson, "Toward an Understanding of the Origins of Crime," in *Crime and the Responsible Community: A Christian Contribution of the Debate about Criminal Justice*, eds. John Stott and Nick Miller (London: Hodder and Stoughton, 1980); Daniel W. Van Ness, *Crime and Its Victims: What We Can Do* (Downers Grove, IL: InterVarsity Press, 1986).

47. Daniel W. Van Ness and Karen Heetderks Strong, *Restoring Justice*, 2nd ed. (Cincinnati: Anderson Publishing Co., 2002), 27.

48. Albert Eglash, "Beyond Restitution: Creative Restitution," in *Restitution in Criminal Justice*, eds. Joe Hudson and Burt Galaway (Lexington, MA: D.C. Heath, 1977), 91-92.

49. Howard Zehr, *Changing Lenses: A New Focus for Crime and Justice* (Scottsdale, PA: Herald Press, 1990).

50. Howard Zehr, *Changing Lenses: A New Focus for Crime and Justice* (Scottsdale, PA: Herald Press, 1990), 181.

51. Howard Zehr, *Changing Lenses: A New Focus for Crime and Justice* (Scottsdale, PA: Herald Press, 1990), 181.

52. Todd R. Clear and Eric Cadora, *Community Justice* (Belmont, CA: Wadsworth, 2003).

53. Exodus 20:12 and Deuteronomy 5:16 (*The New American Bible*).

54. Mark 12:28-31. (*The New American Bible*).

55. Romans 13: 8-10 (*The New American Bible*).

56. Leviticus 19:18 (*The New American Bible*).

57. Colossians 4:1 (*The New American Bible*).

58. Catholic Church, *Catechism of the Catholic Church,* 2nd ed. (Washington, D.C.: United States Catholic Conference, Inc., 1997), 530.

59. St. Thomas Aquinas, *Summa Theologiae. Latin text and English translation, introductions, notes, appendices, and glossaries Thomas, Aquinas, Saint, 1225?-1274* (New York: McGraw Hill, 1964), IIa IIae Q 58 Art I ad 6.

60. St. Thomas Aquinas, *Summa Theologiae. Latin text and English translation, introductions, notes, appendices, and glossaries Thomas, Aquinas, Saint, 1225?-1274* (New York: McGraw Hill, 1964), IIa IIae Q 58 Art I ad 6.

61. St. Thomas Aquinas, *Summa Theologiae. Latin text and English translation, introductions, notes, appendices, and glossaries Thomas, Aquinas, Saint, 1225?-1274* (New York: McGraw Hill, 1964), IIa IIae Q 61 Art 1, Art 2.

62. St. Thomas Aquinas, *Summa Theologiae. Latin text and English translation, introductions, notes, appendices, and glossaries Thomas, Aquinas, Saint, 1225?-1274* (New York: McGraw Hill, 1964), IIa IIae Q 61 Art 1, Art 2.

63. St. Thomas Aquinas, *Summa Theologiae. Latin text and English translation, introductions, notes, appendices, and glossaries Thomas, Aquinas, Saint, 1225?-1274* (New York: McGraw Hill, 1964), IIa IIae Q 29 Art 3 ad 3.

64. See also Cardinal Joseph Ratzinger, *Instructions on Christian Freedom and Liberation,* Congregation for the Doctrine of Faith, http://www.vatican.va/roman_curia/congregations/cfaith/documents/rc_con_cfaith_doc_19860322_freedom-liberation_en.html

65. Pope John XXIII, *Pacem in Terris: Encyclical of Pope John XXIII on Establishing Universal Peace in Truth, Justice, Charity and Liberty,* http://www.vatican.va/holy_father/john_xxiii/encyclicals/documents/hf_j-xxiii_enc_11041963_pacem_en.html

66. Pope John XXIII, *Pacem in Terris: Encyclical of Pope John XXIII on Establishing Universal Peace in Truth, Justice, Charity and Liberty,* http://www.vatican.va/holy_father/john_xxiii/encyclicals/documents/hf_j-xxiii_enc_11041963_pacem_en.html, paragraph 8.

67. Pope John XXIII, *Pacem in Terris: Encyclical of Pope John XXIII on Establishing Universal Peace in Truth, Justice, Charity and Liberty,* http://www.vatican.va/holy_father/john_xxiii/encyclicals/documents/hf_j-xxiii_enc_11041963_pacem_en.html

68. Pope John XXIII, *Pacem in Terris: Encyclical of Pope John XXIII on Establishing Universal Peace in Truth, Justice, Charity and Liberty,* http://www.vatican.va/holy_father/john_xxiii/encyclicals/documents/hf_j-xxiii_enc_11041963_pacem_en.html

69. Pope John XXIII, *Pacem in Terris: Encyclical of Pope John XXIII on Establishing Universal Peace in Truth, Justice, Charity and Liberty,* http://www.vatican.va/holy_father/john_xxiii/encyclicals/documents/hf_j-xxiii_enc_11041963_pacem_en.html

70. Pope John XXIII, *Pacem in Terris: Encyclical of Pope John XXIII on Establishing Universal Peace in Truth, Justice, Charity and Liberty,* http://www.vatican.va/holy_father/john_xxiii/encyclicals/documents/hf_j-xxiii_enc_11041963_pacem_en.html

71. Pope John XXIII, *Pacem in Terris: Encyclical of Pope John XXIII on Establishing Universal Peace in Truth, Justice, Charity and Liberty,* http://www.vatican.va/holy_father/john_xxiii/encyclicals/documents/hf_j-xxiii_enc_11041963_pacem_en.html

72. Pope John XXIII, *Pacem in Terris: Encyclical of Pope John XXIII on Establishing Universal Peace in Truth, Justice, Charity and Liberty,* http://www.vatican.va/holy_father/john_xxiii/encyclicals/documents/hf_j-xxiii_enc_11041963_pacem_en.html

73. Catholic Church, *Catechism of the Catholic Church,* 2nd ed. (Washington, D.C.: United States Catholic Conference, Inc., 1997), 444.

Chapter 2

Criminal Justice

"We are guided by the paradoxical Catholic teaching on crime and punishment: We will not tolerate the crime and violence that threatens the lives and dignity of our sisters and brothers, and we will not give up on those who have lost their way. We seek both justice and mercy."

-The Catholic Bishops of the United States in *Responsibility, Rehabilitation, and Restoration: A Catholic Perspective on Crime and Criminal Justice,* 2000, p. 55 -

Introduction

Taking into consideration the various definitions of justice, while working with the concepts of justice from a Catholic perspective, the next step is to look at the issue of criminal behavior to understand how those concepts of justice should be applied. To do this it is important that we look at the problem of crime, the application of the law as it applies to criminal behavior, and how the criminal justice system enforces the law in the United States. As criminal behavior drives our application of justice, an understanding of the scope of the problem helps place the problem in perspective. How the law is applied to criminal behavior in the United States is also an element that helps us understand the purpose of the law, yet it is also imperative that the Catholic perspective of the law, derived from its concept of justice, is also reviewed. Finally, explaining what is meant by the criminal justice system and its purpose, values, and goals, assists in understanding how criminal justice, from a Catholic perspective, might be ordered differently. It is to these topics this chapter now turns.

Crime

As the basis for having a legal and criminal justice system is crime itself, it is important to understand what is generally meant by the term. According to the *Dictionary of Criminal Justice*, crime is defined as, "an act committed or omitted in violation of a law forbidding or commanding it, for which the possible penalties upon conviction for an adult include incarceration, for which a corporation can be penalized by fine or forfeit, or for which a juvenile can be adjudged delinquent or transferred to criminal court for prosecution."[1] The key element here is that someone has committed a behavior or action that has been defined by a legislative body as being against the law. Rush defines it even further when he explains that "crimes are defined as offenses against the state and are to be distinguished from violations of the civil law that involves harms done to individuals—such as torts—for which the state demands restitution rather than punishment."[2] The key element in this case is that crimes are violations against the state through criminal legislation and not personal wrongs for which law suits are often brought. A crime, then, is a behavior defined by the legislative body to be a criminal act against the state for which a punishment is attached. For example, murder is defined as being a criminal act against the state for which those convicted are sentenced to prison or, in those states with laws allowing for the death penalty, executed.

It should be noted that crimes are defined by the legislative bodies found at the federal, state, or local level. According to Marion, "crimes are behaviors that are defined as criminal acts by political actors through the political process."[3] Certain behaviors are brought to the attention of legislators, who then must debate whether to pass legislation making such behavior illegal. For instance, a recent issue that has come to the attention of many is the watching of pornography in vehicles driving on the highways. Other people can see these videos from their cars driving on the same highway. The question arises as to whether or not this behavior should be illegal. It is the federal, state, and local legislative bodies that will have to determine if this is illegal behavior and what sanctions would go with a person exhibiting these behaviors in order to make it a crime. Therefore, it should be understood that defining what is a crime in our society is purely a political process.

In order to understand the reality of crime we must turn to those indicators that provide us with a more realistic portrait of the level of crime in the United States and how it has fluctuated from year to year. The primary indicators that are most often utilized in the field are the Uniform Crime Reports (UCR) and the National Crime Victimization Survey (NCVS). Each of these provides a different perspective on the level of crime and assists us in understanding the true nature of crime as they are measures of its prevalence. Taken together, they begin to move us toward a more accurate picture of crime in the United States.

The primary source for crime statistics in the United States is the Uniform Crime Reports (UCR) which are collected, maintained, and reported by the Federal Bureau of Investigation (FBI). The UCR was begun in 1930 at the behest of the International Associations of Chiefs of Police, through the leadership of the FBI director J. Edgar Hoover, and through a Congressional mandate as a method of collecting data from every police agency in the United States in order to report on those crimes "known to the police."[4] The methodology utilized to collect these data has, for the most part, remained the same since the inception of the Uniform Crime Reports and is based upon citizens' reporting crime to the police. Most law enforcement agencies in the United States then collect these crime statistics and report them to a central state location, such as state departments of justice. These agencies then forward the collected information to the FBI. While there is no mandate that a law enforcement agency report its crime data to the FBI, approximately 97 percent of the more than 18,000 agencies in the United States do, yielding a data set that covers over 95 percent of the American population. Once the FBI has collected the information from the agencies, they process it for dissemination to the public through preliminary reports and a final report that is published at the end of each year for the previous year, titled *Crime in the United States: Uniform Crime Reports.*

The reports divide crime into "Part I" and "Part II" offenses. Those crimes considered by the FBI to be the most serious, most frequent in occurrence, and are most often to come to the attention of the police are known as "Part I" offenses or "Index Crimes" and are broken down into violent crimes, which include homicide (murder and non-negligent manslaughter), forcible rape, robbery and aggravated assault; and property crimes, which include burglary, larceny, motor vehicle theft, and arson.[5] The Part I offense statistics include those crimes reported to the police, those crimes cleared by the police (either through arrest of the suspect or through special circumstances such as the death of the suspect), and those in which an arrest was made. It is important to note that for any given year, violent crime makes up between 10 and 20 percent of all Index Crimes, while property crimes compose the rest. The "Part II" offenses include such crimes as fraud and embezzlement, vandalism, prostitution, drug abuse, and gambling; however, this data is only maintained by the number of people arrested for the crime.[6] All of these data are then reported in both raw numbers (the actual number of each crime per year) and as a proportion of the population, to control for changing population rates each year, and is reported as X number of crimes per 100,000 population.

While the UCRs provide us with a measurement of how much crime exists in the United States, one must be aware that there are many problems with the use of the data.[7] The UCR data is often considered to severely underestimate the number of crimes occurring in the United States,[8] not all crimes are covered,[9] and the reporting of certain crimes may rise and fall due to increased awareness and media campaigns.[10] In addition, the amount of discretion that the law enforcement personnel and agencies have in reporting crime may also have an effect on the data such as purposeful over-reporting or under-reporting of crime,[11] bias and discrimination by refusing to take reports from certain categories of people such as the poor, blacks, or immigrants,[12] the heavy enforcement of some crimes that other jurisdictions do not enforce,[13] reporting the wrong type of crime for a specific incident, changes in the way crimes are reported, or simply making a mistake in the reporting of a crime all make compiling accurate crime statistics more difficult.[14] However, the UCR is still the best available indicator of crime in the United States, and it has been shown that the majority of these methodological problems are rare in the case of homicides, and that motor vehicle theft, burglaries involving forcible entry, and robberies generally yield more accurate data.[15] So, while the UCR is the main indicator for assessing the reality of crime in the United States, one must remain vigilant as to the accuracy of these findings.

The second primary source of crime statistic information in the United States comes from the National Crime Victimization Survey (NCVS) formerly known as the National Crime Survey. It was first used in 1973 by the U.S. Department of Justice, in cooperation with the U.S. Bureau of the Census, to address the many problems cited in the UCR by creating an instrument that would obtain better and more accurate information on the number of crimes in the United States. The NCVS obtains information directly from citizens and includes such things as the context in which crimes occurred, the time of day, physical setting, the extent of any injuries, the relationship between the victim and the offender, and the characteristics of the crime victim, including such variables as race, gender, and income. The data are compiled annually and published by the Bureau of Justice Statistics (BJS) in a publication titled *Criminal Victimization*.

The data collection process is somewhat complex. The Census Bureau interviews approximately 110,000 residents, ages 12 and older, from some 55,000 randomly selected households in the United States, every six months. In addition, once a household has been selected for the survey interviews, it remains in the sample for approximately three years, at which point it is removed from the sample and new households are selected. As the survey is concerned with measuring victimizations within a household, if individual members of a household move, the survey does not follow them, but continues to focus on the household and any new occupants. The response rate, due to the fact the surveys are conducted through personal interviews, is more than 95 percent. The respondents are asked whether or not they or anyone in their household had been victimized over the previous six months. The crimes are then described to the respondents, and they include aggravated and simple assault, rape and sexual assault, robbery, burglary, larceny-theft, and motor vehicle theft. For each victimization the respondent is then asked a more detailed set of questions which includes the age, race, gender, ethnicity, marital status, income, and educational level of the victim; the age, race, gender and relationship to the victim of the offender; and the time and place of the crime, the use of weapons, the nature of any injuries, the economic impact of the crime, and whether or not the victimization was reported to the police.

The greatest advantage of the calculation of victimization is that it allows for an understanding of the number of crimes committed in the United States rather than the number of crimes reported to the police. For example, the data collected for the year 1994 show that the UCR reported approximately 14 million crimes in the United States, while the NCVS estimated 42 million. More specifically, the UCR reported nearly two million violent crimes, but the NCVS reported nearly 11 million. In terms of property crimes the UCR reported 12 million incidents, while the NCVS reported 31 million. These differences highlight the fact that many crimes remain unreported to the police; thus, the measurement of crime utilizing the UCR does not provide a complete understanding of the reality of crime.

Though the NCVS does provide us with a better understanding of crime victimization in the United States, it, like the UCR, does have limitations. And, like the UCR, its first problem is that it severely underestimates the number of crimes in the United States because it is focused on individual victimizations and not commercial victimizations such as bank robberies and jewelry store burglaries.[16] In addition, because the NCVS asks respondents about their victimization, respondents may potentially forget a victimization,[17] they may overestimate the number of their victimizations,[18] or they may choose not to reveal their victimization to the data collector.[19] In addition, respondents may overreport their number of victimizations, confusing it with one that occurred outside of the time frame requested by the survey,[20] while others may report their victimizations in the wrong category.

Both the UCR and the NCVS do have methodological problems, but these two indicators present the best data available for assessing the reality of crime in the United States. One must recognize, however, that the two data sets are unique. Whereas the UCR is more concerned with the criminal, the NCVS is more concerned with the victim. Thus, combining the two indicators together presents a more accurate understanding of crime in the United States and can reveal trends across the years. So, what does the data tell us about the reality of crime?

In first looking at the Uniform Crime Reports for the offenses known to the police over time, we discover many interesting trends. First, the crime rates from the early 1930s to the late 1950s remained fairly steady when population growth is taken into account.[21] It was not until the early 1960s, into the early 1970s, that crime rates began to rise dramatically among adults, being preceded by a sharp rise in juvenile offenses in the late 1950s. By the later part of the 1970s there was a leveling off of crime and then a decrease in the early 1980s. Crime began to once more rise slightly, with some fluctuations, and level off in the early

1990s, followed by a steady decrease since 1991. If we break down the crimes into violent and property crimes, we find that violent crime matched the trends of "all crime," but property crime began to level off in the early 1980s and fell in the 1990s. If one were to break down the data even further, one would find violent crimes such as murder and rape have remained fairly constant throughout the 1980s, with significant declines in the 1990s, and crimes such as aggravated assault and robbery remained level through the early 1980s, rising a bit at the end of the 1980s and then falling in the 1990s. Turning to property crimes, like motor vehicle theft and larceny/theft, they have remained level in the 1980s and have dropped in the 1990s, while burglaries have been dropping steadily since the early 1980s.

The UCR provide some very interesting data in regards to the more recent trends in crime, namely in the last decade of the twentieth century and the beginning of the twenty-first. The total crime index, controlling for population by looking at the rate per 100,000 population, has seen a decrease from the all-time highs in 1991 of 758 crimes per 100,000 population to 463 crimes per 100,000 population in 2004. We know that crime dropped by 1 percent from 1991 to 1992 and then began dropping with each following year at an increasing rate. It dropped 3.1 percent between 1992 and 1993, 5.1 percent between 1993 and 1994, 6.8 percent between 1994 and 1995, and 9.8 percent between 1995 and 1996. More importantly, during this same time period, violent crime was also falling with decreases of 1.4 percent from 1992 to 1993, 5.8 percent from 1993 to 1994 and 16.3 percent from 1995 to 1996. These are dramatic drops in the number of crimes in the United States and ones that would indicate a safer nation. Yet, again, public concern for crime continued to rise during this same time period putting crime as the "most important problem facing the country" from 1994 through 1996. After crime was no longer considered such an "important problem," the crime rates continued to fall, consisting of a 7.7 percent decline in the crime rate from 1998 to 1999, a 10.7 percent decrease from 1999 to 2000, and a 9.9 percent decrease from 2000 to 2001. More recently, it would appear that crime has "bottomed out" as the decreases are no longer as dramatic, and there is the suggestion that it is once again starting to rise; however, it is too soon to tell with any assurance.

Recognizing some of the previously identified problems with the UCR data, perhaps it would be better to look at the most reliable crimes, such as murder, robbery, burglary, and motor vehicle theft. Each of these has fallen dramatically since the highs of 1991, such as the 24,700 murders in 1991 which fell to 16,148 murders in 2004. In the case of burglaries, there was a total of 3,157,200 in the United States in 1991. By 2002, the number had dropped to 2,144,446. Robberies also dropped from 687,730 in 1991 to 401,470 in 2004, and motor vehicle thefts dropped from 1,661,700 in 1991 to 1,225,226 in 2004. Even when controlling for rises in the population, we still find significant drops in crime. For instance, the murder rate in 1994 was 9.6 per 100,000 population, and in 2004 it stood at 5.4 per 100,000 population. When looking to robbery data, the rate fell from a 1994 rate of 237.7 per 100,000 population to 136.7 per 100,000 population in 2004. Regardless of how one looks at the data, according to the Uniform Crime Reports, crime has been steadily falling for well over a decade.

Turning to the National Crime Victimization Survey (NCVS) we find very similar trend data for the time period 1973 through 1992.[22] Since the early 1980s, the United States has seen a steady decline in the number of victimizations, from a raw number high of 41,454,180 victimizations in 1981 to 34,649,340 victimizations in 1992. In looking at specific crimes, a similar trend appears, including decreases in the number of rapes and robberies, as well as burglaries and larcenies. Although the NCVS format was changed from the years 1992 to 1993, creating a difference in the methods of data collection and reporting, there continued to be a downward trend in the post 1992 victimization data.[23] The year 1993 witnessed 43,547,000 victimizations, 1994 saw a decrease to 42,359,000 victimizations, and in 1995 this number dropped to 38,447,000. By 2005, the number of victimizations had fallen to 23,440,720. In looking at the category of personal crimes (rape, robbery, assault) we see a decrease from 11,365,080 victimizations in 1993 to 5,173,720 in 2005. In property crimes (burglary, motor vehicle theft, theft) America experienced a decrease from 32,182,320 in 1993 to 18,039,930 in 2005. Overall the trend in victimizations has continued downwards with significant declines throughout the 1990s, giving the lowest recorded number and rates of victimizations since the inception of the NCVS, despite the methodological changes in 1992.

The overall story that the Uniform Crime Reports and National Crime Victimization Survey tell is that crime rose in the late 1960s and early 1970s and began leveling off in the 1980s. Since the early 1980s, crime has been declining with some fluctuations but has been definitively declining since the early 1990s. It is only recently, in 2004 and 2005, that we are seeing some leveling off of the crime rates, and, potentially, a possible rise in 2006 and 2007. Despite these dramatic decreases over the past fifteen years, crime is still a problem in the United States, and in order to understand how the criminal justice system deals with crime one must look to the law.

Law

The concept of the "law" and any definition proffered immediately runs into the problem of ambiguity. Like justice, the term law means many things to many different people and has a long history of use and abuse. Laws are based on the concepts of justice and they are a reaction to the problems of crime. In terms of justice, they are the application of morality to society. Every law has at some rudimentary level a moral element that is being applied to social behavior. Whenever society tells people what they can and cannot do, what is right and what is wrong, they are applying their morality to a specific behavior that is found to be unacceptable. However, note that the application here is by society, often in the form of government, not that of an individual. As the famous saying by John Donne tells us, "no man is an island unto himself, every man is a piece of the continent . . . a part of the main . . . any man's death diminishes me, because I am involved in mankind, and therefore never send to know for whom the bell tolls: it tolls for thee."[24] Donne's seventeenth-century statement expresses the notion that individual behavior not only affects the individual, it impacts all of society. The law, and particularly the criminal law, is the same way. Individual criminal behavior affects all of the society, not just the individuals involved in the criminal event. The law, then, is about the application of society's morality, not an individual's morality. Put more simply in an example: if we chose to follow our own morality when we drove to work or school, we would most likely never arrive at our destination. Societal morality, then, is reinforced through the law.

Perhaps the most important element underlying the law is the idea of harm. The harm principle seeks to prevent harm to persons in order to prevent loss of property, physical injury, and/or death. In each of these cases, the harm is done to an individual or individuals. However, harm can also be committed against a state in that some behavior causes harm to society as a whole. An example of this is treason, where the damage is to the state rather than a specific individual. Although harm is a central justification for the law, there are several others justifications cited as well. Joel Feinberg, writing on the relationship between morality and criminal law, has provided an in-depth exploration of a number of justifications for the law.[25] First and foremost, Feinberg cites that it is reasonably necessary to prevent harm to other persons. Second, he offers the offense principle, which states that laws are enacted to prevent serious offense (as opposed to injury or harm) to others. Third, he argues that it is also reasonably necessary to prevent harm to the very person it prohibits from acting. In other words, laws are established to prevent people from causing physical, psychological, or economic harm to themselves. Feinberg calls this legal paternalism. Fourth, Feinberg argues that it is necessary to prevent inherently immoral behavior from occurring, regardless of whether that conduct is harmful or offensive to others. Finally, like legal paternalism, Feinberg argues that it is often necessary to pass laws that restrict a person's liberty in order to prevent moral harm to the persons themselves. Feinberg calls this moral paternalism.

Understanding the justification for the law provides some understanding as to the law's purpose, but the actual definition of the law still remains somewhat elusive. While definitions of the law have tended to be widely varied, they have typically focused on such things as folkways, mores, and customs that eventually become enacted law. Max Weber took a more authoritarian approach when he defined laws as "norms which are directly guaranteed by legal coercion."[26] Benjamin Cardozo, the legal scholar and former Supreme Court Justice, explained that law "is a principle or rule of conduct so established as to justify a prediction with reasonable certainty that it will be enforced by the courts if its authority is challenged."[27] Summing up elements of a number of these definitions of law, Howard Abadinsky explains that the law appears to consist of four components: "norms regularly enforced by coercion, by persons authorized by society, as stipulated by courts of law."[28] The focus here is the legalization of the norms of society which can then be enforced by the criminal justice system. Yet one element that is missing from this summary of the definitions of laws is how the laws are made in the first place.

In ancient societies the law was generally developed by the king or through some form of oligarchy, but inherently it was developed by the ruling class. In more modern democratic societies, the law is developed indirectly by the people, voting for representatives to the various legislatures who then devise the law. While this development of the law is often painted in grade school books as being a very straight-forward process, the opposite is actually closer to reality. The creation of the law, including the criminal law, is very much a political process. Although the individual legislators have a vote, they often barter and trade for votes on the passage of specific laws. They are influenced in their votes by their respective political parties. They are influenced by various special interest groups, ranging from political action committees, activist groups, and various policy think-tanks. They are influenced by the many bureaucratic agencies that deal with the subject matter at all levels of government, federal, state, local, and tribal. And, of course, they are influenced by public opinion as generally reported by the news media. So, the simple determination of whether a certain behavior is to be classified and defined as a crime is actually determined through a very complex political process in America.

Once crimes are defined through the political process, they become part of our criminal law as found in the criminal statutes or penal code. The federal government maintains its own penal code for defining those behaviors that are violations against federal law. Each state also maintains its own criminal code defining what behaviors are criminal and the punishment that one may receive when found in violation of the law. Most charges against the criminal law are made by using state penal codes. Federal charges are only for federal violations of the law, and most local jurisdictions, cities and towns, typically do not maintain a complete penal code because they enforce the state penal code. However, local jurisdictions often do maintain city ordinances, those behaviors that are violations against the law of the city or town such as local noise violations.

The sources of criminal law in America are quite vast. The origins of American law first began with English common law. As early as A.D. 680, the English created a system of law that was based on English customs, tradition, and rules. Over time as judges decided new cases, they based their decisions on the existing laws, but modified them to reflect the current values, attitudes, and ethics of the people.[29] Common law was largely unwritten law and it was not until

Blackstone's *Commentaries on the Law*, published in four volumes between 1765 and 1769, that the concept of recording the law was advanced. The American colonists, however, unlike their English counterparts, recorded the law from the very beginning with Dale's Law in 1611 in the Virginia Colony. This practice would continue throughout the Colonial era, and when America declared its independence in 1776, the American federal, state, and local levels were given the opportunity to adopt the English common law as their own codified law, modify the English Common law to suit their needs, or abolish the Common law and start all over. Most chose to modify the Common law, and one example of this is Thomas Jefferson's work from 1777-1779 to modify the English Common law for Virginia.[30]

The second basis for our laws today was through the ratification of the United States Constitution in 1788 and the adoption of the Bill of Rights in 1791. The Constitution gave power to law makers to create or define new crimes as needed, but it also puts limits on the power of the federal government and thereby protects our freedom. While the Constitution established the frame work for how government would work in the United States, the Bill of Rights was passed in 1791 to give individuals certain freedoms as a means of protection against the national government. The Bill of Rights, the first ten amendments to the Constitution, delineated these specific rights granted to America's citizens. These include the First Amendments freedoms of speech, press, religion, and assembly. In terms of protecting people from what would clearly be the most intrusive element of government, the criminal justice system, the founders put limits on police behavior (Fourth Amendment), limited the admissibility of confessions that have been obtained unfairly (Fifth Amendment), provided for the rights against self-incrimination (Fifth Amendment), provided for the right to a speedy and public trial, an impartial jury, to confront witnesses, and to the assistance of counsel (Sixth Amendment), and protected against excessive bail, excessive fines, and cruel and unusual punishment (Eighth Amendment).[31] These rights continue to be a key element of citizen protection today, against not only the federal government, but state and local governments as well.

Statutory law, which is generally referred to as criminal law, consists of the federal, state, and local ordinances and legislation that define the law. Statutes are the laws passed by the legislative body of government, such as the U.S. Congress for the federal government and state legislatures for state governments. City councils can also pass ordinances that define local offenses, but as previously stated, state criminal law is commonly enforced at the local level because criminal violations are violations against the state.

Statutory law can be further defined as either being substantive law or procedural law. Substantive law is defined as "the part of the law that creates, defines, and regulates rights."[32] This is generally focused on the guarantees provided to all citizens under the U.S. Constitution, specifically those rights found in the Bill of Rights. These are the protections against unreasonable searches and seizures, the right to a speedy and public trial, and the right against excessive bail and cruel and unusual punishments. Substantive law tells us under what circumstance searches and seizures are unreasonable, what specifically is meant by "speedy," and how we know what is excessive bail or cruel and unusual punishment.

Procedural law refers to the "branch of law that prescribes in detail the methods or procedures to be used in determining and enforcing the rights and duties of persons toward each other under substantive law."[33] Procedural law focuses heavily on the administrative process by which citizen's rights are ensured. A key aspect of procedural law is that no one can be deprived of their life, liberty, or property without due process of law, therefore, procedural law is focused on the administrative process for ensuring these rights are protected. The government (police for instance) cannot simply enter a person's property and seize their property. They must first go before a judge to secure the search warrant. The individual is also afforded the opportunity to have a lawyer defend him or her against the state's charges. All of these rights are focused on procedural law.

Case law is "judicial precedent generated as a byproduct of the decisions that courts have made to resolve unique disputes, as distinguished from statutes and constitutions. Case law concerns concrete facts; statutes and constitutions are written in the abstract."[34] In other words, case law is made by the decisions of judges in deciding cases. Prior to issuing their decisions, judges consult previous case law on the same subject matter and look to see how previous judges have decided. This is known as *stare decisis*. When they issue their decision, they are then contributing to the body of case law that builds over time providing the precedents for future cases. As is often the case, many times judges will arrive at different conclusions, and case law builds in different jurisdictions, different states, or in different circuit courts. If the conflict is found at the district level, often the circuit courts will determine which body of case law is correct, thus contributing to case law that will be used in future cases. In the case of a conflict between circuit courts, it is the Supreme Court that will be the final arbiter as the United States Constitution deems the Supreme Court to be the highest court in the land, hence it has the final say. Their decisions then set precedent for future cases.

Administrative laws are "statutes, regulations, and orders that govern public agencies" and are essentially the "rules governing the administrative operations of the government."[35] These laws are regulatory in nature and are passed by government to control certain sectors. These sectors consist of various industries, businesses, and individuals, and may include such laws aimed at regulating building, health, and environmental codes.[36] Agencies of government are often developed to enforce these particular codes as well, such as the Food and Drug Administration, the Environmental Protection Agency, or the Occupational Health and Safety Administration. These agencies all are given regulatory powers to enforce their sector of administrative law, and individuals, industries, and businesses found guilty often face extensive fines. The power of these regulatory agencies through administrative law, explains why this type of law has often been referred to as the fourth branch of government.

The development of the body of laws in the United States has assuredly changed over time. While early legislative activity also considered natural law in the political process of codifying the law, over time the contemporary legal process has removed much of the biblical understanding of the law. In a sense, it attempted to remove the moral element to the law, the notion of universal application, and, perhaps most seriously, the revealed law of God. Rather than be guided by God's law, the law developed into a body of law that resulted from the popular consent of individuals who formed themselves into a sovereign nation. This later is known as positive law.

Positive law can create a moral dilemma in people. If the law is created by popular consent, then it is argued that the laws must be followed. Regardless if people disagree with the law or find the law to be unjust or immoral, they must abide by the law as they have given their consent to government to enforce those laws. If people are confronted with laws that they believe are unreasonable, unjust, or not in the interest of society as a whole, the question is whether or not these laws should be obeyed. The problem is if people obey every law, regardless, they may be forced to abide by something they believe to be immoral. If on the other hand, they were to challenge every law and only follow those laws with which they agree, society would lose the foundation which holds it together. The Catholic Church sees morality as being that which is in the interest of all of society and reflects the will of God. Hence, natural law should provide the foundation upon which natural rights, and ultimately our Constitution, are based. Natural law, however, is not the only means by which we should determine law, for St. Thomas Aquinas identified four types of law.

The first type of law, according to Aquinas, is eternal law. Eternal laws are God's laws that are not revealed to humankind, but rather, constitute the source of all the other laws. Although we cannot know these laws directly, we can know their effects, for as Paul explains, "even since the creation of the world, his invisible attributes of eternal power and divinity have been able to be understood and perceived in what he has made."[37] These laws are universal and everlasting and are the dictates of divine wisdom. These are often thought of as being the physical laws that govern the universe, the stars, and the planets, but eternal laws may also exist in terms of humankind, inherent within the relationship between God and man.

The second type of law is the divine law. Divine laws are God's laws that are revealed to humankind through divine revelation. These are most evident in both the Old and New Testaments of the Bible and can be found more directly through the Ten Commandments, the Beatitudes, and other teachings of Jesus Christ. They also include the Nicene and Apostle's creeds, church doctrine, the articles of faith, the sacraments, the Pope's encyclicals, and all of the other traditions of the Catholic faith. According to St. Thomas, the purpose of divine law is to "bring man to that end which is everlasting happiness."[38]

The third type of law is, again, natural law. Natural laws are discernible by people by virtue of their relationship with God. If they are rational and listen to God, they have the ability to distinguish between right and wrong, good and evil. These laws are tied to human nature as created by God. As Charles Nemeth, writing about St. Thomas and the Law explains, "as author of nature, God could not and would not forge a creation of disorder and anarchy, but more predictably, infuses and imprints, an orderly, lawful, natural sequence in each of his creatures."[39] In addition to understanding the natural law as the nature of being and the operations of that nature, St. Thomas also points out that the basis of the natural law is to do good and avoid evil, this being the "first principle" of the natural law. If people are truly to live out the natural law, practical reason dictates they listen to God and do what is right and good, avoiding what is wrong and evil.

The fourth type of law, and the embodiment of positive law, is human law. These laws are the laws made by the people to govern the action of others and to represent the will of the people as a whole. These include all of the laws previously discussed, such as the criminal law, civil law, and administrative laws. St. Thomas argues that human law, unlike the other three types of laws, is imperfect but is aimed at ordering human life in order for man to live amongst each other. Human law is necessary for the functioning of social and political living, but it can never supersede the other three types of laws.

Returning to the question raised earlier: can a law be unjust? If so, must one follow an unjust human law? St. Thomas explains that a law can be unjust if it is not directed to the common good, if it is beyond the authority of the law-giver, and if it does not impose properly proportionate burdens. In any of these cases the law loses its ability to be enforced, and man is not bound to obey the unjust law. As he cautiously states, "that which is not just seems to be no law at all."[40] Thus, if a law is contrary to the laws of God and his commandments, St. Thomas recommends direct disobedience to the law.

Adhering to the previously discussed concepts of justice in Chapter One, a Catholic perspective on crime and justice would first look to the behavior that is to be defined as criminal to determine if such behavior was a violation of eternal, divine, and natural law. It would then consider the impact of that behavior on society to determine if a law was necessary and just. Thus, any preexisting law would have to be examined under these same principles to determine if unjust laws currently exist and work to change these laws. Recognizing that just laws exist to do God's will and to regulate behavior among humankind in society, enforcing those just laws becomes the duty of the criminal justice system.

Criminal Justice

The enforcement, prosecution, and punishment of the law are the responsibilities of the American criminal justice system. Criminal justice is generally defined as consisting of three components: police, courts, and corrections. The police are responsible for detecting and apprehending people who are accused of breaking the law. The court system decides if a person is guilty of committing a crime, and the corrections system carries out the sentences imposed on a guilty defendant. Although many refer to this as the criminal justice "system," the three components developed largely independent of each other becoming their own separate institutions. Many, therefore, argue that there are really three separate systems that exist in a network relationship as they deal with the same subject matter: crime and the criminally accused. Others argue that the criminal justice system is truly a system of three working components all functioning together toward the attainment of a common goal.

The phrase "criminal justice" is actually absent throughout most of American history. It was not until the 1967 publication of *The Challenge of Crime in A Free Society* by the President's Commission on Law Enforcement and Administration of Justice that "America's System of Criminal Justice" was referred to as such.[41] The Commission stated the criminal justice system is, in general, "to protect individuals and the community." More specifically, the Commission stated there were three goals of the system: to control crime, prevent crime, and provide and maintain justice. The first goal, to control crime, is fairly straightforward in that the system, through arrest, prosecution, and punishing the guilty, works to control the problem of crime. The second goal, to prevent crime, while being slightly more difficult, is also fairly straight-forward, in that the criminal justice system should work to deter crime before it occurs. The last goal, however, is generally considered to be the most difficult. The idea of providing and maintaining justice becomes complicated, for as Chapter One discussed, there is not necessarily a shared definition of the term justice. Many tend to focus on the concept of fairness and the due process of law as being the definition of providing and maintaining justice. Others take the viewpoint that by punishing and repressing criminal behavior, the criminal justice system is providing and maintaining justice in our society. This split was highlighted by Herbert Packer, a distinguished professor of law at Stanford University in the 1960s, when he explained that there are really two conceptual models of criminal justice at work in the United States.

Packer published an article titled "Two Models of the Criminal Process" which was later included in the book, *The Limits of the Criminal Sanctions.*[42] In these publications, Packer presented two models of the criminal justice system, the crime control model and the due process model. His goal was to present two models that would "give operational content to a complex of values underlying the criminal law."[43] Packer achieved his goal, for these two models have come to reflect the competing ideologies and policies of the criminal justice system.

Packer did not necessarily want these two models to become an oversimplification of the values that underlie the criminal process. Rather, he wanted to be able to communicate the two competing systems of values that created an enormous amount of tension on the development of the criminal process and how it should best be ordered. He did contend that the polarity of the two models was not absolute and that there was some common ground between these competing philosophies. The primary commonality between these two competing models, Packer explained, could actually be found in their adherence to the Constitution. Both adhered to the principles found in the Constitution; however, each does so in its own unique way. In addition, both agree that our system is an adversarial system, pitting the prosecution against the defense. Neither model disagrees with this basic premise, but how they react to the adversarial system of justice is quite diverse. Despite the articulation of this "common ground" between the competing models, it is the polarity of the two models that is most renowned and most discussed in terms of Herbert Packer's models. Therefore, it is to these two competing models we now turn.

The crime control model articulates that the repression of criminal conduct is by far the most important function of the criminal justice system. If the system, and more specifically the police, fail to keep criminal conduct under tight control, then it is believed that this will lead to the breakdown of public order, which will cause the denigration of human freedom. If people are not free to do as they choose for fear of crime, then society suffers. Thus, the criminal justice system becomes a guarantor of human freedom. And in order to achieve this freedom, the crime control model argues that the criminal justice system is charged with arresting suspects, determining guilt, and insuring that criminals are properly punished. Therefore, the crime control model stresses the need for efficiency and speed to generate a high rate of apprehension while dealing with limited resources. The goal is to then process these individuals through the system by moving those who are not guilty out of the process and moving those who are toward some form of sanction. Every step in the system, however, is focused on the successful and speedy prosecution of the offender. To this end, individual constitutional rights must often be seen as secondary to the effective prosecution of offenders. This model assumes that in most cases, people who are brought into the system are in fact guilty, otherwise they would not have been brought into the system in the first place. Thus, a presumption of guilt exists prior to a suspect becoming a defendant. So, one way to achieve successful prosecution of these suspects is for lawyers from both sides to come to an agreement about the case, achieve a guilty plea, and close the case.

The due process model is generally the polar opposite of the crime control model. The ideology behind the model is that due process is "far more deeply impressed on the formal structure of the law"[44] and that the protection of individual and thus, constitutional rights, are paramount. Every effort must be made to guarantee than an individual is not being unfairly labeled and treated as a criminal, especially before being found guilty. Hence, rather than assuming a suspect to be guilty, due process assumes the suspect to be innocent and guilt must be proven by the criminal justice system. The purpose of the system then, is to create a process of successive stages that is "designed to present formidable impediments to carrying the accused any further along in the process."[45] The reason it does this is to prevent and eliminate any mistakes being made in the process, at least to the greatest extent possible. Packer describes the due process model as always being skeptical of the morality and utility of the criminal sanction and is wary of the actors in the criminal justice system. Thus, at each successive stage of the system, roadblocks are created to ensure that the innocent go free and the guilty receive equal protection under the law.

Although Packer did not desire the two models to be seen as entirely polar opposites on an ideological spectrum, it is this aspect of the model that is most attractive to students of criminal justice. The crime control model resembles an assembly line, while the due process model resembles an obstacle course. The crime control model is oriented on being as efficient as possible, while the due process model desires to be equitable. The goal of the crime control model is to punish criminals, while the due process model is aimed at protecting individual rights. The crime control model achieves its ends through tough legislation and strong enforcement through the administrative process. The due process model is more judicially oriented and is legalistic in nature. And, as both models are ideologically driven, they tend to be represented by the two political ideological perspectives as well. The crime control model is adhered to more often by conservatives, and the due process model is more often attributed to liberals. Although there are always exceptions to the rule and these generalizations might not always hold true, they have a strong consistency because they are ideologically based.

Taking Packer's two models a little further was Malcolm M. Feeley, a professor of criminal justice and the law, in a 1973 article titled, "Two Models of the Criminal Justice System: An Organizational Approach."[46] Feeley's purpose was to create a theoretical framework for explaining the organization of criminal justice in order that research could be viewed through these two perspectives. Feeley articulated that there were two models of organization, the rational-goal model and the functional systems model. In order to create his rational-goal model he combined two models that had been previously advanced and merged them into one model. The rational model argues that an organization is focused on the means of accomplishing its mission, while the goals model argues that it is not the means, but the end that is important. Feeley advances the argument that in criminal justice these two concepts, the means and the goals (ends), are often the same thing, for in criminal justice the system seeks justice (means) to obtain justice (goals). The way this is accomplished is through an adherence to strict rules and procedures within the bureaucracy, much in the vein of Max Weber.

Weber is the primary scholar who speaks to the rational organization as being the primary means by which government achieves its goals. Organizations are characterized by several major components which consist of (1) a continuous organization of official functions bound by rules, (2) a specific sphere of competence (obligations) in the division of labor to be performed by a person who is provided with the necessary means and authority to carry out their tasks, (3) the organization of offices following the principle of hierarchy, and (4) a set of technical rules and norms regulating the conduct of the offices.[47] As in the criminal justice system, the system itself is made up of various officials (police, judges, correctional officers, etc.) that are bound by formal rules, given specific responsibilities and authority to carry out their duties, must follow a chain-of-command (especially in policing and corrections), and are guided by policies and procedures in the performance of their duties. By ensuring that the organization is highly effective in the performance of their duties, (the mean) they can ensure that they achieve their ends (goals). Thus, effectiveness, like in Packer's crime control model, is the overriding goal.

The functional-systems model is a different conception of how an organization is employed. The common characteristics of this model are that criminal justice is a "system of action based primarily upon cooperation, exchange and adaptation"[48] and that it emphasizes "these considerations over adherence to formal rules and defined 'roles' in searching for and developing explanations of behavior and discussing organizational effectiveness."[49] In fact, this model would acknowledge the viewpoint that the criminal justice system is not very effective in operating through its rules and that the actual means for obtaining these goals is the adherence to the more informal rules of the game, folkways, personal relationships, and dedicated individuals. Another way of explaining the differences between the two models is that the rational-goal model is focused on creating a rational organization, while the functional-systems model is focused on creating rational individuals, those people who work within the criminal justice system, to be better adept at pursuing goals. Hence, increased discretion is important in the functional-systems model because it allows those actors in the system to make decisions in the application of the law, rather than the rules as would be the case in the rational-goal model.

In Feeley's two models, once again ideology is seen as shaping the viewpoint of how criminal justice should best be organized. Packer's models provided us two viewpoints for understanding the purpose of criminal justice, while Feeley's models provide us a perspective on how best to organize society in order for these ends to be achieved. Thus, it can be seen that those whose ideological beliefs lead them to believe that the crime control model is the proper function of our criminal justice system will also most likely believe that the rational-goal model is the best way to achieve this end. Those who believe in the due process model will likely articulate that the functional-systems model is the best way to organize the criminal justice system. Ideology again shapes our understanding of how criminal justice should best be ordered.

If the complexity of Feeley's two models is lost on the reader then perhaps it can be made clearer through the more recent debates over whether or not criminal justice is a system or non-system. In the criminal justice system model the concept that criminal justice operates as a bona fide system is advanced. A system is made up of interdependent elements that work together to perform one or more tasks or goals. This definition implies first that the component parts or subsystems are working together to reach one ultimate goal, and second, that the system is a sequential, orderly process similar to a factory assembly line, whereby a client must be processed through each stage before entering into the next. There are component parts (the police, courts, and corrections agencies) that work together to reach the goal of reducing or preventing crime. There is also a sequential process that must be followed as one goes through the criminal justice system. When individuals enter the system, they must do so through an arrest: they cannot go straight to the courts or the corrections components. Then, after the arrest stage, a defendant goes through the court component. They cannot go directly to the corrections area. Only after the defendant has been processed through the first two components of the system can they enter the corrections component. In order to get to the next level, an offender must have had contact with all the preceding ones.

Each of the components must work together to achieve a final result, which means they are interdependent. The work of each department, therefore, is heavily influenced by the work of every other department. When one unit changes its policies or practices, other units will be affected. For example, an increase in the number of people arrested by the police will affect the work not only of the judicial subsystem but also of the probation and correctional subsystems. Each part must make its own distinctive contribution; each part must also have at least minimal contact with at least one other component of the system.

From this perspective, the criminal justice system is indeed a "system." However, many people see the criminal justice system as a non-system in which the component parts do not work together to achieve a goal. Each of the components are independent and have their own set of tasks and goals. The police have a goal of bringing people into the system, while the correction's system wants to get them out. Within the courts, the prosecution wants to keep the defendant in the system and the defense wants to get the case dismissed. Each agency acts according to its own rules and norms with its own goals and objectives. In addition, each component struggles to find its own resources, sometimes competing for the same resources. This competition, added to strained relations, poor communications, and a reluctance to cooperate with each other, can generate antagonism between the departments. This, in turn, can lead to poor working relationships and resistance to working with each other and doing what is in the best interest of the client and society. Additionally, people working inside the system, as well as those observing the system, lose their respect for the system, and may be more likely to seek justice in alternative ways.

Another way of thinking about the non-system approach has been advanced by Cox and Wade who argue that the traditional flowchart presentation of the criminal justice system is often misleading and inaccurate.[50] They argue that it fails to indicate the routine pursuit of different, sometimes incompatible goals by various components, the effects of feedback based on personal relationships inside and outside criminal justice, the importance of political considerations by all of those involved, and the widespread use of discretion.[51] Instead, what they argue is that we really do not have a criminal justice *system*, but rather a criminal justice *network*. They advance this non-system concept as "consisting of a web of constantly changing relationships among individuals, some of whom are directly involved in criminal justice pursuits, others whom are not" and that "a network may be thought of as a net with intersecting lines of communication among components designed to function in a specific manner."[52] Cox and Wade argue that each criminal event can be unique and that the network will come to bear on the problem in different ways. A series of simple automobile larcenies may generate a network of police officers, detectives, and prosecutors to address the problem, while a kidnapped child who is taken across state lines will create a network of both criminal justice actors (local police, state police, Federal Bureau of Investigation, prosecutors, etc.) and non-criminal justice actors (victim's family, the media, the National Center for Missing and Exploited Children, etc.). Different actors, agencies, and resources are all brought to bear on a specific problem, but it is not a standard response, nor is it always going to be the same responders. These various criminal justice and non-criminal justice actors employ those aspects of the network that are necessary to address a specific problem. This is why they explain that the criminal justice *network* is a "web of constantly changing relationships among individuals involved more or less directly in the pursuit of criminal justice."[53]

These various models of the criminal justice system (or network) provide varying ideological approaches to criminal justice and help us to understand how we perceive this system. Yet, there is something more to our understanding of criminal justice that is an extension of our ideological approach to justice which tells us the purpose of the system itself. While most would agree that the ultimate goal of the criminal justice system is to seek justice, the term justice can have various meanings to various people. Again, these variations generally proceed from one's ideological perspective. What defines this complexity is most often the discussion of the *goals* of the criminal justice system. It is here that perhaps the greatest conflict begins to arise in policy formulation, and it is to this topic we now turn.

Ideology plays an important role in shaping one's understanding about how the world works, which subsequently shapes their views of the criminal justice system. All of this will then come to bear on the question, "what is the goal of the criminal justice system?" While preventing crime and dealing with the aftermath of crimes is clearly the function of the criminal justice system, how it achieves these ends are embodied in the goals of the system. The goals of the system are many, varied, and often conflicting, largely due to the ideological differences that people have over human behavior and how society should be ordered. Understanding these varying goals is important to our understanding of not only criminal justice policy, but the criminal justice system itself.

The first major goal of the criminal justice system is to deter people from committing crime.[54] There are two types of deterrence: general and specific. General deterrence can be described as punishing an individual so severely that it makes an example of them in order to deter the rest of the public from committing a similar act. Deterrence theory operates on the assumption that people are rational actors and that they weigh the costs and benefits of all their actions. If they factor in the cost of committing a crime, as evidenced by the individual of whom an example was made, then their rational process would conclude that the cost far outweighs any benefit they may obtain from the crime. Thus, they will be deterred. For example, when the newspaper reports that someone was sentenced to serve a ten-year sentence in prison for theft, it is thought that this information will prevent others from committing the same or a similar offense. The reasoning is that they too could be sentenced to ten years in prison if they commit a similar act. Another prime example of general deterrence is found in the death penalty. Many argue that the old method of public executions served as a general deterrent to the rest of the community who witnessed the executions in person in order to deter them from committing such heinous crimes that would merit similar punishment. Although some would argue that moving such executions behind prison walls and limiting the number of witnesses has decreased the effect of deterrence, many still argue that the prospect of being executed for murder will prevent future murders.[55] Another, and more recent, example, is found in a book by Michael G. Santos titled *About Prisons,*[56] where he describes his life of drug dealing in his early twenties, being arrested, and ultimately given a forty-five year sentence of which he would have to serve twenty-seven in a federal penitentiary. The judge fully intended to make an example of Santos by giving him a very severe punishment for his crimes, most likely with the intent of deterring future drug dealers or, at a minimum, deterring Santos from future crimes.

This last case of deterrence, the judge giving Santos a lengthy sentence to prevent *him* from future crimes, is what is known as specific deterrence. The goal of specific deterrence is to make the punishment for committing an offense so negative that the same person does not commit further criminal acts. This can be equated to the common practice among parents who punish their children for bad behavior in the hopes that it will deter them from committing the same bad behavior in the future. Equally, by punishing adults who commit criminal acts through either a heavy fine, jail time, or both, it is the goal of specific deterrence that this experience will be so negative that they will never repeat those same illegal behaviors.

Related to specific deterrence is the goal of incapacitation whereby a criminal is sentenced to a lengthy time in a correctional facility.[57] In this particular goal, "the opportunity for offending again is limited (or eliminated) because the offender's freedom is restricted."[58] Many scholars have suggested that the drop in crime during the 1990s had something to do with the prison expansion of the 1980s.[59] As more prisons were built, this allowed for more criminals to be sentenced to prison and for longer sentences, thus incapacitating them in the 1990s and preventing them from committing more crime. An extreme example of incapacitation is the death penalty. When an offender is sentenced to death, they are virtually unable to commit more offenses while on death row and can obviously commit no other crimes once executed. Judges can also order mandatory life sentences that will reduce the amount of crime they can commit in prison, but eliminate the offender's chances of committing more crimes on the streets. Other correctional options provide fewer restrictions on inmate behavior, including curfews, house arrest, day reporting centers, and probation. Each of these options makes it more difficult for offenders to have the opportunity to commit additional crimes, thus incapacitating them.

Like specific deterrence is to general deterrence, there is a more narrowly focused type of incapacitation known as selective incapacitation. Selective incapacitation refers to "sentencing policies that attempt to distinguish between higher-rate and lower-rate criminal offenders in determining who will be incarcerated and for how long."[60] The idea here is for the criminal justice system to target those who are considered career criminals and repeat offenders (or likely career criminals and likely repeat offenders) in order to prevent these few people from committing future crimes. Adhering to the belief that a few people cause the most problems, the goal is to take the few criminals who cause the most crime, the higher-rate offenders, and severely incapacitate them.

Another goal of the criminal justice system is punishment. This goal is also known as "retribution," "revenge," or the "just deserts" models of criminal justice.[61] All of these simply refer to punishing offenders who have done something wrong so that a specific person learns not to commit the crime again. The concept of punishment is based upon the idea that each individual is responsible for their actions and to the community in which they live. When they violate the laws of that community, they are to be held accountable for their actions through various forms of punishment. The goal of the criminal justice system is to ensure that those who commit crimes are held accountable and, if found guilty, are punished for their crimes. Examples of the punishment orientation abound over the past three decades, such as the growing amount of criminal legislation, legislation that has increased the sentences for various crimes, an increase in the use of the death penalty, the hiring of more police officers, and the prison expansion.

All of this suggests an increased movement toward the goal of punishment. Another goal of the criminal justice system is rehabilitation or the treatment of offenders so that they can rejoin society with the goal of no longer committing crime. This is based on the medical model that assumes that there is something wrong with offenders, or some underlying cause for their behavior, and that they can be diagnosed and treated so they won't commit more crimes, just like someone who is sick and can be treated so they are well again.[62] Many people believe that teaching criminals a specific trade or job skills can give them the means to become productive citizens when they are released from confinement. In other cases, officials believe that behavior modification is the proper response in order to socialize the individual to the proper norms of society, so that, once released, they will not commit further crimes. Another means of rehabilitation is to educate the offender, either through classes to help them earn their G.E.D. or to begin work toward a college degree. Finally, one other means of rehabilitation is a direct application of the medical model, by guiding the individual through either a drug treatment program or providing them with the necessary medication to help control mental illnesses that may have been a contributing factor to the offender's crimes.

An extension of the goal of rehabilitation and treatment is reintegration. The goal here is to continue to work with the offender as they make the transition from life in prison or jail to life back in their community. At this point, the goal is not so much to rehabilitate or treat as it is to help move the offender into a community, provide them with an alternative to criminal behavior, and help them become productive citizens. Examples include correctional programs that slowly wean the offender from prison life by allowing them to work outside of the prison, but return to the prison at night and during the weekends. Eventually, many of these offenders are moved into half-way houses where they are provided a controlled environment outside of prison and are given the assistance they need to make the transition back into a community.

Some have also argued that a goal of the criminal justice system is to teach and enforce morality within the community. Morality, as being the understanding of what is right and what is wrong is inherently a part of our system of criminal laws. All laws tell people what is right and what is wrong behavior. According to Marion, when the state establishes this series of punishments and offenses, citizens can get a sense of what is "right" (proper, moral) and "wrong" (improper, immoral) behavior.[63] For example, when the act of prostitution or gambling is deemed wrong by the government, this is teaching a certain population that those actions are inappropriate. When an individual violates society's morality and they commit a "wrong" behavior, then it is the role of the criminal justice system to enforce society's morality through the application of the criminal (moral) law.

Another goal, and one that has recently become a growing area of interest in criminal justice, is restorative justice, sometimes referred to as simply restoration or community justice.[64] This approach implies that crime is a disruption of the community's peace, and it aims to restore the community to its state before the crime was committed.[65] It does this to some degree by avoiding the traditional criminal justice model and pursuing a civil mediation process. Victims and offenders are brought together with a mediator to work through the violation and attempt to arrive at some form of reparation that restores order. It then moves to reintegrate the victim and offender back into the community, thus allowing them to either become or return to being full participants in their community. Through restoration, the community can attempt to repair the peace rather than punish the offender in response to a crime. Community policing, victim-offender mediation, and community-based corrections are all seen as means toward this end, along with an expansion of these concepts to create a sense of community justice, rather than criminal justice.[66]

Finally, one other goal that has recently emerged is known as the pragmatic goal of criminal justice. Pragmatism is a philosophy that stresses practical consequences as being the most important criterion in determining justice. It is very utilitarian in nature and, again, practical. More recently this has come to be found in the literature that asks, "What works?"[67] The premise here is to ignore ideology, theory, or goals, by simply looking at programs that work in preventing or reducing crime, regardless of the reason why. The predominate literature in this pragmatic approach has looked at crime prevention methods in association with different areas that have been attributed to affecting crime. For instance, schools are often seen as a potential source of spawning crime, but also one for preventing crime. Evaluating various programs, such as drug and alcohol education, counseling and mentoring programs, and after-school programs, and looking at what is effective at reducing crime, provides us with practical solutions to the crime problem. As a result, these programs are then encouraged, replicated, and implemented in other jurisdictions. This has been done in the area of community programs, family-based programs, risk factors associated with labor markets, and in terms of police crime prevention programs and the broader criminal justice programs. The goal of pragmatism then, is to figure out what works and replicate these programs in other jurisdictions.

While some would argue that these goals are compatible and that all of them can be obtained simultaneously, this argument loses credibility as one begins to explore the details of each of these goals. Is it realistic to believe that one can be punished with a lengthy sentence, while at the same time being treated and rehabilitated? Even more difficult are such goals as incapacitation, especially selective incapacitation, when faced with the tenets of restorative justice. Further, when faced with the reality of constrained budgets in the criminal justice system, it is highly unlikely that the system can afford both long prison sentences while providing rehabilitation and treatment programs to each offender for the period of these lengthy sentences. Therefore, one must accept the fact that these goals do in reality conflict with each other.

In looking at the reason for the conflict within the criminal justice system over its intended goals, one has to return to ideology. The goals of deterrence, incapacitation, punishment, and to some degree morality all fit into Packer's crime control model. The goals of rehabilitation, reintegration, and restorative justice all intend a very different purpose of the criminal justice system, and, while not specifically Packer's due process model, they do reflect a more humanitarian approach to justice. Finally, the goal of pragmatism, while trying to divest itself of ideological constraints, generally still finds itself constrained, for the programs themselves are often implemented for very specific ideological reasons.

Perhaps the more important question is a normative one which is whether or not goal conflict is a "good" or "bad" thing in criminal justice. Those that would argue goal conflict is "bad," take the position that conflicting goals prevent a rational system, they strain resources, thus making criminal justice less efficient or effective, and they fail to send clear signals to those working within the system as to what specifically they are trying to accomplish. Those that argue goal conflict is "good," argue that conflict allows for a wide variety of interests (ideologies) to be represented within the system. It creates a sort of checks-and-balances process whereby one goal does not become too excessive in nature, and it in actuality creates a "smoothly operating offender-processing system," because it does not try to unify the criminal justice system causing it to bog-down in bureaucratic inertia.[68] The most likely reason, however, for this difference in perception over goal conflict is again due to ideological differences. Those who perceive goal conflict as bad prefer a neatly ordered world where there is a criminal justice *system* that has a well-ordered and agreed upon goal. Those who perceive goal conflict as good prefer a less orderly world where the criminal justice *network* allows for various goals to be applied to specific cases depending on the circumstances of each incident or event. One desires a highly unified system while the other desires a highly fragmented system. From the perspective of the Catholic Church, as the opening quote suggests, the goal for the criminal justice system should be both justice and mercy, the two not necessarily being mutually exclusive.

Criminal Justice from a Catholic Perspective

The sacred scriptures and the theological and sacramental heritage of the Catholic faith, according to the United States Conference of Catholic Bishops, can provide us with a framework in which the Catholic understanding of justice can be applied to our modern day criminal justice system. They presented this brief overview in their 2000 statement, *Responsibility, Rehabilitation, and Restoration: A Catholic Perspective on Crime and Criminal Justice.*[69] As the opening quote suggests, the Bishops explain that a criminal justice system based on the

Catholic faith generates a paradox. On the one hand, they clearly argue that society cannot tolerate any behavior that threatens the lives, rights, and property of others. On the other hand, the Catholic faith teaches that in spite of the fact that a person has committed a crime, no matter how heinous, society should not give up on that individual. So, while they justify responsibility, accountability, and legitimate forms of punishment for the offender, they also seek rehabilitation and restoration for the offender as well.

The Bishops' statement focuses on many of the aforementioned principles of justice, human rights, and the common good. They focus not only on the scriptural writings, but those of St. Thomas Aquinas and St. Augustine. In addition, they orient their statements to the more recent twentieth-century teachings of subsidiarity (problem-solving at the community level) and solidarity (we are each responsible for all), found in the documents of Vatican II and the encyclicals of the Popes. Perhaps the best example, however, of what the Bishops are trying to articulate is found in their explanation of the four traditional elements of the Sacrament of Reconciliation. They explain that this Sacrament teaches us about "taking responsibility, making amends, and reintegrating into community." They do this by breaking it down into the following:

Contrition: Genuine sorrow, regret, or grief over one's wrongs and a serious resolution to not repeat the wrong.
Confession: Clear acknowledgment and true acceptance of responsibility for the hurtful behavior.
Satisfaction: The external sign of one's desire to amend one's life (this "satisfaction," whether in the form of prayers or good deeds, is a form of "compensation" or restitution for the wrongs or harms caused by one's sins).
Absolution: After someone has shown contrition, acknowledged his or her sin, and offered satisfaction, then Jesus, through the ministry of the priest and in the company of the church community, forgives the sin and welcomes that person back into "communion."[70]

In light of this moral framework and based on the Catholic understanding of justice, the Bishops then set out to present the direction the criminal justice system should take.[71] Reflecting St. Thomas Aquinas who taught that the punishment of wrongdoers is justified, but that punishment is never justified for its own sake, they argue that legitimate punishment must be coupled with treatment and, when and where possible, restitution. They explain that the system should emphasize treatment and restoration for the criminal, but that this must not be in deference to the restitution and healing of the victim who should be allowed to participate more fully in the criminal justice process. They call for restorative justice principles to be applied for they reflect the values and traditions of the Catholic faith, and that mediation programs, along with crime prevention, rehabilitation, education, substance abuse treatment, probation, parole, and reintegration programs should be the primary use of government resources. All of these programs, however, the Bishops state, should be at the community level in keeping with the concepts of subsidarity. In fact, they specifically call for such criminal justice orientations as community policing, victim-offender mediation programs, and community-based corrections. In sum, what the Catholic Bishops have called for is the criminal justice system to shift to a restorative justice approach to all that it does, through an adherence to community justice methods.

Conclusion

Criminal behavior drives the political system to react by creating laws. The criminal justice system must not only react to criminal behavior, it must do so in the framework of the law, encapsulated within a myriad of conflicting goals. While many of America's policies have clearly been focused on crime control (e.g., hiring more police, building more prisons, "three strikes" legislation), many of the policies have been more reflective of due process (e.g., legal protections, cause lawyering, laws of evidence, limits of search and seizure). Neither of these ideological policies have focused with any weight on the issues of responsibility, rehabilitation, and restoration. More specifically, they have not placed a heavy emphasis on the treatment and restoration of the offender and the restitution and healing of the victim. As a result, the U.S. Conference of Catholic Bishops has called for a redirection of criminal justice policy in America, one that focuses on restorative and community justice principles, both of which are in keeping with the values and traditions of the Catholic faith.[72] Understanding what restorative and community justice entail is the focus of the next chapter.

Notes

1. G.E. Rush, *The Dictionary of Criminal Justice,* 5th ed. (New York: McGraw Hill, 2000), 86.
2. G.E. Rush, *The Dictionary of Criminal Justice,* 5th ed. (New York: McGraw Hill, 2000), 86.
3. N.E. Marion, *Criminal Justice in America: The Politics Behind the System* (Durham, NC: Carolina Academic Press, 2002), 58.
4. Title 28, Section 534 of the United States Code.
5. Arson was added to the Uniform Crime Reports Part I offenses in 1979.
6. Part II offenses are as follows: simple assaults, forgery and counterfeiting, fraud, embezzlement, stolen property, vandalism, weapons, prostitution and commercialized vice, sex offenses, drug abuse, gambling, offenses against the family and children, driving under the influence, liquor laws, drunkenness, disorderly conduct, vagrancy.
7. There exists a very large set of literature that explores this topic and the following is merely a sampling of the literature: R. H. Beattie, "Problems of Criminal Statistics in the United States," *Journal of Criminal Law, Criminology, and Police Science* 46 (1955):

Criminal Justice

178-186; A.D. Bidermna and J. P. Lynch, *Understanding Crime Incidence Statistics* (New York: Springer-Verlag, 1991); D. J. Black, "Production of Crime Rates," *American Sociological Review* 35 (1970): 733-748; M. Hindelang, "The Uniform Crime Reports Revisited," *Journal of Criminal Justice* 2 (1974): 1-17; J. L. Kituse and A. V. Cicourel, "A Note on the Use of Official Statistics," *Social Problems* 11 (1963): 131-138; D. Seidman and M. Couzens, "Getting the Crime Rate Down: Political Pressure and Crime Reporting," *Law and Society Review* 8 (1974): 457-493; C. E. Silberman, *Criminal Violence, Criminal Justice* (New York: Random House, 1978); W. G. Skogan, "The Validity of Official Crime Statistics: An Empirical Investigation," *Social Science Quarterly* 55 (1974): 25-38; S. Wheeler, "Criminal Statistics: A Reformulation of the Problem," *Journal of Criminal Law, Criminology, and Police Science* 58 (1967): 317-324.

8. R. Block and C. R. Block, "Decisions and Data: The Transformation of Robbery Incidents into Official Robbery Statistics," *Journal of Criminal Law and Criminology* 71 (1980): 622-636; W. Gove, M. Hughes, and M. Geerken, "Are Uniform Crime Reports a Valid Indicator of the Index Crimes? An Affirmative Answer with Minor Qualifications," *Criminology* 23 (1985): 451-501.

9. J. Reiman, *The Rich Get Richer and the Poor Get Prison*, 4th ed. (Boston, MA: Allyn and Bacon, 1995); S. Simpson, A.R. Harris, and B. A. Mattson, "Measuring Corporate Crime," in *Understanding Corporate Criminality*, ed. M.R. Blakenship (New York: Garland Publishing, 1995); S. Walker, *The Police in America* (New York: McGraw Hill, 1992), 295-296.

10. G. F. Jensen and M. Karpos, "Managing Rape: Exploratory Research on the Behavior of Rape Statistics," *Criminology* 31 (1993): 363-385; J. D. Orcutt and R. Faison, "Sex-Role Attitude Change and Reporting of Rape Victimization, 1973-1985," *Sociological Quarterly* 29 (1988): 589-604.

11. See Lois B. DeFluer, "Biasing Influences on Drug Arrest Records: Implications for Deviance Research," *American Sociological Review* 40 (1975):88-103; Joseph G. Weis, "Crime Statistics: Reporting Systems and Methods," in *Encyclopedia of Crime and Justice*, Vol. 1, ed. Sanford H. Kadish (New York: Free Press, 1983), 378-392; David Seidman and Michael Couzens, "Getting the Crime Rate Down: Political Pressure and Crime Reporting," *Law & Society Review* 8 (1974): 457-493.

12. See Donald J. Black, "The Production of Crime Rates," *American Sociological Review* 35 (1970): 733-748; Pamela I. Jackson and Leo Carroll, "Race and the War on Crime: The Sociopolitical Determinants of Municipal Police Expenditures in 90 Non-Southern U.S. Cities," *American Sociological Review* 46 (1981): 290-305; Allen E. Liska and Mitchell B. Chamlin, "Social Structure and Crime Control Among Macrosocial Unites," *American Journal of Sociology* 98 (1984): 383-395.

13. See Joseph F. Sheley and John J. Hanlon, "Unintended Consequences of Police Decisions to Actively Enforce Laws: Implications for Analysis of Crime Trends," *Contemporary Crises* 2 (1978): 265-275; Lawrence Sherman and Barry D. Glick, *The Quality of Police Arrest Statistics* (Washington D.C.: Police Foundation, 1984); James Q. Wilson, *Varieties of Police Behavior: The Management of Law and Order in Eight Communities* (Cambridge, Massachusetts: Harvard University Press, 1978).

14. See Richard McCleary, Barbara C. Nienstedt, and James M. Erven, "Uniform Crime Reports as Organizational Outcomes: Three Time-Series Experiments," *Social Problems* 29 (1982): 361-372; Presidential Commission on Law Enforcement and the Administration of Justice, *The Challenge of Crime in a Free Society* (Washington D.C.:

57

U.S. GPO, 1967); Wesley Skogan, "Citizen Reporting on Crime: Some National Panel Data," *Criminology* 13 (1976): 535-549.

15. See James Q. Wilson, *Thinking About Crime* (New York: Basic Books, 1975); James Lynch, "Crime in International Perspective," in *Crime*, ed. James Q. Wilson and Joan Petersilia (San Francisco: ICS Press, 1995).

16. See A.D. Biderman and J.P. Lynch, *Understanding Crime Incidence Statistics: Why the UCR Diverges from the NCS* (New York: Springer-Verlag, 1991); Walter R. Gove, Michael Hughes, and Michael Geerken, "Are Uniform Crime Reports a Valid Indicator of the Index Crimes? An Affirmative Answer with Minor Qualifications," *Criminology* 23 (1985): 451-501; Robert G. Lehnen and Wesley G. Skogan, *The National Crime Survey: Working Papers, Volume 1: Current and Historical Perspectives* (Washington D.C.: Bureau of Justice Statistics); Robert O'Brien, *Crime and Victimization Data* (Beverly Hills, California: SAGE Publications, 1985); Anne L. Schneider, "Methodological Problems in Victim Surveys and the Implication for Research in Victimology," *Journal of Criminal Law and Criminology* 72 (1981):818-838.

17. See Michael R. Gottfredson and Travis Hirschi, "A Consideration of Telescoping and Memory Decay Biases in Victimization Surveys," *Journal of Criminal Justice* 5 (1977): 205-216; Panel for the Evaluation of Crime Surveys, *Surveying Crime* (Washington D.C.: National Academy of Sciences, 1976).

18. Donald J. Black, "Production of Crime Rates," *American Sociological Review* 35 (1970): 733-748.

19. See Helen M. Eigenberg, "The National Crime Survey and Rape: The Case of the Missing Questions," *Justice Quarterly* 7 (1990): 655-671; Gary F. Jensen and Maryaltani Karpos, "Managing Rape: Exploratory Research on the Behavior of Rape Statistics," *Criminology* 31 (1993): 363-385; Richard F. Sparks, "Surveys of Victimization–An Optimistic Assessment," in *Crime and Justice: An Annual Review of Research* (Chicago: The University of Chicago Press, 1981), 236.

20. See Paul Brantingham and Patricia Brantingham, *Patterns in Crime* (New York: MacMillan, 1984); Michael R. Gottfredson and Travis Hirschi, "A Consideration of Telescoping and Memory Decay Biases in Victimization Surveys," *Journal of Criminal Justice* 5 (1977): 205-216.

21. The following data is obtained from Federal Bureau of Investigation, *Uniform Crime Reports* (Washington D.C.: U.S. GPO, various years); Kathleen Maguire and Ann L. Pastore, *Bureau of Justice Statistics Sourcebook of Criminal Justice Statistics - 1995* (Washington D.C.: U.S. GPO, 1996).

22. The following Data was obtained from Bureau of Justice Statistics, *Criminal Victimization in the United States: 1973-90 Trends* (Washington D.C.: U.S. GPO, 1992); Bureau of Justice Statistics, *Criminal Victimization in the United States, 1992* (Washington D.C.: U.S. GPO, 1994); Bureau of Justice Statistics, *Highlights from 20 Years of Surveying Crime Victims: The National Crime Victimization Survey, 1973-92* (Washington D.C.: U.S. GPO, 1993).

23. Data collected from Bureau of Justice Statistics, *Criminal Victimization in the United States, 1995* (Washington D.C.: U.S. Department of Justice, 1997). Some of these recent changes in the National Crime Victimization Survey include a revised "screening" strategy, additional questions on rape and family violence, as well as the use of computer-assisted telephone interviewing (CATI) and computer-assisted personal interviewing (CAPI) systems.

24. Ernest Hemingway, *For Whom the Bell Tolls* (New York: Scribner, 1995).

25. Joel Feinberg, *Harm to Others* (New York: Oxford University Press, 1984); Joel Feinberg, *Offense to Others* (New York: Oxford University Press, 1985); Joel Feinberg, *Harm to Self* (New York: Oxford University Press, 1986); Joel Feinberg, *Harmless Wrongdoings* (New York: Oxford University Press, 1988).

26. Cited in Howard Abadinsky, *An Introduction to Law and Justice,* 4th ed. (Chicago: Nelson-Hall Publishers, 1998), 2.

27. Cited in Howard Abadinsky, *An Introduction to Law and Justice,* 4th ed. (Chicago: Nelson-Hall Publishers, 1998), 3.

28. Cited in Howard Abadinsky, *An Introduction to Law and Justice,* 4th ed. (Chicago: Nelson-Hall Publishers, 1998), 4.

29. N.E. Marion, *Criminal Justice in America: The Politics Behind the System* (Durham, NC: Carolina Academic Press, 2002).

30. W.M. Oliver and J.F. Hilgenberg, Jr., *A History of Crime and Criminal Justice in America* (Boston: Allyn & Bacon Publishers, 2006).

31. N.E. Marion, *Criminal Justice in America: The Politics Behind the System* (Durham, NC: Carolina Academic Press, 2002).

32. G.E. Rush, *The Dictionary of Criminal Justice,* 5th ed. (New York: McGraw Hill, 2000), 311.

33. G.E. Rush, *The Dictionary of Criminal Justice,* 5th ed. (New York: McGraw Hill, 2000), 270.

34. G.E. Rush, *The Dictionary of Criminal Justice,* 5th ed. (New York: McGraw Hill, 2000), 44.

35. G.E. Rush, *The Dictionary of Criminal Justice,* 5th ed. (New York: McGraw Hill, 2000), 193.

36. N.E. Marion, *Criminal Justice in America: The Politics Behind the System* (Durham, NC: Carolina Academic Press, 2002).

37. Romans 1:20 (*The New American Bible).*

38. St. Thomas Aquinas, *Summa Theologiae. Latin text and English translation, introductions, notes, appendices, and glossaries Thomas, Aquinas, Saint, 1225?-1274* (New York: McGraw Hill, 1964), I-II, Q. 98, Art. 1, ad. c.

39. C.P. Nemeth, *Aquinas in the Courtroom: Lawyers, Judges, and Judicial Conduct* (Westport, CT: Praegar Publishers, 2001), 32.

40. St. Thomas Aquinas, *Summa Theologiae. Latin text and English translation, introductions, notes, appendices, and glossaries Thomas, Aquinas, Saint, 1225?-1274* (New York: McGraw Hill, 1964), I-II, Q. 95 Art. 2 & Q. 96 Art. 4.

41. President's Commission on Law Enforcement and Administration of Justice, *The Challenge of Crime in a Free Society* (New York: Avon Books, 1968), 70.

42. H.L. Packer, "Two Models of the Criminal Process," *University of Pennsylvania Law Review* 113 (1964); H.L. Packer, *The Limits of the Criminal Sanction* (Stanford: Stanford University Press, 1968).

43. H.L. Packer, *The Limits of the Criminal Sanction* (Stanford: Stanford University Press, 1968).

44. H.L. Packer, *The Limits of the Criminal Sanction* (Stanford: Stanford University Press, 1968).

45. H.L. Packer, *The Limits of the Criminal Sanction* (Stanford: Stanford University Press, 1968).

46. M.M. Feeley, "Two Models of the Criminal Justice System: An Organizational Approach," *Law and Society Review* 7 no. 3 (1973): 407-425.

47. M.M. Feeley, "Two Models of the Criminal Justice System: An Organizational Approach," *Law and Society Review* 7 no. 3 (1973): 407-425.

48. M.M. Feeley, "Two Models of the Criminal Justice System: An Organizational Approach," *Law and Society Review* 7 no. 3 (1973): 407-425.

49. M.M. Feeley, "Two Models of the Criminal Justice System: An Organizational Approach," *Law and Society Review* 7 no. 3 (1973): 407-425.

50. S. M. Cox and J. E. Wade, *The Criminal Justice Network: An Introduction,*. 3rd ed. (Boston: McGraw Hill, 1998).

51. S. M. Cox and J. E. Wade, *The Criminal Justice Network: An Introduction,*. 3rd ed. (Boston: McGraw Hill, 1998), 4.

52. S. M. Cox and J. E. Wade, *The Criminal Justice Network: An Introduction,*. 3rd ed. (Boston: McGraw Hill, 1998), 4.

53. S. M. Cox and J. E. Wade, *The Criminal Justice Network: An Introduction,*. 3rd ed. (Boston: McGraw Hill, 1998), 19.

54. N.E. Marion, *Criminal Justice in America: The Politics Behind the System* (Durham, NC: Carolina Academic Press, 2002); F.E. Zimring, and G.J. Hawkins, *Deterrence: The Legal Threat in Crime Control* (Chicago: University of Chicago Press, 1973).

55. W.J. Bowers and G.L. Pierce, "Deterrence or Brutalization? What is the Effect of Executions?" *Crime and Delinquency* 26 (1980): 453-484.

56. M. G. Santos, *About Prisons* (Belmont: Wadsworth Publishers, 2004).

57. J. Cohen, "Incapacitation as a Strategy for Crime Control: Possibilities and Pitfalls," in *Crime and Justice: An Annual Review of Research,* eds. M. Tonry and N. Morris (Chicago: University of Chicago Press, 1983), 1-48.

58. N.E. Marion, *Criminal Justice in America: The Politics Behind the System* (Durham, NC: Carolina Academic Press, 2002), 25.

59. A. Blumstein and J. Wallman, *The Crime Drop in America* (Cambridge: Cambridge University Press, 2000); J. E. Conklin, *Why Crime Rates Fell* (Boston: Allyn & Bacon, 2003).

60. P. Greenwood, *Selective Incapacitation* (Santa Monica: RAND Corporation, 1982), 15.

61. A. Von Hirsch, *Doing Justice: The Choice of Punishments* (New York: Hill & Wang, 1976).

62. N.E. Marion, *Criminal Justice in America: The Politics Behind the System* (Durham, NC: Carolina Academic Press, 2002).

63. N.E. Marion, *Criminal Justice in America: The Politics Behind the System* (Durham, NC: Carolina Academic Press, 2002).

64. P. H. Hahn, *Emerging Criminal Justice: Three Pillars for a Proactive Justice System* (Thousand Oaks: SAGE Publications, 1998); D. Van Ness and K. H. Strong, *Restoring Justice* (Cincinnati: Anderson Publishing, 1997).

65. N.E. Marion, *Criminal Justice in America: The Politics Behind the System* (Durham, NC: Carolina Academic Press, 2002).

66. T.R. Clear and E. Cadora, *Community Justice* (Belmont: Wadsworth, 2003).

67. Examples include G. W. Cordner and D.C. Hale, *What Works in Policing?* (Cincinnati: ACJS/Anderson Publishing, 1992); A. Etzioni, *What Can the Federal Government Do To Decrease Crime and Revitalize Communities?* (Washington, D.C.: U.S. Department

of Justice, 1998); L. Sherman et al., *Preventing Crime: What Works, What Doesn't, What's Promising* (Washington, D.C.: U.S. Department of Justice, 1997).

68. K. N. Wright, "The Desirability of Goal Conflict Within the Criminal Justice System," *Journal of Criminal Justice* 9 no. 3 (1981): 209-218.

69. United States Conference of Catholic Bishops, *Responsibility, Rehabilitation, and Restoration: A Catholic Perspective on Crime and Criminal Justice* (Washington, D.C.: United States Catholic Conference, Inc., 2000).

70. United States Conference of Catholic Bishops, *Responsibility, Rehabilitation, and Restoration: A Catholic Perspective on Crime and Criminal Justice* (Washington, D.C.: United States Catholic Conference, Inc., 2000), 20.

71. United States Conference of Catholic Bishops, *Responsibility, Rehabilitation, and Restoration: A Catholic Perspective on Crime and Criminal Justice* (Washington, D.C.: United States Catholic Conference, Inc., 2000), 27-45.

72. United States Conference of Catholic Bishops, *Responsibility, Rehabilitation, and Restoration: A Catholic Perspective on Crime and Criminal Justice* (Washington, D.C.: United States Catholic Conference, Inc., 2000).

Chapter 3

Restorative and Community Justice

"We believe a Catholic ethic of responsibility, rehabilitation, and restoration can become the foundation for the necessary reform of our broken criminal justice system."

-The Catholic Bishops of the United States in *Responsibility, Rehabilitation, and Restoration: A Catholic Perspective on Crime and Criminal Justice*, 2000, p. 55 -

Introduction

In 2000, the United States Conference of Catholic Bishops issued a statement calling for a Catholic perspective on crime and criminal justice based on the scriptural, theological, and sacramental heritage of the Catholic Church. The Bishops, drawing upon the Catholic understanding of ethics, the virtues, and specifically the virtue of justice, detailed a moral framework upon which a Catholic perspective of criminal justice could be built. In addition, they presented a number of policies that could be implemented to guide and direct such an endeavor in order to create a "broader social fabric of respect for life, civility, responsibility, and reconciliation."[1] In order to achieve this, the Bishops avoided the ideological polarization of calling for either crime control or due process by essentially calling for both. They acknowledge that this may seem rather paradoxical. The Bishops are stating that on the one hand, they are not willing to tolerate behaviors that threaten the lives, rights, and property of others. On the other hand, they are also not willing to give up on either the victims or the offenders when seeking justice. The Bishops made a clarion call for the implementation of programs that seek restitution for the victim, rehabilitation for the offender, and ultimately restoration for the community. What the Bishops were calling for, and what they clearly believe to be the most appropriate goal of the criminal justice system, is the implementation of both restorative and community justice concepts and programs.

63

Restorative and community justice are two terms that have come to be used interchangeably, are sometimes ambiguous, and often overlap in their construct.[2] Restorative justice concepts are built on the premise that the government is not necessarily the only arbiter for appropriate responses to crime. Rather, restorative justice looks to community-based initiatives that bring the victim and offender together in order to repair, rebuild, and restore the community. Restorative justice methods and programs are clearly community-based, but this should not be confused with the concepts of community justice. Community justice adheres to the belief that crime and disorder erodes the quality of life in a community. In order to deal with these problems it advocates the use of the criminal justice system by refocusing and broadening their commitment to crime prevention, dealing with social disorder, and actively engaging citizens through community-based initiatives. Hence, restorative justice involves community-based programs independent of the criminal justice system, while community justice uses community-based programs that are dependent upon the criminal justice system and citizens actively working together in partnership.

In order to understand more fully what the United States Conference of Catholic Bishops was calling for in their statement, this chapter will first review the policy foundations and directions they proposed. After highlighting their various calls for restorative and community justice initiatives, this chapter will then detail a more comprehensive understanding of both these concepts. It will deal with the definition, theoretical foundations, values, principles, goals, practices, and problems for each. In doing so, the chapter will provide a fuller treatment of what criminal justice from a Catholic perspective would entail.

Catholic Bishops' Call for Restorative Justice

The Catholic Church has long held teachings regarding the concepts of justice. While the teaching of the virtue of justice can be applied to the issue of crime, for most of Church history there has never been a direct application to social policies. This has also been true in the United States. In fact, as Professor J. Brian Benestad has pointed out, the United States Bishops realized in the latter half of the twentieth century that "the Gospel and Catholic social thought—a teaching that is shaped mainly by papal writings from 1891 to the present and by the documents of the Second Vatican Council—do not provide specific recipes for resolving public policy dilemmas."[3] Thus, the United States Bishops began drawing upon Catholic social teaching in the post Vatican II era to issue policy statements related to various social topics.

Some of the first areas of attention given to the issue of crime focused on "The Reform of Correctional Institutions in the 1970s" (1973) and the problems of "Community and Crime."[4] In the former, the Bishops issued twenty-two recommendations to improve prison facilities, and in the latter, the Bishops issued an equal number of recommendations to address the problem of crime. On the topic of capital punishment, the Bishops issued a one-line statement in opposition to the death penalty in 1974, which was followed up with their reasoning in 1978 in the aforementioned statement on "Community and Crime."[5]

Several additional statements would be issued by the U.S. Catholic Bishops regarding issues related to crime and justice (e.g., the death penalty,[6] domestic violence[7]), but it was not until they issued their pastoral message titled "Confronting a Culture of Violence: A Catholic Framework for Action"[8] in 1994 that the Bishops would discuss more directly the criminal justice system. It is in this document the Bishops argued "our social fabric is being torn apart by a culture of violence that leaves children dead on our streets and families afraid in our homes."[9] They articulated the "Catholic community brings strong convictions and vital experiences which can enrich the national dialogue on how best to overcome the violence that is tearing our nation apart."[10] Despite the sensational language employed, the Bishops asserted that the example of Jesus Christ, the biblical values of peace and justice, the Catholic teaching on human life and human dignity, its traditions, and its ethical framework, could provide a framework for a Catholic response to violence. The framework for action addressed a number of methods by which the Catholic community could be involved, ranging from prayer to global disarmament. Specific recommendations regarding criminal justice were mostly limited to "supporting community approaches to crime prevention and law enforcement, including community policing, neighborhood partnership with police," "greater citizen involvement," "pursuing swift and effective justice without vengeance," and "support for efforts to attack root causes of crime and violence."[11] For the most part, however, this pastoral message was focused on the global problem of violence, not inherently on the problems associated with the criminal justice system at home.

A growing concern with criminal justice reform took hold amongst many of the Bishops in the late 1990s, and several State Boards of Bishops issued statements. One example is the September 2000 pastoral statement by the Catholic Bishops of New York titled, "Restoring All to the Fullness of Life."[12] In this document the New York Bishops called for a Christian perspective of criminal justice to be adopted, and they advocated for the implementation of a restorative approach to justice. In this statement they also called for public safety to apply the concepts of community justice, for the criminal justice system to respect human life and dignity, for the fair and equal treatment of all, and for a system of incarceration that attempts to treat and rehabilitate those imprisoned. It was clearly this document that provided a foundation for the United States Bishops to issue their statement in November of 2000 regarding a Catholic perspective on crime and criminal justice.

In the statement titled *Responsibility, Rehabilitation, and Restoration: A Catholic Perspective on Crime and Criminal Justice* (2000) the United States Conference of Catholic Bishops clearly make the call for restorative and community justice concepts to be adopted by the criminal justice system.[13] Drawing upon the scriptural, theological, and sacramental heritage of the Church, they lay out the policy foundations and directions that they believe a Catholic perspective on crime and criminal justice should take. The eleven policy proposals are derived from what they believe to be the moral foundations of our American society, and they propose that restorative and community justice approaches to crime should build upon these foundations.

The first recommendation the Bishops make is that any changes to the criminal justice system must always consider that its fundamental charge is "protecting society from those who threaten life, inflict harm, take property, and destroy the bonds of community."[14] As the Bishops further explain:

> The protection of society and its members from violence and crime is an essential moral value. Crime, especially violent crime, not only endangers individuals, but robs communities of a sense of well-being and security, and of the ability to protect their members. All people should be able to live in safety. Families must be able to raise their children without fear. Removing dangerous people from society is essential to ensure public safety. And the threat of incarceration does, in fact, deter some crime (e.g., tougher sanctions for drunk drivers along with a public education campaign seem to have dramatically reduced the numbers of intoxicated drivers on our roadways). However, punishment for its own sake is not a Christian response to crime. Punishment must have a purpose. It must be coupled with treatment and, when possible, restitution.[15]

The second recommendation the Bishops make is that criminal justice policy makers must reject "simplistic solutions such as 'three strikes and you're out' [legislation] and rigid mandatory sentencing."[16] There is a desire among the legislators to look for easy solutions with catchy slogans that resonate with the American people, but these do not necessarily make for good criminal justice policy.[17] As the Bishops lament:

> The causes of crime are complex and efforts to fight crime are complicated. One-size-fits-all solutions are often inadequate. Studies and experience show that the combination of accountability and flexibility works best with those who are trying to change their lives. To the extent possible, we should support community-based solutions, especially for non-violent offenders, because a greater emphasis is placed on treatment and restoration for the criminal, and restitution and healing for the victim. We must renew our efforts to ensure that the punishment fits the crime. Therefore, we do not support mandatory sentencing that replaces judges' assessments with rigid formulations.[18]

The third recommendation that the Bishops make is in an area that lies largely outside of the control of the criminal justice system, but it is one recognized by most who work in the criminal justice system as being the answer to the crime problem. The Bishops call for the promotion of "serious efforts toward crime prevention and poverty reduction."[19] Although the prevention of crime is assuredly a goal of the criminal justice system, these policies often must be dealt with by other institutions such as the labor market, schools, and the family. Many criminologists have come to recognize this reality of the crime nexus and so, too, have the Bishops as they explain:

> Socio-economic factors such as extreme poverty, discrimination, and racism are serious contributors to crime. Sadly, racism often shapes American attitudes and policies toward crime and criminal justice. We see it in who is jobless and who is poor, who is a victim of crime and who is in prison, who lacks adequate counsel and who is on death row. We cannot ignore the fact that one fifth of our preschoolers are growing up in poverty and far too many go to bed hungry. Any comprehensive approach to criminal justice must address these factors, but it should also consider the positive impact of strong, intact families. Parents have a critical and irreplaceable role as primary guardians and guides of their children. One only has to observe how gangs often provide young people with a sense of belonging and hope when grinding poverty and family disintegration have been their only experience. And while it is true that many poor children who are products of dysfunctional families never commit crimes, poverty and family disintegration are significant risk factors for criminal activity. Finally, quality education must be available for all children to prepare them for gainful employment, further education, and responsible citizenship. The failure of our education system in many communities contributes to crime. Fighting poverty, educating children, and supporting families are essential anti-crime strategies.[20]

The fourth policy recommendation made by the Catholic Bishops is "challenging the culture of violence and encouraging a culture of life."[21] They call for finding ways to turn the tide against the culture of violence in America that not only must deal with excessive violence on the streets, but throughout all facets of life, including venues such as television, movies, and books that engage in gratuitous violence. A culture of death adhering to things dark and evil, the Bishops argue, has pervaded our American culture. This has led to the allowance of excessive gun violence, abortion, euthanasia, and the destruction of human embryos. The Bishops are, in essence, calling for an American society that embraces a culture of non-violence and life. In terms of the real violence, they offer support for "measures that control the sale and use of firearms and make them safer (especially efforts that prevent their unsupervised use by children or anyone other than the owner)" as well as for "sensible regulation of handguns."[22] They also renew their call for an end to the death penalty in the United States (see Chapter 7). In regard to the culture of death, they encourage "the media to present a more balanced picture, which does not minimize the human dignity of the victim or that of the offender."[23] As the Bishops so profoundly conclude, "we often fail to value life and cherish human beings above our desires for possessions, power, and pleasure."[24]

The fifth recommendation from the Bishops is focused on the victims of crimes in America when they call for the criminal justice system to offer "victims the opportunity to participate more fully in the criminal justice process."[25] As the Bishops see it, the victims and their families must play a more central role in a reformed criminal justice system. The current system often ignores the victim by not only minimizing the physical trauma they may suffer, but more importantly the emotional trauma caused by their victimization. At worst, the system uses the victim for political purposes to parade around to the detriment of the offender, or the victim is shut out of the system altogether, because their compassion does not conform well to a punitive system. As the Bishops explain:

> This vital concern for victims can be misused. Some tactics can fuel hatred, not healing: for example, maximizing punishment for its own sake and advancing punitive policies that contradict the values we hold. But such abuses should not be allowed to turn us away from a genuine response to victims and to their legitimate and necessary participation in the criminal justice system. Victims of crime have the right to be kept informed throughout the criminal justice process. They should be able to share their pain and the impact of the crime on their lives after conviction has taken place and in appropriate ways during the sentencing process. If they wish, they should be able to confront the offender and ask for reparation for their losses. In this regard, we offer general support for legislation to respond to the needs and the rights of victims, and we urge every state to strengthen victims' advocacy programs.[26]

The sixth recommendation that the Bishops make is very much a call for restorative justice concepts when they encourage "innovative programs of restorative justice that provide the opportunity for mediation between victims and offenders and offer restitution for crimes committed."[27] The Bishops advocate the implementation of restorative justice principles because they reflect the values and traditions of the Catholic Church. They explain that the Catholic faith "calls us to hold people accountable, to forgive, and to heal."[28] They argue that restorative justice achieves this because:

> restorative justice focuses first on the victim and the community harmed by the crime, rather than on the dominant state-against-the-perpetrator model. This shift in focus affirms the hurt and loss of the victim, as well as the harm and fear of the community, and insists that offenders come to grips with the consequences of their actions. These approaches are not "soft on crime" because they specifically call the offender to face victims and the communities. This experience offers victims a much greater sense of peace and accountability. Offenders who are willing to face the human consequences of their actions are more ready to accept responsibility, make reparations, and rebuild their lives.[29]

The seventh recommendation made by the Catholic Bishops is "insisting that punishment has a constructive and rehabilitative purpose."[30] The Bishops argue that the criminal justice system should punish offenders by imprisoning them, but only when it is necessary to protect society. Imprisonment, however, should be more concerned with changing the behaviors and attitudes of the offender while in prison, for the Bishops recognize that the vast majority (approximately 95 percent) of incarcerated offenders will eventually be released back into society. As a result, it is imperative that these individuals be given the skills and tools necessary to become productive members of society, rather than a continued threat to the community. Thus, the Bishops call upon government to:

> redirect the vast amount of public resources away from building more and more prisons and toward better and more effective programs aimed at crime prevention, rehabilitation, education efforts, substance abuse treatment, and programs of probation, parole, and reintegration. Renewed emphasis should be placed on parole and probation systems as alternatives to incarceration, especially for non-violent offenders. Freeing up prison construction money to bolster these systems should be a top priority. Abandoning the parole system, as some states have done, combined with the absence of a clear commitment to rehabilitation programs within prisons, turns prisons into warehouses where inmates grow old, without hope, their lives wasted . . . Finally, we must welcome ex-offenders back into society as full participating members, to the extent feasible, and support their right to vote.[31]

The eighth recommendation extends the previous recommendation by not only calling for the incarcerated offenders' rehabilitation based on conventional criminal justice programs, but also calling for rehabilitation of the soul. The Bishops encourage "spiritual healing and renewal for those who commit crime."[32] In this prison ministry, the Bishops are clearly reflecting the words of Jesus when, addressing the judgment of the nations, he explained "For I was . . . in prison and you visited me."[33] Thus, reflecting on the teachings of Jesus, they encourage healing not only from a secular standpoint, but from a spiritual standpoint as well. As they explain:

> Prison officials should encourage inmates to seek spiritual formation and to participate in worship. Attempts to limit prisoners' expression of their religious beliefs are not only counterproductive to rehabilitation efforts, but also unconstitutional. As pastors, we will continue to press for expanded access to prisoners through our chaplaincy programs, including by dedicated volunteers. We oppose limitations on the authentic religious expression of prisoners and roadblocks that inhibit prison ministry. The denial of and onerous restrictions on religious presence in prisons are a violation of religious liberty. Every indication is that genuine religious participation and formation is a road to renewal and rehabilitation for those who have committed crimes. This includes contact with trained parish volunteers who will help nourish the faith life of inmates and ex-offenders.[34]

The ninth recommendation made by the Catholic Bishops is to make "a serious commitment to confront the pervasive role of addiction and mental illness in crime."[35] It has been noted that over one-third of those who are in prison are solely there because of drugs and drug addictions.[36] The Bishops advocate that these individuals, rather than being incarcerated where they typically receive poor treatment, should be given the proper treatment outside of the prison setting. The Bishops advocate that:

> Persons suffering from chemical dependency should have access to the treatment that could free them and their families from the slavery of addiction, and free the rest of us from the crimes they commit to support this addiction. This effort will require adequate federal, state, and local resources for prevention and treatment for substance abusers. Not providing these resources now will cost far more in the long run. Substance abusers should not have to be behind bars in order to receive treatment for their addictive behavior.[37]

The tenth recommendation by the Bishops is an issue that the criminal justice system deals with on a routine basis, and that is immigration. The Bishops call for "treating immigrants justly."[38] While many of the issues related to the treatment of immigrants lie outside of the control of the criminal justice system, the Bishops urge that when the system does come in contact with immigrants they be treated as human beings and provided the same just treatment that our own citizens receive. While they acknowledge the laws do in fact treat immigrants and citizens differently, they also argue that no one, regardless of status, should be denied the right to fair judicial proceedings. Thus, they urge

> the federal government to restore basic due process to immigrants (including a repeal of mandatory detention) and allow those seeking asylum a fair hearing. Migrants who cannot be deported because their country of origin will not accept them should not be imprisoned indefinitely. Legal immigrants who have served sentences for their crimes should not be re-penalized and deported, often leaving family members behind. Many of these immigrants have become valuable members of their communities. Likewise, we oppose onerous restrictions on religious expression and pastoral care of detained immigrants and asylum seekers under [U.S. Customs and Border Protection (UCBP)] jurisdiction and urge the [UCBP] to guarantee access to qualified ministerial personnel.[39]

Finally, the eleventh recommendation on the part of the Catholic Bishops speaks to the concepts of community justice when it encourages the criminal justice system to place "crime in a community context" and to build "on promising alternatives that empower neighborhoods and towns to restore a sense of security."[40] The importance of community is central to the Catholic faith, and the Bishops highlight this when they explain that:

> 'Community' is not only a place to live; the word also describes the web of relationships and resources that brings us together and helps us cope with our everyday challenges. Fear of crime and violence tears at this web. Some residents

of troubled neighborhoods are faced with another kind of community, that of street gangs. These residents feel powerless to take on tough kids in gangs and have little hope that the situation will ever improve. But there are communities where committed individuals are willing to take risks and bring people together to confront gangs and violence. Often organized by churches—and funded by our Catholic Campaign for Human Development—these community groups partner with local police to identify drug markets, develop specific strategies to deal with current and potential crime problems, and target at-risk youth for early intervention. Bringing together many elements of the community, they can devise strategies to clean up streets and take back their neighborhoods.[41]

The Bishops take this recommendation further by actually naming some of the strategies that have developed over the past several decades which are community-based, such as the "broken windows" model of policing and community policing. The Bishops explain that:

proponents contend that tolerance of lesser crimes (such as breaking windows of cars and factories) undermines public order and leads to more serious crimes. Stopping crime at the broken-windows stage demonstrates that a low-cost, high-visibility effort can be effective in preventing crime. Community policing and neighborhood-watch groups have proven to be effective models of crime control and community building, empowering local leaders to solve their own problems. These efforts reflect the Catholic social teaching principles of solidarity, subsidiarity, and the search for the common good.[42]

The U.S. Catholic Bishops' eleven recommendations are largely centered on the relationship between the criminal justice system and the community. They recognize that there are facets of the criminal justice system that need to be changed in order to develop a system that is more responsive to the needs of the community. They do not, however, neglect the realization that much of the responsibility falls on the community itself and, particularly, to the Bishops and the Catholic community. They further explain in their statement that the Catholic faithful must be involved in the restorative process, and they detail several ways in which this can be done.

First, they explain that the Catholic faithful must "teach right from wrong, respect for life and the law, forgiveness and mercy."[43] Reflecting on the sacramental heritage and Church teachings, they explain that the sanctity of human life and dignity "must be at the center of our approach to these issues," and this respect applies to "both victims and offenders . . . [for] both victims and perpetrators of crime are children of God."[44] It is up to the laity to draw on their Catholic faith (ethics) to continually teach what is right and wrong (morals), so that men and women make the right choice in all that they do (virtues). When crimes do occur, these self-same principles should allow the faithful to show forgiveness and mercy to the offender, as well as compassion for the victim. This is why the Bishops also call for the Catholic faithful to encourage the Catholic

71

community to "reach out to offenders and their families, advocate for more treatment, and provide for the pastoral needs of all involved," while at the same time strongly encouraging them to "stand with victims and their families."[45]

In encouraging the laity to provide for both the offenders and the victims in the wake of a crime, the Catholic Bishops are again advocating the concepts of restorative justice. The center of restorative justice is assuredly the sanctity of the community, and this is why the Bishops encourage the faithful to deal with the problems of crime by advocating that they "build community."[46] As the Bishops explain:

> Every parish exists within a community. When crime occurs, the whole community feels less safe and secure. Parishes are called to help rebuild their communities. Partnerships among churches, law enforcement, businesses, and neighborhood-watch groups, as well as social service, substance abuse, and mental health agencies, can help address crime in the neighborhood.[47]

The Bishops further advocate "policies that help reduce violence, protect the innocent, involve the victims, and offer real alternatives to crime."[48] In order to build community, citizens must be involved in the development of a civil society that reflects good values. Unfortunately, this is often not the case in terms of crime and justice policies in the United States. As the Bishops explain:

> We should resist policies that simply call for more prisons, harsher sentences, and increased reliance on the death penalty. Rather, we should promote policies that put more resources into restoration, education, and substance-abuse treatment programs. We must advocate on behalf of those most vulnerable to crime (the young and the elderly), ensure community safety, and attack the leading contributors to crime, which include the breakdown of family life, poverty, the proliferation of handguns, drug and alcohol addiction, and the pervasive culture of violence. We should also encourage programs of restorative justice that focus on community healing and personal accountability.[49]

To this end, the Bishops advocate that not only should all components of the criminal justice system work together in consultation to address these needs, but that the dioceses, parishes, and various Catholic action groups, such as committees on social justice, should share in the development of these new programs. Thus, the Bishops advocate that all Catholics, both inside and outside of the criminal justice system, should work toward reforming America's policies on crime and justice, by advocating for restorative and community justice programs. Understanding these two policies and their programs is the goal of the rest of this chapter.

Restorative Justice

According to Van Ness and Strong, the first use of the term "restorative justice" was by Albert Eglash in 1958 when he described three types of criminal justice: retributive justice, distributive justice, and restorative justice.[50] The first was said to be based on punishment, the second on treatment, and the last on restitution.[51] The restorative justice approach, as articulated by Eglash, focuses primarily on the harm caused by the offender's actions and incorporates both victims and offenders into the restorative process. Although Eglash apparently helped to develop this concept throughout his career, it was the seminal publication by Howard Zehr, titled *Changing Lenses,*[52] that legitimated the concepts of restorative justice. In his book, Zehr described restorative justice in the following manner:

> Crime is a violation of people and relationships. It creates obligations to make things right. Justice involves the victim, the offender, and the community in a search for solutions which promote repair, reconciliation, and reassurance.[53]

Later, Zehr would offer a comparison of the traditional criminal justice system, which he argued engaged in retributive justice, with that of the restorative model, which assists in defining restorative justice.[54] He explained that the criminal justice system tends to define infractions solely through the legal process, while the restorative model recognizes that crime is a violation of people and it is important to understand the overall context of the problem. He also explained that the retributive model views the offender as a passive recipient of justice, while the restorative model believes the offender plays a key role in restoring order. In regard to the process itself, Zehr sees the criminal justice system as authoritarian, technical, and impersonal, while the restorative model is focused on participation, needs, and obligations. Finally, Zehr argues that the retributive model is focused on punishment, while the restorative model is focused on correcting the problem.

Others have contributed their definitions of restorative justice such as Tony Marshal who describes it as "a process whereby all the parties with a stake in a particular offense come together to resolve collectively how to deal with the aftermath of the offender and its implications for the future."[55] While other authors have offered similar definitions, many have offered alternative names to the same process, such as transformational justice,[56] relational justice,[57] and restorative community justice.[58] However, the authors Daniel W. Van Ness and Karen H. Strong provide a generally accepted definition when they state that:

> Restorative justice is a theory of justice that emphasizes repairing the harm caused or revealed by criminal behavior. It is best accomplished through cooperative processes that include all stakeholders.[59]

Restorative justice is based on a number of theories that grew out of the social movements of the 1960s and 1970s.[60] The theories that underlie restorative justice include the informal justice movement, the restitution movement, the victim's movement, the victim-offender reconciliation movement, as well as the social justice movement. The informal justice movement focused on the need for alternative dispute resolution and more community access to the legal system by shifting more of the responsibility to the people. The restitution movement of the 1960s focused on the needs of the victims after a crime had occurred, while the victim's movement focused more on including the victim in the criminal justice process. The reconciliation movement was grounded in two methods of implementing restorative justice, and these were victim-offender mediation and family group conferencing (discussed below). Finally, the social justice movement was a loosely coupled grouping of people concerned with moving away from retributive justice and the practical implementation of Rawl's social justice theory.

What each of these has in common is what is often referred to as a "grass-roots," bottom-up approach to justice. Rather than community abdicating its authority and responsibility for neighborhood safety and general order to the government, these various theories all are premised on the principle that the community itself should restore social order when order has been violated. Only in the cases of seriously violent offenders and unwilling offenders should the community defer individuals to the government criminal justice system.

According to Leena Kurki, a Senior Research Associate at the University of Minnesota Law School, there are five basic ideas behind these various theories of restorative justice.[61] The first is that a criminal act is not merely a violation of the criminal law and a disregard for the government's authority. Rather, it is, second, a belief that a criminal act involves a three-way relationship between the offender, the victim, and the community. Third, as the criminal act harms both the victim and the community, it is important that not only justice be restored to the victim, but to the community as well. Thus, it is the fourth shared belief that the only way to restore justice to both the victim and the community is if all three work together, independent of government. Fifth, and finally, restitution should be based more heavily on the needs of the victim and the community than on the offender's needs.

Van Ness and Strong articulate there are four normative values of restorative justice.[62] These entail the values that restorative justice *should* reflect. These include active responsibility, peaceful social life, respect, and solidarity. The first value of restorative justice, they argue, is that these programs should take a very proactive approach in terms of making amends for any harm brought to an individual and the community. The second is that restorative justice should build "harmony, contentment, security, and community well-being."[63] The third value, respect, is oriented on treating both the victim and offender humanely in the process and never losing sight of their dignity and worth to society. Finally, the authors argue that restorative justice must never lose sight of the value of solidarity, recognizing that everyone is connected to the larger community and that relationships are the foundation of this value.

As an extension of these values, Carey outlines four principles of restorative justice. The first is that restorative justice must "hold the offender directly accountable to the individual victim and the specific community affected by the criminal act."[64] Second, he argues that restorative justice must also "require the offender to take direct responsibility"[65] in order to restore things to their rightful order. The third principle Carey articulates is that restorative justice must "provide the victims purposeful access to the courts and correctional processes, which allows them to assist in shaping offender obligations."[66] Finally, the fourth principle is that all restorative justice programs must "encourage the community to become directly involved in supporting victims, holding offenders accountable, and providing opportunities for offenders to reintegrate into the community."[67]

The goals of restorative justice, then, are derived from these values and principles and are focused on building relationships within the community by creating a process and a mechanism of response to a criminal event. The goal of these processes is to repair the harm caused by the criminal event, specifically in regard to the victim, but also to the community. Further, the goal is to heal the parties (again, victim, offender, and community) by mending the broken relationships, and thus, building community. In order to achieve this goal, it is imperative that family, friends, and various community residents become engaged in the healing process and help work toward this rebuilding of the community. The Vermont Department of Corrections attempted to encapsulate these goals in its statement regarding the desired outcomes of a reparative sentence when it sought to restore and make whole the victims, make amends to the community, learn about the impact of crime, and learn ways to avoid re-offending.[68] Another example is Pranis's list of goals for the implementation of restorative justice, and these included: services and support for victims, victim opportunity for involvement in decision making, offender encouragement to take responsibility, offender involvement in repairing the harm, community members' involvement in decision making, and the use of processes which build connections among community members.[69]

While these are clearly worthy goals, the processes become most important for the actual implementation of restorative justice. The practices of restorative justice tend to consist of the following: Victim-offender mediation programs, family group conferencing, sentencing circles, and reparative boards. Victim-offender mediation programs entail an entirely community-driven response to crime and disorder.[70] When a crime or disorder has occurred, the victim and offender are brought together with a mediator in order to discuss the crime, determine a way that restitution can be made, repair the harm, and restore both the victim and the community. Victim-offender mediation programs have been used in the United States, but they are more widely accepted in Europe and other countries. In fact, in many European countries, victim-offender mediation is not relegated to minor crimes and disorder, but is also used in relation to more serious and violent crimes as well. Once mediation has taken place and all agree on the disposition of how the offender will perform restitution, there is typically a follow-up period that ensures restitution has been made. Again, the critical element to this type of restorative justice program is the restoration of relationships in order to build community.

Family group conferencing is similar in many ways to victim-offender reconciliation, only here the emphasis is placed on the family being the proper unit to restore justice, often as it relates to juveniles.[71] In addition, family group conferencing does not limit itself to the victim and the offender with a mediator, but rather opens up more broadly to include other individuals who are willing to share in the collective responsibility of restoring order. These may be counselors, psychologists, psychiatrists, clergy, family action groups, school teachers, and others that impact the juvenile's life and that of the family. Moreover, family group conferencing, unlike victim-offender programs, typically must draw more upon members of official agencies, including representatives of such agencies as social services, the police, and juvenile probation.

Sentencing circles is merely an extension of victim-offender reconciliation programs that adopt the wider network seen in family group conferencing.[72] Here, the victim and offender are brought together with the mediator, along with representatives from the community, which may include members of both government (e.g., police, social services, family court, etc.) and non-government (e.g., psychologists, clergy, community action groups, etc.) agencies. And, finally, reparative probation and citizen boards operate in a similar manner, with multiple representatives, but they do so on a more permanent basis, rather than the ad-hoc style of the sentencing circles.[73]

Much of the research conducted to date has found those participating in restorative justice programs to be satisfied with the experience. For example, in victim-mediation reconciliation programs in Indiana and Ohio, 83 percent of the offenders reported satisfaction with the process.[74] In addition, Braithwaite found in a cross-site study that 89 percent of offenders involved in victim-mediation programs felt that their treatment was fair.[75] Still further, and perhaps most important, is the fact that these programs have typically demonstrated less recidivism on the part of the offenders than found in traditional criminal justice practices.[76]

Despite these positive reports, this does not mean that restorative justice is free of problems.[77] One issue that has been raised is the definition of restorative justice. It is unclear what type of programs fall under the rubric of restorative justice and what type of sanctions are actually part of the restorative justice methods. In addition, the restorative justice approaches have been highly confused with community justice methods, raising some questions as to which are being implemented. Moreover, although many restorative justice programs have been implemented, there has not been near enough research to determine their outcomes and impact on crime and disorder. While much of the research has found satisfaction among the participants, the research has not adequately explained if restorative justice reduces crime and disorder, truly repairs the victims in the long-term, and prevents recidivism on a larger scale.

There are other problems that have been raised with restorative justice, and these include an abandonment of what many believe to be a key foundation of the criminal justice system, and that is the application of the "just deserts" model and structured sentencing. Because restorative justice is on a highly individualized basis, this may lead to very different dispositions of similar cases, potentially leading to unfair and unequal punishments for similar crimes. In addition, because these outcomes are largely conducted through a process of binding arbitration, there are no procedural safeguards built into many restorative justice programs in order to protect the victim from receiving unfair treatment and the offender from walking away from his or her punishment. Despite these problems, there have been many who have argued for restorative justice to become the primary means by which to deal with the problems of crime and disorder. They articulate that it is more humane than the current criminal justice system, that restorative justice values would better serve the current system, and that the criminal justice system should help to develop restorative justice programs. The United States Conference of Catholic Bishops is clearly one group that has advocated the adoption of restorative justice practices.

Community Justice

Community justice has been defined by Karp and Clear as broadly referring to "all variants of crime prevention and justice activities that explicitly include the community in its processes and set the enhancement of community quality of life as a goal."[78] The difference between restorative justice and community justice is the role of government in the process of improving life in the community. Restorative justice attempts to minimize, if not eliminate, government involvement, while community justice acknowledges government's role, but ensures that it is through government-community partnerships that justice is served. It is understood that no longer should the community abdicate its moral responsibility of community safety and quality of life to the criminal justice system, but rather, they should take an active part through a process referred to as the co-production of order.[79]

In general, then, the defining features of community justice include: a view of the community as an active agent in the partnership, public safety through problem solving, building community capacity to deal with crime, analysis of outcomes at the community level, and a restorative justice orientation.[80] Taken together, according to Clear and Cadora, these features provide a general understanding of community justice as both a philosophy and a strategy. As a philosophy, "community justice seeks to be evaluated for the way it responds to criminal events or even problems of public safety," and "it also accepts responsibility for helping to improve the quality of life and building social capital in the locations where community justice is most needed."[81] The philosophical approach is strongly rooted in the concepts of both restorative and social justice.

The strategy of community justice, according to Clear and Cadora, is to broaden "the responsibility of traditional criminal justice agencies to make room for partnerships with various citizen groups and other service providers so that a more comprehensive level of activity is sustained in the high-impact areas."[82] More specifically, they detail the community justice strategy as having three priorities, and they are:

> 1. Community justice selects high-impact locations—places where there is a concentration of crime and criminal justice activity—for special strategies designed to improve the quality of community life, especially by promoting public safety.
> 2. Community justice approaches its tasks in these areas by working to strengthen the capacity of informal systems of social control: families, neighborhood groups, friends, and social supports. This means that instead of adopting the usual *reactive* strategy of merely responding to criminal cases as they occur, community justice undertakes a *proactive* strategy designed to work in partnership with these informal social control sources to strengthen the foundation for public safety.
> 3. In order to strengthen community capacity, community justice initiatives develop partnerships with residents, businesses, and other social services to coordinate the way public safety problems are addressed.[83]

Understanding community justice as both a philosophy and strategy assists in understanding the concept more broadly, but understanding the theories behind this new perspective of justice provides an understanding of what is driving the move to this new approach for criminal justice.

Community justice, because it is closely related to restorative justice concepts, is in reality driven by a number of highly related theories. All of these theories have a shared approach, and that is to view crime as a social problem.[84] The problem is that the criminal justice system, as it developed throughout the twentieth century, came to view the problem of crime as simply an incident, committed by an offender that mandated an administrative response. The system worked to detect, arrest, prosecute, and punish the offender after a crime had been committed. The system was largely reactive and it primarily applied its administrative response in the wake of a crime. Perhaps more importantly, it came to be viewed in the Post World War II era, as government began to grow and citizens became more mobile, that the responsibility for neighborhood safety was relegated to the police. Citizens abdicated their authority as guardians of the community to the police, making it the police officer's "job" to control the problems of crime and disorder.

All theories of community justice reject these two premises, that the criminal justice system should be reactive and that citizens have abdicated their responsibility of neighborhood safety to the police. Rather, community justice adheres to the belief that crime prevention is an important part of the criminal justice system's responsibilities and that the community must be part of the solution. Yet, how to go about these two critical responses under the auspices of community justice is often debated. According to Kurki, there are four underlying theories of community justice.[85]

One theory of community justice advocates the participation of citizens in the coproduction of order through community empowerment. The underlying assumption for this theory is that if citizens begin to reassert their authority and take up their responsibility as citizens in a community, they will be able to prevent crime by working closely with the criminal justice system, mainly the police. This will allow the police to be more proactive in their responses to neighborhood problems of crime and social disorder, thus allowing for the implementation of community-based crime prevention programs. While in theory this makes intuitive sense, in practice it is unclear as to the roles the police and community are to play and how much authority the community truly has. More importantly, it is rare to actually find a community strong enough and cohesive enough to assert this type of authority. As a result, citizens tend to lapse into being the "eyes and ears" for the police and are relegated to a role of "see a problem, call the police."[86]

Another theory of community justice is premised on James Q. Wilson and George L. Kelling's "Broken Windows theory."[87] This theory, published in 1982 in the *Atlantic Monthly*, argued that minor disorders, such as broken windows, abandoned vehicles, potholes, etc., if not immediately addressed by the community, will broadcast a signal that no one cares about the community. As a result, further disorder, neighborhood deterioration, and crime will ultimately occur. This downward spiral will also lead to increased levels of fear among residents further exacerbating the problems. The goal is to fix the broken windows before they have a chance to send out the wrong signals, and if a community has already started on a downward spiral, to reassert community control by enforcing the laws related to minor crimes and disorders through the use of the police and community reasserting its control over the neighborhoods. Some argue that this type of zero-tolerance policing has created more problems than it has solved and has taken away the liberties and rights of local citizens, all in the name of crime control.

Still another theory of community justice advocates the methods of problem solving. Herman Goldstein, in his seminal article and later book on problem-oriented policing, advocates for problem-solving methods to be applied to policing.[88] Typically police have tended to respond to each and every incident as if it has no past and no future and was in no way connected with other calls-for-service they may have responded to. The proper means for handling calls was simply to respond, deal with the situation, and when warranted, write a report. Any attempt to link calls-for-services or to explore underlying causes was lost upon the police acting in their administrative role. Thus, Goldstein argued that calls-for-services should be seen as symptoms of some underlying problem and that through a more thorough investigation into causes, solutions to the problem can be generated and implemented. While problem-solving appeared to be a police-only change in behavior, the need for cooperation with other criminal justice agencies and community groups to help solve the underlying problems, forced the police to adopt a cooperative effort that would allow for the creation of partnerships. The actual practices of problem-oriented policing and community partnerships under community policing, have had mixed results. Reduction in citizen fear of crime has been most evident, but reduction in actual crime has not.

The final theoretical framework for community justice, according to Kurki, is the focus on geographic location.[89] Part of the premise is that it is important to define neighborhoods from social perspectives and not preexisting geographical boundaries such as roads and rivers. The other part of this premise is that criminal justice agencies should work to apply their trade at the lowest level of community possible in order to enhance the sense of community. Police officers should be assigned to specific neighborhoods and establish substations in and around local communities. Corrections should adopt a stronger community-based approach that attempts to keep non-violent offenders in the community rather than isolating them in jails and prisons often far removed from the neighborhoods in which they reside. In practice, it is difficult to assess the impact that these types of programs have had on crime and disorder. These programs are so widely varied and implemented that a generalization is difficult. In addition, the results of many evaluations must be treated with some reservations as they may highlight a reduction in citizen fear of crime, but not crime itself, or they may demonstrate a reduction in crime, but cannot state with any definitive assurance that the reduction came about as a result of the program being implemented.

Derived from these various theories, Ed Barajas of the National Institute of Corrections, has articulated four key values that underlie community justice.[90] The first is that community justice benefits the community by promoting community protection and service. The second value is that it prevents crime and its harmful effects. The third value is that community justice repairs the damage caused by crime to individual victims and communities. Finally, the fourth value is that it promotes universal justice and fairness through proactive, problem-solving practices focused on creating and maintaining safe, secure, and just communities. The first two values largely encapsulate the values of the traditional criminal justice system, while the latter two values are reflective of the restorative justice values. However, because community justice is somewhat the application of restorative justice concepts to the criminal justice system, this makes intuitive sense.

Further derived from both the theoretical underpinnings of community justice and its key values, Barajas has also identified four key principles of community justice.[91] The first is that the community, which includes victims and offenders, is the ultimate customer as well as partner of the criminal justice system. The second principle is that the criminal justice system and citizens, actively working together, share the common goal of maintaining a peaceful community. Third, the criminal justice system confronts crime by addressing social disorder, criminal activities and behavior, and by restoring victims and communities to the fullest extent possible. Finally, the fourth principle of community justice is that the criminal justice system components should collaborate in doing what is appropriate, just, and necessary to preserve community safety and well-being.

The goals of community justice can thus be derived from its theoretical foundation, values, and principles. Community justice is aimed at reducing crime and disorder at the lowest possible level—the neighborhood. It is about improving the neighborhoods, both the social ties as well as the environment in order to improve the quality of life in each neighborhood. This means that one of its key goals is to have the formal criminal justice system components, police, courts, and corrections, partner with citizens in order to address the problems of crime and disorder. This means that a further goal of community justice is to increase citizen satisfaction with their neighborhood, the police, and the criminal justice system as a whole. In addition, one of its key goals is to reduce fear of crime in the neighborhoods along with a reduction in crime and disorder. These are all worthy goals, but in order for them to be achieved it takes the cooperative effort between the citizens and the police, putting programs into action, and carrying them through to fruition. The specific practices of community justice, as related to each component of the criminal justice system includes implementing community policing, community prosecution, and community-based corrections.

Community policing has become an umbrella term that describes a variety of initiatives that involve both the police and community working in partnerships, in order to reduce the problems of crime and social disorder, reduce the level of fear of crime, and, ultimately, improve the quality of life.[92] By combining the resources of the police and local government with the vested interest that citizens have in their own neighborhood, it is believed that these types of partnerships can co-produce these goals. The mechanisms for implementing community policing consist of targeting specific crime problems, or "hot spots," in order to alleviate crime and disorder in the worst areas of the neighborhoods. Then, when the police and community work together through partnerships, they can begin to "take back the neighborhoods," restoring order, and improving the quality of life. These partnerships can be police-citizen patrols, community meetings, foot and bicycle patrols, and various forms of neighborhood watch. In addition, applying the concepts of problem-solving to neighborhood problems, police and local citizens can identify the most serious problems, develop solutions for the problems, and implement and evaluate their success.

The concept of community prosecution has come to be defined as that which "focuses on targeted areas and involves a long-term, proactive partnership among the prosecutor's office, law enforcement, the community and public private organizations, whereby the authority of the prosecutor's office is used to solve problems, improve public safety, and enhance the quality of life in the community."[93] It involves many of the same goals and means as community policing, but it emphasizes the relationship between the prosecutor's office and local citizens working together in partnership. The mechanisms for implementing community prosecution also include the use of targeting specific problems, working in partnerships, and using the problem-solving methods in order to reduce crime and disorder and improve the quality of life.

Community-based corrections is another umbrella term that has come to be defined as any means of dealing with offenders other than sending them to jail or prison.[94] While probation and parole do fall under the term community-based corrections, the concept is to deal with non-violent offenders through intermediate sanctions in order to rehabilitate and reintegrate them back into the community. Prisons and jails tend to isolate the individuals sentenced to them. It is known that approximately 95 percent of all offenders will eventually return to society. The goal for community-based corrections is to find ways of keeping many of these individuals from entering prisons or jail by strengthening their ties to the community. The mechanisms for accomplishing this include various means of keeping them in the community, ranging from simple contacts with probation officers, intensive supervision, day-reporting centers, home confinement, electronic monitoring devices, and engaging them in community service. The programs aimed at rehabilitation and reintegration include treatment, education, job placement, skills training, and various interventions and networks that build family and communal ties (e.g., business, religious, fraternal groups, etc.).

According to Clear and Cadora, community justice, when implementing these types of programs, attempts to focus its tactics on two types of operational-strategies. The first is community-oriented strategies. There are a number of ways in which these programs should be implemented, and the first is by focusing on "places, not just cases." Rather than focusing on specific circumstance of a criminal case, community justice should focus on the places involved, thus taking a broader community approach. Community justice must also be proactive in its approaches to crime and disorder, rather than what is considered to be the traditional criminal justice approach of being reactive. In addition, Clear and Cadora argue that criminal justice has for too long tried to blame others for the problem of crime. While the blame may be justified, it is not productive. Clear and Cadora urge the criminal justice system to engage in problem solving to improve the quality of life in neighborhoods. Finally, from a structural standpoint, they encourage greater decentralization of criminal justice services, avoiding the traditional hierarchical approach, and, along with that, to allow for more fluid organizational boundaries between not only criminal justice agencies, but all government and social service agencies.

The second operational-strategy that Clear and Cadora articulate for community justice is to focus on comprehensive community change initiatives. Here, they advocate that multiple problems cannot necessarily be solved by one criminal justice agency, but rather, must take a multiple-agency approach to solving problems. In addition, what is needed is the political empowerment of citizens, which can be derived from their inclusion in the criminal justice process. It is through this power of local control that citizens come to understand more fully the difficulties faced by the criminal justice system, the complexities of their community, and, ultimately, a greater satisfaction through both their participation and understanding. Citizen empowerment is also encouraged in order to have the community working toward economic development and service sector improvement. In other words, Clear and Cadora understand that many criminal and social disorder problems are multi-faceted and take a multi-faceted approach. Community justice should be implemented through a co-productive effort on the part of the community and government, and through a reorientation of the criminal justice system to a community-orientation.

Despite the development of community justice programs like restorative justice, there have been a number of problems associated with its implementation.[95] While restorative justice suffers from a definitional problem, community justice is even less well defined and includes an amalgam of various programs. In addition, it is unclear if community justice can be successfully implemented, that the various components will work together toward a systemic process of community justice, and if it can, in the end, successfully reduce crime and disorder. Research to date on the success of community policing, community prosecution, and community-based corrections is mixed or inadequate. Moreover, many have argued that the application of many of the theories have created problems in the community, rather than alleviating them. Crackdowns on minor nuisance crimes and disorders has increased fear, driven up local crime rates, and caused undue attention to social problems, thus raising fear of crime. One author, McCold, has argued that the adoption of community justice programs threatens the implementation of restorative justice programs, rather than compliments them, as government begins to encroach on the otherwise government-free programs of restorative justice.[96] Others have argued that these programs have violated individuals' constitutional rights and that procedural safeguards are being impaired as a result of overzealous policing. It has been said that community prosecution has been relegated only to minor and insignificant cases, while community-based corrections is being used to move offenders out of overcrowded prisons and because they are poorly monitored, increasing the problems of crime and disorder through recidivism. Finally, another argument has been that these types of community justice programs benefit the white and middle to upper class neighborhoods, while all others are excluded.

Conclusion

In the Bishops' statement titled *Responsibility, Rehabilitation, and Restoration: A Catholic Perspective on Crime and Criminal Justice* (2000), the United States Conference of Catholic Bishops made the call for a renewed approach to how our criminal justice system operates in America.[97] They articulated a number of policy directions that the criminal justice system should adopt, and they detailed how the Catholic community, and really all communities, should respond to the problems of crime and disorder. Underlying the responses, both of the criminal justice system and the laity, were the calls for restorative and community justice concepts to be adopted by the criminal justice system.

Restorative justice has focused primarily on relationships and encourages a process in which the humanity of the victim and the offender is clearly recognized and a reconciliation between the two can be made. It is only then that the restoration of the community can be achieved. Community justice, adhering to many of the principles and theories behind restorative justice, encourages criminal justice and community partnerships in order to deal with the problems of crime and disorder. These two approaches to community problems are highly interrelated, and it has been said that, because community justice has largely incorporated the theoretical underpinnings of restorative justice, this has made "it difficult to determine where one begins and the other ends."[98] Any attempt to try and separate these two approaches to crime and disorder is somewhat of a moot point in regard to a Catholic perspective of crime and justice. It is clear from the Bishops' statement that both should be incorporated into the criminal justice approach to the problems of crime and disorder and that the community must be a part of this process. Thus, it is perhaps Young's synthesis of the two concepts into one, labeled "restorative community justice," that is the most appropriate for a Catholic perspective of criminal justice.[99] What then would the criminal justice system look like if it adopted the concepts of restorative community justice?

The criminal justice system, if molded on the Catholic concepts of justice and the teachings of the Church, would move toward the adoption of restorative justice programs through criminal justice and citizen partnerships to specifically address the problems of crime and disorder in their neighborhoods. The police would adopt the police-citizen partnerships called for under community policing, and it would use the problem-solving methods to improve the quality of life in the neighborhoods. The courts would more broadly adopt the concepts of community prosecution, along with the use of various forms of victim-offender mediation in order to resolve problems at the community level. Finally, corrections would be oriented around taking those measures necessary to bring offenders back into the folds of society through such mechanisms as community-based corrections, as well as treatment and rehabilitation programs. These changes in the criminal justice system will be addressed in the next three chapters in order to more fully understand the Catholic perspective of crime and justice.

Notes

1. United States Conference of Catholic Bishops, *Responsibility, Rehabilitation, and Restoration: A Catholic Perspective on Crime and Criminal Justice* (Washington, D.C.: United States Catholic Conference, Inc., 2000), 27.

2. Leena Kurki, "Restorative and Community Justice in the United States, " *Crime & Justice* 27 (2000): 235-303.

3. J. Brian Benestad, *The Pursuit of a Justice Social Order: Policy Statements of the U.S Catholic Bishops, 1966-1980* (Washington, D.C.: Ethics and Public Policy Center, 1982), 4.

4. See J. Brian Benestad and Francis J. Butler, *Quest for Justice: A Compendium of Statements by the American Catholic Bishops on the Political and Social Order, 1966-1980* (Washington, D.C.: United States Catholic Conference, 1981).

5. See J. Brian Benestad and Francis J. Butler, *Quest for Justice: A Compendium of Statements by the American Catholic Bishops on the Political and Social Order, 1966-1980* (Washington, D.C.: United States Catholic Conference, 1981).

6. United States Conference of Catholic Bishops, *A Good Friday Appeal to End the Death Penalty* (Washington, D.C.: United States Conference of Catholic Bishops, 1999).

7. United States Conference of Catholic Bishops, *When I Call for Help: A Pastoral Response to Domestic Violence Against Women* (Washington, D.C.: United States Conference of Catholic Bishops, 1992).

8. U.S. Catholic Bishops, *Confronting a Culture of Violence: A Catholic Framework for Action* (Washington, D.C.: United States Conference of Catholic Bishops, 1994).

9. U.S. Catholic Bishops, *Confronting a Culture of Violence: A Catholic Framework for Action* (Washington, D.C.: United States Conference of Catholic Bishops, 1994), 2.

10. U.S. Catholic Bishops, *Confronting a Culture of Violence: A Catholic Framework for Action* (Washington, D.C.: United States Conference of Catholic Bishops, 1994), 3.

11. U.S. Catholic Bishops, *Confronting a Culture of Violence: A Catholic Framework for Action* (Washington, D.C.: United States Conference of Catholic Bishops, 1994), 13.

12. The Catholic Bishops of the State of New York, *Restoring All to the Fullness of Life* (New York: The Catholic Bishops of the State of New York, 2000).

13. United States Conference of Catholic Bishops, *Responsibility, Rehabilitation, and Restoration: A Catholic Perspective on Crime and Criminal Justice* (Washington, D.C.: United States Catholic Conference, Inc., 2000).

14. United States Conference of Catholic Bishops, *Responsibility, Rehabilitation, and Restoration: A Catholic Perspective on Crime and Criminal Justice* (Washington, D.C.: United States Catholic Conference, Inc., 2000), 27.

15. United States Conference of Catholic Bishops, *Responsibility, Rehabilitation,*

and Restoration: A Catholic Perspective on Crime and Criminal Justice (Washington, D.C.: United States Catholic Conference, Inc., 2000), 27.

16. United States Conference of Catholic Bishops, *Responsibility, Rehabilitation, and Restoration: A Catholic Perspective on Crime and Criminal Justice* (Washington, D.C.: United States Catholic Conference, Inc., 2000), 28.

17. Nancy E. Marion and Willard M. Oliver, *The Public Policy of Crime and Criminal Justice* (Upper Saddle River, NJ: Prentice Hall, 2006).

18. United States Conference of Catholic Bishops, *Responsibility, Rehabilitation, and Restoration: A Catholic Perspective on Crime and Criminal Justice* (Washington, D.C.: United States Catholic Conference, Inc., 2000), 28.

19. United States Conference of Catholic Bishops, *Responsibility, Rehabilitation, and Restoration: A Catholic Perspective on Crime and Criminal Justice* (Washington, D.C.: United States Catholic Conference, Inc., 2000), 29.

20. United States Conference of Catholic Bishops, *Responsibility, Rehabilitation, and Restoration: A Catholic Perspective on Crime and Criminal Justice* (Washington, D.C.: United States Catholic Conference, Inc., 2000), 29.

21. United States Conference of Catholic Bishops, *Responsibility, Rehabilitation, and Restoration: A Catholic Perspective on Crime and Criminal Justice* (Washington, D.C.: United States Catholic Conference, Inc., 2000), 29.

22. United States Conference of Catholic Bishops, *Responsibility, Rehabilitation, and Restoration: A Catholic Perspective on Crime and Criminal Justice* (Washington, D.C.: United States Catholic Conference, Inc., 2000), 29.

23. United States Conference of Catholic Bishops, *Responsibility, Rehabilitation, and Restoration: A Catholic Perspective on Crime and Criminal Justice* (Washington, D.C.: United States Catholic Conference, Inc., 2000), 29.

24. United States Conference of Catholic Bishops, *Responsibility, Rehabilitation, and Restoration: A Catholic Perspective on Crime and Criminal Justice* (Washington, D.C.: United States Catholic Conference, Inc., 2000), 31.

25. United States Conference of Catholic Bishops, *Responsibility, Rehabilitation, and Restoration: A Catholic Perspective on Crime and Criminal Justice* (Washington, D.C.: United States Catholic Conference, Inc., 2000), 31.

26. United States Conference of Catholic Bishops, *Responsibility, Rehabilitation, and Restoration: A Catholic Perspective on Crime and Criminal Justice* (Washington, D.C.: United States Catholic Conference, Inc., 2000), 35.

27. United States Conference of Catholic Bishops, *Responsibility, Rehabilitation, and Restoration: A Catholic Perspective on Crime and Criminal Justice* (Washington, D.C.: United States Catholic Conference, Inc., 2000), 36.

28. United States Conference of Catholic Bishops, *Responsibility, Rehabilitation, and Restoration: A Catholic Perspective on Crime and Criminal Justice* (Washington, D.C.: United States Catholic Conference, Inc., 2000), 36.

29. United States Conference of Catholic Bishops, *Responsibility, Rehabilitation, and Restoration: A Catholic Perspective on Crime and Criminal Justice* (Washington, D.C.: United States Catholic Conference, Inc., 2000), 36.

30. United States Conference of Catholic Bishops, *Responsibility, Rehabilitation, and Restoration: A Catholic Perspective on Crime and Criminal Justice* (Washington, D.C.: United States Catholic Conference, Inc., 2000), 39.

31. United States Conference of Catholic Bishops, *Responsibility, Rehabilitation,*

and Restoration: A Catholic Perspective on Crime and Criminal Justice (Washington, D.C.: United States Catholic Conference, Inc., 2000), 39-41.

32. United States Conference of Catholic Bishops, *Responsibility, Rehabilitation, and Restoration: A Catholic Perspective on Crime and Criminal Justice* (Washington, D.C.: United States Catholic Conference, Inc., 2000), 41.

33. Matthew 26:35-36 (*The New American Bible*).

34. United States Conference of Catholic Bishops, *Responsibility, Rehabilitation, and Restoration: A Catholic Perspective on Crime and Criminal Justice* (Washington, D.C.: United States Catholic Conference, Inc., 2000), 41.

35. United States Conference of Catholic Bishops, *Responsibility, Rehabilitation, and Restoration: A Catholic Perspective on Crime and Criminal Justice* (Washington, D.C.: United States Catholic Conference, Inc., 2000), 41.

36. James Austin and John Irwin, *It's About Time: America's Imprisonment Binge,* 3rd ed. (Belmont, CA: Wadsworth, 2001).

37. United States Conference of Catholic Bishops, *Responsibility, Rehabilitation, and Restoration: A Catholic Perspective on Crime and Criminal Justice* (Washington, D.C.: United States Catholic Conference, Inc., 2000), 42.

38. United States Conference of Catholic Bishops, *Responsibility, Rehabilitation, and Restoration: A Catholic Perspective on Crime and Criminal Justice* (Washington, D.C.: United States Catholic Conference, Inc., 2000), 43.

39. United States Conference of Catholic Bishops, *Responsibility, Rehabilitation, and Restoration: A Catholic Perspective on Crime and Criminal Justice* (Washington, D.C.: United States Catholic Conference, Inc., 2000), 43-44.

40. United States Conference of Catholic Bishops, *Responsibility, Rehabilitation, and Restoration: A Catholic Perspective on Crime and Criminal Justice* (Washington, D.C.: United States Catholic Conference, Inc., 2000), 44.

41. United States Conference of Catholic Bishops, *Responsibility, Rehabilitation, and Restoration: A Catholic Perspective on Crime and Criminal Justice* (Washington, D.C.: United States Catholic Conference, Inc., 2000), 44.

42. United States Conference of Catholic Bishops, *Responsibility, Rehabilitation, and Restoration: A Catholic Perspective on Crime and Criminal Justice* (Washington, D.C.: United States Catholic Conference, Inc., 2000), 45.

43. United States Conference of Catholic Bishops, *Responsibility, Rehabilitation, and Restoration: A Catholic Perspective on Crime and Criminal Justice* (Washington, D.C.: United States Catholic Conference, Inc., 2000), 47.

44. United States Conference of Catholic Bishops, *Responsibility, Rehabilitation, and Restoration: A Catholic Perspective on Crime and Criminal Justice* (Washington, D.C.: United States Catholic Conference, Inc., 2000), 47-48.

45. United States Conference of Catholic Bishops, *Responsibility, Rehabilitation, and Restoration: A Catholic Perspective on Crime and Criminal Justice* (Washington, D.C.: United States Catholic Conference, Inc., 2000), 49.

46. United States Conference of Catholic Bishops, *Responsibility, Rehabilitation, and Restoration: A Catholic Perspective on Crime and Criminal Justice* (Washington, D.C.: United States Catholic Conference, Inc., 2000), 50.

47. United States Conference of Catholic Bishops, *Responsibility, Rehabilitation, and Restoration: A Catholic Perspective on Crime and Criminal Justice* (Washington, D.C.: United States Catholic Conference, Inc., 2000), 50-51.

48. United States Conference of Catholic Bishops, *Responsibility, Rehabilitation, and Restoration: A Catholic Perspective on Crime and Criminal Justice* (Washington, D.C.: United States Catholic Conference, Inc., 2000), 52.

49. United States Conference of Catholic Bishops, *Responsibility, Rehabilitation, and Restoration: A Catholic Perspective on Crime and Criminal Justice* (Washington, D.C.: United States Catholic Conference, Inc., 2000), 52.

50. Daniel W. Van Ness and Karen H. Strong, *Restoring Justice: An Introduction to Restorative Justice,* 3rd ed. (Cincinnati: Lexis Nexis/Anderson Publishing, 2006).

51. See Albert Eglash, "Beyond Restitution: Creative Restitution," in *Restitution in Criminal Justice,* eds. Joe Hudson and Burt Galaway (Lexington, MA: D.C. Heath, 1977).

52. Howard Zehr, *Changing Lenses: A New Focus for Crime and Justice* (Scottsdale, PA: Herald Press, 1990).

53. Howard Zehr, *Changing Lenses: A New Focus for Crime and Justice* (Scottsdale, PA: Herald Press, 1990), 181.

54. Howard Zehr, *Restorative Justice Symposium: Summary of the Proceedings* (Washington, D.C.: U.S. Department of Justice, 1996).

55. Tony Marshall, *Restorative Justice: An Overview* (London, England: Home Office Research Development and Statistics Directorate, 1999), 5.

56. Ruth Morris, *A Practical Path to Transformational Justice* (Toronto, Canada: Rittenhouse, 1994).

57. Jonathan Burnside and Nicola Baker, *Relational Justice: Repairing the Breach* (Winchester, England: Waterside Press, 1993).

58. Marlene A. Young, *Restorative Community Justice: A Call to Action* (Washington, D.C.: National Organization for Victim Assistance, (1995).

59. Daniel W. Van Ness and Karen H. Strong, *Restoring Justice: An Introduction to Restorative Justice,* 3rd ed. (Cincinnati: Lexis Nexis/Anderson Publishing, 2006), 43.

60. Daniel W. Van Ness and Karen H. Strong, *Restoring Justice: An Introduction to Restorative Justice,* 3rd ed. (Cincinnati: Lexis Nexis/Anderson Publishing, 2006).

61. Leena Kurki, "Restorative and Community Justice in the United States," *Crime & Justice* 27 (2000): 235-303. See also Daniel W. Van Ness and Karen H. Strong, *Restoring Justice: An Introduction to Restorative Justice,* 3rd ed. (Cincinnati: Lexis Nexis/Anderson Publishing, 2006).

62. Daniel W. Van Ness and Karen H. Strong, *Restoring Justice: An Introduction to Restorative Justice,* 3rd ed. (Cincinnati: Lexis Nexis/Anderson Publishing, 2006).

63. Daniel W. Van Ness and Karen H. Strong, *Restoring Justice: An Introduction to Restorative Justice,* 3rd ed. (Cincinnati: Lexis Nexis/Anderson Publishing, 2006), 49.

64. M. Carey, "Restorative Justice in Community Corrections," *Corrections Today* 58 (1996): 152-155.

65. M. Carey, "Restorative Justice in Community Corrections," *Corrections Today* 58 (1996): 152-155.

66. M. Carey, "Restorative Justice in Community Corrections," *Corrections Today* 58 (1996): 152-155.

67. M. Carey, "Restorative Justice in Community Corrections," *Corrections Today* 58 (1996): 152-155.

68. Vermont Department of Corrections, *Sentencing Options: Restructuring Corrections for the 21st Century* (Waterbury, VT: Vermont Department of Corrections, 1995).

69. K. Pranis, "Restorative Justice: The Next Stage in Responding to Crime?" *Corrections Alert* 3, no. 5 (1996): 6.

70. Daniel W. Van Ness and Karen H. Strong, *Restoring Justice: An Introduction to Restorative Justice,* 3rd ed. (Cincinnati: Lexis Nexis/Anderson Publishing, 2006).

71. Daniel W. Van Ness and Karen H. Strong, *Restoring Justice: An Introduction to Restorative Justice,* 3rd ed. (Cincinnati: Lexis Nexis/Anderson Publishing, 2006). See also Allison Morris and Gabrielle Maxwell, "Restorative Conferencing," in *Restorative Community Justice: Repairing Harm and Transforming Communities* (Cincinnati, OH: Anderson Publishing Company, 2001).

72. Daniel W. Van Ness and Karen H. Strong, *Restoring Justice: An Introduction to Restorative Justice,* 3rd ed. (Cincinnati: Lexis Nexis/Anderson Publishing, 2006). See also Barry Stuart, "Guiding Principles for Peacemaking Circles," in *Restorative Community Justice: Repairing Harm and Transforming Communities* (Cincinnati: Anderson Publishing Company, 2001).

73. David R. Karp and Lynne Walther, "Community Reparative Boards in Vermont: Theory and Practice," in *Restorative Community Justice: Repairing Harm and Transforming Communities* (Cincinnati: Anderson Publishing Company, 2001).

74. John Braithwaite, *Crime, Shame, and Reintegration* (New York: Cambridge University Press, 1999).

75. John Braithwaite, *Crime, Shame, and Reintegration* (New York: Cambridge University Press, 1999).

76. See John Braithwaite, *Restorative Justice and Responsive Regulation* (Oxford: Oxford University Press, 2002).

77. Leena Kurki, "Restorative and Community Justice in the United States," *Crime & Justice* 27 (2000): 235-303.

78. David R. Karp and Todd R. Clear, "Community Justice; A Conceptual framework," in *Boundary Changes in Criminal Justice Organizations* (Washington, D.C.: National Institute of Justice, 2000), 323-368.

79. See for instance William Wells, Joseph A. Schafer, Sean P. Varano, and Timothy S. Bynum, "Neighborhood Residents' Production of Order: The Effects of Collective Efficacy on Responses to Neighborhood Problems," *Crime & Delinquency* 52, no. 4 (2006): 523-550.

80. Caterina G. Roman, Gretchen E. Moore, Susan Jenkins, and Kevonne M. Small, *Understanding Community Justice Partnerships: Assessing the Capacity to Partner* (Washington, D.C.: Urban Institute, Justice Policy Center, 2003).

81. Todd R. Clear and Eric Cadora, *Community Justice* (Belmont, CA: Wadsworth, 2003), 3.

82. Todd R. Clear and Eric Cadora, *Community Justice* (Belmont, CA: Wadsworth, 2003), 3.

83. Todd R. Clear and Eric Cadora, *Community Justice* (Belmont, CA: Wadsworth, 2003), 2-3.

84. Leena Kurki, "Restorative and Community Justice in the United States," *Crime & Justice* 27 (2000): 235-303.

85. Leena Kurki, "Restorative and Community Justice in the United States," *Crime & Justice* 27 (2000): 235-303.

86. Michael E. Buerger, "A Tale of Two Targets: Limitations of Community Anti-crime Actions," *Crime & Delinquency* 40 (1994): 411-436.

87. James Q. Wilson and George L. Kelling, "Broken Windows: The Police and Neighborhood Safety," *The Atlantic Monthly* (March, 1982): 29-38.

88. Herman Goldstein, "Improving Policing: A Problem-Oriented Approach," *Crime & Delinquency* 25 (1979): 236-258; Herman Goldstein, *Problem-Oriented Policing* (New York: McGraw Hill, (1990).

89. Leena Kurki, "Restorative and Community Justice in the United States," *Crime & Justice* 27 (2000): 235-303.

90. Eduardo Barajas, Jr., "Moving Toward Community Justice," *Topics in Community Corrections, Community Justice* (Washington, D.C.: U.S. Department of Justice, National Institute of Justice, 1995).

91. Eduardo Barajas, Jr., "Moving Toward Community Justice," *Topics in Community Corrections, Community Justice* (Washington, D.C.: U.S. Department of Justice, National Institute of Justice, 1995).

92. Willard M. Oliver, *Community-Oriented Policing: A Systemic Approach to Policing,* 4th ed. (Upper Saddle River, NJ: Prentice Hall, 2007).

93. American Prosecutors Research Institute, *Community Prosecution Implementation Manual* (Alexandria, VA: American Prosecutors Research Institute, 1995), 1.

94. Joan Petersilia, *Community Corrections* (New York: Oxford University Press, 1998).

95. Leena Kurki, "Restorative and Community Justice in the United States," *Crime & Justice* 27 (2000): 235-303.

96. P. McCold, "Paradigm Muddle: The Threat to Restorative Justice Posed by its Merger with Community Justice," *Contemporary Justice Review* 7 (2004): 13-35.

97. United States Conference of Catholic Bishops, *Responsibility, Rehabilitation, and Restoration: A Catholic Perspective on Crime and Criminal Justice* (Washington, D.C.: United States Catholic Conference, Inc., 2000).

98. Gordon Bazemore and Mara Schiff, "Understanding Restorative Community Justice: What and Why Now?" in *Restorative Community Justice: Repairing Harm and Transforming Communities* (Cincinnati: Anderson Publishing Company, 2001). See also Clear, Todd and David Karp, *The Community Justice Ideal: Preventing Crime and Achieving Justice* (Boulder, CO: Westview Press, 1999).

99. Marlene A. Young, *Restorative Community Justice: A Call to Action* (Washington, D.C.: National Organization for Victim Assistance, (1995).

Part Two

Criminal Justice

Chapter 4

Community Policing

"Blessed are the peacemakers, for they will be called children of God."
- Matthew 5:9 -

Introduction

The United States Conference of Catholic Bishops has twice called for the police to adopt the philosophy and strategy of community policing in their pastoral statements. The first was in their message *Confronting A Culture of Violence: A Catholic Framework for Action,* where they supported community approaches to crime prevention and law enforcement, specifically calling for "community policing, neighborhood partnerships with police, and greater citizen involvement."[1] The second time was when the Bishops issued their statement on *Responsibility, Rehabilitation, and Restoration: A Catholic Perspective on Crime and Criminal Justice,* where they urged the criminal justice system to place crime within the context of a community and build on those promising alternatives to crime control that have focused on empowering neighborhoods in order to restore a sense of security.[2]

The Bishops specifically mentioned community policing as one such alternative that has proven to be an effective model "of crime control and community building," that empowers "local leaders to solve their own problems."[3] In addition, they asserted that another community-based strategy in the prevention of crime, which is closely associated with community policing, is based on the "broken windows" theory which contends that tolerance of lesser crimes undermines public order and ultimately leads to more serious crime. The Bishops highly encouraged the adoption of community policing, partnerships, and use of the broken-windows model, because as they explained, "these efforts reflect the Catholic social teaching principles of solidarity, subsidiarity, and the search for the common good."[4] These words, written by the American Bishops, are not simple words to be taken lightly, for the Catholic faith teaches that these three principles are fundamental to how people live the vocation of humanity.

The principle of solidarity is often articulated in the terms "friendship" or "social charity,"[5] and is predicated on the teachings of Jesus Christ in his affirmation of the second greatest commandment, "love your neighbor as yourself."[6] Solidarity, according to Pope John Paul II is a direct demand of human and Christian Brotherhood.[7] It is often thought of as manifesting itself in the distribution of goods and remuneration for work, fair prices and a just wage. According to the Catechism of the Catholic Church, however, "it also presupposes the effort for a more just social order where tensions are better able to be reduced and conflicts more readily settled by negotiation."[8] Thus, the virtue of solidarity goes far beyond material goods in that it is more about the spreading of the spiritual goods of faith.

The principle of subsidiarity, as detailed by the Church, states that "a community of a higher order should not interfere in the internal life of a community of a lower order, depriving the latter of its functions, but rather should support it in case of need and help to co-ordinate its activity with the activities of the rest of society, always with a view to the common good."[9] The key, then, lies in the fact that each community must be given a purpose which means they will consequently have to obey specific rules that it establishes to achieve order. However, the Church also stresses that "the human person . . . is and ought to be the principle, the subject and the end of all social institutions."[10] As a result, subsidarity is opposed to all forms of collectivism, but rather supposes that the lowest level of community should be responsible for mediating its own relationships. Thus, individuals, communities, and societies should be harmonized to create and maintain the social order.

The principle or concept of the "search for the common good" is clearly spelled out by the Catholic faith.[11] The Catechism of the Catholic Church explains that "in keeping with the social nature of man, the good of each individual is necessarily related to the common good, which in turn can be defined only in reference to the human person."[12] The common good is understood as "the sum total of social conditions which allow people, either as groups or as individuals, to reach their fulfillment more fully and more easily."[13] Thus, the common good is concerned with the life of all.

The Catholic Church further defines the common good as consisting of three essential elements. First, "the common good presupposes respect for the person"[14] in that public authorities must respect the rights of human persons at all times and that society should allow each person to fulfill his or her vocation. Second, "the common good requires the social well-being and development of the group itself."[15] While the common good must afford individuals respect and allow them to seek out their vocation, these things must also work toward the good of all society, not to its detriment. Finally, the third element of "the common good requires peace, that is, the stability and security of a just order."[16] As the Catechism further elaborates, it also presupposes that the public authority should ensure, by morally acceptable means, "the security of society and its members."[17]

The United States Bishops, in their statement on crime and criminal justice, have articulated that community policing, through its partnerships, problem-solving, and use of the "broken windows" theory, reflects these three Catholic social teachings. In order to understand how and why the Bishops believe community policing reflects these principles, it is important to understand more fully what community policing entails. Furthermore, this will assist in understanding why criminal justice from a Catholic perspective encourages the police to move toward the adoption of the community policing philosophy and the implementation of its strategic programs.

This chapter, then, will focus on placing the development of community policing in the United States in a historical context, showing how this particular policing strategy has evolved. It will also explain what is meant by the term community policing, detailing the vast array of strategies, policies, and programs that have fallen under this umbrella term. Further, it will detail the crucial elements of police and community partnerships, describing what these entail, which will be followed by a discussion of the benefits and success community policing has achieved over the past twenty years. Finally, it will conclude with a brief discussion detailing how community policing compliments the larger goal of moving criminal justice toward a restorative and community justice approach, as called for by the U.S. Conference of Catholic Bishops.

History of Policing

The history of policing in the United States is a highly complex amalgam of varying agencies from all levels of government that have not always developed entirely in concert.[18] Police-like agencies in early America were often a replication of the English means of maintaining order, consisting of the day ward, night watch, constables, and sheriffs, or some combination thereof. In the early South, with the rise of slavery, slave-patrols became a de facto police force. However, it was not until a decade after the establishment of the first police department in the world, the London Metropolitan Police in 1829, that America would see the establishment of its first bona fide police department in Boston, Massachusetts. The Boston Police Department was officially established in 1838, arising out of several previous police-like agencies as a result of a series of three riots that went unchecked between 1834 and 1838.[19] Despite the London Police Department beginning with over 1,000 armed and uniformed officers, the Boston Police started off small, wearing street clothes, and officers were not officially armed. Although several cities would emulate the Boston Police Department, the proliferation of police departments in the United States did not take place until the post-Civil War era.

Police departments developed along a variety of lines in the nineteenth century, ranging from sheriff's departments to police departments. These agencies were oftentimes small agencies, purposefully kept small so as to not wield much control over the local populace. In other cases, the agencies were well-staffed so as to be well-entrenched in the community. Early police, however, were not established to serve the community, so much as to serve the political machine. They were most often mechanisms for graft, corruption, and brutality. They served the political machine by rolling graft up to the police leadership, who then sent it on to the political machines, and they served as a protectorate of big business interests in order to, again, serve the political machines. This is why Kelling and Moore, two leading police scholars, recognize this as the Political Era of policing.[20]

The Political Era of policing ranged from 1838, with the establishment of the first police department, to the 1930s. The early American police were authorized by local municipalities and derived their authority and resources from local political leaders, often ward politicians. They were guided by the law as to what tasks they were authorized to perform and what powers they could utilize, but the oversight by local politicians was so strong that many police historians have stated they were simply adjuncts to local political machines. Political machines recruited and maintained police in office and on the beat, while police helped ward political leaders maintain their political offices by encouraging citizens to vote for certain candidates, discouraging them from voting, and rigging elections.

The police function during the Political Era was varied, because until the close of the nineteenth century there were no other social agencies available to provide services. The police bore the brunt of these calls for service. Police often ran soup lines, housed the homeless, and assisted newly arriving immigrants in finding jobs. These early police departments, although organized along military lines, did not have a unified chain-of-command, were highly decentralized, and, due to a lack of communication technology, often acted independently of police management. Thus, citizens often made demands directly to the police officers on the beat, and these officers simply had to manage on their own with no guidance or supervision.

The Political Era of policing was not bleak, as it was marked by several strengths. First, the police were well-integrated into neighborhoods and enjoyed the support of the citizens—at least the support of the dominant political interests. Second, and as a direct result of the first strength, policing provided some useful services to the community, as again, there were no other agencies to do so. However, the reality of all this points to a number of weaknesses in early American policing. First, the intimacy with the community, the closeness to political leaders, and the decentralized organizational structure, with its inability to provide supervision of its officers, gave rise to police corruption. Second, close identification of police with neighborhoods and neighborhood norms often resulted in discrimination against strangers and others who violated those norms, especially minority ethnic and racial groups. Finally, the lack of organizational control over officers resulting from both decentralization and the political nature of many appointments to police positions caused inefficiency and disorganization.

The Reform Era of policing ranged from the early 1930s through the 1970s, and was largely promulgated by one man: Berkeley, California, Police Chief August Vollmer. Vollmer first rallied police executives around the idea of reform during the 1920s and early 1930s, and his vision of policing was the trumpet call: Police in the post-flapper generation were to remind American citizens and institutions of the moral vision that had made America great and of their responsibilities to maintain that vision. Vollmer's protégé, O.W. Wilson, also took Vollmer's vision, coupled it with the efficient transformation of the Federal Bureau of Investigation by J. Edgar Hoover, and became a leading administrative architect of the police reform organizational strategy.

Police reformers rejected politics as the basis of police legitimacy for, as they viewed it, politics and political involvement *was* the problem in American policing. They moved to end the close ties between local political leaders and police. Law, especially criminal law, became the basis for all enforcement, and a strict adherence to this enforcement became the justification for the role of police in society. Police departments, in a sense, became law enforcement agencies with the sole goal of controlling crime. In order to achieve this, the early twentieth-century theories of scientific management were adopted, and police departments became highly centralized with strict chains-of-command. Police work became routine and standardized, and discretion was limited and controlled. The relationship with the community became more remote as the police professional model redefined the citizen role in crime control, relegating it to simply the eyes and ears of the police and to defer to the police in all matters related to crime and disorder. The strengths of the Reform Era included better organizational administrative structure, better organizational control over the police, and a profession highly centered on controlling crime through law enforcement.

The weaknesses of the Reform Era did not show until the 1960s and 1970s, for prior to that, especially in the immediate aftermath of World War II, there existed a strong economy, and the political and social institutions were extraordinarily stable. The police professionalism movement of the Reform era seemed to be a success. In the 1960s and 1970s, however, with increasing social unrest, destabilizing institutions, and a declining economy, hidden weaknesses were exposed. The first was the fact that, despite the emphasis on crime control, crime in America began to rise quite dramatically. Second, fear of crime rose rapidly in concert with crime, and the police were not able to abate this fear. Third, although police professionalism called for fair and impartial delivery of police services to all, the reality became very clear that, like the rest of America, the police discriminated against minority citizens, especially blacks. Fourth, the civil rights and anti-war protests challenged the legitimacy of the police by often ignoring the demands of the police to disperse or cease their protests. Fifth, the routinization and standardization of policing, which meant that the police exercised little discretion in their job, was found to be a myth. Sixth, while the reform ideology gained traction with the police chiefs, it was largely rejected by the line officers. Finally, due to a declining economy, the police lost much of their financial support as cities became strapped for cash and many began cutting the ranks in order to save money. In sum, the police reform movement failed to achieve its promises when faced with the political, social, and economic realities of the 1960s and 1970s; thus further reform of the police became a common demand by both politicians and citizens.

These growing demands for further reform resulted in the Community Problem-Solving Era of the late 1970s and early 1980s that continues today, only questioned by a movement toward the tenets of homeland security. The early calls for a community orientation came out of the Police-Community Relations movement, first addressed in 1955 and brought to the forefront of policy in the wake of the rising social unrest of the 1960s. In addition, expenditures on crime by the federal government allocated funding for research, and that research began to call into question long held practices of the Reform Era. Random police patrols were found to have little impact on crime. Rapid response to calls-for-service by citizens did not reduce crime. Enhancement of police detectives through training and technology was found to have little impact on crime. Police remoteness to the community was also called into question as it was found that citizens were generally the ones that solved most crimes. Police routinization and standardization was called into question as it simply dealt with the symptoms of crime rather than the underlying problem. In sum, the standard discussion of the 1970s was that nothing the police did works.

The Community Problem-Solving Era of policing thus called for a renewed emphasis on community or political authorization for many police tasks, along with law and professionalism. Law continues to be the major legitimating basis of the police function as it defines police power. However, it does not fully direct police activities in efforts to maintain order, negotiate conflicts, or solve community problems. That, according to the new reforms should be through police-community partnerships. Thus, the police function was broadened to include order maintenance, conflict resolution, problem-solving, and provision of services. Although crime control is still a part of policing, crime prevention, order maintenance, and reducing fear of crime are also important police functions. In order to achieve this, the organizational structure has moved toward the decentralization of the police, placing them closer to the community through foot patrols, permanently assigned beat officers, and neighborhood police substations. In addition, participatory management has become an integral part of the police organization. All of these changes are oriented on the community in order to develop police-community partnerships that work to solve problems specific to each neighborhood in which the police patrol.

The strengths of the Community Problem-Solving Era have been the increased satisfaction of citizens with police, an increased satisfaction among police officers in their jobs, and a reduction in the levels of fear related to crime. Problems are often being solved, rather than their symptoms, and communities are working to take back control of their neighborhoods by reasserting control. The weaknesses of the Community Problem-Solving Era would appear to be, once again, little to no overall impact on actual crime, an inequity in the delivery and quality of community policing, and a bandwagon effect created by federal grant money being offered in record amounts during the 1990s.[21] Despite these drawbacks, the community-policing and problem-solving aspects of this era have become the overriding philosophy and strategy of policing in America today.

It should be noted that the Community Problem-Solving Era developed largely out of the Police-Community Relations movement. While it continues to incorporate many of the policies and concepts of this movement, community policing has developed and advanced well beyond the programs implemented in the late 1960s and early 1970s. Many of the programs implemented during this time frame were said to have been conducted for nothing more than public relations purposes. In some cases, they were implemented simply for political purposes. One primary method of delivering police-community relations services was the concept of "team policing," implemented in various communities across the nation in the early 1970s. Although touted as one of the most prominent police-community relations programs, it failed. The premise of team policing was to make the team of police officers part of the community and in turn make the community they policed more valuable to them on a personal level. According to Lawrence Sherman, a preeminent police scholar, team policing failed because management created the teams and controlled them, but failed to provide the proper support.[22] Jack R. Greene, another police scholar, summarized why team policing failed in this way: "it required a rethinking of the social and formal organization of policing on a massive scale,"[23] which was something that did not fit the organizational climate of the times.

Other programs of the police-community relations movement were aimed at various aspects of creating an alliance with the community. The programs were divided into different aspects of the police-community relations ideology consisting of the public relations programs such as "wave at a cop" and "ride-alongs," crime prevention and safety education programs such as theft prevention lectures and neighborhood watch, youth programs such as community-police service corps and law enforcement explorer programs, and core police-community relations programs such as community service units and various volunteer committees oriented on key social issues. All of these programs were a demonstration of the police-community relations ideology.

The police-community relations ideology was centered on the goal of changing attitudes and projecting a positive image of the police in order to improve relations with citizens. Officers would have occasional contact with citizens, based on need. The police department would establish a police-community relations unit to handle the improved police-community relations, while the rest of the department remained "business as usual." This unit would be controlled from the top down, in order for the police administration to determine what they considered to be the best means of improving police-citizen relations. Citizens often established blue ribbon committees that would identify problems with the police, and, in the event of an actual problem, citizen review boards would recommend officers be held accountable. Citizens were asked to volunteer, but it was primarily to perform clerical functions within the police department, rather than focusing on community safety and crime prevention.

The failures of police-community relations became all too evident throughout the 1970s and into the early 1980s.[24] The irregular contacts with the police created dissatisfaction on the part of the community. A good example is found in the establishment of neighborhood watch. After police officers helped a neighborhood establish the watch program, by bringing the community together and electing individuals to fill various roles, the police would abandon the program and leave it entirely in the hands of the citizens. These programs often floundered and failed, and the only thing remaining to prove the program had once existed was the neighborhood watch signs on the street corners. When the police department did communicate to the public that the police department cared about their relationship with the community, generally through the police-community relations units, it sent a false signal, the reality being that for the rest of the police agency nothing had changed. In some cases, the effort to improve relations actually backfired, especially when the blue ribbon committees preached to the police or when the citizen review boards became confrontational with the police. Finally, because police success was still measured by traditional methods, such as the number of arrests and tickets, it did not foster an improved relationship between the police and community.

As the problems of the police-community relations movement became evident, there began a reformulation of many of the police-community relations concepts. What the police did not abandon was the necessity of improving relations with the community, but rather, what they moved to change were the goals, methods, and programs employed under the new rubric, community policing. [25] The goal of community policing was to work with citizens in partnership in order to solve problems related to crime and disorder in specific neighborhoods. Officers would have regular contact with citizens by working with them to identify and solve problems. If officers established programs such as neighborhood watch, they would not abandon the program after its inception, but rather they would remain an integral part of the group, attending meetings, working alongside the volunteers, and providing them with information and data from the police perspective. The police would thus be held accountable by the citizens they served, and because officers would be permanently assigned to specific neighborhoods, they would not be able to escape the problems, and citizens would know who to deal with directly in regard to police services. Citizens would work alongside the police in helping to identify problems of crime and social disorder and work toward resolving them in their own neighborhoods. In addition, community policing would be systemic in that it would affect the entire police department, rather than simply adopting a new appendage to handle community relations. Finally, the goal of the police, which depended in part on the success of the community, was to reduce citizen fear, neighborhood disorder, and crime. These were the concepts that ushered in the Community Problem Solving Era of the early 1980s.

Policing has clearly moved through three eras—the political, reform, and community eras—and we are currently in this last era. However, this last era has lasted for well over twenty-five years now, and it is not accurate to portray this era in general terms, for much has changed over the ensuing years. Community policing in the early 1980s was vastly different from community policing at the turn of the millennium. Because of these differences, one author has described the movement from the early 1980s through the present as consisting of three generations of the community era: the innovation (1979-1986), the diffusion (1987-1994), and the institutionalization (1995 to present) generations.[26]

The first generation of community policing spans the time period 1979 through 1986 and is labeled the innovation generation. Although the start date is somewhat arbitrary, it is based on the realization in the 1970s that few of the long-held beliefs in policing actually worked, and a search for the answer to "What works in policing?" began. The publication of Herman Goldstein's important article on problem-oriented policing seems to have sparked the initiative for answering that question. This, coupled with the publication of Wilson and Kelling's seminal article "Broken Windows," would become the primary theoretical basis for several significant innovations in policing.

The early concepts of community policing were most often termed experiments, test sites, and demonstration projects. They were mainly restricted to larger metropolitan cities such as Flint, Michigan; Newark, New Jersey; Newport News, Virginia; Baltimore, Maryland; and Houston, Texas. These experiments were typically funded through federal and state grants as well as through funding by a number of foundations. The style of community policing that was generally employed during this generation consisted of a single method such as foot patrols, problem solving, or community substations. Finally, the methods of evaluating these early community policing programs were mostly through the case study method.

The second generation of community policing spans the time period of 1987 through 1994 and is considered the diffusion generation because as community policing became more widely known, it began to diffuse, or spread, to other police agencies across the country. Community policing during this generation was largely organized through various programs that consisted of newly created units or extensions of previously existing organizational units. Some examples of the newly created units included the Cartographic Oriented Management Program for the Abatement of Street Sales (COMPASS) in Hartford, Connecticut; the Community Oriented Policing and Problems Solving (COPPS) program in Hayward, California; the Community Police Officer Program (CPOP) in New York City; and the Citizen Oriented Police Enforcement (COPE) program in Baltimore County, Maryland. Like the first generation, many of these programs were funded by federal and state grants, but additional police agencies were making the move toward these innovations without external financial assistance. Many agencies simply retooled some of their existing units in order to adapt to the community policing methods.

Community policing during the diffusion generation, was still mainly restricted to large urban metropolitan areas but was working its way into medium-sized cities. The diffusion to these other agencies was due to the greater access of information, larger budgets to absorb any additional costs associated with community policing, and the preexisting structures of these agencies in which community policing was often placed, such as the former police-community relations units. Although some small-town and rural agencies did adopt community policing, they were the exception and not the rule. In addition, many of these new or evolved community policing programs were no longer relegated to one type of function (e.g., foot patrol, problem solving) but were now incorporating several components for a more expanded community policing program. Finally, evaluation of community policing improved in terms of the number of evaluations, and while many were still case studies, numerous surveys were beginning to be conducted, although primarily on the police, not the citizens.

The third generation of community policing spans the time period of 1995 to the present. The term *institutionalization* is used to denote the fact that community policing has become so widespread within American policing that a vast majority of agencies lay at least some claim to having implemented community policing. The adoption of community policing initiatives by police departments was significantly increased with the passage of the Violent Crime Control and Law Enforcement Act of 1994. This bill, which aimed to place "100,000 cops on the streets" under the community policing concepts, amounted to federal grants of nearly $10 billion to police departments throughout the United States over the time frame of 1994 to 2000. In addition, in the year 2000, Congress appropriated additional funds to hire another 50,000 police officers for community policing and to continue funding a number of programs instituted under the original crime bill. All of these grants were to assist law enforcement with the adoption and implementation of community policing, thus the federal government contributed greatly to the institutionalization of this policing philosophy.

The institutionalization generation of community policing is heavily marked by agencies shifting to or further developing their community policing programs because of the federal grant money. Not only could large and medium-sized cities now implement community policing more easily, but small-town and rural agencies were beginning to implement it as well. While many small-town and rural agencies did in fact adopt community policing prior to this generation, the vast majority of them made the move because of the availability of the aforementioned grant dollars. Thus, community policing now cast a much wider net than it did in the early 1980s when it was in the innovation generation.

In addition to the widespread adoption of community policing, the concepts behind community policing had become more refined, and agencies adopting community policing were beginning to employ multiple integrated strategies consisting of such tactics as aggressive and saturation patrols, foot patrols and community substations, and problem-solving methods. Under the institutionalization generation, the adoption of community policing was no longer seen as simply the adoption of a foot or bike patrol officer, but had come to entail numerous innovations, all aimed at enhancing the relationship between the police and community, reducing citizen fear of crime, and addressing the problems of not only crime, but social disorder. Finally, evaluations of community policing have become more widespread and much more sophisticated, utilizing a multitude of methods available from case studies and surveys to quantitative statistical analysis drawing upon data from both police and citizens all aimed at determining the success of community policing.

Community Policing

Although it is recognized that policing today finds itself in the community era, and throughout this era there have been a number of generations of community policing development, perhaps the most interesting aspect of community policing is its lack of a generally shared definition. Community policing is not a simple and clear-cut approach to policing. Rather, it has become an amalgam of programs and tactics that share the umbrella term: community policing. This is largely because community policing was developed out of a number of disparate ideas and theories, was advanced by a variety of advocates, has been defined by a number of core themes, and has been delivered through a patchwork quilt of programs. While the search for a common definition may seem more academic and wholly unnecessary, the need for a shared definition becomes evident when agencies and researchers try to determine if community policing "works." If agencies and researchers are not even sure what community policing is, then how do they know whether or not it works?

One reason for some of the confusion over the definition of community policing lies in the fact that several ideas were being advanced at approximately the same time, and these disparate ideas became merged together to present a new method of policing.[27] The first was the development of problem-oriented policing, when Herman Goldstein advocated the use of problem-solving methods in order to improve policing.[28] Goldstein argued that police often treat calls-for-service as isolated incidents having no past or future. Rather, he argued, police should begin to look for connections among calls-for-service to see if there are relationships among the people, places, and events. If connections are made, the underlying problem that results in the police being called should be identified and solutions developed to address the problem, not its symptoms. Starting in the early 1980s, in Newport News, problem-oriented policing became widely popular among the police through the adoption of the SARA Model, which stands for Scanning, Analysis, Response, and Assessment. Police were taught to look for connections among calls-for-service, analyze the problem and develop a solution, implement the solution, and then evaluate the response to see if it had any impact on the problem.

The other development in policing, based on a 1982 *Atlantic Monthly* article by James Q. Wilson and George L. Kelling titled "Broken Windows," was an emphasis on order maintenance policing. The broken windows theory of policing advances the argument that communities that present signs of social decay, like broken windows, abandoned cars, etc., send a clear communication that the people who live there do not care about their neighborhood. This signals that it is acceptable to break more windows, commit minor acts of vandalism, and it gives an invitation for an unattractive element to enter the neighborhood. When vagrants, derelicts, and homeless begin entering a community, this is often followed by drug dealers, prostitutes, and various criminals, which then attract or create situations for more serious crimes such as burglaries, robberies, and homicides. The key to preventing this type of neighborhood decay is to fix the broken windows and send a signal that people care about their neighborhood, or, if the community has already spiraled out of control, to begin reasserting control of the neighborhood through the reestablishment of order maintenance. The broken windows theory led many in policing to begin creating a variety of programs aimed at either preventing the encroachment of minor disorders (e.g., zero-tolerance policing) or fixing up neighborhoods and then putting community controls in place (e.g., the weed and seed program).

These two advances in policing came about at the same time that a decade of research had challenged long-held assumptions of what works in policing.[29] The Kansas City Preventive Patrol experiment found that random police patrols had no impact on crime. A study analyzing the rapid response by police found that, on average, enhanced police response times had no impact on crime. Finally, the RAND Corporation's study on police detectives and both their training and technology found little impact on crime. Police patrols, rapid response, and the power of the detectives all had no impact on crime, but underlying each of these was the realization that it was the community that mattered. In the preventive patrol experiment it was found that the police through their enhanced pres-

ence could reduce the fear citizens had of crime. The rapid response of the police did not solve more crimes, because the response times were contingent upon the public contacting the police department immediately, and often there was a lengthy delay before people called the police. In part, this may have been because police and citizen relationships were considered poor. Finally, the detective study found that detectives and technology did not solve most crimes; citizens coming forward with information tended to solve most crimes. All of these studies, and others, suggested that the cooperation of the community was imperative and both the broken windows theory and problem-oriented policing had the potential of including citizens in their implementation. Thus was born the community era of policing, an amalgam of concepts that all fell under the rubric of "community policing."

In addition to the various concepts that helped develop community policing, it has been suggested there were also a variety of sources for the intellectual development of community policing.[30] In other words, there were individuals and consortiums that were working to advance the concepts of community policing. Robert C. Trojanowicz of Michigan State University founded the National Center for Community Policing which conducted some of the earliest research on community policing and helped to develop many of the community policing programs. Another researcher, out of Harvard's Kennedy School of Government, was Mark Moore, who also worked to advance the practices of community policing. In addition, George L. Kelling worked hard to advance the programs that encapsulated the broken windows theory, while Herman Goldstein worked with others, William Eck and John Spelman, to develop programs that incorporated the concept of problem-solving into policing. Finally, a consortium of various police associations came together to create the Community Policing Consortium. This consortium received funding from the U.S. Department of Justice and consisted of the International Association of Chiefs of Police (IACP), the Police Executive Research Forum (PERF), National Sheriff's Association (NSA), and the Police Foundation. Through the Community Policing Consortium, these various agencies were able to pool their resources to help advance the research and training of community policing. Yet, again, it should be noted that each of these individuals and the consortium were advancing very different concepts, but concepts that were easily adaptive to the underlying concept of the time: police-community partnerships.

In light of the numerous concepts that were developing under the umbrella term of community policing, the creation of a shared and agreed-upon definition became tenuous at best. Writing in the earlier years of the community policing movement, Bayley explained the issue with defining community policing:

Despite the benefits claimed for community policing, programmatic implementation of it has been very uneven. Although widely, almost universally said to be important, it means different things to different people—public relations campaigns, shop fronts and mini-stations, rescaled patrol beats, liaison with ethnic groups, permission for rank and file to speak to the press, neighborhood watch, foot patrol, patrol detective team, and door-to-door visits by police officers. Community policing on the ground often seems less a program than a set of aspirations wrapped up in a slogan.[31]

As community policing continued to progress out of the 1980s and into the 1990s, writing six years later, Bayley continued to find the same problems amplified when he explained that:

> Community policing means too many things to different people. Its practices are so varied that any evaluation will be partial or challengeable as not being authentic 'community policing.' Furthermore, because the mix of practices is so great, any evaluation will be *sui generis*, making generalization to other situations problematic.[32]

Bayley was not the only policing scholar to challenge the wide diversity of programs and practices being tied to the rubric of community policing. Many scholars argued there was no cohesive program, practice, or strategy that could readily be identified as community policing, and that what was being offered was most likely to have little impact upon police performance.[33] In other words, implementing some of the programs, such as neighborhood watch or foot patrols, were not likely to make the police department as a whole more community-oriented. However, one scholar saw the variety of programs and the ambiguity of the definition of community policing as an asset, not a liability. Moore explains that:

> It is partly the ambiguity of the concept that is stimulating the wide pattern of experimentation we are observing. In this sense, it is important that the concept mean something, but not something too specific: The ambiguity is a virtue.[34]

Another author, Friedmann, explains that the ambiguity of the term is exactly what gives community policing its appeal and makes it so popular, when he states:

> What is possibly so fascinating about community policing is that it is not easily amenable to a particular definition . . . but it is clearly a highly appealing concept.[35]

There were a number of attempts to clear the air and definitively define community policing. Perhaps the first was made by Robert Trojanowicz and Bonnie Bucqueroux in their book *Community Policing,* where they define it as:

> a new philosophy of policing, based on the concept that police officers and private citizens working together in creative ways can help solve contemporary

community problems related to crime, fear of crime, social and physical disorder, and neighborhood decay.[36]

However, the realization that community policing could be defined from a variety of perspectives, ranging from the rhetorical and philosophical to the programmatic, caused one author to argue that even this definition is too general in its approach and ignores other aspects of community policing.[37]

As a result of the often confusing collection of programs and ideas, some early attempts to define community policing simply searched for common elements. The International City/County Management Association (ICMA), which was actively involved in the movement among not only police to the community orientation but to city and county government as well, attempted to summarize the common elements as follows:

> Whether they are called 'community-oriented policing' or 'neighborhood policing' or 'problem-oriented policing,' the idea is to take the police officer out of isolation as a lone crime-fighter and make him or her part of a team that includes not only the staff resources of the police department, but also the resources of the local government and the resources of private citizens. Traditional lines of command are replaced with new group arrangements that emphasize problem solving and personal interaction.[38]

The ICMA definition, although focused on core elements rather than a specific name for community policing, was considered too general. What became very popular after this, however, was the attempt to specifically identify the core elements of community policing in order to demonstrate that regardless of the name being applied or the programs being employed, community policing did have a shared set of concepts that could be identified and evaluated.

The Community Policing Consortium published a document titled, "Understanding Community Policing: A Framework for Action,"[39] where they attempted to identify the goal and core components of community policing. The consortium explained that the goal of community policing was "to reduce crime and disorder by carefully examining the characteristics of problems in neighborhoods and then applying appropriate problem-solving remedies."[40] They, therefore, saw the two core components of community policing as consisting of community partnerships, where police and community work together, in order to solve problems, the second core component.

Additional authors began to identify core elements of community policing by categorizing common themes, programs, and practices among police agencies implementing community policing and analyzing community policing evaluations conducted by police scholars, researchers, and academics. Skolnick and Bayley described four elements of community policing as consisting of police-community reciprocity (e.g., partnerships), area decentralization of command, reorientation of patrol toward more preventive tactics, and civilianization.[41]

These elements meant that the police would have to become more community focused by moving from a highly centralized force structure to one that works closely with and is accessible to the community. Police would work with the community on mostly crime prevention methods, rather than the reactive measures, and, in order to achieve this redistribution of patrol officers, more of the functions of policing would have to be placed into the hands of civilian workers. These themes, while prevalent in the community policing movement, are heavily focused on the management aspects of community policing.

Bayley, on his own, identified four elements that are somewhat related, but are more oriented on the nature of implementing community policing at the neighborhood level. He sees community policing as consisting of police consultation with communities (again, partnerships), adaptation of police resources to local needs, mobilization of public and private resources, and addressing specific community problems by remedying the conditions that give rise to crime. Herman Goldstein also found four elements of community policing, but he lists these as

> the involvement of the community in getting the police job done; the permanent assignment of police officers to a neighborhood in order to cultivate better relationships; the setting of police priorities based on the specific needs and desires of the community; and the meeting of these needs by the allocation of police resources and personnel otherwise assigned to responding to calls for police assistance.[42]

While both Bayley and Goldstein do describe elements of community policing, the deficiencies related to their lists are that they are too narrowly focused and address more police tactics, rather than operations or strategies.

In an attempt to go the other way, by focusing on the concepts of community policing from a broader perspective, Gary Cordner, a renowned police scholar, identified four dimensions of community policing and asserted that there were common elements in each of these dimensions.[43] The first dimension was the philosophical, where community policing tended to focus on a broader view of policing which incorporated citizen input and developed more personalized (at the neighborhood level) service. The second dimension, the strategic, describes the common elements of refocusing police operations from the general, random patrols, to the specific, directed geographic enforcement, with a stronger emphasis on crime prevention. The tactical dimension is the third dimension, and Cordner describes it as being heavily focused on positive police-citizen partnerships that emphasize problem solving. Finally, the fourth dimension, the organizational, is concerned with restructuring the police agency to better manage community policing and its implementation.

Another preeminent police scholar, Jack Greene, identified community policing as operating at three different levels and that the changes required in each anticipated different outcomes. The first level of community policing intervention is the environmental level. It is here that the police form relationships and partner with local organizations, ranging from formal organizations, such as businesses and the chambers of commerce, to concerned citizens from a specific neighborhood. These partnerships are aimed at reducing crime and citizen fear of crime, developing increased levels of trust between police and citizens through better communication, and working toward better problem solving. The organizational level of community policing is focused on how the department structures and manages itself in order to advance community policing; it is concerned with improving training, developing better methods for acquiring and sharing information, and enhancing communication within the agency. Finally, the individual level of community policing is concerned with developing officers through their interpersonal skills, knowledge, and personal attachment to the community.

In light of the fact there is no agreed upon definition of community policing, it still seems possible that there are aspects of community policing that run through all of these definitions and attempts to identify core elements. Police-community partnerships are at the core of community policing. Everything stems from this concept, ranging from how the police department is structured, how it reaches out to the community, right down to how police are evaluated in the performance of their job. The actual implementation of community policing seems to fall into three categories. First, there is the implementation of strategic and targeted measures to reduce crime, disorder, and fear of crime. Second, opening up the lines of communication between the police and the community, whether it is merely a picnic or something more complex such as a working community action group, would appear to be a necessary part of community policing. Finally, the use of problem-solving techniques is the other ingredient necessary to implement community policing. Therefore, community policing can be said to be the triangulation of police-community partnerships that utilize targeted methods (broken windows) and problem-solving techniques (problem-oriented policing).[44]

Partnerships

It should be clear at this point that the centerpiece of community policing is the police-community partnership. While it is easy to recognize a police agency by the uniform and all the organizational trappings, it is less easy to define the concept of community. To clearly define the term community is difficult because of the conceptual ambiguity of the term itself.[45] The ability to look to one strict analysis and definition of community is of no benefit to community policing, for there are always communities within communities. As Goldstein explains, "communities are shifting groups, defined differently depending on the problem that is addressed."[46] Therefore, it is necessary to define community as it is defined by various members of the community, including how it is defined by the police, citizens, and government. Geography often helps us form a conceptualization of community and police boundaries, as well as neighborhood and business districts can assist in this endeavor. However, within these confines, community can only be defined as consisting of a group of people who interact and have some shared attitudes and beliefs, whether they are criminal or law-abiding, residential or business-oriented, socially acceptable or not acceptable.

Community policing, then, perceives the community as whatever collective group it is dealing with to address a criminal or order maintenance issue. As Mastrofski points out, a minimum standard for community policing is a "demonstration that a group of people—say a neighborhood—shares a definition of what constitutes right order, threats to it, and appropriate methods for maintaining it."[47] He further states that "to the extent that community implies a basis for citizens to work collectively with police to restore and preserve order, it also requires a sense of group identity or attachment—a 'we-ness' derived from shared experience and interaction."[48] In a perfect setting, this may already exist, but in a conceptual sense, it may require the creation of community where none exists.

It is indeed important to define who the community is, but more important is the conceptualization and recognition of the community's role in community policing. Eck and Rosenbaum identified five ways in which citizens of a community can effectively deal with the criminal and order maintenance issues that face their neighborhoods.[49] They identified the first and primary function to be the "eyes and ears" of the community. The second function is for citizens to form patrols, confront criminal and disorderly individuals, and drive them from the community. Although this function was generally discouraged in the past, some police came to encourage such bold action under community policing. The third function of the community is to reduce its citizens' chances of victimization, reduce the opportunity for crime, reduce the actual amount of crime, and reduce the fear of crime. The fourth function is for citizens to "put pressure on others to act." As Eck and Rosenbaum explain:

> They can demand more police resources, they can pressure businesses to change their practices, they can lobby local government agencies to obtain services and get favorable rulings from regulators, and they can threaten property owners and organizations with civil suits to change behaviors and physical conditions.[50]

The fifth function Eck and Rosenbaum discuss is allowing "the police to act on their behalf."[51] The police, through meetings with the community can gather the opinions of the community members and obtain their authorization to extend their capabilities beyond the normal routines of policing.

The authors, however, leave out one important function of the community under community policing, and that is the leadership role they must play. The community, made up of indigenous citizens from a specific neighborhood, must be given the authority to determine what the criminal and order maintenance problems are in their community, their priority, and the type of programs that should be implemented. Citizens must be given a leadership role in taking back control of their community. As Friedman explains, "the community must have a voice in the forums that define community policing itself, must be a ready and knowledgeable ally to the forces of reform, and, in the neighborhood, where the benefits are supposed to be delivered, must have a serious part in implementing solutions as well as nominating problems."[52] In fact, recent research has demonstrated that the most effective communities have utilized their community organizations to apply pressure through activism to obtain changes in policing practices that are more in line with the philosophy of community policing.[53] To accomplish this goal, the community must have a shared form of leadership in both the policy-making and decision-making processes, and like the police, the community's citizens should be held accountable for their actions. When the community works with the police in this shared leadership role, the citizens have not only a vested interest in how the police perform their role, but also a responsibility for their role that has not existed since the decline of civic engagement and civic responsibility starting in the 1950s.

One method for creating a shared power role for the community has been through the establishment of citizens' steering committees or councils. Osborne and Gaebler, in their book *Reinventing Government*,[54] go so far as to call for a system of "public safety coordinating councils" at the state and local level, which would consist of representatives of the providers (government) and the customers (local citizens). These councils would oversee all of government, according to Osborne and Gaebler, including the police. There is a strong need for a similar entity specifically for the police, for as Guyot has pointed out, "listening to the many voices of the community is essential for police officers and police managers in their striving for fairness," and "police departments need structures that can encourage officers to be more attentive to the diversity of views in a neighborhood."[55] If Zhao and Thurman are accurate in their analysis—that it is external environment that brings about organizational change in police departments—then it is clear that these types of councils should be a focal point of community policing.[56] In addition, community policing should be primarily a means for community empowerment rather than a means for extending the power of police, which can often be the case.[57] Although this issue can be a source of contention for chiefs who do not embrace sharing power with the community, if adopted properly, it would be as Osborne and Gaebler envision where the councils "would steer their local systems, but would not row."[58]

The workhorse of community policing, however, should be the neighborhood committee which would consist of citizens from a specific neighborhood, working with a permanently assigned police officer or officers. These committees would meet on a regular basis to determine the specific needs of the neighborhood, and to identify which criminal and/or social disorder problems need to be addressed. This forum gives the community an opportunity to voice its concerns, as well as giving the officer a chance to articulate the police department's perspective on crime and disorder. These concerns and issues can then be prioritized, and innovative solutions to the problems can be developed through this police-community partnership. It is in these meetings that the problem-solving methods can be applied, innovations implemented, and programs evaluated for their effectiveness. Most important, these types of neighborhood forums provide all of the stakeholders a chance to become involved in improving the quality of life in their neighborhood.

Benefits

Research regarding the benefits afforded the police by community policing has generally been consistent in its findings over the past several decades. Early studies, in the 1980s, tended to be anecdotal references to police satisfaction with community policing or were derived from extensive case studies, but an extensive review of all of these early studies found consistencies among the reports. For example, one of these early studies in Flint, Michigan, analyzed police satisfaction with the implementation of the Neighborhood Foot Patrol Program (NFPP) and they found when compared with those officers riding in routine motor vehicle patrols, foot patrol officers had a much higher job satisfaction because "officers were more likely to perceive that they were doing an important job in the department and in their patrol areas, improving police-community relations, performing a job that the police department view[ed] as important, and working as part of a police team."[59] Another study in San Diego found that officers were "more likely to report that their job was interesting and less likely to report that their job was frustrating,"[60] and in Baltimore County, in their Citizen-Oriented Police Enforcement (COPE) program, they found that "those officers who participated in [the program] had higher levels of reported job satisfaction, more cooperative and service-oriented attitudes about the police role, more positive attitudes toward the community, and more positive evaluations of the COPE project's effects."[61]

As community policing began to see more wide-spread implementation in the 1990s, the studies of police satisfaction became much more robust in their analysis. Rather than simply looking at programs where community policing had been implemented, many studies began focusing on pre-implementation analysis, as well as pre- and post-tests of officer satisfaction. The results, again, were generally very consistent. What these studies found was that officers tended to be very skeptical of the program prior to implementation, and remained tentative to the concept as the programs were being implemented, usually in the first year. However, as the programs began to take hold and as their experience with the implementation of community policing increased, their attitudes typically shifted to the more positive, especially when they experienced the positive effects first-hand. For instance, in Joliet, Illinois, officers reported an increase in job satisfaction in the first year for those in the Neighborhood-Oriented Policing (NOP) program; in the second year, officers working in the program and outside the program reported a more positive change in both the characteristics of their job and their level of satisfaction.[62] Key to this success was found in such studies as the one in Kalamazoo, Michigan, where a study of officers' attitudes revealed that there was a positive attitude toward community policing when citizens were involved in the process, when they had job involvement, and when community policing officers were like other officers (i.e., it was implemented department-wide).[63]

In terms of police officer satisfaction, it also does not appear to matter whether the officers are serving in large metropolitan agencies,[64] in public housing agencies,[65] or in police departments located throughout small-town and rural America.[66] All of the findings remain consistent that when community policing is legitimately implemented, officer satisfaction increases, officers demonstrate higher levels of self-initiated policing, they receive fewer citizen complaints, and essentially community policing officers are more likely to meet the needs of the citizens they police.[67] As Russell and MacLachlan concluded in their study on officer satisfaction, "the evidence supports the hypothesis that community policing will improve employee satisfaction in a law enforcement agency."[68] Thus, it is relatively clear after more than twenty-five years of research that a bona fide shift to community policing enhances officer satisfaction in the long term, which results in better policing and greater citizens' satisfaction. Recognizing that police are more satisfied in their jobs with the implementation of community policing, it is to the citizen satisfaction research we now turn.

While the research related to police officer attitudes toward community policing has been broadly explored, until more recent years, little was known about community attitudes toward community policing. Although conventional wisdom articulated that citizens would be in favor of the police and community engaging in partnerships, it was simply that, conventional wisdom. When the issue of community was explored, the starting point tended to be the extensive research related to fear of crime as well as citizens' perceptions of the police. A natural extension was to begin looking at these two bodies of research from a community policing perspective.

In regard to fear of crime, traditional policing did not focus on reducing fear of crime by targeting fear, rather it did so by trying to target crime itself. A variety of studies have demonstrated that actual crime and fear of crime are not necessarily associated with one another. Hence in the late 1970s and early 1980s, police attention began to focus on citizen fear of crime, not just the crime itself. According to Dietz, this concept has been associated with community policing for the "reduction of fear of crime has been associated with community police programs since their inception."[69] As the community policing philosophy and its strategies developed, crime reduction, fear reduction, and improved quality of life all became central tenets of this systemic approach to policing. Today, it is well understood that one of the goals of community policing is to reduce the fear of crime among citizens.

The past twenty-five years have yielded an extensive amount of research focused on fear reduction by the police. Zhao and his associates recently conducted an analysis of all of the studies available, using quasi-experiments, to determine if police could, in fact, reduce citizen fear of crime.[70] Out of the 50 studies included in their analysis, they found 31 studies had demonstrated that police were able to reduce the fear of crime, 18 found no changes in the level of fear, and only one study was reported to have found an increase in citizen fear. The study also suggested that simple police presence is not as effective as the pro-active interventions and partnerships that are part of community policing.

The more important question, then, is whether or not community policing can reduce citizen fear of crime. One study that analyzed twelve cities in the United States, found that perceptions of community policing do have a strong positive effect on citizen satisfaction with the police, but that citizen perceptions of community policing do not directly affect levels of fear.[71] Follow up research, utilizing the same data, advanced on the notion that community policing did not directly affect levels of fear, but may have somehow indirectly reduced fear among citizens.[72] This research found that community policing has a direct impact on the perceptions of incivilities by citizens and dissatisfaction with their quality of life. Community policing works toward reducing incivilities and improving the quality of life, which in turn leads toward a reduction in fear. Thus, the study found, like so many others, that community policing does decrease fear of crime.

Additional research into citizens' perceptions has continued to yield an enormous body of literature that points toward the success of community policing. For instance, in an analysis conducted across five small cities in North Carolina, citizen awareness of the implementation of community policing contributed to reduced fear of crime, stronger feelings of community attachment, and citizens engaging in self-protection efforts more often.[73] In addition, programs such as Citizen Police Academies have been found to generate a more positive attitude toward the police, along with the willingness to assist the police in community policing programs.[74] This also creates somewhat of a feedback cycle, making the relationship between police and citizens stronger, for other research has found that those who do volunteer to assist the police in community policing programs have a higher confidence in their police.[75] Moreover, other research has found that the positive impact of community policing is not necessarily limited to affluent or well-off neighborhoods, but can apply at all levels on the socio-economic scale.[76] In fact, the researchers in this last study conclude that "citizens' perceptions of police actions that are consistent with the principles of community policing are associated with individual interpretive processes of local conditions and may enhance quality of life assessments."[77] Another way of saying this is when community policing is truly implemented, people see the results, and their quality of life improves. Citizen perceptions do change when faced with honest community policing.

The benefits to the police and the citizens, especially in the area of fear reduction and enhanced quality of life, are most assuredly important benefits derived from the implementation of community policing. However, when one considers the role of police in society, one generally considers their role in crime reduction. So, a natural extension of this consideration is to ask if community policing reduces crime. It should be stated first that the majority of research into police reduction of crime in general has concluded that the police have very limited control over crime. There are numerous causes of crime, most of which are far beyond the reach of the police, such as schooling, the economy, family, and the labor market. Recognizing the limitations of the police overall, one must still ask if the traditional methods of crime control are more or less effective in controlling crime than community policing. The answer, unfortunately, appears to be largely mixed.

A recent report that analyzed all of the research to date in an attempt to ascertain community policing's efficacy found that many of the programs were wholly ineffective at reducing crime itself, but highly effective when it came to increasing citizen satisfaction with the police, quality of life in a community, and reducing fear of crime. The report did indicate that some programs demonstrated mixed results, while others appeared to be very promising in potentially reducing crime.[78] Studies related to neighborhood watch programs, community meetings, newsletters, and police storefronts, did not find them to have any impact on crime rates. Various crackdowns by the police on specific targets were found to have an impact on crime, but it was typically short-lived, and crime often returned to previous rates within days, weeks, or months. The concepts of problem-oriented policing, where police used problem-solving measures to address crime, seemed to be effective at reducing such crimes as gun crimes, drunk driving, and domestic assault. Finally, those programs where there was an asserted effort by the police to treat citizens with respect and programs that were focused on being responsive to citizen concerns found that the legitimacy of the police increased, contributing to a decrease in crime rates. Unfortunately, community policing does not appear to generate a blanket reduction in crime, but there are certain aspects of the community policing philosophy and program that do. Mixed with the other benefits, however, it would appear that community policing is a proper direction for dealing with problems of both crime and disorder.

It can be summarized, then, that community policing offers benefits to both the police and the community, and in some instances can contribute to a reduction in crime.[79] For the police it means they will receive greater community support in their role in society, they are able to share the responsibility for the control of crime and disorder with citizens, they have increased job satisfaction because they are able to see the results of their efforts, and communication and cooperation among units in the police department is enhanced. For the community it means that the police are making a commitment to prevent crime, rather than simply reacting to it, public scrutiny of the police is improved as citizens know more about what the police do and why, police officer accountability not only to the department but to the citizens is improved, police services are tailored to the needs of each neighborhood, and citizens become more involved in their communities. And for all, it can lead to a reduction in crime rates, resulting in further benefits for both the police and community. Clearly then, there are many benefits that can be derived from police-community partnerships. This is assuredly why the U.S. Conference of Catholic Bishops specifically advocated the adoption of community policing as a means of implementing criminal justice from a Catholic perspective.

Conclusion

According to the U.S. Conference of Catholic Bishops in their publication *Responsibility, Rehabilitation, and Restoration: A Catholic Perspective on Crime and Criminal Justice*, community policing programs that employ police-community partnerships have proven to be effective models of crime control and community building, empowering local leaders to solve their own problems with the assistance of the police. These types of programs truly reflect the Catholic social teaching principles of solidarity, subsidarity, and the search for the common good.[80] In terms of implementing a new and bold criminal justice system that reflects Catholic social teaching and values, the Bishops make clear that the first component of the system, the police, should adopt the philosophy, policies, and programs of community policing.

Still further, it is very clear that the larger concepts the Bishops have called for, namely the adoption of restorative and community justice, are compatible with the police moving to community policing. As Nicholl has explained, both restorative justice and community policing "emphasize participation and citizen engagement, cooperative and collaborative approaches, and problem solving" and that "operating restorative justice [and] community policing enables learning, understanding, respect, and shared responsibility."[81] All factors that have motivated the Bishops to specifically name a program that they believe is in alignment with Catholic principles.

It should be expressly stated that community policing should not be implemented without adopting and adhering to the concepts of restorative justice. As Bazemore and Griffiths explain, "what restorative justice brings to community and problem-oriented policing is a set of tools or 'levers' for building social capital and efficacy around the direct response to specific incidents of crime, conflict, and harm."[82] As they further state, "whereas generic community policing offers opportunities for citizen participation in determining police priorities and invites community involvement in organized group events, restorative policing provides at the case level a decision-making role for citizens in informal sanctioning and the effective resolution of individual incidents of crime that has traditionally been the province of courts and professional court group decision makers (e.g., prosecutors, defenders)."[83] Thus, in order to fully implement the Bishops' recommendations that would transform the criminal justice system, moving the police toward community policing is not enough in and of itself. Rather, the adoption of community policing must be part of a larger initiative of adopting restorative justice for all of the criminal justice system and the community as a whole. As Bazemore and Griffiths elude to in this last quote, this would necessitate not only a change in the role of the police and community under restorative justice practices, but also the role of the courts and the community. It is to this latter issue the next chapter turns.

Notes

1. U.S. Catholic Bishops, *Confronting a Culture of Violence: A Catholic Framework for Action* (Washington, D.C.: United States Conference of Catholic Bishops, 1994), 13.
2. United States Conference of Catholic Bishops, *Responsibility, Rehabilitation, and Restoration: A Catholic Perspective on Crime and Criminal Justice* (Washington, D.C.: United States Catholic Conference, Inc., 2000).
3. United States Conference of Catholic Bishops, *Responsibility, Rehabilitation, and Restoration: A Catholic Perspective on Crime and Criminal Justice* (Washington, D.C.: United States Catholic Conference, Inc., 2000), 45.
4. United States Conference of Catholic Bishops, *Responsibility, Rehabilitation, and Restoration: A Catholic Perspective on Crime and Criminal Justice* (Washington, D.C.: United States Catholic Conference, Inc., 2000), 45.
5. Catholic Church, *Catechism of the Catholic Church,* 2nd ed. (Washington, D.C.: United States Catholic Conference, Inc., 1997), 471.
6. Mk 12:29-31; cf. Deut 6:4-5; Lev 19:18; Mt 22:34-40; Luke 10:25-28 (*The New American Bible*).
7. Pope John Paul II, *Solicitude Rei Socialis* (Encyclical: Vatican, 1987), http://www.vatican.va/holy_father/john_paul_ii/encyclicals/documents/hf_jp-ii_enc_3012198 7_sollicitudo-rei-socialis_en.html
8. Catholic Church, *Catechism of the Catholic Church,* 2nd ed. (Washington, D.C.: United States Catholic Conference, Inc., 1997), 471.
9. Pius XI, *Quadragesimo Anno* (Encyclical: Vatican, (1931), http://www.vatican.va/holy_father/pius_xi/encyclicals/documents/hf_p-xi_enc_19310515 _quadragesimo-anno_en.html
10. Catholic Church, *Catechism of the Catholic Church,* 2nd ed. (Washington, D.C.: United States Catholic Conference, Inc., 1997), 460.

Chapter Four

11. Catholic Church, *Catechism of the Catholic Church,* 2nd ed. (Washington, D.C.: United States Catholic Conference, Inc., 1997), 464-466.

12. Catholic Church, *Catechism of the Catholic Church,* 2nd ed. (Washington, D.C.: United States Catholic Conference, Inc., 1997), 464.

13. Catholic Church, *Catechism of the Catholic Church,* 2nd ed. (Washington, D.C.: United States Catholic Conference, Inc., 1997), 465.

14. Catholic Church, *Catechism of the Catholic Church,* 2nd ed. (Washington, D.C.: United States Catholic Conference, Inc., 1997), 465.

15. Catholic Church, *Catechism of the Catholic Church,* 2nd ed. (Washington, D.C.: United States Catholic Conference, Inc., 1997), 465.

16. Catholic Church, *Catechism of the Catholic Church,* 2nd ed. (Washington, D.C.: United States Catholic Conference, Inc., 1997), 465.

17. Catholic Church, *Catechism of the Catholic Church,* 2nd ed. (Washington, D.C.: United States Catholic Conference, Inc., 1997), 465.

18. Willard M. Oliver and James F. Hilgenberg, Jr., *A History of Crime and Criminal Justice in America* (Boston: Allyn & Bacon, 2006).

19. Willard M. Oliver and James F. Hilgenberg, Jr., *A History of Crime and Criminal Justice in America* (Boston: Allyn & Bacon, 2006).

20. George L. Kelling and Mark H. Moore, "The Evolving Strategy of Policing," *Perspectives on Policing,* No. 4 (Washington, D.C.: National Institute of Justice, 1988).

21. Willard M. Oliver, *Community-Oriented Policing: A Systemic Approach to Policing,* 3rd ed. (Upper Saddle River, NJ: Prentice Hall, 2004).

22. Lawrence W. Sherman, "Middle Management and Democratization," *Criminology* 12, no. 4 (1975): 363-377.

23. Jack R. Greene, "Foot Patrol and Community Policing: Past Practices and Future Prospects," *American Journal of Police* 6, no. 1 (1987): 1-15.

24. Robert C. Trojanowicz, "Community Policing is Not Police-Community Relations," *FBI Law Enforcement Bulletin* (October 1990): 10.

25. Robert C. Trojanowicz, "Community Policing is Not Police-Community Relations," *FBI Law Enforcement Bulletin* (October 1990): 10.

26. Willard M. Oliver, "The Third Generation of Community Policing: Moving Through Innovation, Diffusion, and Institutionalization," *Police Quarterly* 3, no. 4 (2000): 367-388.

27. Willard M. Oliver, *Community Policing: Classical Readings* (Upper Saddle River, NJ: Prentice Hall, 2000).

28. H. Goldstein, "Improving Policing: A Problem-Oriented Approach," *Crime & Delinquency* 25 (1979): 236-258.

29. Willard M. Oliver, *Community-Oriented Policing: A Systemic Approach to Policing,* 3rd ed. (Upper Saddle River, NJ: Prentice Hall, 2004).

30. Todd R. Clear and Eric Cadora, *Community Justice* (Belmont, CA: Wadsworth, 2003).

31. D. H. Bayley, "Community Policing: A Report from the Devil's Advocate," in *Community Policing: Rhetoric or Reality?,* eds. J.R. Greene and S.D. Mastrofski (New York, NY: Praeger Publishers, 1988), 225.

32. D.H. Bayley, "International Differences in Community Policing," in *The Challenge of Community Policing: Testing the Promises* ed. D. P. Rosenbaum (Thousand Oaks, CA: Sage Publications, 1994), 279.

33. J.R. Greene and S.D. Mastrofski, *Community Policing: Rhetoric or Reality?* (New York: Praeger Publishers, 1988); C.B. Klockars, "Order Maintenance, the Quality of Urban Life and Police: A Different Line of Argument," in *Police Leadership in America: Crisis and Opportunity,* ed. W.A. Geller (New York: Praeger Publishers, 1985); Manning, P.K. (1984). "Community Policing." *American Journal of Police,* 3: 205-227.

34. Mark H. Moore, "Community Policing," in *Modern Policing,* eds. M. Tonry and N. Morris (Chicago, IL: University of Chicago Press, 1992), 290.

35. R.R. Friedmann, *Community Policing: Comparative Perspectives and Prospects* (New York: St. Martin's Press, 1992), 3.

36. Robert C. Trojanowicz and Bonnie Bucqueroux, *Community Policing: A Contemporary Perspective* (Cincinnati: Anderson Publishing, 1990), 5.

37. Jayne Seagrave, "Defining Community Policing," *American Journal of Police* 15, no. 2 (1996): 1-22.

38. International City Management Association, *Management Information Service Report.* Vol. 21 No. 9 (Washington, D.C.: International City Management Association, 1989).

39. Community Policing Consortium, *Understanding Community Policing: A Framework for Action* (Washington, D.C.: Bureau of Justice Assistance, 1994).

40. Community Policing Consortium, *Understanding Community Policing: A Framework for Action* (Washington, D.C.: Bureau of Justice Assistance, 1994), 10-11.

41. J. H. Skolnick and D. H. Bayley, *The New Blue Line: Police Innovations in Six American Cities* (New York: Free Press, 1986), 211-220.

42. H. Goldstein, "Toward Community-Oriented Policing: Potential, Basic Requirements and Threshold Questions," *Crime & Delinquency* 33 (1987): 6-30.

43. Gary Cordner, "Community Policing: Elements and Effects," in *Critical Issues in Policing: Contemporary Readings,* . 5th ed., eds. R.G. Dunham and G.P. Alpert. Long Grove, IL: Waveland Press, Inc., 2005).

44. Willard M. Oliver, *Community-Oriented Policing: A Systemic Approach to Policing,* 3rd ed. (Upper Saddle River, NJ: Prentice Hall, 2004).

45. Mark E. Correia, "The Conceptual Ambiguity of Community in Community Policing: Filtering the Muddy Waters," *Policing: An International Journal of Police Strategies and Management* 23, no. 2 (2000): 218-232.

46. Herman Goldstein, *Problem-Oriented Policing* (New York: McGraw Hill, 1990), 26.

47. Stephen D. Mastrofski, "Community Policing as Reform: A Cautionary Tale," in *Community Policing: Rhetoric or Reality?,* eds. Jack R. Green and Stephen D. Mastrofski (New York: Praeger Publishers, 1988), 49.

48. Stephen D. Mastrofski, "Community Policing as Reform: A Cautionary Tale," in *Community Policing: Rhetoric or Reality?,* eds. Jack R. Green and Stephen D. Mastrofski (New York: Praeger Publishers, 1988), 49.

49. Eck, John E. and Dennis P. Rosenbaum. (1994). "The New Police Order: Effectiveness, Equity, and Efficiency in Community Policing." In Dennis P. Rosenbaum (Ed.) *The Challenge of Community Policing: Testing the Promises.* Thousand Oaks, CA: Sage Publications.

50. John E. Eck and Dennis P. Rosenbaum, "The New Police Order: Effectiveness, Equity, and Efficiency in Community Policing," in *The Challenge of Community Policing: Testing the Promises,* ed. Dennis P. Rosenbaum (Thousand Oaks, CA: Sage Publica-

tions, 1994), 14-15.

51. John E. Eck and Dennis P. Rosenbaum, "The New Police Order: Effectiveness, Equity, and Efficiency in Community Policing," in *The Challenge of Community Policing: Testing the Promises,* ed. Dennis P. Rosenbaum (Thousand Oaks, CA: Sage Publications, 1994), 15.

52. Warren Friedman, "The Community Role in Community Policing," in *The Challenge of Community Policing: Testing the Promises,* ed. Dennis P. Rosenbaum (Thousand Oaks, CA: Sage Publications, 1994), 263.

53. See for instance Sandra Bass, "Negotiating Change: Community Organizations and the Politics of Policing," *Urban Affairs Review* 36, no. 2 (2000): 148-177; David E. Duffee, Reginald Fluellen, and Brian C. Renauer, "Community Variables in Community Policing," *Police Quarterly* 2, no. 1 (1999): 5-35.

54. David Osborne and Ted Gaebler, *Reinventing Government: How the Entrepreneurial Spirit is Transforming the Public Sector* (Reading, MA: Addison-Wesley, 1992).

55. Dorothy Guyot, *Policing as Though People Mattered* (Philadelphia, PA: Temple University Press, 1991).

56. Jihong Zhao and Quint Thurman, *The Nature of Community Policing Innovations: Do the Ends Justify the Means* (Washington, D.C.: Police Executive Research Forum, 1996).

57. William Lyons, *The Politics of Community Policing: Rearranging the Power to Punish* (Ann Arbor, MI: University of Michigan Press, 1999); Wilson E. Reed, *The Politics of Community Policing: The Case of Seattle* (New York: Garland, 1999).

58. David Osborne and Ted Gaebler, *Reinventing Government: How the Entrepreneurial Spirit is Transforming the Public Sector* (Reading, MA: Addison-Wesley, 1992), 320.

59. Arthur J. Luigio and Dennis P. Rosenbaum, "The Impact of Community Policing on Police Personnel: A Review of the Literature," in *The Challenge of Community Policing: Testing the Promises,* ed. Dennis P. Rosenbaum (Thousand Oaks, CA: Sage Publications, 1994), 152.

60. Arthur J. Luigio and Dennis P. Rosenbaum, "The Impact of Community Policing on Police Personnel: A Review of the Literature," in *The Challenge of Community Policing: Testing the Promises,* ed. Dennis P. Rosenbaum (Thousand Oaks, CA: Sage Publications, 1994), 152.

61. D.W. Hayeslip, Jr., and Gary W. Cordner, "The Effects of Community-Oriented Patrol on Police Officer Attitudes," *American Journal of Police* 6, no. 1 (1987): 95-119.

62. Dennis P. Rosenbaum, Sandy Yeh, and Deanna L. Wilkinson, "Impact of Community Policing on Police Personnel: A Quasi-Experiment," *Crime & Delinquency* 40, no. 3 (1994): 331-353.

63. Todd J. Dicker, "Tension on the Thin Blue Line: Police Officer Resistance to Community-Oriented Policing," *American Journal of Criminal Justice* 23, no. 1 (1998): 59-82.

64. Arthur J. Luigio and Dennis P. Rosenbaum, "The Impact of Community Policing on Police Personnel: A Review of the Literature," in *The Challenge of Community Policing: Testing the Promises,* ed. Dennis P. Rosenbaum (Thousand Oaks, CA: Sage Publications, 1994); Debroah G. Wilson and Susan F. Bennett, "Officers' Response to Community Policing: Variations on a Theme," *Crime and Delinquency* 33, no. 1 (1994): 53-70.

65. Jack R. Greene, Patricia Collins, and Robert Kane, "Policing Public Housing in Philadelphia: Public Safety Perspectives of the Police and the Community," *Police Practice* 1, no. 3 (2000): 397-434; Jack R. Greene, Alex R. Piquero, Patricia Collins, and Robert J. Kane, "Doing Research in Public Housing: Implementation Issues from Philadelphia's 11th Street Corridor Community Policing Program," *Justice Research and Policy* 1, no. 1 (1999): 67-95.

66. Timothy C. O'Shea, "Community Policing in Small Town Rural America: A Comparison of Police Officer Attitudes in Chicago and Baldwin County, Alabama," *Policing and Society* 9, no. 1 (1999): 59-76.

67. Jack R. Greene, Patricia Collins, and Robert Kane, "Policing Public Housing in Philadelphia: Public Safety Perspectives of the Police and the Community," *Police Practice* 1, no. 3 (2000): 397-434; David A. Kessler, "The Effects of Community Policing in Complaints Against Officers," *Journal of Quantitative Criminology* 15, no. 3 (1999): 333-372; Stephen D. Mastrofski, Jeffrey B. Snipes, Roger B. Parks, and Christopher D. Maxwell, "The Helping Hand of the Law: Police Control of Citizens on Request," *Criminology* 38, no. 2 (2000): 307-342.

68. Gregory D. Russell and Susan MacLachlan, "Community Policing, Decentralized Decision Making, and Employee Satisfaction," *Journal of Crime & Justice* 22, no. 2 (1999): 31-54.

69. Steven A. Dietz, "Evaluating Community Policing: Quality Police Service and Fear of Crime," *Policing An International Journal of Police Strategy and Management* 20, no. 1 (1997): 83-100.

70. J. Zhao, M. Scheider, and Q. Thurman, "The Effect of Police Presence on Public Fear Reduction and Satisfaction: A Review of the Literature," *The Justice Professional* 15 (2002): 273-299.

71. M. C. Scheider, T. Rowell, and V. Bezdikian, "The Impact of Citizen Perceptions of Community Policing on Fear of Crime: Findings from Twelve Cities," *Police Quarterly* 6, no. 4 (2003): 363-386.

72. Sunghoon Roh and Willard M. Oliver, "Effects of Community Policing Upon Fear of Crime: Understanding the Causal Linkage," *Policing: An International Journal of Police Strategies and Management* 28, no. 4 (2005): 670-683.

73. R.E. Adams, W. M. Rohe, and T.A. Arcury, "Awareness of Community-Oriented Policing and Neighborhood Perception in Five Small to Midsize Cities," *Journal of Criminal Justice* 33, no. 1 (2005): 43-54.

74. J. Brewster, M. Stoloff, and N. Sanders, "Effectiveness of Citizen Police Academies in Changing the Attitudes, Beliefs, and Behaviors of Citizen Participants," *American Journal of Criminal Justice* 30, no. 1 (2005): 21-34.

75. L. Ren, L. Cao, N. Lovrich, and M. Gaffney, "Linking Confidence in the Police with the Performance of the Police: Community Policing Can Make a Difference," *Journal of Criminal Justice* 33, no. 1 (2005): 55-66.

76. Michael D. Reisig and Roger B. Parks, "Can Community Policing Help the Truly Disadvantaged?" *Crime & Delinquency* 50, no. 2 (2004): 139-167.

77. Michael D. Reisig and Roger B. Parks, "Can Community Policing Help the Truly Disadvantaged?" *Crime & Delinquency* 50, no. 2 (2004): 160.

78. Lawrence W. Sherman, et al. *Preventing Crime: What Works, What Doesn't, What's Promising* (Washington, D.C.: U.S. Department of Justice, Office of Justice Programs, 1997).

79. Lee P. Brown, "Community Policing: A Practical Guide for Police Officials," *Perspectives on Policing* (Washington, D.C.: National Institute of Justice, 1989).

80. United States Conference of Catholic Bishops, *Responsibility, Rehabilitation, and Restoration: A Catholic Perspective on Crime and Criminal Justice* (Washington, D.C.: United States Catholic Conference, Inc., 2000), 45.

81. Caroline G. Nicholl, *Community Policing, Community Justice, and Restorative Justice: Exploring the Links for the Delivery of a Balanced Approach to Public Safety* (Washington, D.C.: Office of Community Oriented Policing Services, 1999), 105.

82. Gordon Bazemore and Curt Griffiths, "Police Reform, Restorative Justice, and Restorative Policing," *Police Practice and Research* 4, no. 4 (2003): 337.

83. Gordon Bazemore and Curt Griffiths, "Police Reform, Restorative Justice, and Restorative Policing," *Police Practice and Research* 4, no. 4 (2003): 337.

Chapter 5

Community Courts

"You shall appoint judges and officials throughout your tribes to administer true justice for the people in all the communities which the Lord, your God, is giving you. You shall not distort justice; you must be impartial."
- Deuteronomy 16:18-19 -

Introduction

In the United States Conference of Catholic Bishops' statement on crime and criminal justice, they repeatedly call for the criminal justice system to adopt more "community-based solutions" and the principles of "restorative justice."[1] This is highly reflective of the scriptural, theological, and sacramental heritage of the Catholic Church, despite the fact that the concepts of community justice and restorative justice tend to have a more modern connotation. For instance, according to Charles Nemeth, St. Thomas Aquinas explained that judges and the courts "should focus on not only the individual dilemma but the need for a restoration of personal or community equality," and that the courts' judgment "is just if it is restorative to the individual harmed or beneficial to the common good."[2] However, in criminal justice the concepts of community justice and restorative justice have developed into two inter-related, but distinct concepts of how the criminal justice system should be ordered.

Community justice has been defined as a new and innovative method for carrying out criminal justice.[3] The emphasis of community justice is on the criminal justice system developing community partnerships. Community justice also attempts to adopt and implement the concepts of restorative justice (as detailed in Chapter 3). What sets it apart from true restorative justice, or restorative justice mediation, is that the concepts are adopted and implemented by the criminal justice system itself. So, in the case of the courts, it is taking the current existing framework and having it move toward the adoption of restorative justice principles. While this will include developing partnerships with various members of the court process (e.g., prosecutors, judges, defenders) and those of the community (e.g., citizen action groups, interested neighbors, social workers), the programs are still run by the local government. Community justice, then, is about the formal justice system adopting restorative justice principles to deal more effectively with the problems of crime and disorder.

Restorative justice, or more specifically restorative justice mediation, is about the development of various programs that also draw upon the restorative justice principles (again see Chapter 3). It is relatively new and innovative in the criminal justice field as well, and it too seeks to develop partnerships with community members to work toward the resolution of conflicts in the neighborhood. Restorative justice, however, unlike community justice, has come to be more readily defined as eschewing the courts (government) altogether or, at least, minimizing the amount of contact it has with the local court system. This is done to ensure that the mediation process is a grass-roots approach and truly has the best interest of the community in mind when it seeks a resolution to a crime problem. Restorative justice mediation, then, is about local community groups adopting restorative justice principles to deal with the problem of crime and disorder.

In order to more clearly define how both community justice and restorative justice programs have developed in the courts, this chapter will first focus on community courts and then on restorative justice mediation. In the case of the former, it will discuss what community courts are, how they have been implemented, and the roles that both the prosecutor and defense play in such a system. In the case of the latter, it will discuss how restorative justice mediation can be used in place of the traditional court system, and it will detail the various methods that have been used throughout the United States and around the world. In sum, it will detail how the second component of the criminal justice system, the courts, would change if a Catholic perspective of the courts, drawing upon community-based solutions and restorative justice principles, were adopted.

Community Courts

According to Clear and Karp, under the concept of community justice, criminal events are considered and dealt with as social acts that shatter community life.[4] They are not simply violations of the law but renunciation by offenders of their moral and social obligations to the community as a whole, as well as to the victim. When crime is viewed this way, it shows the state's role as sole arbiter of the offender-victim conflict to be flawed, because community members are isolated from that conflict.

At the heart of community justice is civic participation.[5] Through the problem-solving process, all parties carry out tasks derived from their relationship to the criminal event. These tasks are based on principles that define an essentially democratic vision of justice: Citizens participate in processes that affirm community standards of conduct, restore the quality of community life, and reduce the likelihood of further crime. The tasks of each party are reciprocal, linking them in a network of mutual obligation.

The offender must strive for readmission to the community.[6] This involves admitting the wrong, working to undo the effects of the offense, and taking steps to convince the community that the crime will not occur again. Victims, too, have responsibilities. In community justice their goal is to recover their capacity to fully function in the community. Recovery begins when the victim articulates the losses, intangible as well as tangible, and estimates the resources, financial and otherwise, needed to restore the losses.

Because community laws have been violated and community life disrupted, it is incumbent on community institutions to play a role in recovery.[7] That may involve clarifying norms and standards of conduct, expressing to the offender in particular what is and is not acceptable. The community provides opportunities for making restitution and offers the support and supervision needed for the offender to live in the community crime-free. To the victim, the community provides support in achieving recovery.

For the criminal justice system, the role shifts from that of defender of law and order to that of resource to the community, bearing ultimate responsibility for the justice process.[8] In the community justice model, the justice system helps the victim, community, and offender carry out their tasks by designing and managing a process that facilitates participation. Unlike the restorative justice approach which attempts to employ a community model that avoids contact with the criminal justice system, the community justice model moves to incorporate restorative justice practices into traditional criminal justice practices. For instance, the adoption of restorative justice principles in policing leads to the concepts of community policing (See Chapter 4). In the area of traditional corrections, it moves this institution toward a more community-based corrections approach (See next chapter). And, in the area of courts, the concern of this chapter, it moves the traditional courts toward a "community courts" model.[9]

During the 1960s and 1970s, according to Rottman, the national commissions on crime promoted a quest for the justice system's community roots by espousing citizen participation.[10] Harbingers of a renewed community focus can be found within the traditional court structure from the 1960s onward. Court-watching programs, judicial disciplinary commissions, and permanent court advisory committees flourished. The primary goal of most of these early efforts was limited to serving as "conduits of information" between the courts and the community. If by the 1980s, opportunities for citizen participation in the courts were not plentiful, they were expanding. During the 1990s, the widespread adoption of community policing (Again see Chapter 4) encouraged extension to the courts of similar approaches.

A community-focused court is a more expansive effort still, requiring ongoing collaboration between a trial court and one or more community groups either for a specific purpose or in a major aspect of the court's adjudicatory scope.[11]

This definition does not generally encompass programs that consist primarily of court outreach, such as public education. On the other hand, court "inreach" (e.g., court monitoring by citizens) comes closer to meeting the definition, particularly if its objective is to forge a more broadly-based connection between court and community.

Two examples of the community court model include the Midtown Community Court (MCC) in New York City and the Red Hook Community Justice Center in Brooklyn, New York. These two programs are just some of the ways that community courts can be achieved.[12] The MCC exemplified the renewed interest in bringing high-volume, short-duration criminal cases back to communities through satellite and branch courts.[13] MCC, however, added a significant community component. The community is viewed as having a major stake in how well the courts adjudicate cases involving quality-of-life crime. Launched in 1993, the MCC targets quality-of-life offenses such as prostitution, illegal vending, graffiti, shoplifting, fare beating, and vandalism in midtown Manhattan.[14] Often in such cases judges are forced to choose between a few days of jail time and no sentence at all—results that fail to impress the victim, the community, or the defendant that these offenses are taken seriously. In contrast the MCC sentences low-level offenders to pay back the neighborhood through community service while offering them help with problems (e.g., addictions, mental illness, lack of job skills) that underlie their criminal behavior. Residents, businesses, and social service agencies collaborate with the court by supervising community service projects and by providing onsite social services, including drug treatment, health care, and job training.

Social services are available onsite at the MCC, providing the judge a range of services to include in a mandate, such as onsite drug treatment, a health education class for prostitutes and "johns," one-on-one counseling for young offenders and mentally ill persons, and employment training.[15] For defendants with a long criminal record and a history of substance abuse, the court offers an alternative-to-incarceration program that sentences defendants to long-term drug treatment. Many defendants return to court voluntarily to take advantage of services offered at the court, including the English as a second language and General Education Development (GED) classes. The court also uses an award-winning computer application to craft individualized sanctions for each offender and monitor compliance. The system also provides police officers with regular feedback about the outcomes of their arrests.

Community involvement is extensive at the MCC.[16] According to Rottman, the MCC "is a community court, most fundamentally because of its contributions to the broader array of partnerships and collaborations among local organizational and residents' groups in Midtown Manhattan that are dedicated to the general betterment of the area."[17] Some of these partnerships include the community advisory board, which reviews court operations and results and which meets quarterly, and the community conditions panel, which keeps the court abreast of local problems and emerging hot spots and which meets monthly.[18] Community members participate in impact panels, meeting face-to-face with offenders to discuss how their behavior harmed the community. The court also publishes a newsletter to keep stakeholders informed about its work. The court also seeks to solve community problems through a partnership with the police known as the Social Outreach Services program. To address problems before they result in arrest, social workers from the court join police officers on the beat. Together, they engage the homeless and other street people and encourage them to come to the court voluntarily for social services.

In the case of the Red Hook Community Justice Center in Brooklyn, New York, the community court concept has been implemented in a somewhat different manner. Operating in the heart of a low income neighborhood, the Red Hook Community Justice Center has allowed judges to transform their responses to the people who appear before the court. Surrounded by water on three sides and an elevated highway on its fourth side, Red Hook is an isolated community served by two police precincts.[19] Decades of marginalized community of low-income residents, most of whom (more than 70 percent) live in an old, massive public housing complex. The Justice Center is housed in a former parochial high school in the center of this community, a site that was selected by community members. New York City financed the cost of renovating the long-vacant building.

At Red Hook, a single judge hears neighborhood cases that ordinarily are heard in three different courts—civil, family, and criminal.[20] This model did not emerge by accident. Justice center planners felt that the problems faced by families and individuals do not conform to jurisdictional boundaries. By having a single judge handle matters traditionally heard by different decision makers at different locations, the justice center offers a swift and coordinated judicial response.

The Red Hook judge has an array of sanctions and services available, including community restitution projects, onsite job training, drug treatment, and health counseling—all of which are rigorously monitored to ensure accountability and to encourage individual responsibility. Court staff supervise offenders performing community service, and state-of-the-art technology helps the judge monitor compliance.

In addition, the courthouse is the hub of programs that engage local residents in "doing justice." These programs include mediation, community service projects that put local volunteers to work repairing conditions of disorder, and a youth court where teenagers resolve actual cases involving their peers. Through these initiatives, Red Hook seeks to engage the community in aggressive crime prevention. Planners see this strategy working in two ways: by solving local problems before they become a court problem and by helping knit together the fabric of the neighborhood.

By using its coercive power to link defendants to drug treatment and by providing onsite services like domestic violence counseling, health care, and job training. Red Hook seeks to strengthen families and help individuals avoid further involvement with the court system. Services are not limited to court users but are available to anyone in the community who needs help.

The MCC and Red Hook are both examples of the possibilities for how community courts could be implemented by adapting restorative justice principles to existing court structures. As in any type of serious change, however, there are key players that must be included in the process in order for this type of change to take place. At the center of the law are the lawyers. This is why any movement to the concept of community courts necessitates the adoption of what has come to be known as "community-oriented lawyering."[21]

Community-oriented lawyering is, in a sense, an expansion of the concepts of community-oriented policing (Discussed in Chapter 4) by applying them to the courts component of the criminal justice system. Community-oriented lawyering is distinctive in integrating a new approach with the conventional advocate's role.[22] Rather than focusing on the traditional method of lawyering in America, such as crimes, cases, and complaints, community-oriented lawyering, like community policing, is focused on people, problems, and relationships. Instead of using the traditional tools of investigation, negotiation, and litigation, it tries to mobilize the community, generate civil remedies to problems, and tries to negotiate voluntary compliance. Perhaps the most important aspect lies in the relationship between lawyers and the community.

The traditional court model has used the community as a source of clients and witnesses, handled the cases of complainants, and, beyond this, has merely relied on the general political support of the community. In the case of community-oriented lawyering, the focus shifts to including the community as a partner in the courts process, having the community help to define what constitutes success in the courts, and to influence the priorities of the court. Essentially, the community takes an active role and works toward not simply winning cases, but finding ways to reduce the severity of the problems that come before the court, improving the quality of life for all in the community, and restoring relationships that are at the heart of a healthy community.

The application of community-oriented lawyering is not limited to the prosecution, but can include city and county attorneys, police legal advisors, lawyers from other city agencies, public-interest law groups, legal services, pro bono lawyers, law school clinics, defense lawyers, and judges. All of these individuals trained in the law are members of the community and have a stake in the communities in which they serve. Hence community-oriented lawyering, like community policing, is seen as an opportunity to advance the quality of life in a community by focusing on the adoption of restorative justice principles in the legal world.

Despite the examples just listed of what lawyers could be involved in community-oriented lawyering, the primary application from a criminal justice standpoint has to be the community prosecutor and, in kind, the defense attorneys. This is why the concepts of community prosecution and community defense have become widely discussed since the turn-of-the-century. Beginning with the concept of community prosecution, it is noted that this concept is an organizational response to the grassroots public safety demands of neighborhoods, as expressed in highly concrete terms by the people who live in them.[23] Community prosecution invites citizens to participate in establishing crime-fighting priorities and collaborating with prosecutors.[24] By clearly defining an area in which to implement community-based programs, committing resources for the long term, and being sensitive to residents' concerns, prosecutors can target key problems identified by residents.

Community prosecution contrasts sharply with the traditional method of setting prosecutorial priorities by assessing the seriousness of the crime, the weight of the evidence, and the threat that defendants pose to the public or to themselves.[25] Community prosecution often addresses less serious crimes, such as prostitution or loitering, that threaten to deteriorate the quality of life in communities.

In September 1993, and February 1995, the American Prosecutors Research Institute (APRI) convened focus groups to discuss the concept of community prosecution.[26] Both groups consisted of prosecutors actively involved in community prosecution programs and other allied professionals, including law enforcement officials, with expertise on the subject. The groups defined community prosecution, identified key components of a successful program, discussed the issues that prosecutors should consider when planning and implementing a program and determined the relationship of community prosecution to community policing.

While perspectives varied among jurisdictions, the groups agreed that community prosecution focuses on targeted areas and involves a long-term, proactive partnership among the prosecutor's office, law enforcement, the community, and public and private organizations in order to solve problems, improve public safety, and enhance the quality of life in the community.

Building on this definition, the focus groups identified nine key components that embody the general concept of community prosecution.[27] The first component is the need for a proactive approach. A community prosecution strategy must enforce the law and prevent crime. Rather than merely waiting for a crime to occur, prosecutors work with the target community to prevent crime. The second component is that the prosecutor must choose a site and focus all efforts into that area. The area may encompass one city block, a housing development, or a police district.

The third component, and perhaps the hallmark of community prosecution, is forming partnerships. In a position to affect policy, prosecutors, law enforcement leaders, and public and private sector officials must work together to thoughtfully consider the community's public safety and quality-of-life concerns. As a group, they fashion an effective, coordinated approach and ensure the successful use of all legal tools. In close connection with the third component, the fourth component is the need for community input. Successful community prosecution also depends on the direct interaction between the prosecutor and the community, as well as the incorporation of the community's input into the courtroom. Prosecutors may keep residents apprized of pending felony and misdemeanor charges against offenders in their neighborhoods. At the same time, residents may provide information that strengthens the evidence against a specific defendant (e.g., community impact statements).

The fifth component is communication. Maintaining open community with residents of the target area and officials from other entities in the partnership remains crucial to the success of the program. Through problem solving, prosecutors learn which issues most trouble citizens so they can address these priorities accordingly. Often, these priorities include public safety and quality-of-life issues.

The sixth component is the use of varied methods, methods that lie outside of the traditional prosecutorial model. In conjunction with the other entities involved in the partnership, prosecutors can incorporate varied strategies, such as civil sanctions and nuisance abatement, to strictly enforce the law. These varied enforcement strategies can eliminate problems without actually prosecuting defendants. For example, responding to residents' complaints about drug dealing in a restaurant or bar, health department inspectors may enter the establishment and search for health code violations. Upon discovering a sufficient number of violations, the inspectors can close the business, effectively shutting down the illegal drug operations. In addition to the varied methods, prosecutors must also think in terms of the seventh component: long-term strategies. Prosecutors must dedicate themselves to the community prosecution concept and demonstrate this firm commitment in the long run. Only in this way can community prosecution establish credibility and acceptance among community residents and achieve its objectives.

The eighth component is commitment. As with all new programs, support from the prosecutor, as well as from other partnership policy makers, is critical to success. Only when the district attorney demonstrates a steadfast commitment to the effort and clearly communicates this dedication to middle managers, will those on the front lines be convinced that their efforts are priorities. Finally, the ninth component is the continuous evaluation of the community prosecution program. The district attorney must provide for the collection of data at all stages of the community prosecution. Careful and continuous evaluation of a program is important for monitoring the delivery of services, identifying program strengths and weaknesses, and providing evidence of the effectiveness of the program strategy.

According to Weinstein, in theory, a community prosecution program is easy to implement.[28] In practice, however, the transition may prove difficult and tedious. Prosecutors may face numerous obstacles from inside and outside their organizations. One potential roadblock involves the residents of the target area. Initially, they may be suspicious of outsiders whom they perceive as insincere in their attempts to "help" them. Often residents see prosecutors as enemies in business suits who send friends and loved ones to jail. Prosecutors must build trust carefully with these individuals.

Another possible hurdle is that the culture of district attorneys' offices does not always lend itself to this type of work. Many attorneys choose careers in prosecution to enforce laws and lock up "bad guys." Often, they view community involvement as "touchy-feely" or the job of social workers. Prosecutorial leaders must select staff members who remain open to the new concept and possess unique skills to act as community problem solvers. Not every assistant district attorney will be suited for the new endeavor, and the prosecutor must recognize this.

Turf battles represent the third obstacle, as they are inevitable in any partnership. Boundaries erected by and between various entities must be torn down. For example, the historically conflict-prone relationship between police and prosecutors must give way to a team approach.

Indeed, collaborative efforts work best when each member of the partnership understands that achieving the goals of public safety and crime prevention requires a team effort. Policy makers must cast aside stereotypes and acknowledge the abilities and limitations of their organizations. Open communication among all of the partners is essential.

Because of these and other challenges, prosecutors planning to make the transition to community prosecution should follow a specific approach. In general, instituting a community prosecution program involves eight steps: (1) selecting a target area, (2) conducting a needs assessment, (3) identifying resources and garnering the support and commitment of policy makers, (4) identifying funding sources, (5) organizing program players and internal staff, (6) developing the community prosecution program plan, (7) implementing the program, and (8) evaluating the program.

One example where this has been successful is in Multnomah County, Oregon.[29] In 1990, the Multnomah district attorney, Michael Shrunk, "enjoyed the wide respect of the electorate, the confidence of business leaders, and political independence."[30] However, he faced some of the highest crime in one area of Portland, the Lloyd District, and most people had little confidence that the District Attorney's (DA) Office would actually do anything to address the problem. Shrunk began exploring ways in which the services of his office could augment Portland's community policing effort. He formed a coalition of resources, both public and private, to fund a community prosecution program. Members of his staff, together with residents of various neighborhoods in the county, developed several ways of improving life in targeted areas. They call it the Neighborhood DA Program.

As part of the program, the DA assigns one deputy district attorney to each of the six geographic areas within Multnomah County. The deputy DAs work from offices in their assigned areas, making them readily accessible to residents. At the same time, the deputy can conduct a host of activities, from teaching citizens about restraining orders to reviewing criminal cases that originate in the district.

The District Public Safety Committee works in conjunction with the Neighborhood DA Program to provide a forum for collaboration and information dissemination among residents, business owners, and the Neighborhood DA. The committee meets monthly to identify quality-of-life issues and crime problems that are important to the area and devises strategies to address these problems.

For example, the Neighborhood DA distributes "trouble-shooter cards" at each committee meeting and on each block throughout the neighborhood. These cards, which contain questions on drug-related crimes and public safety issues, enable the deputy DA to obtain timely and accurate information on community observations. The prosecutor compiles the information, distributes it to the district police officers, and uses it to develop crime prevention strategies.

The Neighborhood DA Program is focused and long-term. It demonstrates the community-based commitment of the district attorney to solving public safety and quality-of-life problems in innovative ways.

Turning to the other side of community lawyering, the concept of community defense attorneys has only been recently explored as a means of bringing the concepts of community justice to bear on the problems of criminal defense. Stone has pointed out that for public defenders the transformation of the other parts of the criminal justice system from a series of offender-processing machines to a set of community justice services presents both a welcome opportunity and a challenge.[31] The machines were designed to respond to 911 calls, make arrests, produce convictions, and punish offenders. Ironically, their efficiency can improve even while crime soars. Public defenders working in such a system sometimes conceive of their mission as gumming up the works, although a more objective assessment would recognize them as primarily another link in the offender-processing chain.

Community justice services, by contrast, aim to identify and solve the problems that foster crime and injustice. The transformation from machine to service is most advanced, as we have seen, in the police departments; although it is also under way in prosecution, court management, and corrections. For defendants, if the change means new opportunities to solve structural problems that have compromised public defense for the past 30 years, the community justice movement may be the best thing to come along in a long time.

According to Strickland, there are three approaches that defense attorneys can employ under the concepts of community justice, and they include: 1) whole client representation, 2) defender cooperation with other criminal justice stakeholders, and 3) community outreach activities."[32] The whole client representation is a method by which the defense attorney does not simply represent the client in the courtroom, but rather takes a more holistic approach to the needs of the client. The defense attorney looks to all of the needs of the client and assists them in getting the help and support they need. Whether it is health care, food stamps, housing, counseling, or other types of needs, the community defense attorney works with the client to represent all of their needs.

The second method, defender cooperation with the other criminal justice stakeholders, consists of the defense attorney not just working with clients, but taking a role in dealing with all of the agencies their clients are exposed to in order to develop working relationships. They may include the creation of programs aimed at helping those addicted to drugs, victims of domestic violence, or special courts to deal with gun-related crimes. In addition, it may also place the defender in the position of lobbying and advocating for certain programs and building coalitions to advocate new policies.

The third approach is the defense community outreach. In this approach, community defenders reach out to various communities and groups in order to educate them regarding the work of the public defender. In addition, it may include volunteering in the school system or other programs that work with various groups in the community that may be impacted. Moreover, it may be specifically addressing the needs of individual offenders and their families, by working with them and other community groups to create a working link between the client and community.

One example of the community defense concept can be found in the Neighborhood Defender Services (NDS) in Harlem, New York.[33] The NDS was an experiment aimed at developing and testing new ways of organizing and deploying public defenders that can solve problems of justice in the community while providing high-quality representation at a cost government can afford. Begun in 1990 by the Vera Institute of Justice in partnership with the city and State of New York, the 5-year project operated alongside the far larger Legal Aid Society, New York City's institutional defender.

Like any public defender, NDS has represented individuals accused of crimes who could not afford private lawyers. But while traditional public defenders are based at courthouses to handle court business, NDS has been based in the community. Instead of waiting for the court to assign NDS to represent clients, NDS has encouraged Harlem residents to call the office any time, the way more affluent people would call their attorneys. This relatively minor change in intake procedure has given NDS a few more hours before a client is in court to gather information and, more significantly, has created a wholly different attorney-client relationship that continued to pay dividends long after the case was over.

In contrast to the usual practice of assigning each client a single attorney, each NDS client has been represented by a team. Each team has consisted of attorneys, community workers, an administrative assistant, an intern, and a senior attorney who served as team leader. One attorney has had principal responsibility for each case, but everyone on the team was aware of the activity in each of the team's cases. If a client ever had another case, it was handled by the same team.

NDS adopted this structure to increase efficiency by making extensive use of non-lawyers and to ensure continuity of representation over time. In addition to producing these benefits, the structure also unexpectedly heightened accountability. In traditionally structured offices only the attorneys know what they are or are not doing on a case, and they answer principally to themselves. At NDS, team members, whether lawyers or not, challenged each other in a common effort to represent each client as well as possible.

In a traditional defender office, the highest priority is given to cases about to go to trial, with little priority given to cases just begun, and none given to former clients or anyone who does not have an active criminal case in court. NDS turned this priority system on its head, assigning the highest priority to clients at the start of their cases, sometimes even before arrest. Teams were held accountable for the amount of work accomplished early in the case—in the first four weeks. Community workers gave priority to helping former clients avoid problems on probation and parole that might otherwise produce new cases.

Changing priorities in professional organizations is difficult and is one source of resistance to community justice. For public defenders, assigning priority to trials reflects their pride in this work more than their judgment about what benefits the most clients. NDS also took pride in winning trial cases, and trial work still received a higher priority than many other stages of representation; however, trial work was removed from the pinnacle of NDS office culture, just as arrests and convictions have been demoted as part of community policing and prosecution reforms. The concepts of community defense under community justice appear to have some promise of being effective, but due to the fact the program is not widespread and has only been recently implemented, it is too soon to tell.

Restorative Justice Mediation

Restorative justice has long advocated the use of what has been referred to as Alternative Dispute Resolution (ADR). Over time, the concept of ADR has come to have multiple meanings and encompasses a wide variety of methods, ranging from negotiations to reconciliation, and mediation to arbitration. These methods, however, are all focused on preventing a grievance, dispute, or conflict, from reaching the most formal means of resolution, and that is the formal court adjudication process.[34] There is a growing body of literature that has focused on Alternative Dispute Resolution (ADR) and the various methods that can be employed,[35] but the majority has focused on mediation and arbitration as the key alternatives to court adjudication.[36] Mediation can be defined as "an effort by a neutral third party to resolve a dispute through the conduct of a face-to-face meeting between the disputing parties," while arbitration is defined as "a dispute resolution process whereby a neutral third party is empowered to impose a settlement upon disputing parties following a hearing between the parties."[37] The difference is subtle, but very distinct; in the former the parties are encouraged to come to their own resolution, whereas in the latter, the third party determines the binding outcome.

In addition to the concept of Alternative Dispute Resolution, there is another concept that is very similar and often indiscernible from ADR, and that is the concept of Community Dispute Resolution.[38] Community Dispute Resolution, often referred to as "community mediation," "neighborhood justice," or "community boards," focuses on a wide variety of programs that present an alternative to court adjudication and are found at the neighborhood and community level.[39] According to McGillis, many of these programs began with the emphasis on criminal cases and subsequently adopted the practices in civil cases.[40] The cases typically come from issues that have a criminal justice focus, and the goal is to resolve the dispute through these various methods at the community and neighborhood level. Although many of the Community Dispute Resolution programs are based on receiving referrals from the court system, they have also been known to receive referrals from police and corrections as well.[41]

As the Alternative Dispute Resolution and Community Dispute Resolution models have grown, the idea of victim-offender mediation and reconciliation has become more prominent in terms of dealing with crimes and criminal justice related cases. The first such program is believed to have been developed in 1978 and was known as the Victim-Offender Reconciliation Program (VORP).[42] It was created out of dissatisfaction with the traditional criminal justice system, primarily because the system focused too heavily on the offender and punishment. The Victim-Offender Reconciliation Programs, rather, focused on a balanced approach to achieving justice that attempted to consider the accountability to the victims, developing the offender in order to reintegrate them into society, and promoting overall community safety.[43] The goals of the Victim-Offender Reconciliation Programs were also different in that they sought to achieve three basic objectives: identifying the injustice, making things right, and considering future implications of the offense.[44]

The four idealized models of the Victim-Offender Reconciliation Programs, according to Coates and Gehm, include: (1) the normalize community conflict resolution model, where people would bring conflicts to community mediation centers before invoking the law, (2) diversion from the formal criminal justice systems model, which is based upon referrals to mediation at the point of arrest or pre-trial hearings, (3) alternatives to incarceration model, which allows post-conviction offenders to enter into mediation, and (4) the justice model, which focuses on restitution as an alternative or additional sanction to adjudication.[45]

Each of these models presents an ideological model to the Victim-Offender Mediation concept, all of which are acceptable under the community justice concept. However, it should be noted that, under true restorative justice concepts, the formal criminal justice system would not be involved, hence the first model would be the idealized model for restorative justice.

Another researcher in the field of Community Dispute Resolution, Mark Umbreit, details four program models for who would actually implement these types of programs, and they are: (1) church-related programs, those taking a religious perspective in mediation, (2) community-based criminal justice private agencies, the largest portion of programs, which are non-profit organizations that receive referrals from the criminal justice system, (3) probation-based agencies, a method for moving people into probation through mediation with the victim, and (4) dispute settlement centers, which are neighborhood "justice centers" where both victim and offender can go to enter into mediation as an alternative to adjudication. Each of these presents a variation on the same theme, but each also factors in different goals and objectives into the mediation process.

Finally, it should be noted that there are a number of Community Dispute Resolution and mediation models that exist for how victim-offender reconciliation can be achieved. Although there are many models, the four most predominate models include what have been categorized as (1) victim-offender mediation, (2) community reparative boards, (3) family group conferencing, and (4) circle sentencing. Each of these models will be discussed in depth with a focus on how they have been implemented, their procedures and goals, the victim's role in the process, what type of preparation and follow-up is necessary under each of these models, and finally, whether or not these programs have been found to be effective, efficient, and equitable, based upon the research to date.

Victim-Offender Mediation

Although still unfamiliar to many mainstream juvenile and criminal justice audiences and marginal to the court process in some jurisdictions where they do operate, victim-offender mediation programs—referred to in some communities as "victim offender reconciliation programs" and, increasingly, as "victim offender dialog programs"—have a respectable 20-year track record in the United States, Canada, and Europe.[46] As of 2001, there were approximately 320 victim-offender mediation programs in the United States and Canada and more than 700 in Europe. Several programs in North America currently receive nearly 1,000 case referrals annually from local courts. Although the greatest proportion of cases involves less serious property crimes committed by young people, the process is used increasingly in response to serious and violent crimes committed by both juveniles and adults.[47]

The victim-offender mediation process offers victims an opportunity to meet offenders in a safe, structured setting and engage in a mediated discussion of the crime. In the case of juvenile offenders, the parent becomes part of the process as well. In either case, with the assistance of a trained mediator, the victim is able to tell the offender about the crime's physical, emotional, and financial impact; receive answers to lingering questions about the crime and the offender; and be directly involved in developing a restitution plan for the offender to pay back any financial debt to the victim. The process is different from mediation as practiced in civil or commercial disputes, because the involved parties are in agreement about their respective roles in the crime. Also, the process is not primarily focused on reaching a settlement, although most sessions do, in fact, result in a signed restitution agreement. It should also be noted that not all restitution agreements result in a financial restitution, but may consist of service to the victim or service to the larger community. Because of these fundamental differences, the terms "victim-offender meeting," "conferencing," and "dialog" are becoming increasingly popular to describe variations from standard mediation practices.

Cases may be referred to victim-offender mediation programs by judges, probation officers, victim advocates, prosecutors, defense attorneys, and law enforcement. In some programs, cases are primarily referred as a diversion from prosecution (assuming that any agreement reached during the mediation session is successfully completed). In other programs, cases are usually referred after a formal admission of guilt has been accepted by the court, with mediation being a condition of probation or other disposition (if the victim has volunteered to participate). Some programs receive case referrals at both stages.

During mediation sessions, victims explain how the crime affected them and are given the opportunity to ask questions about the incident and help develop a plan for restoring losses. Offenders are given the opportunity to tell their stories and take direct responsibility through making amends in some form.[48] The goals of victim-offender mediation include the following: (1) supporting the healing process of victims by providing a safe, controlled setting for them to meet and speak with offenders on a strictly voluntary basis; (2) allowing offenders to learn about the impact of their crimes on the victims and take direct responsibility for their behavior; (3) providing an opportunity for the victim and offender to develop a mutually acceptable plan that addresses the harm caused by the crime.[49]

An example of a victim-offender mediation session illustrates how the program works. In an example provided by Bazemore and Umbreit, the victim was a middle-aged woman.[50] The offender, a 14-year-old neighbor of the victim, had broken into the victim's home and stolen a VCR. The mediation session took place in the basement of the victim's church. In the presence of a mediator, the victim and offender talked for 2 hours. At times, their conversation was heated and emotional. When they finished, the mediator felt that they had heard each other's stories and learned something important about the impact of the crime and about each other. The participants agreed that the offender would pay $200 in restitution to cover the cost of damages to the victim's home resulting from the break-in and would also reimburse the victim for the cost of the stolen VCR (estimated at $150). They also worked out a payment schedule. During the session, the offender made several apologies to the victim and agreed to complete community service hours working in a food bank sponsored by the victim's church. The victim said that she felt less angry and fearful after learning more about the offender and the details of the crime. She also thanked the mediator for allowing the session to be held at her church.

When implementing any victim-offender mediation program, such as the one above, Bazemore and Umbreit explain that it is critically important to maintain sensitivity to the needs of the victim.[51] First and foremost, the mediator must do everything possible to ensure that the victim will not be harmed in any way. Additionally, the victim's participation must be completely voluntary. The offender's participation should also be voluntary. Offenders are typically given the option of participating in mediation or dialog as one of several dispositional choices. Although offenders almost never have absolute choice (e.g., the option of no juvenile justice intervention), they should never be coerced into meetings with victims. The victim should also be given choices, whenever possible, about procedures, such as when and where the mediation session will take place, who will be present, and who will speak first. Cases should be carefully screened regarding the readiness of both victim and offender to participate. The mediator should conduct in-person pre-mediation sessions with both parties to clarify the issues to be resolved. The mediator should also make follow-up contacts and monitor any agreement reached.

Mediation programs offer victims an opportunity to tell offenders how the crime has affected them, give victims maximum input into plans for holding offenders responsible, and ensure that victims are compensated for their losses to the greatest extent possible. The programs also provide victims with referrals for needed services and assistance. Victims frequently are given the opportunity to speak first in mediation sessions, which helps them feel empowered, or at least not overwhelmed or abused by the process. Mediation programs give the needs of victims and offenders priority over the needs of other participants in the process (e.g., parents and other relatives), but victims receive extra attention to ensure that they are not revictimized by the process itself. Victim participation in the mediation process is voluntary. Most programs also are voluntary for offenders and attempt to engage their participation in the least coercive manner possible;[52] in some jurisdictions, however, offenders are often less-than-willing participants.[53] Increasingly, mediation programs seek to offer their services in a victim-sensitive manner. In contrast to other models, most research studies report that victim satisfaction with victim-offender mediation has been uniformly high.

Mediation programs stress the importance of extensive victim and offender preparation prior to the mediation session. The most widely accepted model encourages mediators to hold at least one separate, face-to-face discussion with the offender and the victim. During these discussions, the mediator listens to each person describe how the crime affected him or her, gives an overview of the mediation process, identifies its potential benefits, and invites each person to participate. If the offender and victim agree to participate, the mediator introduces them to the process in a way that minimizes anxiety and maximizes the likelihood that the two parties will engage in direct dialog with minimal intervention by the mediator. Many practitioners argue that up-front preparation is often more important than the session itself in bringing about a successful result.

Victim-offender mediation programs vary in their approach to monitoring and enforcement. In many programs, mediators usually help session participants devise a reparation schedule and may even ask them to agree to a follow-up meeting to review progress. In some programs, follow-up may be the responsibility of probation or diversion staff (depending on the offender's court status), other paid staff, community volunteers, or student interns; in others, victim-offender mediation may be one part of a larger restitution program responsible for development and enforcement of reparation agreements.

A large multi-site study of victim-offender mediation programs with juvenile offenders found the following: (1) in cases referred to the four study-site programs during a 2-year period, 95 percent of mediation sessions resulted in a successfully negotiated restitution agreement to restore the victim's financial losses; (2) victims who met with offenders in the presence of a trained mediator were more likely to be satisfied with the justice system than were similar victims who went through the standard court process (79 percent versus 57 percent); (3) after meeting offenders, victims were significantly less fearful of being revictimized; (4) offenders who met with victims were far more likely to successfully complete their restitution obligation than were similar offenders who did not participate in mediation (81 percent versus 58 percent); (5) recidivism rates were lower among offenders who participated in mediation than among offenders who did not participate (18 percent versus 27 percent); furthermore, participating offenders' subsequent crimes tended to be less serious.[54]

Several multi-site studies by researchers Coates and Gehm, and another by Mark Umbreit, also found that although restitution was an important motivator for victim participation in mediation sessions, victims consistently viewed actual receipt of restitution as secondary to the opportunity to talk about the impact of the crime, meet the offender, and learn the offender's circumstances.[55] The studies also found that offenders appreciated the opportunity to talk to the victim and felt better after doing so.

A statewide survey of victim service providers in Minnesota found that 91 percent believed that victim-offender mediation should be available in every judicial district because it represents an important victim service.[56] The American Bar Association has also endorsed victim-offender mediation and recommended its use throughout the United States. As of 1997, victim-offender mediation programs have been identified in nearly every state.[57]

Community Reparative Boards

The community reparative board is a recent version of a much older and more widespread community sanctioning response to youth crime, generally known by such terms as "youth panels," "neighborhood boards," or "community diversion boards."[58] These panels or boards have been in use in the United States since the 1920's, and their contemporary counterparts, reparative boards, have been in use since the mid-1990's, principally in Vermont. There, the boards are primarily used with adult offenders convicted of nonviolent and minor offenses; more recently, the boards have also been used with juvenile offenders. Reparative boards typically are composed of a small group of citizens, prepared for their function by intensive training, who conduct public, face-to-face meetings with offenders ordered by the court to participate in the process. The boards develop sanction agreements with offenders, monitor compliance, and submit compliance reports to the court.

During reparative board meetings, board members discuss with the offender the nature of the offense and its negative consequences. Then board members develop a set of proposed sanctions, which they discuss with the offender until an agreement is reached on the specific actions the offender will take within a given time period to make reparation for the crime. Subsequently, the offender must document his or her progress in fulfilling the terms of the agreement. After the stipulated period of time has passed, the board submits a report to the court on the offender's compliance with the agreed-upon sanctions. At this point, the board's involvement with the offender ends.

The goals of community reparative boards include the following: (1) promoting citizens' ownership of the criminal and juvenile justice systems by involving them directly in the justice process; (2) providing an opportunity for victims and community members to confront offenders in a constructive manner about their behavior; (3) providing opportunities for offenders to take personal responsibility and be held directly accountable for the harm they caused to victims and communities; (4) generating meaningful community-driven consequences for criminal and delinquent actions, thereby reducing costly reliance on formal justice system processing.

The Vermont Department of Corrections implemented its Reparative Probation Program in 1995, in response to a 1994 public opinion survey (conducted by John Doble and Associates) in which citizens indicated broad support for programs with a reparative emphasis and active community involvement. The program's reparative boards are part of a mandated separation of probation into community corrections service units (designed to provide supervision for more serious cases) and court and reparative service units (which coordinate and provide administrative support to reparative boards).

In order to illustrate how a community reparative board would work, an example from Vermont provides a beneficial illustration. A Vermont reparative board convened to consider the case of a 17-year-old who had been caught driving with an open can of beer in his father's pickup truck. The youth had been sentenced by a judge to reparative probation, and it was the board's responsibility to decide what form the probation should take. For about 30 minutes, the citizen members of the board asked the youth several simple, straightforward questions. The board members then went to another room to deliberate on an appropriate sanction for the youth. The youth awaited the board's decision nervously, because he did not know whether to expect something tougher or much easier than regular probation. When the board returned, the chairperson explained the four conditions of the offender's probation contract: (1) begin work to pay off his traffic tickets, (2) complete a state police defensive driving course, (3) undergo an alcohol assessment, and (4) write a three-page paper on how alcohol had negatively affected his life. The youth signed the contract, and the chairperson adjourned the meeting.

Based on Vermont's experience, such as the illustration above, the following factors have been identified by the Vermont Department of Corrections as important in implementing community-driven reparative board programs: (1) marketing the program effectively to the justice system (to judges, prosecutors, and defense attorneys); (2) having a committed, well-trained staff; (3) working with victim organizations and ensuring that victims are represented and provided adequate opportunity to participate; (4) processing cases expeditiously and in a manner that is easy for community members to understand; (5) facilitating a positive experience for the board members; (6) providing quality training for the boards; (7) supporting the program with adequate resources (e.g., space, time, and staff); (8) striving for successful outcomes for offenders, victims, and community participants in the board's initial cases; and (9) getting support from judges in limiting the time the offender is in the program and on probation.

The design of Vermont's reparative boards was shaped to a large extent by restorative justice concepts and state officials who developed and now monitor the boards and strongly encourage an emphasis on victim participation.[59] Nevertheless, in the early months of operation, victim involvement in most local boards was minimal. Some boards appear to have increased victim involvement, but it remains to be seen to what extent citizen board members will want to take on the demanding task of contacting crime victims and engaging their participation in the justice process.[60] Some boards have demonstrated a strong commitment to making certain that offenders repay victims; ultimately, this commitment might motivate increased involvement of victims as the value of all forms of victim-offender dialog in improving restitution completion rates becomes clearer.[61] State administrators have also encouraged boards to refer victims and offenders to victim-offender mediation or family group conferencing programs, if such programs are available in the community and if victims agree to participate.

In Vermont's reparative board programs, case preparation usually is limited to brief intake interviews with offenders to gather information about the offense for the board hearings. Boards can obtain basic information about victim losses from police, court, or probation records. Nevertheless, some board programs increasingly are attempting to contact victims prior to hearings.

Monitoring and enforcement policies and procedures are more formally developed in reparative boards than in other models. Board members themselves have enforcement responsibilities (i.e., recommending revocation or termination of offender contracts as necessary), although they do not make final enforcement decisions. A reparative coordinator, who is a state corrections' employee, is responsible for monitoring offender contract compliance. If offenders do not meet contract conditions, the coordinator may recommend that they be charged with violation of probation or conditions of the diversion agreement and/or that the court take additional corrective action.

Only limited quantitative data have been collected on the effectiveness of community reparative boards. There is growing concern that evaluations of reparative board programs should consider measures beyond the standard offender-focused measure of recidivism. Additional measures should include responsiveness to victim and community needs, victim and community satisfaction, and impact on the community (including physical improvements resulting from board-imposed community work sanctions and indicators of healthy relationships among citizens). At this point, experiential and anecdotal information indicates that reparative boards show much promise as an effective response to non-violent crime.[62]

Family Group Conferencing

Family group conferencing is based on centuries-old sanctioning and dispute resolution traditions of the Maori of New Zealand.[63] In its modern form, the model was adopted into national legislation in New Zealand in 1989, making it the most systemically institutionalized of any of the four models. In South Australia, family conferencing is now widely used in modified form as a police-initiated diversion approach known as the Wagga Wagga model. Developed by the Wagga Wagga Police Department, this model uses police officers or school officials to set up and facilitate family conferencing meetings. Conferencing is also being used in U.S. cities in Minnesota, Montana, Pennsylvania, Vermont, and several other states and in parts of Canada. The Wagga Wagga model is the primary approach that has taken hold in North America. A variety of offenses have been resolved through family group conferencing, including theft, arson, minor assaults, drug offenses, vandalism, and, in a number of states, child maltreatment cases. In New Zealand, conferencing is used in the disposition of all but the most violent and serious delinquency cases.

Family group conferencing involves the community of people most affected by the crime—the victim, the offender, and the family, friends, and key supporters of both—in deciding the resolution of a criminal or delinquent incident. The affected parties are brought together by a trained facilitator to discuss how they and others have been harmed by the offense and how that harm might be repaired. The conference facilitator contacts the victim and offender to explain the process and invite them to the conference. The facilitator also asks the victim and offender to identify key members of their support systems, who also will be invited to participate. The conference typically begins with the offender describing the incident. The other participants then describe the impact of the incident on their lives. Some argue that it is preferable to allow the victim to start the discussion, if he or she wishes to do so. Through these narrations, the offender is faced with the impact of his or her behavior on the victim, on those close to the victim, and on the offender's own family and friends, and the victim has the opportunity to express feelings and ask questions about the incident. After a thorough discussion of impacts, the victim is asked to identify desired outcomes from the conference; in this way, the victim can help to shape the obligations that will be placed on the offender. All participants contribute to the problem-solving process of determining how the offender might best repair the harm he or she has caused. The session ends with participants signing an agreement that outlines their expectations and commitments.

The goals of family group conferencing include the following: (1) providing an opportunity for the victim to be directly involved in the discussion of the offense and in decisions regarding appropriate sanctions to be placed on the offender; (2) increasing the offender's awareness of the human impact of his or her behavior and providing the offender an opportunity to take full responsibility for it; (3) engaging the collective responsibility of the offender's support system for making amends and shaping the offender's future behavior; and (4) allowing both offender and victim to reconnect to key community support systems.

An example of a family group conferencing session helps to illustrate how this program is intended to work. A family conferencing group convened in a local school to consider a case in which a student had injured a teacher and broken the teacher's glasses in an altercation. Group members included the offender, his mother and grandfather, the victim, the police officer who made the arrest, and about 10 other interested parties (including 2 of the offender's teachers and 2 friends of the victim). The conferencing process began with comments by the offender, his mother and grandfather, the victim, and the arresting officer. Each spoke about the offense and its impact. The youth justice coordinator next asked for input from the other group members and then asked all participants what they thought the offender should do to pay back the victim and the community for the damage caused by his crime. In the remaining 30 minutes of the hour-long conference, the group suggested that the offender should make restitution to the victim for his medical expenses and the cost of new glasses and that the offender should also perform community service work on the school grounds.

The family group conferencing process, like the example above, has been implemented in schools, police departments, probation offices, residential programs, community mediation programs, and neighborhood groups. Conferencing is most often used as diversion from the court process for juveniles but can also be used after adjudication and disposition to address unresolved issues or determine specific terms of restitution. Conferencing programs have been implemented within single agencies and developed collaboratively among several agencies. After completing a training course, either volunteers or paid employees can serve as conference facilitators. Participation by all involved in conferences is voluntary. In addition to the victim and offender and their family members, a conference might involve teachers, other relatives, peers, special adult friends, and community resource people.

The dimensions of victim protection and empowerment are more complex in models that move beyond the small group or dyad to the larger community. Family group conferencing is perhaps the strongest of all the models in its potential for educating offenders about the harm their behavior causes to others. Concerns have been expressed, however, about the role of victims in this model. Among these concerns are the following: (1) Emphasis on offender education may cause victim needs to be overshadowed or trivialized as appears to have been the case when conferences have been held with little or no victim input or involvement; (2) standard protocol for family group conferences requires that offenders speak first which may affect victims' participation in the discussion; and (3) some interpretations of family group conferencing place primary emphasis on getting offenders to experience shame; in such interpretations, victim benefits are limited to an apology and perhaps material restitution.

Either or both of these benefits may meet the main needs of many victims, but other needs may be neglected. Moreover, if forgiveness is a primary goal, the process may be slanted toward eliciting apologies from offenders, victims may feel pressured to offer forgiveness and resentful of the implication that they should do so, and resentment may cause some victims to refuse to participate. Other criticisms of victim treatment in the family group conferencing model cite a lack of concern with victim empowerment, lack of protection against abuse or retaliation, and use of victims to serve as "props" or to meet offender needs.

Victim participation and satisfaction were indeed significant problems during the early development of family group conferencing in New Zealand, but it is wrong to conclude that most advocates of the conferencing model are not concerned with victims' needs. Recent studies, of family group conferencing programs in Minnesota, Pennsylvania, and South Australia have found higher rates of victim participation and satisfaction than when the model was first introduced in New Zealand.[64]

Such criticism of victim treatment in family group conferencing (or in any alternative model) should have as its context the extent to which the current formal system does or does not provide for victim reparation, empowerment, and support. Nevertheless, as family group conferencing models evolve, it will be important to keep in mind that emphasis on offender shaming and reintegration may limit the model's capacity to meet the needs of crime victims.

In New Zealand, preparation is viewed as critical for the success of family group conferences. Preconference face-to-face meetings generally are held with offenders and their families, and victims are contacted by phone. The Australian Wagga Wagga model places much less emphasis on preparation, apparently in the belief that spontaneity is important. Some coordinators, for example, argue that hearing victims' and offenders' stories prior to the conference may even diminish the impact and focus of the stories. Recently, however, some proponents of the Wagga Wagga model are placing greater emphasis on the need to ensure accuracy of facts, check with participants, develop plans, and ensure that key participants and their support groups attend conference sessions.

Family group conferencing programs generally have often left responsibility for compliance to the offender, although the New Zealand model does provide for reconvening conferences in the event of non-compliance. Conferencing programs generally do not make monitoring and enforcement responsibilities explicit, although Australia's Wagga Wagga model anticipates that police officers are ultimately responsible for enforcement and that juvenile justice staff may also play a role. In the United States, the enforcement function is evolving and varies from jurisdiction to jurisdiction. Although preferred practice calls for encouraging voluntary compliance and assigning monitoring roles to conference participants, final enforcement authority rests primarily with the police agencies that convene the conferences; however, the extent of actual follow-up varies.

To date, there have only been a few studies that have been conducted to assess the impact of family group conferencing with young offenders. One study by Maxwell and Morris assessed the impact of New Zealand's law mandating the widespread use of conferencing.[65] It found that families of offenders in conferencing programs are more frequently and actively involved in the justice process than are families of offenders whose cases are handled by standard procedures. It also found that offenders, victims, and their families described the conference process as helpful. Preliminary evaluations of conferencing programs in the United States also indicate high levels of victim satisfaction with the conference process and high rates of offender compliance with agreements reached during conferences.[66]

Practitioners involved in family group conferencing programs have observed reductions in fear for many victims. When used as a diversion from court, conferencing can provide a much speedier and more satisfying resolution of incidents than would otherwise be the case. Family group conferencing also builds community skills in conflict resolution and participatory decision-making.

Circle Sentencing

Circle sentencing is an updated version of the traditional sanctioning and healing practices of aboriginal peoples in Canada and American Indians in the United States.[67] Sentencing circles—sometimes called peacemaking circles—were resurrected in 1991 by judges and community justice committees in the Yukon Territory and other northern Canadian communities. Circle sentencing has been developed most extensively in Saskatchewan, Manitoba, and the Yukon and has been used occasionally in several other communities. Its use spread to the United States in 1996, when a pilot project was initiated in Minnesota. Circle sentencing has been used for adult and juvenile offenders, for a variety of offenses, and in both rural and urban settings.

Circle sentencing is a holistic reintegrative strategy designed not only to address the criminal and delinquent behavior of offenders but also to consider the needs of victims, families, and communities. Within the "circle," crime victims, offenders, family and friends of both, justice and social service personnel, and interested community residents speak from the heart in a shared search for an understanding of the event. Together they identify the steps necessary to assist in healing all affected parties and prevent future crimes. The significance of the circle is more than symbolic: all circle members—police officers, lawyers, judges, victims, offenders, and community residents—participate in deliberations to arrive at a consensus for a sentencing plan that addresses the concerns of all interested parties.

Circle sentencing typically involves a multistep procedure that includes (1) application by the offender to participate in the circle process, (2) a healing circle for the victim, (3) a healing circle for the offender, (4) a sentencing circle to develop consensus on the elements of a sentencing plan, and (5) follow-up circles to monitor the progress of the offender. In addition to commitments by the offender, the sentencing plan may incorporate commitments by the justice system, community, and family members. Specifics of the circle process vary from community to community and are designed locally to fit community needs and culture.

The goals of circle sentencing include the following: (1) promoting healing for all affected parties; (2) providing an opportunity for the offender to make amends; (3) empowering victims, community members, families, and offenders by giving them a voice and a shared responsibility in finding constructive resolutions; (4) addressing the underlying causes of criminal behavior; (5) building a sense of community and its capacity for resolving conflict; and (6) promoting and sharing community values.

In order to understand how a circle sentencing session would work, the following example by Bazemore and Umbreit provides a good illustration.[68] The victim was a middle-aged man whose parked car had been badly damaged when the offender, a 16-year-old, crashed into it while joyriding in another vehicle. The offender had also damaged a police vehicle. In the circle, the victim talked about the emotional shock of seeing what had happened to his car and his costs to repair it (he was uninsured). Then, an elder leader of the First Nations community where the circle sentencing session was being held (and an uncle of the offender) expressed his disappointment and anger with the boy. The elder observed that this incident, along with several prior offenses by the boy, had brought shame to his family. The elder also noted that in the old days, the boy would have been required to pay the victim's family substantial compensation as a result of such behavior. After the elder finished, a feather (the "talking piece") was passed to the next person in the circle, a young man who spoke about the contributions the offender had made to the community, the kindness he had shown toward elders, and his willingness to help others with home repairs.

Having heard all this, the judge asked the Crown Council (Canadian prosecutor) and the public defender, who were also sitting in the circle, to make statements and then asked if anyone else in the circle wanted to speak. The Royal Canadian Mounted Police officer, whose vehicle had also been damaged, then took the feather and spoke on the offender's behalf. The officer proposed to the judge that in lieu of statutorily required jail time for the offense, the offender be allowed to meet with him on a regular basis for counseling and community service. After asking the victim and the prosecutor if either had any objections, the judge accepted this proposal. The judge also ordered restitution to the victim and asked the young adult who had spoken on the offender's behalf to serve as a mentor for the offender. After a prayer in which the entire group held hands, the circle disbanded and everyone retreated to the kitchen area of the community center for refreshments.

The success of the circle sentencing process depends to a large extent on a healthy partnership between the formal juvenile justice system and the community. Participants from both need training and skill building in the circle process and in peacemaking and consensus building. It is critically important that the community's planning process allow sufficient time for strong relationships to develop between justice professionals and community members. Implementation procedures should be highly flexible, because the circle process will evolve over time based on the community's knowledge and experience. As it gains experience, the community can customize the circle process to fit local resources and culture.

In many communities that have implemented the circle sentencing concept, direction and leadership have come from a community justice committee that decides which cases to accept, develops support groups for the victim and offender, and helps to conduct the circles. In most communities, circles are facilitated by a trained community member, who is often called a keeper.

Although circles have been used as a response to serious and violent crimes, circle sentencing is not an appropriate response to all offenses. Key factors in determining whether a case is appropriate for the circle process include the offender's character and personality, sincerity, and connection to the community; the victim's input; and the dedication of the offender's and victim's support groups. Moreover, circles are often labor intensive and require a substantial investment of citizen time and effort; circles should not, therefore, be used extensively as a response to first offenders and minor crime.

The capacity of the circle to advance solutions capable of improving the lives of participants and the overall well-being of the community depends on the effectiveness of the participating volunteers. To ensure a cadre of capable volunteers, the program should support a paid community-based volunteer coordinator to supply logistical support, establish linkages with other agencies and community representatives, and provide appropriate training for all staff.

Proponents of circle sentencing are concerned with protecting victims, providing them with support, and hearing their stories. Circle organizers avoid an unbalanced focus on offenders' issues, which may cause victims to withdraw or react by challenging offenders.[69] Victims' telling of their stories is viewed as important not only for victims, offenders, and their supporters, but also for the community as a whole. If a victim is unwilling to participate in a circle, the organizer may encourage a friend or relative to speak on the victim's behalf; however, organizers emphasize the value of community residents hearing victims' stories firsthand whenever possible.[70]

Because the circle sentencing process is so open and community driven, a potential concern is that the importance given to victims' needs may vary widely. The seriousness of offenders' needs may slant the focus of some circles toward offender rehabilitation, service, and support and away from victims' needs, as also appears to occur in some family group conferences. In addition, because the circle sentencing model requires extensive preparation on the offender's part before the circle convenes, some circles become "stacked" with offender supporters who have little relationship to victims.

Initially unique to the circle sentencing model of conferencing is the concept of victim support groups. Support groups are formed by community justice committees, which are responsible for achieving an appropriate balance among victim, offender, and community needs and representation. Usually a support group is formed at the time an offender petitions for admission to the circle, but the group may expand at any time (including during the circle ceremony itself).

Perhaps because its community empowerment and healing goals are most ambitious, the circle sentencing model demands the most extensive presession preparation. As a condition of admission to a circle, offenders are required to petition the community justice committee, visit an elder or other respected community member for a conference, begin work on a reparative plan that may involve some restitution to the victim and community service, and identify a community support group. This presession process serves as a screening device and an indicator that offenders are serious about personal change. It is not uncommon for circles to be canceled or postponed if offenders fail to complete the preliminary steps. When the screening process works well and offenders meet the presession obligations, however, a circle can actually be less a hearing about disposition requirements than a celebration of the offender's progress and an opportunity for victim and offender to tell their stories.

Follow-up should be as intensive as preparation in the circle sentencing model. Circle participants are expected to take responsibility for monitoring and enforcing the conditions of the circle sentence, which often include an extensive list of reparative responsibilities, treatment requirements, and (in aboriginal communities) traditional healing and community-building rituals. Support groups for offenders and victims, which are formed through community justice committees, also monitor offenders and act as victim advocates to ensure that agreements made within the circle are carried out. Sentencing circle agreements are subject to review by a judge, who asks for routine reports from the justice committee and support groups. At the conclusion of a circle, the judge may assign further monitoring responsibilities to members of the community and may withhold a final decision about detention terms or other sanctions pending the offender's completion of obligations as verified at a follow-up hearing.

Very little research has been conducted to date on the effectiveness of circle sentencing. One study conducted by Judge Barry Stuart in Canada in 1996 indicated that recidivism was less likely among offenders who had participated in circles than among offenders who were processed traditionally.[71] Those who have been involved with circles report that circles empower participants to resolve conflict in a manner that promotes sharing of responsibility for outcomes, generates constructive relationships, enhances respect and understanding among all involved, and fosters enduring, innovative solutions.

Conclusion

According to the U.S. Catholic Bishops, the concepts inherent within community justice and restorative justice reflect the values and traditions of the Catholic Church. Adopting both of these perspectives, community justice and restorative justice mediation, works toward changing the criminal justice system from one that is punitive in nature and process oriented, to one that takes into consideration the victim, the offender, and the harm caused to the community, and puts its emphasis on the human element. Although many of these programs are still new and untested, they do provide promise for moving the criminal justice system forward, while at the same time moving it toward a Catholic perspective. As both the police and courts begin to adopt a community perspective in regard to their roles in the criminal justice system, so too must the third component of the criminal justice system—corrections. This, the movement toward community-based corrections, is the subject of the next chapter.

Notes

1. U.S. Catholic Bishops, *Confronting a Culture of Violence: A Catholic Framework for Action* (Washington, D.C.: United States Conference of Catholic Bishops, 1994). See for instance p. 28 regarding "community justice" and p. 36 regarding "restorative justice."

2. Charles P. Nemeth, *Aquinas in the Courtroom* (Westport, CT: Praeger Publishers, 2001), 129, citing St. Thomas Aquinas, *Summa Theologica, II-II, Q. 64, a. 4*.

3. Todd R. Clear and Eric Cadora, *Community Justice* (Belmont, CA: Wadsworth Publishing, 2003).

4. T.R. Clear and D.R. Karp, "Toward the Ideal of Community Justice," *National Institute of Justice Journal* (October 2000): 21-28.

5. T.R. Clear and D.R. Karp, "Toward the Ideal of Community Justice," *National Institute of Justice Journal* (October 2000): 21-28.

6. T.R. Clear and D.R. Karp, "Toward the Ideal of Community Justice," *National Institute of Justice Journal* (October 2000): 21-28.

7. T.R. Clear and D.R. Karp, "Toward the Ideal of Community Justice," *National Institute of Justice Journal* (October 2000): 21-28.

8. T.R. Clear and D.R. Karp, "Toward the Ideal of Community Justice," *National Institute of Justice Journal* (October 2000): 21-28.

9. E. Lee, "Community Courts: An Evolving Model," *Community Justice Series, #2* (Washington, D.C.: Bureau of Justice Assistance, 2000).

10. D.E. Rottman, "Community Courts: Prospects and Limits," *National Institute of Justice Journal* (August 1996): 46-50.

11. T.R. Clear and D.R. Karp, "Toward the Ideal of Community Justice," *National Institute of Justice Journal* (October 2000): 21-28.

12. E. Lee, "Community Courts: An Evolving Model," *Community Justice Series, #2* (Washington, D.C.: Bureau of Justice Assistance, 2000); D.E. Rottman, "Community Courts: Prospects and Limits," *National Institute of Justice Journal* (August 1996): 46-50.

13. D.E. Rottman, "Community Courts: Prospects and Limits," *National Institute of Justice Journal* (August 1996): 46-50.

14. E. Lee, "Community Courts: An Evolving Model," *Community Justice Series, #2* (Washington, D.C.: Bureau of Justice Assistance, 2000).

15. E. Lee, "Community Courts: An Evolving Model," *Community Justice Series, #2* (Washington, D.C.: Bureau of Justice Assistance, 2000).

16. E. Lee, "Community Courts: An Evolving Model," *Community Justice Series, #2* (Washington, D.C.: Bureau of Justice Assistance, 2000).

17. D.E. Rottman, "Community Courts: Prospects and Limits," *National Institute of Justice Journal* (August 1996): 49.

18. E. Lee, "Community Courts: An Evolving Model," *Community Justice Series, #2* (Washington, D.C.: Bureau of Justice Assistance, 2000).

19. D.E. Rottman, "Community Courts: Prospects and Limits," *National Institute of Justice Journal* (August 1996): 46-50.

20. E. Lee, "Community Courts: An Evolving Model," *Community Justice Series, #2* (Washington, D.C.: Bureau of Justice Assistance, 2000).

21. Roger Connor, "Community Oriented Lawyering: An Emerging Approach to Legal Practice," *National Institute of Justice Journal* (January 2000): 26-33.

22. Roger Connor, "Community Oriented Lawyering: An Emerging Approach to Legal Practice," *National Institute of Justice Journal* (January 2000): 26-33.

23. Barbara Boland, "What is Community Prosecution?" *National Institute of Justice Journal* (August 1996): 35-40.

24. Susan P. Weinstein, "Community Prosecution: Community Policing's Legal Partner," *FBI Law Enforcement Bulleting* (April 1998): 19-23.

25. Susan P. Weinstein, "Community Prosecution: Community Policing's Legal Partner," *FBI Law Enforcement Bulleting* (April 1998): 19-23.

26. M. Blaine Nugent, *What Does It Mean to Practice Community Prosecution?* (Alexandria, VA: American Prosecutors Research Institute, 2004).

27. M. Blaine Nugent, *What Does It Mean to Practice Community Prosecution?* (Alexandria, VA: American Prosecutors Research Institute, 2004); Susan P. Weinstein, "Community Prosecution: Community Policing's Legal Partner," *FBI Law Enforcement Bulletin* (April 1998): 19-23.

28. Susan P. Weinstein, "Community Prosecution: Community Policing's Legal Partner," *FBI Law Enforcement Bulletin* (April 1998): 19-23.

29. Susan P. Weinstein, "Community Prosecution: Community Policing's Legal Partner," *FBI Law Enforcement Bulletin* (April 1998): 19-23.

30. Todd R. Clear and Eric Cadora, *Community Justice* (Belmont, CA: Wadsworth Publishing, 2003), 59.

31. Christopher Stone, "Community Defense and the Challenge of Community Justice," *National Institute of Justice Journal* (August 1996): 41-45.

32. Ruth Ann Strickland, *Restorative Justice* (New York: Peter Lang, 2004), 71.

33. Christopher Stone, "Community Defense and the Challenge of Community Justice," *National Institute of Justice Journal* (August 1996): 41-45.

34. J.W. Cooley, *Mediation Advocacy* (South Bend, IN: National Institute for Trial Advocacy, 1996).

35. E.J. Costello, *Controlling Conflict* (Chicago, IL: CCH Inc., 1996); S.B. Goldberg, E.D. Green, and F.E.A. Sanders, *Dispute Resolution* (Boston, MA: Little, Brown, 1985); C.B. Harrington, *Shadow Justice* (Westport, CT: Greenwood Press, 1985); S.M. Leeson and B.M. Johnston, *Ending It: Dispute Resolution in America* (Cincinnati: Anderson Publishing, 1988); L.R. Singer, *Settling Disputes* (Boulder, CO: Westview Press, 1994).

36. T.E. Carbonneau, *Alternative Dispute Resolution* (Urbana, IL: University of Illinois Press, 1996); J.W. Cooley, *Mediation Advocacy* (South Bend, IN: National Institute for Trial Advocacy, 1996); J.M. Nolan-Haley, *Alternative Dispute Resolution in a Nutshell* (Minneapolis, MN: West Publishing Co., 1992).

37. D. McGillis, *Community Dispute Resolution Programs and Public Policy* (Washington, D.C.: National Institute of Justice, 1986), 32.

38. F. Dukes, "Understanding Community Dispute Resolution," *Mediation Quarterly* 8, no. 1 (1990): 27-37.

39. F. Dukes, "Understanding Community Dispute Resolution," *Mediation Quarterly* 8, no. 1 (1990): 27-37; R. Hofrichter, *Neighborhood Justice in a Capitalist Society*

Chapter Five

(New York: Greenwood Press, 1987); D. McGillis, *Community Dispute Resolution Programs and Public Policy* (Washington, D.C.: National Institute of Justice, 1986).

40. D. McGillis, *Community Dispute Resolution Programs and Public Policy* (Washington, D.C.: National Institute of Justice, 1986).

41. L. H. Cole, *Alternative Dispute Resolution Mechanisms for Prisoner Grievances* (Washington, D.C.: U.S. Department of Justice, 1983); L.R. Singer, "The Quiet Revolution in Dispute Settlement," *Mediation Quarterly* 7, no. 2 (1989): 105-113; M.R. Volpe, "The Police Role," in *Mediation in Criminal Justice*, eds. M. Wright and B. Galaway (Newbury Park, NJ: Sage Publications, 1989).

42. M.S. Umbreit, *Crime and Reconciliation: Creative Options for Victims and Offenders* (Nashville, TN: Abingdon Press, 1985); H. Zehr, *Changing Lenses: A New Focus for Crime and Justice* (Scottsdale, PA: Herald Press, 1995); H. Zehr and M. Umbreit, "Victim Offender Reconciliation: An Incarceration Substitute?" *Federal Probation* 46, no. 4 (1982): 63-68.

43. C.G. Nicholl, *Community Policing, Community Justice, and Restorative Justice* (Washington, D.C.: U.S. Department of Justice, 1999).

44. D.W. Van Ness and K.H. Strong, *Restoring Justice: An Introduction to Restorative Justice*, 3rd ed. (Cincinnati: Anderson Publishing, 2006).

45. R.B. Coates and J. Gehm, "An Empirical Assessment," in *Mediation in Criminal Justice*, eds. M. Wright and B. Galaway (Newbury Park, NJ: Sage Publications, 1989).

46. See Gordon Bazemore and Mark Umbreit, "A Comparison of Four Restorative Conferencing Models," *Juvenile Justice Bulletin* (February 2001): 1-20.

47. Mark Umbreit, "Humanistic Mediation: A Transformation Journey of Peacemaking," *Mediation Quarterly* 14, no. 3 (1997): 201-213.

48. Mark Umbreit, *Victim Meets Offender: The Impact of Restorative Justice in Mediation* (Monsey, NY: Criminal Justice Press, 1994).

49. Gordon Bazemore and Mark Umbreit, "A Comparison of Four Restorative Conferencing Models," *Juvenile Justice Bulletin* (February 2001): 1-20.

50. Gordon Bazemore and Mark Umbreit, "A Comparison of Four Restorative Conferencing Models," *Juvenile Justice Bulletin* (February 2001): 1-20.

51. Gordon Bazemore and Mark Umbreit, "A Comparison of Four Restorative Conferencing Models," *Juvenile Justice Bulletin* (February 2001): 1-20.

52. Mark Umbreit and J. Greenwood, *Victim Sensitive Guidelines for Victim Offender Mediation* (Washington, D.C.: U.S. Department of Justice, 1998).

53. Gordon Bazemore and Mark Umbreit, "A Comparison of Four Restorative Conferencing Models," *Juvenile Justice Bulletin* (February 2001): 1-20.

54. Mark Umbreit, *Victim Meets Offender: The Impact of Restorative Justice in Mediation* (Monsey, NY: Criminal Justice Press, 1994).

55. R. Coates and J. Gehm, "An Empirical Assessment," in *Mediation and Criminal Justice*, eds. M. Wright and B. Galaway (London, England: Sage Publications, 1989); Mark Umbreit, *Victim Meets Offender: The Impact of Restorative Justice in Mediation* (Monsey, NY: Criminal Justice Press, 1994).

56. Mark Umbreit and B. A. Schug, *Directory of Victim Offender Mediation Programs in the U.S.* (St. Paul, MN: Center for Restorative Justice and Mediation, University of Minnesota, 1997).

57. Gordon Bazemore and Mark Umbreit, "A Comparison of Four Restorative Conferencing Models," *Juvenile Justice Bulletin* (February 2001): 1-20.

58. Gordon Bazemore and Mark Umbreit, "A Comparison of Four Restorative Conferencing Models," *Juvenile Justice Bulletin* (February 2001): 1-20.

59. M. J. Dooley, *Reparative Probation Program* (Waterbury, CT: Vermont Department of Corrections, 1995); M.J. Dooley, *Restoring Hope Through Community Partnerships: The Real Deal in Crime Control* (Lexington, KY: American Probation and Parole Association, 1996).

60. D. Karp and L. Walther, "Community Reparative Boards: Theory and Practice," in *Restorative Community Justice: Cultivating Common Ground for Victims, Communities, and Offenders*, eds. G. Bazemore and M. Schiff (Cincinnati: Anderson Publishing, (2001).

61. M. Umbreit and R. Coates, "Impact of Mediating Victim-Offender Conflict: An Analysis of Programs in Three States," *Juvenile and Family Court Journal* 43, no. 1 (1993): 21-28.

62. Gordon Bazemore and Mark Umbreit, "A Comparison of Four Restorative Conferencing Models," *Juvenile Justice Bulletin* (February 2001): 1-20.

63. Gordon Bazemore and Mark Umbreit, "A Comparison of Four Restorative Conferencing Models," *Juvenile Justice Bulletin* (February 2001): 1-20.

64. Gordon Bazemore and Mark Umbreit, "A Comparison of Four Restorative Conferencing Models," *Juvenile Justice Bulletin* (February 2001): 1-20.

65. G. Maxwell and A. Morris, *Family Participation, Cultural Diversity, and Victim Innovation in Youth Justice: A New Zealand Experiment* (Wellington, New Zealand: Victoria University, 1993).

66. C. Farcello and M. Umbreit, *Client Evaluation of Family Group Counseling* (St. Paul, MN: Center for Restorative Justice and Mediation, University of Minnesota, 1999); P. McCold and B. Wachtel, *Restorative Policing Experiment: The Bethlehem, Pennsylvania, Police Family Group Conferencing Project* (Pipersville, PA: Community Service Foundation, 1998).

67. Gordon Bazemore and Mark Umbreit, "A Comparison of Four Restorative Conferencing Models," *Juvenile Justice Bulletin* (February 2001): 1-20.

68. Gordon Bazemore and Mark Umbreit, "A Comparison of Four Restorative Conferencing Models," *Juvenile Justice Bulletin* (February 2001): 1-20.

69. B. Stuart, "Circle Sentencing—Turning Swords into Ploughshares," in *Restorative Justice: International Perspectives*, eds. B. Galaway and J. Hudson (Monsey, NY: Criminal Justice Press, 1996), 193-206.

70. B. Stuart, "Circle Sentencing—Turning Swords into Ploughshares," in *Restorative Justice: International Perspectives*, eds. B. Galaway and J. Hudson (Monsey, NY: Criminal Justice Press, 1996), 193-206.

71. B. Stuart, "Circle Sentencing—Turning Swords into Ploughshares," in *Restorative Justice: International Perspectives*, eds. B. Galaway and J. Hudson (Monsey, NY: Criminal Justice Press, 1996), 193-206.

Chapter 6

Community Corrections

"For I was hungry and you gave me food, I was thirsty and you gave me drink, a stranger and you welcomed me, naked and you clothed me, ill and you cared for me, in prison and you visited me."

- Matthew 25:35-36 -

Introduction

In the fall of 2000, the National Conference of Catholic Bishops took a good, hard look at America's criminal justice system. In their statement *Responsibility, Rehabilitation, and Restoration: A Catholic Perspective on Crime and Criminal Justice*, the Bishops spoke very directly about what Catholics can and should do about America's prisons—and its prisoners.[1]

The Bishops pointed out that there are currently more than two million people incarcerated in the United States, and that more than $35 billion is spent annually on corrections. These figures represent a significant increase over previous years. From the early 1930s until the 1980s, the prison population remained at about 115 inmates for every 100,000 U.S. residents. By 1980, the prison population rose to 138 inmates per 100,000 residents. The figure hit 297 per 100,000 in 1990, and in 2000 reached a staggering 478 inmates per 100,000 residents.

The explosion in America's prison population is often attributed to the growth in prison space. There has indeed been a steady upward trend in prison construction since the 1960s. In the movie *Field of Dreams*, the ghost tells the protagonist to build a baseball field in the middle of a corn field and repeats the line: "If you build it, they will come." Unfortunately, that same logic applies to the building of prisons, for every time a prison is built, it quickly fills and eventually becomes overcrowded. It certainly seems reasonable to assume that judges and juries will more readily send criminals to prison when they know there is a prison to send them to. However, a closer look at the characteristics of criminals entering the corrections system sheds more light onto the question.

In their statement, the Bishops pointed out some basic facts about today's inmates. Approximately 24 percent are incarcerated solely for drug offenses and no other crime, while nearly half were under the influence of drugs and alcohol at the time they committed their crimes. The Bishops also pointed out that nearly three-quarters are high-school dropouts, more than 200,000 suffer from some type of mental illness, and an unknown number are victims of past abuse. The Bishops also stated that, contrary to popular perception, most inmates are in for petty crime, which criminal justice research confirms.[2]

But perhaps the most important point the Bishops made was that nearly all of the nation's present inmates will, at some point, be released back into society. The average sentence in the United States is little less than four years. And, once they are released, the majority will recidivate—commit more crimes. Most will return, sooner or later, to jail.

The Catechism builds on our Lord's explicit reference to incarcerated criminals when he stated, "I was in prison and you visited me."[3] The Catechism explains that visiting the imprisoned is a work of mercy—a "charitable action by which we come to the aid of our neighbor in his spiritual and body necessities."[4] The Bishops elaborated on this theme in their statement when they explained that a "community has a right to establish and enforce laws to protect people and to advance the common good, [but] at the same time, a Catholic approach does not give up on those who violate these laws."[5]

The Bishops see the potential salvation of inmates through the sacraments of the Eucharist and Reconciliation. Giving oneself up to God and coming closer to Jesus through the Eucharist is, according to the Bishops, the quickest way to physical, behavioral, and emotional healing that will have a lasting effect. And, through the sacrament of Penance, sinners can learn how to show contrition, how to take responsibility for their own actions, how to restore justice, and how to rejoin the community.

The Catholic response to prisoners should, then, reflect Pope John Paul II's words in his message on the Jubilee of Prisons, delivered July 9, 2000: "Assuring the men and women who are in prison throughout the world that I am close to them in spirit, I embrace them all as brothers and sisters in the human family."[6] As the Holy Father frequently articulated throughout his pontificate, what is needed is the evangelization of all our brothers and sisters—including those in prison.

Russell L. Ford, an inmate in Alabama who converted to the Catholic faith and who is the author of *The Missionary's Catechism*, highlights the fact that one of the only sure ways to prevent recidivism among inmates is for them to embrace a life in Christ. If this is achieved, he wrote in the *Homilectic and Pastoral Review*, "the recidivism rate for converts to genuine Catholicism is zero."[7] Recent scientific research in criminal justice supports Ford's assertions. Studies have shown that inmates who commit to some form of Christian prayer or Bible-study group while in prison are more likely to continue with those activities upon release. This involvement, in turn, appears to make them less likely, as a group, to commit post-release crimes. Meanwhile, inmates who do not participate in religious activities while incarcerated, or those who participate only sporadically, tend to recidivate within the first year of release.

A number of organizations have sprung up over the past few decades to bring Christ to the incarcerated. Charles "Chuck" Colson, a former White House aide who served prison time for his role in the Watergate scandal, started Prison Fellowship Ministries in 1976; today, it is the largest prison-outreach and criminal-reform organization in the world, operating in all 50 states and in other countries. Russell L. Ford also started a ministry for Catholic conversion of inmates called First Century Christian Ministries. In addition, many dioceses have, through their social-justice offices, created prison ministries. The Bishops in their statement also called for the creation of parish-outreach programs for those parishes located near jails and prisons.

In order to understand a Catholic perspective to corrections, and more specifically the issues surrounding community corrections, it is important first to understand the scope of the problem. In America we have over two million people incarcerated in prisons and jails, and nearly six million more Americans serving some type of probation or parole. Once this is understood, trying to reconcile that with the Catholic perspective of dealing with offenders, in particularly imprisonment, helps us to understand where the criminal justice system should be heading, namely toward community corrections. Thus, a review of incarceration in America, understanding the Catholic perspective on corrections, and learning what community corrections has to offer is the focus of this chapter.

Prisons & Jails

There are currently over two million people incarcerated in America's prisons and jails. Prisons house those sentenced to more than one year in confinement, while jails house those who are sentenced to one year or less in confinement. There are approximately 84 federal prisons, 1,320 state prisons, and 3,376 jails throughout the United States. The number of inmates in prison does not typically include the number of people currently on probation or parole, and often does not include those who are sentenced to community-based corrections programs. Because of the constant state of flux among the correctional facilities, it is difficult to assess the actual number of those imprisoned, on parole/probation, or in community-based programs at any given time, however, the U.S. Bureau of Justice Statistics does try to track the actual numbers. The most recent data available is at midyear in 2004.

At midyear 2004 the nation's prisons and jails incarcerated 2,131,180 persons.[8] Prisoners in the custody of the 50 states and the federal system accounted for two-thirds of the incarcerated population (1,410,404 inmates). The other third were held in local jails (713,990), not including persons in community based programs. In the first 6 months of 2004, the nation's population increased 24,079 (1.7 percent). Since mid-year 2003, the total incarcerated population has increased 2.3 percent. Including inmates in public and privately-operated facilities, the number of inmates in state prisons increased 1.3 percent; in federal prisons, 6.3 percent; and in local jails 3.3 percent. At midyear 2004, federal prisons (including all secure and non-secure public and private facilities) held 8.3 percent of all inmates, up from 5.6 percent in 1995.

Between year-end 1995 and midyear 2004, the incarcerated population grew an average of 3.5 percent annually. During this period the federal and state prison populations and the local jail population grew at the average annual rates of 7.8 percent, 2.7 percent, and 4.1 percent respectively. In the 12 months before midyear 2004, the number of inmates in prison and jail rose an estimated 48,452 inmates or 932 inmates per week. The rate of incarceration in prison and jail in 2003 was 726 inmates per 100,000 U.S. residents—up from 716 at midyear 2003. At midyear 2004, 1 in every 138 U.S. Residents was in prison or jail.

On June 30, 2004, 1,494,216 prisoners were under federal and state jurisdiction, which includes inmates in custody and persons under the legal authority of a prison system but held outside its facilities. During the 12 month period ending June 30, 2004, the number under state jurisdiction rose 1.6 percent, while the number under federal jurisdiction rose 5.1 percent. Minnesota (up 13.2 percent), Montana (up 10.5 percent), Arkansas (up 8.9 percent), and Kentucky (up 8.5 percent) had the largest percentage increases. Twelve states had decreases, including Alabama (-6.7 percent), Connecticut (-2.5 percent), Ohio (-2.3 percent), and New York (-2.0 percent).

At midyear 2004 local jail authorities held or supervised 784,538 offenders. Nine percent of these offenders (70,458) were supervised outside jail facilities in programs such as community service, work release, weekend reporting, electronic monitoring, and other alternative programs.

The rate of growth of the state prison population slowed between 1995 and 2001 and then began to rise. During this time, the percentage change in the first six months of each year steadily decreased, reaching a low of 0.6 percent in 2001, and then rising to 1.5 percent in 2004. The percentage change in the second 6 months of each year showed a similar trend, resulting in an actual decrease in state prison populations for the second half of 2000 and 2001.

Since 1995, the federal system has grown at a much higher rate than the states, peaking at 6 percent growth in the first 6 months of 1999. In the first 6 months of 2004, the number of federal inmates increased 3.6 percent (more than twice the rate of state growth). Some of the federal growth since 1999 has been the result of the transfer of responsibility for housing sentence felons from the District of Columbia. The transfer to federal facilities was completed by year-end 2001. Since then, the federal system has continued to receive sentenced felons from D.C. Superior Court.

In absolute numbers, the total increase of 30,019 state and federal prison inmates between July 1, 2003, and June 30, 2004, was significantly lower than the growth during the previous 12-month period (44,260 inmates). The percentage change from mid-year 2003 to mid-year 2004 (2.1 percent) was also smaller than the 2002-03 increase (3.1 percent). The average annual growth from 1995 to 2004 was 3.4 percent.

Twenty-nine percent of the nation's prison population during the 12 months ending June 30, 2004, was accounted for by the 8,749 additional inmates under jurisdiction of the federal system. During this 12-month period, several states also experienced substantial growth, including Minnesota (13.2 percent), Montana (10.5 percent), and Arkansas (8.9 percent). Twelve states experienced a decline in their prison population. Alabama had the largest percentage decrease (-6.7 percent), followed by Connecticut (-2.5 percent), Ohio (-2.3 percent), and New York (-2.0 percent).

The incarceration rate of state and federal prisoners sentenced to more than one year was 486 per 100,000 U.S. residents on June 30, 2004, up from 482 per 100,000 on December 31, 2003. At midyear 2004, 12 states, led by Louisiana (814 sentenced prisoners per 100,000 state residents), Texas (704), and Oklahoma (684), exceeded the national rate. Nine states, including Maine (149), Minnesota (169), and North Dakota (189)—had rates that were less than half of the national rate. Overall, the state incarceration rate rose about 14 percent between year-end 1995 and mid-year 2004, from 379 to 433 prisoners per 100,000 U.S. residents. At the same time, the federal incarceration rate rose almost 66 percent, from 32 to 53 prisoners per 100,000 U.S. residents.

Since year-end 1995 the total number of sentenced inmates per 100,000 residents has risen from 411 to 486. During this period prison incarceration rates rose the most in the Midwest (from 310 to 378), followed by the West (from 358 to 421) and the South (from 483 to 543). The rate in the Northeast decreased slightly from 301 to 299.

In the first 6 months of 2004, the number of prisoners held in privately-operated facilities increased from 95,522 to 98,791, an increase of 3.4 percent. Overall, private facilities held 6.6 percent of all state and federal inmates, up from 6.5 percent at mid-year 2003. The federal system (24,506), Texas system (16,906), Oklahoma (5,675), and Tennessee (5,121) reported the largest number of inmates in private facilities at midyear 2004. Five states, all in the West, had at least a quarter of their prisoners in private facilities.

From June 30, 2003, to June 30, 2004, the number of women under the jurisdiction of state and federal prison authorities grew from 100,384 to 103,310, an increase of 2.9 percent. The number of men rose 2.0 percent, from 1,363,813 to 1,390,906. At mid-year 2004, California, Texas, Florida, and the federal system housed 4 of every 10 female inmates. Since 1995 the annual rate of growth in the number of female inmates has averaged 5.0 percent, higher than the 3.3 percent average increase of male inmates. Women accounted for 6.9 percent of all inmates at midyear 2004, up from 6.1 percent at year-end 1995.

A total of 2,477 state prisoners were under age 18 on June 30, 2004, down nearly 10 percent from 2,740 at midyear 2003. The number of minors held in state prisons peaked in 1995 at 5,309, and has since decreased every year. Overall, 0.2 percent of all state prisoners were under age 18. Eight states reported more than 100 prisoners under age 18 at mid-year 2004, led by Connecticut (321), New York (225), Florida (214), and Texas (210). Three of these states reported an increase in their under age 18 populations held in prison during the 12 months ending June 30, 2004, while the rest experienced declines. Six states reported no inmates under age 18, and another twelve states had fewer than 10 inmates under age 18.

On June 30, 2004, 91,789 non-citizens were in the custody of state or federal correctional authorities, up from 90,566 at midyear 2003. Overall, 6.5 percent of state and federal inmates at midyear 2004 were not U.S. citizens. The noncitizen prisoner population increased between 1998 and 1999, and since then has remained nearly stable, increasing about 3.4 percent between mid-year 1999 and mid-year 2004. At mid-year 2004, 34,422 federal inmates were non-citizens, representing over 20 percent of all prisoners in federal custody. California (17,890), Texas (9,048), New York (8,027), Florida (4,834), and Arizona (3,924) held over 75 percent of all non-citizens confined in state prison. Noncitizen prisoners accounted for over 10 percent of the prison populations of Arizona, New York, Nevada, and California.

From 2000 to 2003 admissions to state prison rose 9.1 percent (from 581,487 in 2000 to 634,149 in 2003). During 2003, 612,185 sentenced prisoners were released from state prisons, up from 569,599 in 2000—an increase of 7.5 percent. Admissions to the federal prison system increased 19.6 percent between 2000 and 2003 (from 43,732 to 52,288); releases increased 25.2 percent (35,259 to 44,135). The number of admissions to federal prison in 2003 exceeded releases by more than 8,000 inmates.

Prior to 1998, growth in prison admissions reflected increasing numbers of offenders returning for parole violations. Between 1990 and 1998, the number of returned parole violators increased 54 percent (from 133,870 to 206,152) while the number of new court commitments increased 7 percent (from 323,069 to 347,270). However, since 1998 parole violators returned to prison increased by less than 2 percent, while new court commitments rose 5.1 percent.

Based on the 2004 Annual Survey of Jails, the nation's local jails, the destination for those who are sentenced to less than one year confinement, held or supervised 784,538 offenders on June 30, 2004. Jail authorities supervised 9 percent of these offenders (70,548) in alternative programs outside the jail facilities. A total of 713,990 persons were housed in local jails.

Among persons under community supervision by jail staff in 2003, 19 percent were required to perform community service (13,171), and 16 percent participated in a weekend reporting program (11,589). Seventeen percent of offenders in the community were under electronic monitoring; 20 percent were under other pretrial supervision; 3 percent were in a drug, alcohol, mental health, or other type of medical treatment program; and 14 percent were participating in a work release or other alternative work program.

Between July 1, 2003, and June 30, 2004, the number of persons held in local jail facilities grew 3.3 percent—from 691,301 to 713,990. The 12-month increase was similar to the average annual growth (3.9 percent) from midyear 1995 to midyear 2004. The 3.3 percent growth in 2003 was less than the 2004 increase of 3.9 percent. In absolute numbers, the total increase of 22,689 inmates in 2004 was 3,100 less than the increase in 2003.

The sheer number of people being held in American prisons and jails is astounding, but the number of people estimated to be on probation or parole in America is even more astounding. According to the Bureau of Justice Statistics, there were 4,162,536 people on probation and another 784,408 people on parole in the United States. Both of those figures have more than doubled in the twenty years since 1985. Not only does America have more people incarcerated, but it has more and more people under the supervision of the criminal justice system at federal, state, and local levels. How to deal with this problem has been the consideration of penology in America, and typically the response has been to warehouse prisoners and to loosely manage those on probation and parole. And even when the system has been well intentioned, the sheer numbers described above have always managed to overwhelm the system, thus the end result has often been, again, warehousing inmates and loosely managing offenders on probation and parole.

Catholic Perspective

Jesus mentions in the opening quote the issue of prison by way of stating that what one does for the least of humanity, they do for him. The full passage is important for understanding what Jesus is trying to convey to his disciples. For it states:

> But when the Son of Man comes in his glory, and all the angels with him, then he will sit on his glorious throne. All the nations will be gathered before him; and he will separate them from one another, as the shepherd separates the sheep from the goats; and he will put the sheep on his right, and the goats on the left. Then the King will say to those on his right, 'Come, you who are blessed of my Father, inherit the kingdom prepared for you from the foundation of the world. 'For I was hungry, and you gave me something to eat; I was thirsty, and you gave me something to drink; I was a stranger, and you invited me in; naked,

and you clothed me; sick, and you visited me; I was in prison, and you came to me.'

"Then the righteous will answer him, "Lord, when did we see you hungry, and feed you, or thirsty, and give you something to drink? And when did we see you a stranger, and invite you in, or naked, and clothe you? When did we see you sick, or in prison, and come to you?"

"The King will answer and say to them, 'Truly I say to you, to the extent that you did it to one of these brothers of mine, even the least of them, you did it to me."[9]

By caring for the poor and the sick, and visiting the imprisoned, we are in Jesus' words, caring and visiting him. Although there are many mentions of prison and people being imprisoned in the Bible, it is this quote that entails how society should treat its prisoners. The *Catechism of the Catholic Church,* under a discussion of the Fifth Commandment "thou shall not kill," details the importance of having respect for the human dignity of people, even those who have committed crimes and are in prison. In this case, the *Catechism* refers to this as "scandal."[10]

Scandal is defined as an "attitude or behavior which leads another to do evil." When a person tempts his neighbor or does something to damage their virtue and integrity, this creates a situation where one person does not respect another, hence they have committed a sin. When a person derides one who is imprisoned or throws invectives toward them, they are engaging in scandal.

Scandal, however, is not limited to the attitudes and behaviors of an individual, but can be provoked by our institutions and the laws put into place to oversee those institutions. If the institution (e.g., corrections) supports the attitude or behavior that prisoners are less than human or does anything to damage the respect for the person, they are guilty of scandal. Scandal is defined as those who establish laws or social structures leading to the decline of morals and the corruption of religious practice. And, according to Pope Pius XII, they are also engaging in scandal when "social conditions that, intentionally or not, make Christian conduct and obedience to the Commandments difficult and practically impossible." All of these are issues in the way in which our correctional institutions in America are formed and run. The focus is generally not on the respect for the humanity of the individual imprisoned, but they are rather focused on warehousing and processing prisoners. The aforementioned data on the number of prisoners in America, well over two million, highlights the fact that the system does not and cannot care for the needs of each individual, nor can it show the respect and dignity to each person when faced with such an overburdened system.

On July 9, 2000, John Paul II issued a message for the Jubilee in Prisons, served mass for the inmates of "Regina Caeli" Prison, and delivered a homily regarding the "Day of Jubilee for Prisoners."[11] He spoke to a number of these issues and highlighted the proper Catholic perspective toward prisoners. His words are a clarion call for the American corrections system adopting a Catholic perspective in corrections.

In his homily, Pope John Paul II opened with the passage from Matthew, "I was in prison." The Pope then reflected that

these words of Christ re-echoed for us today in the Gospel . . . they set before our mind's eye the image of Christ actually imprisoned. We can almost see him again on Holy Thursday in Gethsemane: he, innocence personified, surrounded like a criminal by an armed band from the Sanhedrin, captured and brought before the court of Annas and Caiaphas. The long hours of the night follow, as he awaits trial in Pilate's Roman court. The trial takes place on Good Friday morning in the praetorium: Jesus stands before the Roman procurator, who questions him. Over his head hangs the request for the death penalty by the torture of the cross. We next see him tied to a pillar to be scourged. Then he is crowned with thorns . . . *Ecce homo*—"Here is the man." Pilate said these words, counting perhaps on a humane reaction from those present. The answer was: "Crucify him, crucify him!" And when at last they untied his hands, it was to nail them to the cross.[12]

The Pope then explains:

Dear brothers and sisters, Jesus Christ—*the prisoner*—appears before us who are gathered here. 'I was in prison and you came to me.' He is asking to be found in you and in so many other people touched by various forms of human suffering: "As you did it to one of the least of these my brethren, you did it to me." These words . . . invite us to live them as a commitment to the dignity of all people, that dignity which flows from God's love for every human person.

Those in prison look back with regret or remorse to the days when they were free, and they experience their time now as a burden which never seems to pass. In this difficult situation, a strong experience of faith can greatly help in finding the inner balance which every human being needs."

Even time in prison does not escape God's dominion. Public authorities who deprive human beings of their personal freedom as the law requires, bracketing off as it were a longer or shorter part of their life, must realize that they are not masters of the prisoner's time. In the same way, those who are in detention must not live as if their time in prison had been taken from them completely: even time in prison is God's time. As such it needs to be lived to the full; it is a time which needs to be offered to God as an occasion of truth, humility, expiation and even faith.

If the Great Jubilee is a chance for those in prison to reflect upon their situation, the same may be said of civil society as a whole, which every day has to come to grips with the reality of crime. It can be said of the authorities who have to maintain public order and promote the common good, and of those in the legal profession, who ought to reflect on the meaning of inflicting punishment and suggest better proposals for society to aim at.

These issues have been addressed often enough in history, and substantial progress has been made in conforming the penal system both to the dignity of the human person and to the effective maintenance of public order. But the unease and strains felt in the complex world of the administration of justice and, even more, the suffering attached to prison life show that there is still much to be done. We are still a long way from the time when our conscience can be certain of having done everything possible to prevent crime and to control it effectively so that it no longer does harm and, at the same time, to offer to those who commit crimes a way of redeeming themselves and making a positive return to society. If all those in some way involved in the problem tried . . . to develop this line of thought, perhaps humanity as a whole could take a great step forward in creating a more serene and peaceful society.

Imprisonment as punishment is as old as human history. In many countries, prisons are very overcrowded. Some of them are equipped with good facilities, but living conditions in others are very precarious, not to say altogether unworthy of human beings. What is clear to all is that this kind of punishment generally succeeds only in part in addressing the phenomenon of crime. In fact, in some cases detention seems to create more problems than it solves. This must prompt rethinking with a view to some kind of reform.

According to God's plan, all must play their part in helping to build a better society. Obviously, this includes making a great effort in the area of crime prevention. In spite of everything criminal actions are committed. For all to play their part in building the common good they must work, in the measure of their incompetence, to ensure that prisoners have the means to redeem themselves, both as individuals and in their relations with society. Such a process is based on growth in the sense of responsibility. None of this should be considered utopian. Those who are in positions to do so must strive to incorporate these aims in the legal system.

In this regard, therefore, we must hope for a change of attitude, leading to an appropriate adjustment of the juridical system. Clearly this presupposes a strong social consensus and the relative professional skills. A strong appeal of this kind comes from the countless prisons throughout the world, in which millions of our brothers and sisters are held. Above all they call for a review of prison structures, and in some cases a revision of penal law. Regulations contrary to the dignity and fundamental rights of the human person should be definitively abolished from national legislation, as should laws which deny prisoners religious freedom. There will also have to be a review of prison regulations where they give insufficient attention to those who have serious or terminal illnesses. Likewise, institutions offering legal protection to the poor must be further developed.

But even in cases where legislation is satisfactory, much suffering comes to prisoners from other sources. I am referring in particular to the wretched state of some of the places of detention where prisoners are forced to live, and the harassment to which they are sometimes subjected because of ethnic, social, economic, sexual, political, and religious discrimination. Sometimes prisons can become places of violence resembling the places from which the inmates not infrequently come. Clearly this nullifies any attempt to educate through imprisonment.

People in prison also find it difficult to maintain regular contact with their families and loved ones, and structures intended to help those leaving prison in their re-entry into society are often seriously flawed.

To make prison life more human it is more important than ever to take practical steps to enable prisoners as far as possible to engage in work which keeps them from the degrading effects of idleness. They could be given access to a process of training which would facilitate their re-entry into the workforce when they have served their time. Nor should the psychological assistance which can help resolve personality problems be overlooked. Prison should not be a corrupting experience, a place of idleness and even vice, but instead a place of redemption.

To this end, it will certainly help if prisoners are offered the chance to deepen their relationship with God and to become involved in charitable projects and works of solidarity. This will help to speed up their social recovery and to make prisons more livable places.[13]

The Pope highlighted a number of issues of concern, many centered on the respect for the dignity of the humanity of those imprisoned. In particular, he addressed the problem of prison overcrowding, the state of the facilities, and the environment in which prisoners live. Often these three factors go hand and hand to diminish any potential education or rehabilitation of the individual within prison. Corrections must ensure, in cooperation with the courts, that prisons do not become overcrowded, that the facilities are kept in a decent state of repair, and that prison life does not devolve into a socially immoral and violent environment. In fact, the call is for the opposite, and that is an environment where prisoners can be safe and one in which their individual needs for education, counseling, and rehabilitation are met. Still further, the rules, policies, and laws of the prison should not violate the rights of prisoners, nor subject them to scandal. And finally, the Pope rails against the common practice of building large penitentiaries in locations that are far removed from the public and the prisoners families and friends, thus further isolating them from society, an environment into which over 95 percent of prisoners will eventually return. This is not healthy for the prisoner, nor is it healthy for the community into which prisoners subjected to this type of isolation are to be released.

In the late 1960s and early 1970s, there was a series of U.S. Supreme Court decisions that began looking at the rights of prisoners. Prior to the 1960s, the basic doctrine toward prisoners was one of "hands-off" by the state, essentially making the argument that prisoners had no rights. It was the case of *Ruffin v. Commonwealth of Virginia* (1871) that ruled that prisoners were "slaves of the state," which had essentially solidified the concept of no rights for prisoners. This would remain the accepted doctrine for nearly one hundred years until the U.S. Supreme Court issued their decision in the case of *Cooper v. Pate* (1964), which ended the "hands-off" doctrine and allowed prisoners to bring civil action (law suits) against prison authorities when they believed that their rights had been violated. This would open up a series of Supreme Court decisions and placed the issue of prisoners' rights in the forefront of the social justice movement. Recognizing the needs of prisoners, several U.S. Bishops began to address this issue and eventually all of the American Bishops would address this issue.

The United States Catholic Conference of Bishops in 1973 recognized in their statement *The Reform of Correctional Institutions in the 1970s*[14] that rehabilitation, not punishment, should be the primary goal of correction facilities. They noted that "there is an increasing and strongly convincing evidence that a large center of incarceration should not be the major instrument for dealing with convicted offenders" and that "bigger, better, more modern buildings is not the answer."[15] They advocated for smaller, community-based facilities that would try to keep most offenders connected with society, thus avoiding many of the social ills associated with the warehousing of prisoners in large, isolated facilities.

The Bishops realized that many of the solutions for the rehabilitation of inmates lie outside of the prison facility itself. In order to achieve a prisoner's rehabilitation they took a holistic and restorative approach to correctional reform. They argued that victims should be compensated for the injuries they received, that correctional officers should receive a just wage, and that society should be more compassionate in their acceptance of released prisoners back into society. It is only when these reforms are achieved that the prisoner can be truly seen as a human being and treated as one in the likeness of God.

The Bishops outlined twenty-two recommendations for reform in order to achieve this, and, despite the rather dated statement (1973), most of the recommendations remain relevant today:

1) *Correctional institutions whose residents come mainly from urban centers should usually be located near these centers.*

The Bishops raise the issue that too many prisons and jails are built outside of the urban area from which the offenders are derived. This is perhaps more true today than it was in the 1970s, for as we witnessed a prison expansion throughout the 1980s and 1990s, most of the new prisons were built in isolated areas. This makes it difficult for family and friends to visit the prisoners, thus ties to family and friends on the outside get severed and the inmate becomes isolated.

Knowing that over 95 percent of prisoners ultimately get released, this is a dangerous practice.[16]

2) *Staffs should be recruited on the basis of ability, training, and experience without reference to partisan politics.*

This is less of a problem today than it was in the 1970s, and it is less of a problem in prisons than in jails. However, many small jails are run by sheriffs who are elected, and there is room for political corruption to take place.

3) *In developing programs and facilities careful consideration to the varying needs of men and women is important.*

Most prisons and jails have separate facilities, but as more and more women (and children) are being sentenced to prison, this is becoming, once again, a growing concern.[17] However, many of the women sentenced to prison have children and, in some cases, are pregnant, thus making the situation of imprisonment all the more difficult. In addition, women have special medical needs and they often have greater needs for psychiatric services, highlighting the need for special programs and facilities.[18]

4) *Discrimination because of race, religion or national or ethnic background is never tolerable.*

Today, there are more programs in prisons and jails oriented on religion, but problems do still exist where inmates are discriminated against because of their race, ethnicity, and religion. Not to mention that in many cases, the discrimination comes from other inmates. Correctional facilities must always be aware of these issues and take every measure to prevent against such discrimination.

5) *Free exercise of religion should be guaranteed in every institution.*

The activities of such groups as Chuck Colson's Prison Fellowship Ministries[19] have brought to light the rights of prisoners to practice their religion, and many rehabilitation programs have developed around religion. A recent prison was opened in Texas where the entire facility is based on the Christian principles of rehabilitation and church services and prayers are part of the everyday routine. Despite these types of advances, there is still a need for correctional institutions to protect this right.

6) *All residents should be given the regulations of the institutions in writing. They should be advised of their rights and privileges, their responsibilities and obligations, punishments to which they are subject for infractions of regulations and established grievance procedures.*

Today, this has become part of the operational procedures of most prisons, and the American Correctional Association has led the way in promoting model policies and procedures for correctional institutions.[20]

7) *Residents should never be authorized to punish one another.*

Although historically an occasional practice in America's prisons, this is far more rare today. Prison management should, however, continue to maintain strong oversight to ensure that correctional officers adhere to accepted policies and procedures.

8) *All residents should be afforded protection against all assaults, sexual or otherwise, even if this requires a transfer.*

Assaults in prison are known to occur, but most prisoners are not subjected to violent incidents. In fact, the majority of violence in prisons, oddly enough, tends to be found in high-security units, where violence is quite common.[21] However, rates of violence tend to be no higher in prison than they are on the outside, despite having the most violent group—young males—concentrated in one location.

9) *At least elementary and secondary education and vocational training that is truly useful in free society should be provided all residents who wish to take advantage of these opportunities.*

Prisoners today tend to have access to education, but are limited usually to Adult Basic Education (ABE) or a General Education Degree (GED). In fact, in 1995, 46,000 inmates received some level of education with 83 percent of them receiving ABE, 75 percent receiving pre-GED education, and 35 percent enrolled in the GED program.[22] The ability to engage in higher education, however, is typically very limited, and many prisons that had programs of higher education have discontinued them in recent years.

10) *The work to which a resident is assigned should be—and appear to be— worthwhile and compatible with the dignity of a human being.*

Again, the Bishops highlight the dignity of the human being and recognize that work assignments that have no meaning and are useless in terms of their function can have a devastating impact upon a person's dignity. The Bishops also call for a fair wage when prisoners do perform work.

11) *National standards should be adopted and promulgated regarding residents' diets, the lighting and ventilation of their living and work environments, their access to toilet and bathing facilities.*

While national standards were not developed by either Congress or the Department of Justice, they were eventually mandated by various decisions of the United States Supreme Court, which eventually were written into various Department of Corrections policies. However, these standards are often challenged by prison overcrowding and should be safeguarded.

12) *A resident should be free to refuse treatments, aimed at social rehabilitation, whose appropriateness can be called into question by reasonable persons in and outside the institution.*

Again, this has been an area of corrections that has developed since the Bishops wrote their policy statement. Today, through a series of U.S. Supreme Court decisions, prisoners do have the right to refuse not only social rehabilitation programs, but medical treatment as well.[23]

13) *National standards should be adopted and promulgated regarding the residents' right to send and receive mail, censorship of mail, access to printed literature within the institution and from without, and opportunities to listen to the radio and watch television.*

As the past two have developed through U.S. Supreme Court and Court of Appeal decisions, so too has the right to receive mail and other printed literature. These court decisions typically have supported the rights of the prisoners, but as the medium for information changes, so do the cases of civil rights suits. Most recently the issue has revolved around the ability of inmates to receive internet materials.

14) *Authorities should encourage visiting by residents' relatives, friends, and acquaintances.*

In many cases, prison authorities do everything they can to limit contact as these visits create a drain on staffing resources. However, again, this is critical to the social well-being of the prisoner, and it encourages the ties that they have to the outside, keeping those ties strong until they are released. Unfortunately, as in the first recommendation by the Bishops, often it is merely the location of the prison that keeps family and friends from visiting the inmates.

15) *A national committee of lawyers, state and federal legislators, members of correctional staffs, offenders and ex-offenders and other knowledgeable citizens should be assigned the task of establishing a national code of civil rights for the incarcerated and the development of standardized grievance and due-process procedures as well as a bill of rights clearly defining the extent of duties and limits of obligations of the incarcerated.*

This has not been done to date despite several organizations advancing this idea of a prisoner bill of rights. Again, this has largely been left to the courts to decide what rights prisoners have.

16) *National standards should be adopted and promulgated regarding the inspection of correctional institutions.*

The American Correctional Association has developed policies related to correctional inspections[24] and the National Institute of Corrections (NIC), housed within the U.S. Department of Corrections has issued recommended guidelines for the conduct of inspections,[25] but the standards have not been adopted on a national basis to date.

17) *No resident should be detained simply because employment is not available.*

The Bishops have advocated that if employment opportunities are not available for the inmate upon their release, this should not be a justification for retaining the prisoner.

18) *A resident should be informed of the date beyond which further detention demands another intervention of the court.*

While this typically does occur today, it is imperative that prison management attend to the rights of prisoners in regard to their access to the courts.

19) *Parole is a vital function, both for the offender and for society.*

Since the publication of the Bishops' statement, many states, and the federal government, have worked to pass laws that abolish parole. The Bishops see parole not as a means of emptying overcrowded prisons, but rather as a means of providing hope to prisoners that one day they will be released. In addition, it is believed that there is more compliance with prison life if prisoners know that there is the potential they may be released early, on parole, if their behavior is exemplary while in prison. As the old saying states, "hope springs eternal."

20) *Congress should investigate the feasibility of extending the Social Security Act coverage to residents of correctional institutions.*

The Bishops advanced this idea to ensure that prisoners were treated as their fellow citizens and that they too would be eligible for benefits under the OASDI portion of the Social Security Act. In fact, when the Social Security Administration became an independent agency, they promulgated the Prisoner Incentive

Payment Program to pay prisons a fee for providing inmate registries to ensure that inmates were not receiving OASDI payments.

21) *After release, ex-offenders, upon their resumption of life in society, should have their civil rights completely restored.*

The Bishops argued that the reintegration of the offender back into society is important for the offender to move beyond their time imprisoned, as it is important that the community finds ways to receive the individual back into their neighborhoods. The Bishops placed a high priority on the concepts of community-based corrections for achieving this goal.

22) *The use and dissemination of arrest records should be strictly controlled.*

It is here the Bishops voiced concern that information regarding past arrests, where there was no conviction, should be controlled and not available to the public as a means for use as a screening device by employers. Additionally, the employer forms should only ask for legitimate conviction information and not arrest records, as our system is premised on the concept of innocent until proven guilty.

Each of these recommendations remains centered on the humanity of the individual being sent to prison, and they are key to ensuring that prisons treat inmates humanely. While this is critical to adhering to a Catholic perspective on corrections, there is far more to it than ensuring those in prison are treated humanely. Incorporating the concepts of social and community justice into corrections leads to a larger focus than just on prisons and jails. As prisons and jails tend to isolate the individual from society, community-based corrections attempts to bring the offender back into the folds of society. The goal is inclusion, not exclusion. While prison is assuredly one means of punishment, it should be reserved for the serious offender. When possible, alternatives to incarceration should be utilized, and these include many of the community-based corrections mechanisms that are available today.

Community-Corrections

The traditional mechanism for dealing with offenders in America has not always been prisons and jails. Prior to the nineteenth century, offenders were generally punished through various forms of shaming, such as public displays of remorse, locking offenders into the stocks and pillories in the town-square, or through harsher treatments such as public whippings. Jails (spelled "gaols" at the time) were solely a means of pre-trial detention and as a punishment for debtors. Even in the case of the debtor, the individual would be required to work during the day and remain in the gaol at night until the debt was satisfied. It was not until 1790, in Philadelphia's Walnut Street Jail, that jails became a means of punishing offenders. This would give rise to the penitentiary system in the 1820s and 1830s, giving us the most common means of punishment in America—the prison.[26]

In the 1960s, a time period of great social change, there were increasing calls to find alternatives to incarceration. As our society began to rapidly change, the calls for change in penology and our punishment philosophy began to change as well. Under the President's Commission on Law Enforcement and the Administration of Justice, a Corrections Task Force was formed to look at the many issues facing American corrections and to make recommendations for many alternatives.[27] These alternatives to incarceration were intent upon finding ways for offenders to remain in the community, rather than going to prison or jail, and these programs became known as "community-based corrections."

A number of programs were attempted in the late 1960s and 1970s, but crime continued to rise, and the problem remained unabated. In addition, it has been noted that "community corrections in the 1970s were underfunded, understaffed, and poorly administered."[28] In the 1980s, there was a strong movement to decry the past programs and failed attempts at controlling crime, and harsh penalties for various offenses increased, while the use of community-based corrections decreased. As prison and jail populations increased throughout the 1980s, there was a demand for building more prisons, thus rather than drawing upon the concepts of community-based corrections, the emphasis was on incarceration.[29] Despite the growth of what has come to be known as the prison-industrial complex,[30] the building of new prisons and jails could not keep up with the increase in offenders, hence alternative, or intermediate, sanctions needed to be imposed. Community-based corrections became a necessary part of the correctional environment.

Community-based corrections, often simply referred to as community corrections, has been defined as "a nonincarcerative sanction in which offenders serve all or a portion of their sentence in the community."[31] This definition has become the standard type of definition for community-based corrections, which provides a broad category detailing essentially any offender who is not in prison or jail and states that they are under community-based corrections. While this would recognize such programs as half-way houses, drug treatment facilities, and electronic monitoring, it would also incorporate long-standing components of corrections such as probation and parole.

Recognizing this problem of an overly broad definition, other authors have tried to define community-based corrections more succinctly. One written in 1975 by Paul Hahn explains that:

> Community-based corrections is a concept which views the criminal justice system as a whole process, emphasizing due process and the development of service delivery systems at every level, to divert the maximum number of of-

fenders, and which employs a reintegration approach to develop alternatives to incarceration consistent with public safety and local community needs, so that secure facilities can be reduced in size, located close to the offender's community, and utilized only when necessary.[32]

While Hahn's definition is also broad in scope, it does focus primarily on the concepts of diversion and reintegration. Diversion being focused on finding alternatives to sending an offender to jail or prison, while reintegration focuses on bringing those that have been incarcerated back into society. In fact, today, many of the community-based corrections programs are labeled as diversionary because they divert offenders away from prisons and jails. In fact, there are more people in these types of programs today (approximately 6 million), than there are in jails and prisons (approximately 2 million).

Marion highlights a number of advantages to community-based corrections.[33] She explains that these programs help alleviate prison overcrowding by diverting many into community-based probation programs, and allowing others to leave prison early on community-based parole programs. Marion also argues that the cost of monitoring an individual in the community is far less costly than the expense of keeping the offender imprisoned. The third point Marion cites, the fact that socially, for the offender, community-based corrections is a more effective means of keeping the offender's ties to the community through friends and family, rather than isolating them from the community as is typically found in incarceration. She also explains that community-based programs provide more flexibility in sentencing for the judges, thus allowing them to control resources, time, and place of service more effectively and efficiently. In addition, she cites many people's beliefs, and the Bishops would agree, that community-based corrections is far more humane than imprisonment. Moreover, she states that these programs are at least as effective as incarceration when it comes to recidivism rates, and often better. And finally, Marion points out that overall, "when compared to traditional incarceration, alternative sentences are far less destructive to the offender and society."[34]

This is not to say there are not disadvantages to the implementation of community-based corrections programs, for there are many. The first drawback is based upon public perception of the program, and in an environment that mandates punitive measures for its offenders, community-based corrections is often seen as being "soft on crime." In addition, when failures occur in correctional facilities, they tend to be less visible to the public. When they occur in the community-based setting, they tend to be far more visible and can garner more bad press.

Another significant disadvantage to community-based programs, which is largely tied to these first two drawbacks, is the fact that when municipalities, counties, and the states are looking for areas to cut the budget, community-based corrections programs tend to be cut or eliminated. This creates a see-saw effect of creating and abolishing programs, as well as increasing and reducing the funding of many of these programs.

Another drawback to community-based corrections is the fact there is no central advocate or agency that oversees all of the programs. Although we speak of community-based corrections as if it was one concept or one agency, it is in reality a myriad of concepts coupled with a disparate set of agencies, many of which have little communication with one other. Probation, parole, and half-way house programs (all to be discussed below), all may be run by different agencies, with different funding sources, and different goals and objectives, hence this lack of a coordinated effort can lead to inefficiencies, ineffectiveness, and opens up the potential for inequity among those who are enrolled in these types of programs.

Finally, it should be noted that many of these programs are unfavorable to the community, and although the goal is for them to be community-based, the "NIMBY" (Not In My Back Yard) effect occurs, and programs for sex offenders, half-way houses, and homes for the mentally ill find themselves unable to locate in the community setting.

Despite these drawbacks, community-based corrections developed into an integral part of our corrections system by the 1980s. It was about this same time that the concepts of restorative justice were beginning to be introduced into corrections and criminal justice. While restorative justice principles adhere to the community-based approach, what is labeled community-based corrections is not always compatible with restorative justice, hence there has been the need to alter or "revamp"[35] community-based corrections to bring it more into a restorative justice focus.

According to Clear and Cadora,[36] there are five themes that run through community corrections under the community justice concept. These themes highlight how community corrections would differ from community-based corrections. The first focus is on the neighborhood and community. As the neighborhood is the central focus of life, there must be a balance between protecting the neighborhood from further offense, but also incorporating the offender into the neighborhood to keep them integrated into the community. Locking up the offenders, removing them from the community, and severing their ties with family and friends does more harm to the individual and the community in the long run, as the practice of exclusion and isolation often leads to further criminal behavior.

The second focus is on developing partnerships between the community and the criminal justice system. Thus, if the various community agencies can assist the offender, through such things as social services, welfare, and employment, mixed with the criminal justice agencies such as parole and probation services and the local police, these agencies working together can help to improve the offender's situation in the community, but monitor their ability to function in the neighborhood to ensure they contribute in a positive manner to the community.

The third focus is on victims and communities, where the previous two foci, community and partnerships, do not exclude the victim. In addition, the offender making restitution to the victim or the community is an integral part of community corrections. Moreover, the fourth focus is on problem solving, attempting to address the problems that the offender faces in trying to reintegrate into society or for remaining within the community. It is here that the partnerships become imperative for assisting in the identification of the problems the offender and community face, and developing the means to overcome them. Finally, restoration is the ultimate goal for community corrections, restoring the loss not only to the victim, but to the community as well.

There are a number of programs under both community-based corrections and community corrections that can be used to adhere to these five important concepts. The various restorative justice methods previously detailed (See Chapter 5) which included victim-offender mediation, community reparative boards, family group conferencing, and circle sentencing, are all means by which community corrections can be implemented. There are, however, a number of other programs which fall under the community-based corrections label and may be used under the restorative and community justice approach to corrections.

One program that has attempted to move beyond the often very limited probation officer-offender contact is a program known as Intensive Supervised Probation (ISP).[37] In fact, the average probation officer carries a load of 63 cases, and sometimes as high as 150, whereas in ISP, the probation officer will only carry 18, on average.[38] In ISP, the offender will meet with their probation officer three to five times a week, and the probation officer will also make unannounced visits to the offender's home and place of work. In addition, ISP may incorporate community service, impose curfews, and have the offender conduct weekly/monthly drug and alcohol screening tests. While this program was originally developed for high-risk and high-needs offenders, the success of the program has expanded to the inclusion of many other types of offenders or simply drawing participants from a pool of probationers. A recent review of the effectiveness of ISP has found that while ISP does increase probation officer-offender contact, the program does not appear to have any impact on recidivism, and it tends to increase the number of technical violations associated with the ISP program (e.g., curfew violations, etc.).[39]

Another common community-based corrections program is to house offenders in a residential setting, or halfway house, in order to help them transition back into society.[40] The theory is that if the offender can transition more slowly back into the community by having a support system, they are less like to recidivate. Halfway houses are typically found in neighborhoods in a single-family dwelling setting, and they provide a resident staff, counselors, education, employment training, group therapy, and various drug and alcohol treatment programs. The offenders are confined to the house except for engaging in employment, education programs, or treatment and counseling. They have strict curfews and are required to stay in the facility at night and on weekends. Halfway houses have been used for those on parole or those sentenced to probation. They typically are limited in their capacity, with twenty to twenty-five offenders being the maximum number allowed, and the offender will typically stay in the facility for an average of eight to sixteen weeks. Research on the effectiveness of halfway house programs is largely mixed, but the general findings are that they are no more effective in reducing recidivism than other methods for dealing with offenders.[41]

Another community-based corrections program is house arrest and electronic monitoring. The terms "house arrests," "home confinement," and "electronic monitoring," are often used interchangeably; however, it should be noted that the first two are programs, while the latter is a tool used to monitor compliance with the requirements of a sentence. Regardless, all of these are imposed by the court and are often used in conjunction with ISP. In this case, rather than being confined to a halfway house, the offender is confined to their own home.[42] They face the same requirements as in the halfway house where they are limited to leaving only for employment, education, and treatment, and they have strict curfews, unannounced visits and phone calls by their probation officer, and they have to submit to random drug and alcohol tests.

In the case of more serious offenders where surveillance is considered critical, electronic monitoring can occur where the offender must wear an ankle bracelet, and if they attempt to leave the house during a time in which they are not allowed to, the system sends an alert. In addition, computer-assisted checks can make random calls to the offender that they must respond to; otherwise the probation officer is alerted to a possible violation of the offender's parole. The use of electronic monitoring increased dramatically in the 1990s, going from only 2,300 offenders in 1988 to over 95,000 in 1998.[43] There are clearly advantages to this method in that the cost of confinement is significantly reduced over incarceration; it keeps the offender in the community, and in an environment in which they are familiar. The disadvantages, however, are that the offender can become bored confined to their home, they become dependent upon their family and friends for basic needs beyond the house, and the wearing of the ankle bracelet can be humiliating. Although offenders in these programs do tend to have low recidivism rates, it is generally believed that it is because most of those that enter these programs are low-risk offenders to begin with, and when compared with control groups, there is no significant reduction in recidivism.[44]

Another program that has developed over the twentieth century and is typically classified as a community-based corrections program is work release. Since the State of Washington first introduced the program in 1913, correctional facilities have moved toward allowing offenders in the last years of their prison sentences to be released during the day in order that they may engage in legitimate employment outside of the prison.[45] Nearly every state had instituted the use of work release programs by the early 1970s, and it has become a standard program that is aimed at reintegrating the offender back into the community. Research on the State of Washington's work release program has found that very few inmates committed crimes while on work release; however, the recidivism rates for those offenders that participate in the work release program are no different from the general population of released inmates.[46]

Another means of implementing community-based corrections, and one that is predicated on restorative justice principles, is the use of restitution. Restitution is a part of the statutory provisions of all fifty states in the U.S. and it is generally applied as a condition of probation.[47] There have been a number of problems associated with restitution, and they include indigent offenders who cannot raise the money to pay for restitution, the problem of determining how much money is necessary to restore justice, the actual collection of the money, and the use of the money by victims, which in most states, tends to be underutilized. While the public is generally very supportive of restitution programs, the success rate is somewhat limited.[48] Those offenders on probation that do manage to pay their restitution fees do tend to have lower recidivism rates, but that is most likely because they are already well integrated into the community and have the means by which to pay.

Another program that is a combination of both the work release and restitution programs is that of community service. In this case, those offenders on probation are often given the task of serving in some type of community service project as a condition of their probation. The types of projects may include cleaning up and beautifying parks and roadsides of trash, serving meals in a soup kitchen, building or repairing playgrounds, and assisting the poor or homeless. The goal of community service is to keep the offender in the community by having them provide a form of restitution, not necessarily to the victim, but rather to the community at large. Thirty-four states employ community service as a condition of probation, and some states, such as Texas, make it a condition in nearly three-quarters of their probation sentencing.[49] There is generally wide public support for the use of community service as a condition of probation, and generally over half of those sentenced to community service complete their required number of hours before being released.[50]

Another program related to community-based corrections is the employment of Day Reporting Centers. Although widely used in England and throughout Europe, they are only a recent correction option in the United States.[51] This is a nonresidential program that can be used for offenders on probation or parole, who are allowed to remain in the community, but must report to the Day Reporting Center on a daily or weekly basis. The centers are, in a sense, a "one-stop-shop" for all the needs of the offender, ranging from providing information on employment opportunities, career counseling, drug and alcohol counseling, GED classes, and assisting with the application for welfare benefits.[52] At the same time as these centers provide treatment opportunities, they are also providing a form of supervision in order to track the offender while they serve out their probation or parole. As these programs are relatively new, the research is just beginning to paint a picture of their success rate. Most of the studies have found that approximately half of those entering into the Day Reporting Center program will be removed from the program and returned to custody. However, many of the studies have also found evidence that those who are not removed from the program have a slightly lower recidivism rate and tend to go longer without committing an additional offense.[53]

Another form of community-based corrections programs are substance abuse treatment programs. While many of these programs do take place while the offender is incarcerated, many of the programs, like in the Day Reporting Centers, may take place outside of the prison environment. In these cases, the offender is sentenced specifically to a drug or alcohol treatment center, and their attendance in the program is a condition of their probation. In many of these cases, they are coming out of the widely growing number of drug courts in the United States that are handling all cases related to drugs and using drug treatment as a mechanism for probation. There is indeed a growing body of evidence that these programs are successful, and the better, more intense, and longer programs have been found to reduce recidivism by as much as 10 to 20 percentage points.[54]

In addition to all of the programs thus far discussed, there are a number of other programs that are classified under the community-based corrections label, but many tend not to have a truly community-based element and simply fall into the category of "other than prison." A good example of this is the use of boot camps, where offenders are diverted from prison to a military style boot camp that is shorter in duration, but more intense in its treatment of the offenders in the hopes of rehabilitating them along the military model. These boot camps, however, are not community based; they are simply not prison based.

Despite the wide net of programs that fall under the term Community-Based Corrections, there are a number of programs that are aimed at reintegrating the offender into the community by providing treatment and counseling to allow the individual to become a productive member of the community. These types of programs are in keeping with the principles of both community and restorative justice, and under the Catholic perspective of criminal justice should be encouraged. Although not all of these programs have proven to be successful, there are a number that have demonstrated signs of success and should be supported and bolstered to provide a truly community approach to corrections.

Conclusion

Clearly, evangelization, catechesis, and works of mercy are the most merciful and faithful Catholic responses to the problem of fast-rising prison populations. As Pope John Paul II stated in his Jubilee of Prisons message: "The Good

Shepherd is always going in search of the lost sheep, and when he finds them he puts them on his shoulders and brings them back to the flock. Christ is in search of every human being, whatever the situation."[55] There are a number of programs that fall under the concept of community-based corrections that manage to incorporate both the community and restorative justice principles that are in keeping with the Catholic perspective of criminal justice. These programs are critical to adhering to Catholic principles of justice that focus on the needs of the individual and not toward the traditional correctional mechanism of warehousing offenders. As the Bishops so clearly stated in their statement on *Responsibility, Rehabilitation and Restoration:* "We call upon government to redirect the vast amount of public resources away from building more and more prisons and toward better and more effective programs aimed at crime prevention, rehabilitation, education efforts, substance abuse treatment, and programs of probation, parole, and reintegration."[56] Many of the community-based corrections programs now available reflect the emphasis of the Bishops and should be bolstered to more truly reflect a Catholic perspective on crime and criminal justice.

Notes

1. Willard M. Oliver, "Prisons are Golden Opportunities for the Gospel," *National Catholic Register* (2002).

2. James Austin and John Irwin, *It's About Time: America's Imprisonment Binge,* 3rd ed. (Belmont, CA: Wadsworth, 2001).

3. Matthew 25:36 (*The New American Bible*).

4. Catholic Church, *Catechism of the Catholic Church,* 2nd ed. (Washington, D.C.: United States Catholic Conference, Inc., 1997), no. 2447.

5. United States Conference of Catholic Bishops, *Responsibility, Rehabilitation, and Restoration: A Catholic Perspective on Crime and Criminal Justice* (Washington, D.C.: United States Catholic Conference, Inc., 2000).

6. John Paul II, "Message of His Holiness John Paul II for the Jubilee in Prisons," (2000) http://www.vatican.va

7. L. Russell, "Making Coverts in Prisons," *Homilectic and Pastoral Review* (January 1996): 20-22.

8. Paige M. Harrison and Allen J. Beck, "Prison and Jail Inmates at Midyear 2004," *Bureau of Justice Statistics Bulletin* (Washington, D.C.: U.S. Bureau of Justice Statistics, 2005).

9. Matthew 25:31-40 (*The New American Bible*).

10. Catholic Church, *Catechism of the Catholic Church,* 2nd ed. (Washington, D.C.: United States Catholic Conference, Inc., 1997), No. 2284-2287.

11. John Paul II, "Message of His Holiness John Paul II for the Jubilee in Prisons," (2000) http://www.vatican.va

12. John Paul II, "Message of His Holiness John Paul II for the Jubilee in Prisons," (2000) http://www.vatican.va

13. John Paul II, "Message of His Holiness John Paul II for the Jubilee in Prisons,"

(2000) http://www.vatican.va

14. United States Catholic Conference, *The Reform of Correctional Institutions in the 1970s* (Washington, D.C.: U.S. Catholic Conference, 1973).

15. United States Catholic Conference, *The Reform of Correctional Institutions in the 1970s* (Washington, D.C.: U.S. Catholic Conference, 1973).

16. James Austin and John Irwin, *It's About Time: America's Imprisonment Binge*, 3rd ed. (Belmont, CA: Wadsworth, 2001).

17. James Austin and John Irwin, *It's About Time: America's Imprisonment Binge*, 3rd ed. (Belmont, CA: Wadsworth, 2001).

18. James Austin and John Irwin, *It's About Time: America's Imprisonment Binge*, 3rd ed. (Belmont, CA: Wadsworth, 2001).

19. See the Homepage of the Prison Fellowship Ministries at www.pfm.org

20. See the Homepage of the American Correctional Association at http://www.aca.org/

21. James Austin and John Irwin, *It's About Time: America's Imprisonment Binge*, 3rd ed. (Belmont, CA: Wadsworth, 2001).

22. James Austin and John Irwin, *It's About Time: America's Imprisonment Binge*, 3rd ed. (Belmont, CA: Wadsworth, 2001).

23. Rudolph Alexander, Jr., "The United States Supreme Court And An Inmate's Right To Refuse Mental Health Treatment," *Criminal Justice Policy Review* 5, no.3 (1991): 225-240; Daniel P. Wilansky, "Recent Developments in Health Law. Civil Rights: Prisoners' Right to Treatment Information under Pabon v. Wright1," *The Journal of Law, Medicine & Ethics* 34, no. 4 (2006): 831-832.

24. See the American Correctional Association at http://www.aca.org/standards/

25. See the Homepage of the National Institute of Corrections at http://www.nicic.org/

26. Willard M. Oliver and James F. Hilgenberg, Jr., *A History of Crime and Criminal Justice in America* (Boston: Allyn & Bacon, 2006).

27. Nancy E. Marion, *Criminal Justice in America: The Politics Behind the System* (Durham, NC: Carolina Academic Press, 2002).

28. Ruth Ann Strickland, *Restorative Justice* (New York: Peter Lang, 2004), 112.

29. Nancy E. Marion, *Criminal Justice in America: The Politics Behind the System* (Durham, NC: Carolina Academic Press, 2002); Willard M. Oliver and James F. Hilgenberg, Jr., *A History of Crime and Criminal Justice in America* (Boston: Allyn & Bacon, 2006).

30. Eric Schlosser, "The Prison-Industrial Complex," *The Atlantic Monthly* (April 1998): 51-57.

31. Leanne Fiftal Alarid, Paul Cromwell, and Rolando V. Del Carmen, *Community-Based Corrections*, 7th ed. (Belmont, CA: Thomson Wadsworth, 2008), 9.

32. See Paul H. Hahn, *Emerging Criminal Justice: Three Pillars for a Proactive Justice System* (Thousand Oaks, CA: SAGE Publications, 1998), 97-98.

33. Nancy E. Marion, *Criminal Justice in America: The Politics Behind the System* (Durham, NC: Carolina Academic Press, 2002).

34. Nancy E. Marion, *Criminal Justice in America: The Politics Behind the System* (Durham, NC: Carolina Academic Press, 2002), 366.

35. Ruth Ann Strickland, *Restorative Justice* (New York: Peter Lang, 2004), 113.

36. Todd R. Clear and Eric Cadora, *Community Justice* (Belmont, CA: Thomson

Wadsworth, 2003).

37. Leanne Fiftal Alarid, Paul Cromwell, and Rolando V. Del Carmen, *Community-Based Corrections,* 7th ed. (Belmont, CA: Thomson Wadsworth, 2008).

38. Camille Graham Camp, George M. Camp, and Bob May, *The 2002 Corrections Yearbook: Adult Corrections* (Middletown, CT: Criminal Justice Institute, Inc., 2003).

39. Lawrence W. Sherman, et. al., *Preventing Crime: What Works, What Doesn't, What's Promising* (Washington, D.C.: U.S Department of Justice, 1997).

40. Nancy E. Marion, *Criminal Justice in America: The Politics Behind the System* (Durham, NC: Carolina Academic Press, 2002).

41. Leanne Fiftal Alarid, Paul Cromwell, and Rolando V. Del Carmen, *Community-Based Corrections,* 7th ed. (Belmont, CA: Thomson Wadsworth, 2008).

42. Nancy E. Marion, *Criminal Justice in America: The Politics Behind the System* (Durham, NC: Carolina Academic Press, 2002).

43. Ruth Ann Strickland, *Restorative Justice* (New York: Peter Lang, 2004).

44. Lawrence W. Sherman, et. al., *Preventing Crime: What Works, What Doesn't, What's Promising* (Washington, D.C.: U.S Department of Justice, 1997).

45. Leanne Fiftal Alarid, Paul Cromwell, and Rolando V. Del Carmen, *Community-Based Corrections,* 7th ed. (Belmont, CA: Thomson Wadsworth, 2008).

46. Susan Turner and Joan Petersilia, "Work Release in Washington: Effects on Recidivism and Corrections Costs," *The Prison Journal* 76 (June 1996): 138-164.

47. Leanne Fiftal Alarid, Paul Cromwell, and Rolando V. Del Carmen, *Community-Based Corrections,* 7th ed. (Belmont, CA: Thomson Wadsworth, 2008).

48. Burt Galaway, "Restitution as Innovation or Unfilled Promises?" in *Towards a Critical Criminology,* ed. Ezzat A. Fattah (New York: St. Martin's Press, 1992), 347-371.

49. Leanne Fiftal Alarid, Paul Cromwell, and Rolando V. Del Carmen, *Community-Based Corrections,* 7th ed. (Belmont, CA: Thomson Wadsworth, 2008).

50. Anderson, David C. Anderson, *Sensible Justice: Alternatives to Prison* (New York: New Press, 1998).

51. Leanne Fiftal Alarid, Paul Cromwell, and Rolando V. Del Carmen, *Community-Based Corrections,* 7th ed. (Belmont, CA: Thomson Wadsworth, 2008).

52. Leanne Fiftal Alarid, Paul Cromwell, and Rolando V. Del Carmen, *Community-Based Corrections,* 7th ed. (Belmont, CA: Thomson Wadsworth, 2008).

53. Leanne Fiftal Alarid, Paul Cromwell, and Rolando V. Del Carmen, *Community-Based Corrections,* 7th ed. (Belmont, CA: Thomson Wadsworth, 2008); Lawrence W. Sherman, et. al., *Preventing Crime: What Works, What Doesn't, What's Promising* (Washington, D.C.: U.S Department of Justice, 1997).

54. Lawrence W. Sherman, et. al., *Preventing Crime: What Works, What Doesn't, What's Promising* (Washington, D.C.: U.S Department of Justice, 1997).

55. John Paul II, "Message of His Holiness John Paul II for the Jubilee in Prisons," (2000) http://www.vatican.va

56. United States Conference of Catholic Bishops, *Responsibility, Rehabilitation, and Restoration: A Catholic Perspective on Crime and Criminal Justice* (Washington, D.C.: United States Catholic Conference, Inc., 2000), 39.

Part Three

Criminal Justice Issues

Chapter 7

The Death Penalty

"The new evangelization calls for followers of Christ who are unconditionally pro-life; who will proclaim, celebrate, and serve the Gospel of life in every situation. A sign of hope is the increasing recognition that the dignity of human life must never be taken away, even in the case of someone who has done great evil. Modern society has the means of protecting itself, without definitively denying criminals the chance to reform. I renew the appeal I made most recently at Christmas for a consensus to end the death penalty, which is both cruel and unnecessary."

-Pope John Paul II, January 27, 1999-

Introduction

The use of the death penalty in America continues to surface as a social issue that divides Americans. If you ask most Americans for their views on the death penalty you generally see a division of seventy percent favoring the death penalty, while 30 percent are against.[1] If you ask a Catholic for their views on the death penalty, their answers tend to be nearly identical to the national response of most Americans. There are those Catholics who are adamantly opposed to executions and often cite the Fifth Commandment, "though shalt not kill." There are those Catholics that are defiantly in favor of executions and the state's right to impose the death penalty on those convicted of murder and they often cite the biblical reference to "an eye for an eye and a tooth for a tooth." Yet, there is an assumption that this should not be the case, if there is a Catholic social doctrine toward the death penalty. Regardless of what that doctrine is, whether pro- or anti-death penalty, one would expect some deviation between a national response in favoring the death penalty and a Catholic response. According to public opinion polls, however, there is no discernible difference.

185

Public opinion of the death penalty, overall, was rather evenly split in the 1950s and did not begin to rise until the early 1960s and 1970s, corresponding closely with a rise in crime rates across the United States.[2] The average response to the survey question, "do you favor or oppose the death penalty for persons convicted of murder," in the 1970s, had risen to 60 percent of all Americans responding they favored the death penalty. This rose again in the 1980s and early 1990s, to more than 70 percent of Americans voicing they favored the death penalty with 1985 being the peak year when a record 76 percent of Americans voiced support. More recently, beginning in the mid-1990s, the percentages have begun to decline from a low 70 percent down to the mid-60 percentile.

In looking at the differences between the national opinion of the death penalty with Catholic opinion, from the early 1960s to 2002, the largest variation between these categories has only been four percent in the years 1980 (67 percent versus 71 percent) and 1993 (72 percent versus 68 percent).[3] Overall, however, throughout this time period the national response and the Catholic response have been nearly identical. And just as the national response since the mid-1990s has dropped some, so too has the Catholic response. For example, a public opinion poll in 2002, reported that 66 percent of all Americans reported favoring the death penalty, while 68 percent of Catholics reported the same.[4] There simply appears to be no differences between how the American public and American Catholics perceive the death penalty. Although some have indicated there is a new trend at work since the mid-1990s, that Catholic opposition to the death penalty has increased at a faster rate than for the general population,[5] statistically this increase has kept pace with the national opposition as well.

In light of the similarities, one should question if the theology of Catholic doctrine regarding the death penalty is highly related to the attitudes of most Americans. In the case of the Catholic response to the survey question, it would appear that these two are in sync with one another, yet by simply listening to Pope John Paul II's statement at the beginning of this chapter it begins to raise doubts. In fact, when asking Catholics what the Church's teaching on the death penalty actually is, one may find answers at both extremes, as well as everywhere in-between. In order then to fully understand the death penalty from a Catholic perspective, one must understand the use of the death penalty in America, the secular understanding and debate over the death penalty, and, most obviously, the Catholic social teaching on the death penalty.

Therefore, this chapter will provide a brief historical sketch of the death penalty and will then discuss the contemporary application of the death penalty today. It will then discuss the myriad of issues revolving around the death penalty from a purely secular standpoint. The chapter will then shift its focus to Catholic doctrine on the death penalty and the current theological debate as it exists within the Catholic Church today. Finally, the chapter will conclude with a summary of the death penalty from a Catholic perspective.

History of the Death Penalty

The first known death penalty law dates back to the Code of King Hammurabi from the year 1900 B.C.[6] Hammurabi was the ruler of Mesopotamia which was located in modern day Iraq. Hammurabi, having received the law from the "gods," published them in the sandstone pillars in the central temple which codified the death penalty for 25 specific crimes, such as stealing the property of others, runaway slaves, and defacing a religious temple. In 1400 B.C. the Hittite Code, which was similar to the Code of Hammurabi, also had a number of crimes punishable by death. The death penalty was also codified by the Greeks in the Law of Draco (from which we derive the term "Draconian law") in the Seventh Century. Because the only punishment was death in the Law of Draco, the codes were later refined in the Athenian Code of 403/404 B.C.[7] Finally, before the birth of Christ, history shows that the Romans, under the Roman Twelve Tables, had codified the death penalty for a number of crimes such as judges receiving bribes or treason. The means of execution for these crimes depended upon the code, but most of the death sentences were "carried out by such means as crucifixion, drowning, beating to death, burning alive, and impalement."[8]

Clearly the most renowned use of the death penalty came in the year A.D. 30 with the crucifixion of Jesus Christ. The justification for the trial and execution of Jesus came from a series of historical developments that created a unique situation between the Roman rulers and the Jewish leaders. In 63 B.C., the Roman General Pompey captured Jerusalem and ended independent rule of the Jews. Roman law became the law of the land with a Roman Prefect placed in charge to maintain order. Rome appointed the local high priest, and his council of priests, the Sanhedrin, was allowed to oversee their religious laws, but they were not allowed to oversee any form of criminal or political law. When Jesus came to Jerusalem for the feast of the Passover in A.D. 30, the high priest was Caiaphas and the Roman Prefect was Pontius Pilate.

What brought Jesus to the attention of the Sanhedrin and the high priest Caiaphas was his teachings and statements that he was the "Son of Man" and that he could forgive sins in the name of the Father. What most likely brought him to the attention of the Romans was his entry into the Temple where he cried out, "My house shall be a house of prayer, but you are making it a den of thieves."[9] When Jesus overturned the tables of the money-changers, he threatened the order of Jerusalem, thus committing not only a "crime" against the Jewish religion, but also against Roman law.[10] This would lead to the arrest of Jesus in the garden of Gethsemane. Guards dispatched by Caiaphas and aided by Judas arrested Jesus and brought him before the Sanhedrin for questioning. Jesus was asked a number of questions, but ultimately he was asked if he was in fact the Messiah, and he answered, "I am."[11] This was considered blasphemy by Jewish law and deserving of the death penalty, however because Roman law prevented executions by the religious, Jesus was turned over to Pontius Pilate.

Pilate clearly did not want the trial of Jesus to fall into his lap, for his only concern was to maintain order in Jerusalem. Pilate spoke to the crowds that had gathered and attempted to dismiss the case. The response by the crowd was for the death penalty. Pilate attempted to use a local custom of releasing a prisoner on the feast of the Passover and he offered to release either Jesus or Barabbas. Barabbas was a local dissident who had attempted to riot against the local order. The crowd demanded that Barabbas be released, thus tying Pilate's hands to order the execution of Jesus. Stating that he found no case against Jesus, but hoping to maintain order in Jerusalem, he ordered Jesus to be turned over to the Roman guard for execution. Jesus was then scourged, made to carry the cross he would die on, and was executed by crucifixion in a place called Golgotha, just outside of the city walls of Jerusalem. This historical use of the death penalty, along with the resurrection of Jesus, would give rise to the largest religion in history, Christianity.

Despite the execution of Jesus Christ, the death penalty remained a common punishment for a variety of crimes, although the use of crucifixion as a means of execution would lessen in frequency. Death by hanging would become the common method of execution throughout the western world. Although protections against government tyranny would begin to spread throughout Europe with the passage of the Magna Carta in 1215 A.D., executions as a punishment for crimes continued to be common, even in England, which was one of the more advanced countries legally. However, beginning in the late 1600s and continuing through the eighteenth century, England, and especially London, began experiencing a rising problem with crime. England at the beginning of the 1600s had approximately 50 crimes that could result in the death penalty, but as crime continued to rise, they attempted to legislate their way out of the problem, and the number of crimes rose to 222 by the mid-1700s and more than 350 by the time America declared its independence.[12] These crimes included such offenses as treason, murder, manslaughter, rape, robbery, burglary, arson, counterfeiting, theft, cutting down a tree, begging, and robbing a rabbit warren.[13] And, because the American colonies were in fact part of England, the Colonial settlers were supposed to adhere to English law.

The use of the death penalty in America was initially a transplant of English practices to the new world. The first known execution came in the Jamestown Colony just one year after it was established when George Kendall was executed for theft and spying for Spain.[14] Although all of the colonies were supposed to follow English Common law, many attempted to expand their legal code by either enhancing the number of crimes resulting in the death penalty, such as Virginia Governor Sir Thomas Dale in his *Divine, Moral, and Martial Laws,* which listed the death penalty for crimes ranging from adultery to breaking the Sabbath; or by attempting to reduce the number of crimes resulting in the death penalty, such as William Penn's "Great Act," which limited the use of the death penalty to only two crimes: murder and treason (although this limitation was undone in the early 1700s).[15] Despite the wide variety of laws passed in the Colonies, by the time America declared its independence from England, the Colonies had greatly reduced the number of crimes resulting in the death penalty, or they simply refused to enforce the laws as England had attempted to do. One explanation for this refusal to apply the death penalty is that "before the late Eighteenth Century Americans tended to understand criminals as people like themselves,"[16] and were much less likely to impose a death sentence. As America began to separate religion from the state and the government in the late 1700s, it has been argued that American views toward criminals became more hardened and they were seen as alien to the rest of society, so the death sentence was more easily imposed.[17]

As the Colonies became states and America moved into the nineteenth century, the use of the death penalty continued to be a common punishment for more serious crimes, but many states began to curtail its use.[18] The first states to move executions from the public forum to behind prison walls were Connecticut (1830), Pennsylvania (1834), and New York (1835), primarily as a result of their building the earliest penitentiary systems in the United States.[19] Other means of making the death penalty more palatable during this time period included passing laws that made the death penalty a discretionary sentence, rather than a mandatory one, and making executions more humane by switching to the "drop method" which moved death by hanging from one of suffocation over a period of several minutes to near-instantaneous death by snapping the neck using a drop-door platform.[20] In addition, the first state to abolish the death penalty for all crimes except treason and murder would be Michigan in 1846, and later Rhode Island (1852) and Wisconsin (1853) would abolish it for all crimes.[21] Despite these efforts by the abolitionist movement, their real success would not come until after the Civil War, and then it tended to come in waves.

The execution of William Kemmler in 1890, marked the first use of the electric chair in the United States, and very quickly it spread as a means of making executions more "humane."[22] In addition, during this time period a number of states began abolishing the death penalty only to see it reinstated several years later. Examples include Colorado (1897 abolished/1901 reinstated), Iowa (1872/1878), and Maine (1876/1883).[23] This wave of abolitionism would be followed by a similar wave which came in the lead up to World War I during the "Progressive Era," and would see repeals follow in the wake of the War. Examples here include Arizona (1916 abolished/1918 reinstated), Missouri (1917/1919), Oregon (1914/1920), and Washington (1913/1919).[24] As America entered into the decade of the 1920s it would see the use of the death penalty rise and in the following decade it would reach its peak with an average of nearly 200 executions per year in the mid-1930s.[25]

In the post World War II era, America would actually witness the opposite

189

trend as seen in the aftermath of World War I in that public sentiment toward the death penalty and its actual usage began to drop off precipitously. Perhaps the most dramatic evidence is that while "there were 1,289 executions in the 1940s, there were only 715 in the 1950s, and the number fell even further, to only 191, from 1960 to 1976."[26] In addition, a number of states began to abolish the death penalty, including Oregon (1964), New York (1965), Vermont (1965), West Virginia (1965), and New Mexico (1969).[27] What brought about this change was not only decreased support for the death penalty among Americans, but also a series of Supreme Court cases that raised public awareness about the death penalty process.

The first of these cases was *U.S. v. Jackson* (1968)[28] which ruled that the federal provision that only a jury could recommend the death penalty was unconstitutional because it forced defendants to waive their right to a jury trial to avoid execution. Another 1968 case, *Witherspoon v. Illinois,*[29] held that a juror's reservations about the death penalty were not sufficient grounds to prevent the individual from serving. The Court ruled that any reservation would have to prevent the individual from making an impartial decision. These and other cases, however, were only the forerunners to the landmark case of *Furman v. Georgia* (1972),[30] when the Supreme Court ruled that capital punishment, as it was administered at that time, was "arbitrary and capricious" and could result in "cruel and unusual" punishment in violation of the eighth Amendment.[31] As a result, the Supreme Court in a 5 to 4 vote, with 9 separate opinions, commuted the sentences of 629 death row inmates and placed a moratorium on the use of the death penalty in the United States until a system could be established that would avoid the arbitrary sentencing of the past. It would be four more years before the moratorium was lifted and another year before an execution was conducted in America.

Contemporary Application of the Death Penalty

The departure point for the contemporary understanding of the death penalty is generally considered to be the U.S. Supreme Court decision of *Gregg v. Georgia* (1976),[32] which ruled that the revised procedures for the death penalty in Georgia, Florida, and Texas, met the challenges of the *Furman* decision and were once again considered constitutional.[33] This decision resulted in 34 states adopting new legislation similar to the Georgia method for death penalty procedures which included a bifurcated trial where guilt is first determined and, upon a finding of "guilty," the jury deliberates between execution or life imprisonment.[34] In addition, sentencing guidelines for both the judge and the jury were established in an effort to ensure uniformity in the death penalty process. Moreover, the system of automatic appellate review was established as a safeguard over the initial conviction and sentencing. And, finally, the system of proportionality review was established as a means for states to identify and eliminate any sentencing disparities that may arise regarding race or ethnicity. It should be noted that the Supreme Court did not mandate that all of these reforms be adopted, but as the three states, Georgia, Florida, and Texas, had passed constitutional muster, it made sense for other states to simply emulate their death penalty procedures, rather than attempt something different that could potentially open them up to a constitutional challenge.[35]

The first execution to take place after the moratorium was lifted was in Utah, when Gary Gilmore was executed by firing squad on January 17, 1977. The reason the execution proceeded so quickly in the wake of the *Gregg* decision was for the fact Gilmore waived his right to an automatic appeal and did not challenge his execution. However, because all of the states incorporated the automatic appeal's procedure in their death penalty laws, most states were not so quick to return to the conduct of executions. There were no executions in 1978, two in 1979, none in 1980, and only one in 1981.[36] It wasn't until 1983 and 1984 that the number of executions would begin to rise again in America with five and twenty-one executions respectively. Since then, there has been a continual rise in the number of executions in America with the peak year of 1999, observing 98 executions. Although the number of executions in the 1990s was the highest in the past fifty-year period (1950-1999), they were only half of the number for the previous fifty-year period (1900-1949).[37]

Today there are 38 states with the death penalty, and both the federal government and the United States military maintain death penalty laws.[38] The majority of the states tend to reserve capital punishment for capital offenses or what is often referred to as "first degree murder." Many states also include statutes that authorize the death penalty for rape with aggravating circumstances (Kentucky), capital drug trafficking (Florida), or aircraft hijacking (Georgia). The federal government has statutes authorizing the death penalty for murder associated with such things as kidnapping, bank-robberies, or criminal enterprise. In addition, they maintain statutes authorizing executions in three non-homicide crimes: espionage, treason, and trafficking in large quantities of drugs.

Since the reinstatement of the death penalty in 1976 there have been 1,056 executions in the United States.[39] In 2005, there were 60 executions, and as of November 14, 2006, there have been 52 executions in 2006.[40] The majority of the death penalty states have executed less than ten offenders since 1976, with states such as Colorado, Idaho, and Wyoming having only executed one individual. In addition, five states have not executed a single person since the reinstatement of the death penalty, despite maintaining death penalty laws on the books. Another way of looking at the death penalty in the United States is by region. What is most interesting here is that the majority of executions have occurred in the South (864), with the Midwest (122) and the West (66) showing far fewer, and the Northeast (4) almost none.[41] The top five states, all of which are largely located in the South, are Texas (379), Virginia (98), Oklahoma (83),

Missouri (66), and Florida (63). In fact, if one were to combine the number of executions in Texas and Virginia, these two states account for 477 executions or nearly half of all executions since the *Gregg* decision. If one were to isolate Texas, with its 379 executions, they account for 35 percent of the same total.[42] And, still further, within Texas, only a handful of jurisdictions account for most of the 379 executions: Harris County (Houston) with 67, Dallas with 26, Fort Worth with 22, and San Antonio with 18. [43] Taken together, these four jurisdictions account for 42 percent of all Texas executions or 15 percent of all executions in the United States since 1976.

The number of executions, while informative, tends to mask the larger number of current death row inmates. As of July 1, 2006, there were 3,366 inmates on death row awaiting execution. The majority of these inmates come from three states: California (657), Texas (401), and Florida (396).[44] The majority of states tend to have less than 50 inmates on death-row, with the federal government having 43 and the U.S. military nine. The racial breakdown of those on death-row is 45 percent White (1,525), 41 percent Black (1,407), 10 percent Hispanic (356), and two percent "other" (78). The breakdown for those actually executed since the *Gregg* decision is 57 percent White, 34 percent Black, six percent Hispanic, and two percent "other."[45] While the breakdown between those on death-row and those executed appear to be fairly consistent, many point to the racial breakdown of victims in murder cases and particularly the race of the victim for those actually executed. The race of all murder victims from 1977 to 2006 consisted of 79 percent White and 14 percent Black.[46] The method for execution since the reinstatement of the death penalty has largely been that of death by lethal injection.[47] All of the states that have death penalty legislation, except Nebraska, as well as the federal government and the U.S. military, maintain death by lethal injection as their primary means of execution. Ten states still maintain laws that authorize death by electrocution, five states still authorize the gas chamber, three authorize firing squad (Idaho, Oklahoma, and Utah) and two authorize executions by hanging (New Hampshire and Washington).[48] Recent legislation has also seen some changes in state laws regarding the death penalty, and they include Alabama's move away from mandatory electrocution to the option of lethal injection or electrocution (July 2002), and Georgia recently ruled that the use of the electric chair was "cruel and unusual" and thus unconstitutional according to the Georgia State Constitution (October 2001).[49]

One more reality of the death penalty which has become more evident since the *Gregg* decision is the fact the death penalty process and the executions themselves are not perfect. Because of advancements in technology during the 1980s, DNA evidence has come to be used in more and more cases to help determine whether those inmates serving on death-row committed their crimes or not. Since 1976, 123 people in 25 different states have been released from death-row because DNA evidence has proven they could not have committed the crime. [50] Although the majority of these 25 states have released less than five death-row inmates, four states have accounted for nearly half of the total, and they are Florida (21), Illinois (18), Louisiana (8), and Texas (8).[51] In addition, despite the lack of any proof that an innocent person has been executed to date, the fact that 123 people have been released from death row because evidence proved them innocent is a disturbing fact. Finally, one other disturbing fact is that despite contemporary belief that executions in the United States are simple and fast, there have been at least 37 "botched" executions since the *Gregg* decision which have included declarations of death when the person was still alive, lethal injections that did not render the individual unconscious, and difficulty in finding a vein in lethal injections due to past drug use. [52]

Secular Debate over the Death Penalty

There is an enormous debate over the death penalty in the secular world. Many of the topics previously discussed have raised a number of these issues, but even the so-called "facts" can be very misleading. For instance, it was stated that the differences between Americans' support of the death penalty and Catholic support is negligible and that these figures since the early 1980s have run at approximately 75 percent of both favoring the death penalty for those convicted of murder.[53] This would seem to suggest that there is little debate in the venue of public opinion. However, several studies have demonstrated that when respondents are given the opportunity to choose between the death penalty and life in prison without the chance of parole (LWOP), the number of those supporting the death penalty tends to drop below 50 percent.[54] This means that when offered a choice, more than 20 percent of respondents back away from the death penalty. One study concluded that very few Americans overwhelmingly support the death penalty, but that most simply accept it as part of the criminal justice system.[55]

Another aspect of the death penalty previously discussed is the imbalanced distribution of its application. As previously stated, 12 states and the District of Columbia currently do not have death penalty statutes. In addition, because there are five states that haven't executed anyone since the *Gregg* decision and 14 states have executed less than five inmates, this leaves only nineteen states that have actively used the death sentence. Finally, because the majority of these states tend to be in the South with the states of Texas, Virginia, Oklahoma, Missouri, and Florida, accounting for the majority of executions,[56] these facts raise a fundamental question. If the death penalty is so well supported in America, why is it relegated to only a handful of states located in one particular region? It would seem that this disparity between states and their use of the death penalty is in itself part of the larger debate over the death penalty.

Another issue that continues to raise the debate is the fact that DNA evidence has exonerated 123 people since 1973 who were on death row awaiting execution. In each of these cases, faulty investigations and circumstantial evidence led to their convictions, but DNA evidence, which did not become widely available until the 1990s, has provided proof that these individuals did not commit the crime. This has raised increased awareness in the problems with the death penalty process and has increased the debate over this ultimate sanction. Another current issue has centered on those individuals that were either mentally ill or mentally incompetent when they committed their crimes. In fact, the controversy found its way to the United States Supreme Court in the case of *Atkins v. United States* (2002), in which the Court ruled that it is a violation of the Eighth Amendment ban on cruel and unusual punishment to execute death row inmates who are mentally retarded. However, because the Supreme Court did not define mental retardation, the controversy over this issue has moved to one of definition: who is considered to be "mentally retarded."

Another issue that continues to be debated revolves around the issue of social standing. Although the *Furman* decision was based on racial discrimination, and the *Gregg* decision stated that the new death penalty process was impartial, the problem of race continues to be raised in regard to the death penalty. Again, the data has shown that 80 percent of the capital cases involve a white victim, while only 50 percent of all murders involve white victims[57] and that for all of the executions involving interracial murders since *Gregg*, 213 of them have consisted of a black defendant with a white victim and only 15 have been white defendants and blacks victims,[58] which at least raises such questions over the disparity of the death penalty sentence. Going beyond simply race, it has also been pointed out by many that all of the people executed since *Gregg* have been from the lower class and that although women account for 15 percent of the annual murders, they account for less than 1 percent of the annual executions,[59] again raising some issues about the equity of the death penalty.

Perhaps the most controversial of the issues regarding the death penalty is whether or not it serves as a deterrent. An extensive debate over this topic was opened up in 1975, when economist Isaac Ehrlich published a study that stated executions between 1930 and 1969 deterred between seven and eight future murders.[60] When several follow-up studies were conducted by various researchers and they removed the turbulent 1960s from his analysis, Ehrlich's explanatory factors no longer had any explanatory value.[61] Since then, the debate has led to numerous studies attempting to determine if the death penalty has a deterrent effect on other criminals, and the evidence has overwhelmingly offered no support.[62] As one author has summarized, "it does not matter if one compares states with and without the death penalty, nations with and without the death penalty, or if one studies jurisdictions before and after executions—all methods show *no valid empirical evidence* that the death penalty deters murders."[63]

Another of the secular debates revolves around the cost of the death penalty. Many argue that by executing an offender it will save the state money because of the fact he is no longer sitting on death row costing the state money year after year. The fact of the matter is, because of the amount of expenditures in a death penalty case, on average it costs the state between two and three million dollars. Taking the highest estimate of the cost to maintain one prisoner for one year as $30,000 per year, and assuming the murder was committed by the offender at age 18 and he will live to the average age of 74, that figure comes to approximately 1.7 million dollars, still well short of the 2-3 million dollars it costs to sentence an offender to death. And, because the *Gregg* decision established mandatory appeals of all death penalty cases, the costs often rise in excess of 40 million dollars. The reality over this debate is that, despite conventional wisdom to the contrary, the death penalty process is very expensive.[64]

Finally, it has been said that the greatest argument for support of the death penalty in this debate comes in the form of both retribution and incapacitation. The concept of retribution is simply a means of restoring justice for an offense by giving the offender their "just deserts." Because the reasoning for this is largely one of morality (i.e., one finds it either morally acceptable or morally unacceptable) this will largely be discussed below. The other argument in favor of the death penalty is that by incapacitating the offender through execution, he or she will never be able to commit future crimes. The support for this appears sound, for a study by James W. Marquart found that for those inmates released from death row, for various reasons such as commutations, judicial reversals, or dismissals, nearly 25 percent went on to commit violent crimes.[65] However, what many from the anti-death penalty side argue is that simply sentencing murderers to life in prison without the chance of parole would achieve the same goal of incapacitation without resorting to executions. The counter to this, and a belief held by many people, is that if criminals were sentenced to LWOP, there is always the chance they may be given parole at some point in their life, even if it is in their seventies or eighties, and this is simply unacceptable.

Catholic Doctrine on the Death Penalty

The Bible as a source of understanding about the death penalty is not necessarily a clearly-defined source. Those who favor the death penalty often cite the passage "an eye for an eye," while those who are against the death penalty often cite the Fifth Commandment "thou shalt not kill." This raises issues over which teaching from the Bible is correct. The answer is partly dependent upon the context in which each of these passages is written and also partly dependent upon how the ecclesiastical authority has both translated and defined the passages within the historical context. Therefore, any understanding from a Catholic point of view cannot rely solely on a literal translation of the biblical text, but must take into consideration the context in which the passage was written and the Church's translation and interpretation of each passage.

The majority of pro death penalty passages in the Bible tend to be found in the Old Testament. It has been noted that the Old Testament "specifies no less than thirty-six capital offenses for execution by stoning, burning, decapitation, or strangulation"[66] which includes profaning the Sabbath (Exodus 35:2, Exodus 31:14-15; Numbers 15:32-36), blasphemy (Leviticus 24:11-14; Exodus 22:20), dishonoring one's parents, priests, or elders (Exodus 21:15; Leviticus 20:9; Deuteronomy 17:12; Deuteronomy 21:18-21; Proverbs 20:20), worship with human sacrifices (Leviticus 20:2), violations of a temple (Numbers 1:51; Numbers 3:10; Numbers 18:7), sorcery (Exodus 22:18; Leviticus 20:27), and "a variety of familial and sexual violations, including adultery, incest, homosexuality, and bestiality"[67] (Leviticus 20:9-1). Despite the high number of death penalty crimes or the various means by which one could be executed, one analysis of capital punishment in the Bible has shown that of the twenty-two murders depicted in the Bible, only four[68] resulted in executions by the state.[69] However, it is clear that the Old Testament does reserve the right of the state to execute offenders for various crimes, especially murder.

The first biblical reference in the Old Testament comes in Genesis (9:6), when God establishes the new covenant with Noah after the Great Flood by stating, in part, "If anyone sheds the blood of man, by man shall his blood be shed; For in the image of God has man been made."[70] God clearly defines the right of man to govern the acts of man, thus humanity is instilled with free will to manage their own affairs. Authorizing capital punishment is clearly one of these rights. However, in Exodus (20:13) we see God give the Ten Commandments to Moses of which the Fifth Commandment clearly states, "You shall not kill." What is critical here is the translation and understanding of this specific Commandment, for literally it would seem to imply a direct contradiction to God's covenant with Noah. The Hebrew word for "kill" that has been translated in this passage is meant to imply "killing under the law," or more specifically, "it represents the wanton killing of the innocent for prurient or sadistic reasons."[71] This is further evidenced by the next chapter in Exodus (21:12-14) when God states that "whoever strikes a man a mortal blow must be put to death. He, however, who did not hunt a man down, but caused his death by an act of God, may flee to a place which I will set apart for this purpose. But when a man kills another after maliciously scheming to do so, you must take him even from my altar and put him to death." The Book of Exodus continues to provide the word of God which lays out further cases of crimes and punishments, including the penalty for when a person strikes his Father or Mother, as death.

These crimes are then followed by the oft-recited line in Exodus (21:24) which states that punishment should be "eye for eye, tooth for tooth." However, it is important to look at the context in which this phrase is stated, for there is far more to the passage than the scriptural sound-bite:

> When men have a fight and hurt a pregnant woman, so that she suffers a miscarriage, but no further injury, the guilty one shall be fined as much as the

woman's husband demands of him, and he shall pay in the presence of the judges. But if injury ensues, you shall give life for life, eye for eye, tooth for tooth, hand for hand, foot for foot, burn for burn, wound for wound, stripe for stripe. [72]

This section, which is commonly referred to as the *lex talionis,* is not meant to merely reinforce the right of the state to execute an offender, but rather it was meant as a limit on the power of man. In other words, "the purpose of this law was not merely the enforcement of rigorous justice, but also the prevention of greater penalties than would be just."[73] Therefore, the passage reigns in punishments and makes them more proportioned to the crime. Thus, executions were limited to cases of loss of life or "life for life."

The *lex talionis* passage does not mandate the use of executions for all crimes, but it does not negate the fact that executions in the case of murder can be lawful. However, the Lord clearly spells out other instances in which the death penalty can be applied. In Leviticus (24:16-21), God states that

Whoever blasphemes the name of the Lord shall be put to death. The whole community shall stone him; alien and native alike must be put to death for blaspheming the Lord's name. Whoever takes the life of an animal shall make restitution of another animal. A life for life! Anyone who inflicts an injury on his neighbor shall receive the same in return. Limb for limb, eye for eye, tooth for tooth! The same injury that a man gives another shall be inflicted on him in return. Whoever slays an animal shall make restitution, but whoever slays a man shall be put to death.

God also tells Moses in Numbers (35:16) that

If a man strikes another with an iron instrument and causes his death, he is a murderer and shall be put to death. If a man strikes another with a death-dealing stone in his hand and causes his death, he is a murderer and shall be put to death. If a man strikes another with a death-dealing club in his hand and causes his death, he is a murderer and shall be put to death. The avenger of blood may execute the murderer, putting him to death on sight.

The punishment for the crime of what we would today call "first degree murder" or "capital murder" in the Old Testament was most evidently execution.

In the New Testament, however, there are no direct statements authorizing the state to use the death penalty, but then again, there are no statements that reject the use of capital punishment either.[74] Taking this further, many acknowledge the fact that even at the point of knowing he was going to be executed on the cross, Jesus never spoke out against the state's right to execute him under the law. At any point, Jesus could have raised the issue regarding the validity of the death penalty, but he never did so. In fact, in two cases, Jesus acknowledged the Mosaic laws that authorized the death penalty. Thus, by not speaking directly to them in terms of the sanctity of the death penalty, this may very well constitute "an implicit endorsement of capital punishment by Jesus."[75] The first instance of this was on an occasion when the Pharisees were questioning Jesus.

> So the Pharisees and scribes questioned him, "Why do your disciples not follow the tradition of the elders but instead eat a meal with unclean hands?" He responded, "Well did Isaiah prophesy about you hypocrites, as it is written:

> 'This people honors me with their lips,
> But their hearts are far from me;
> In vain do they worship me,
> Teaching as doctrines human precepts.'

> You disregard God's commandment but cling to human tradition." He went on to say, "How well you have set aside the commandment of God in order to uphold your tradition! For Moses said, 'Honor your father and your mother,' and 'Whoever curses father or mother shall die.' Yet you say, 'If a person says to father or mother, "Any support you might have had from me is qorban"' (meaning, dedicated to God), you allow him to do nothing more for his father or mother. You nullify the word of God in favor of your tradition that you have handed on. And you do many such things."[76]

The second instance of this endorsement may be found in Jesus' handling of the accusers of the adulterous woman. Jesus, as was his custom, had gone to the Mount of Olives, but had returned early one morning to the temple in Jerusalem and began teaching the people.

> Then the scribes and the Pharisees brought a woman who had been caught in adultery and made her stand in the middle. They said to him, "Teacher, this woman was caught in the very act of committing adultery. Now in the law, Moses commanded us to stone such women. So what do you say?" They said this to test him, so that they could have some charge to bring against him. Jesus bent down and began to write on the ground with his finger. But when they continued asking him, he straightened up and said to them, "Let the one among you who is without sin be the first to throw a stone at her." Again he bent down and wrote on the ground. And in response, they went away one by one, beginning with the elders. So he was left alone with the woman before him. Then Jesus straightened up and said to her, "Woman, where are they? Has no one condemned you" She replied, "No one, sir." Then Jesus said, "Neither do I condemn you. Go, and from now on do not sin any more."[77]

Jesus had the opportunity to raise the issue that the death penalty was a sin, in and of itself, that it violated God's commandments, or that the Mosaic law was in error, misunderstood, or simply no longer valid. But, he did not do this. Rather, Jesus implied that the law was a valid law, but questioned the integrity of those who would judge others. Yet, herein lies the difficulty of this passage.

While it may appear to validate the death penalty, for Jesus did not raise issue with the law, it may also bring into question the ability of man to pass the sentence of death upon another. Jesus, in this story, implies that only those who are without sin can cast judgment on a fellow human being, yet since every human being is a sinner, that would imply that no person can pass this judgment onto another and that it is reserved for God and God alone. It is difficult to surmise then, whether this story truly supports or refutes the state's right to executions.

There are other similar instances in the New Testament that raise issue with the Mosaic Laws and the tradition of state's rights to executions. For instance, Jesus repeatedly tells his disciples to forgive others, especially when he explains, "For if you forgive men their trespasses, your heavenly Father will also forgive you. But if you do no forgive men their trespasses, neither will your Father forgive you your trespasses."[78] While this does not address the death penalty directly, forgiveness of those who commit the most heinous crime, murder, is central to the issue. Unless of course, forgiveness and punishment are two separate issues. Can one forgive a murderer for his crime, but still demand justice and punishment be served? Jesus would appear to address this issue when he discusses the teaching of *lex talionis,* when he explains:

> You have heard that it was said, "An eye for an eye and a tooth for a tooth," but I say to you, offer no resistance to one who is evil. When someone strikes you on your right cheek, turn the other one to him as well. If anyone wants to go to law with you over your tunic, hand him your cloak as well. Should anyone press you into service for one mile, go with him for two miles. Give to the one who asks of you, and do not turn your back on one who wants to borrow. You have heard that it was said, "You shall love your neighbor and hate your enemy." But I say to you, love your enemies, and pray for those who persecute you, that you may be children of your heavenly Father, for he makes his sun rise on the bad and the good, and causes rain to fall on the just and the unjust.[79]

Jesus repeats here the concepts of forgiveness, but also highlights the fact that the *lex talionis* was not meant as a system of revenge, but rather one of fairness. While it would seem to indicate that people should "love thy neighbor," even when those neighbors might potentially bring harm to you, it does not directly refute the right of the state to execute. In the form of a question: is it possible to love thy enemy, forgive thy enemy, but still execute thy enemy?

One more passage from the New Testament, may serve to answer some questions about the state's right to execute murderers and to enforce the Mosaic laws. It comes in Romans, Chapter 13, and addresses the issue of obedience to authority or, more importantly, obedience to the state. The passage states:

> Let every person be subordinate to the higher authorities, for there is no authority except from God, and those that exist have been established by God. Therefore, whoever resists authority opposes what God has appointed, and those who oppose it will bring judgment on themselves. For rulers are not a cause of fear

to good conduct, but to evil. Do you wish to have no fear of authority? Then do what is good and you will receive approval from it, for it is a servant of God for your good. But if you do evil, be afraid, for it does not bear the sword without purpose; it is the servant of God to inflict wrath on the evildoer.[80]

This New Testament passage explains that government is granted its authority through God and exists to do God's work on earth. When the government enforces the law, it is in reality enforcing God's law. So, if someone is good, they will have nothing to fear from the government, but if someone is bad they will face the laws and punishments of the government, who is acting on God's behalf. Thus, it could be understood that when the government employs capital punishment to execute an offender, it is not the impassioned individual seeking revenge for a murder, but rather, "it is the servant of God" who inflicts "wrath on the evildoer."

It would appear, then, that within the Old Testament, capital punishment was sanctioned by God and was an accepted punishment for certain crimes. In the New Testament, while the laws favoring capital punishment are not refuted, there does appear to be a lessening of the strict adherence to executions as a means of punishment in the name of forgiveness. However, at the same time, the state, acting on behalf of God, does reserve the right to punish evildoers, and one means by which this can be carried out is through capital punishment. As one researcher, exploring the issue throughout the New Testament concluded, "Jesus accepted the Mosaic Code, complete with capital punishment, and did nothing, by word or deed, to abrogate the death penalty."[81]

Another means of sorting the issue out within the Catholic faith is to turn to the Christian traditions and look at what the Fathers and Doctors of the Church have said in regard to the use of the death penalty. Two people, declared Saints by the Catholic Church, have been instrumental in furthering our understanding of the state's right to use capital punishment, and they are St. Augustine and St. Thomas Aquinas. For instance, in his seminal book, *The City of God,* St. Augustine explains that

the same divine law which forbids the killing of a human being allows certain exceptions, as when God authorizes killing by a general law or when He gives an explicit commission to an individual for a limited time. Since the agent of authority is but a sword in one hand, and is not responsible for the killing, it is in no way contrary to the commandment, "Thou shalt not kill" to wage war at God's bidding, or for the representatives of the State's authority to put criminals to death, according to law or the rule of rational justice.[82]

St. Augustine is obviously citing the passage in Romans which states that governments, acting on behalf of God's authority, do retain the right to capital punishment and that this is not contrary to the Fifth Commandment.

St. Thomas Aquinas echoes this sentiment, but further develops the

Church's understanding of the death penalty by explaining that the state does reserve the right to execute a criminal but that the primary concern should be for "the needs and wants of those other than the executed" for "by slaying the wicked, we enhance the safety of the virtuous."[83] Aquinas explains in his *Summa Theologica* that "when . . . the good incur no danger, but rather are protected and saved by the slaying of the wicked, then the latter may be lawfully put to death."[84] Aquinas reasons that one of the purposes of the death penalty is to protect the citizenry from further crimes committed by the criminal. As Nemeth has explained, "to justify the infliction, Thomas argues that the common good replaces the individual need for self-preservation, and even though self-preservation is an inherent, natural-law precept, forfeiture of that right occurs by the conduct committed."[85] In fact, Aquinas is so strict on this point that he is almost defiantly pro-death penalty. One example is found in his *Commentary on the Nicomachean Ethics,* when he states that "the insubordinate and the degenerate are allotted physical punishments like beatings and other chastisements, censure and loss of their possessions. However, the absolutely incurable are exterminated—the bandit, for instance, is hanged."[86]

Despite the appearance of being "overly" pro-death penalty, Aquinas does acknowledge several qualifications to the state's right to use the death penalty. First, he articulates that punishments should be proportioned to both the passion of the crime as well as the acts, and that executions for such crimes as thievery would be unjust.[87] Second, he clearly states that the right of capital punishment is only extended to those whose "office it is to impose the law; indeed, lawmakers enforce observance of the law by means of rewards and punishments."[88] This is in keeping with the passage from Romans, which highlights that the state receives its authority through God. Individuals who would exact the same punishment for a crime are not acting on behalf of God, but rather of their own passions. And, just to be sure that no one believes that the judge, who ultimately passes the sentence of death is acting as an individual, Aquinas states that the judge is not guilty of this because it is not "he that puts the innocent man to death, but they who state him to be guilty."[89]

The third qualification Aquinas imposes is that such factors as mitigating circumstances, justifiable defense, and exculpatory rationales should be considered when determining the proper punishment in a death penalty case.[90] Finally, Aquinas strongly voices that the death penalty is only reserved for the guilty and that conviction based upon faulty facts and unsubstantiated allegations is in and of itself a transgression, for "if the judge knows that a man who has been convicted by false witnesses is innocent he must, like Daniel, examine the witnesses with great care, so as to find a motive for acquitting the innocent; but if he cannot do this he should remit him for judgment by a higher tribunal."[91] So, while Aquinas does take various factors into consideration regarding the death penalty, he, as one of the Church's greatest scholars, adheres to the principal right of the state to execute offenders.

This same adherence to the right of the state can be found among numerous other scholars and documents within the history of the Roman Catholic Church. Cardinal Avery Dulles highlights that there are numerous cases of the Church itself adhering to this right when he states that, "in the high Middle Ages and early modern times the Holy See authorized the Inquisition to turn over heretics to the secular arm for execution," that "in the Papal States the death penalty was imposed for a variety of offenses," and that "the Vatican City State from 1929 to 1969 had a penal code that included the death penalty for anyone who might attempt to assassinate the pope."[92] He also cites many of the early Church documents such as "the Roman Catechism, issued in 1566, three years after the end of the Council of Trent, [which] taught that the power of life and death had been entrusted by God to civil authorities and that the use of this power, far from involving the crime of murder, is an act of paramount obedience to the fifth commandment."[93] Finally, he has explained that "in modern times Doctors of the Church such as Robert Bellarmine and Alphonse Liguori held that certain criminals should be punished by death" and that "John Henry Newman, in a letter to a friend, maintained that the magistrate had the right to bear the sword" and that the Church should sanction its use, in the sense that Moses, Joshua, and Samuel used it against abominable crimes."[94] Cardinal Dulles thus demonstrates yet again, that the Catholic Church has provided a very consistent teaching on capital punishment throughout much of its two-thousand year history. However, more recent Church teaching and language have raised some questions among many within the Church over what appears to be an inviolable right of the state under Church doctrine.

A key source for understanding modern Church doctrine comes from the *Catechism of the Catholic Church*. Released in 1992 and revised in 1997, it has provided a source for understanding Church doctrine and the Catholic faith. It has also raised some controversies in understanding the Church's teaching on the death penalty. In the first edition, the section reviewing the Fifth Commandment (Article 5), explained that

> Preserving the common good of society requires rendering the aggressor unable to inflict harm. For this reason the traditional teaching of the Church has acknowledged as well-founded the right and duty of legitimate public authority to punish malefactors by means of penalties commensurate with the gravity of the crime, not excluding, in cases of extreme gravity, the death penalty.[95]

The section goes on to state that "the primary effect of *punishment* is to redress the disorder caused by the offense." However, in the next section (2267) the *Catechism* more directly addresses the issue of the death penalty by emphasizing how its use should be restricted when it explains that

> If bloodless means are sufficient to defend human lives against an aggressor and to protect public order and the safety of persons, public authority should

limit itself to such means, because they better correspond to the concrete

conditions of the common good and are more in conformity to the dignity of the human person.[96]

This is still in keeping with the passage from Romans, which authorizes the state to use capital punishment, but incorporates Aquinas' concept that capital punishment should be concerned primarily with the safety of the citizenry. Thus, the state reserves the right to executions for the safety of the people.

What is interesting in the revised (second) edition of the *Catechism of the Catholic Church*, regarding the death penalty, is the change in language, the moving of certain passages among these two sections, and the insertion of new language. In the first section (CCC No. 2266), language expressly dealing with the death penalty is dropped, and the section deals primarily with proportioning punishment to the crime and that "punishment has the primary aim of redressing the disorder introduced by the offense." The dropped language reappears in the next section (CCC No. 2267), albeit altered somewhat, but the defined purpose of punishment remains largely the same. Curiously, however, this section does drop the language in the 1992 edition which stated, "not excluding, in cases of extreme gravity, the death penalty." This clause, which disappears in the second edition of the *Catechism,* highlighted the fact that the death penalty was an acceptable punishment.

Section 2267 in the revised edition is not only changed, but largely revamped. It states:

> Assuming that the guilty party's identity and responsibility have been fully determined, the traditional teaching of the Church does not exclude recourse to the death penalty, if this is the only possible way of effectively defending human lives against the unjust aggressor.

Again the passage reserves the right of a public authority, the government, to use the death penalty, but primarily emphasizes the safety of the public. It further states,

> If, however, non-lethal means are sufficient to defend and protect people's safety from the aggressor, authority will limit itself to such means, as these are more in keeping with the concrete conditions of the common good and more in conformity with the dignity of the human person.

The same passage was found in the first edition; however, the language was altered from "bloodless" to "non-lethal" means in describing alternatives to executions. Finally, a new paragraph was added to the section which stated,

> Today, in fact, as a consequence of the possibilities which the state has for effectively preventing crime, by rendering one who has committed an offense in-

capable of doing harm—without definitively taking away from him the possibility of redeeming himself—the cases in which the execution of the offender is an absolute necessity "are very rare, if not practically non-existent."

This passage has a footnote which cites Pope John Paul II's *Evangelium Vitae* as its source. This is interesting, because in the revision, rather than focusing on issues of translation, the authors of the *Catechism* have chosen to incorporate the language from an Encyclical written by the Pope in the time period between the two editions. Because the writing is from an Encyclical, which is a document for Catholic Social Teaching, and because it is found in the *Catechism of the Catholic Church*, essentially a compendium of the teachings of the Catholic Church, this added paragraph cannot be ignored as being the definitive teachings of the Catholic Church. Therefore, it is important to understand the origins of this specific passage.

Evangelium Vitae (The Gospel of Life)[97] was published in 1995, by Pope John Paul II, which attempted to further define a consistent ethic of life for the modern, or "post-modern," world. The Pope set out to instruct the faithful in the Gospel of Life as taught by Jesus Christ in order to provide a definitive document on how Catholics should perceive life. In it he encouraged Catholics to embrace a Culture of Life and rail against the Culture of Death that seems so persuasive within modern society. Early in the document he specifically addressed the issue of the death penalty by stating that "not even a murderer loses his personal dignity," and he uses the story of Cain and Abel to show that God, through exile and the mark of Cain, "preferred the correction rather than the death of a sinner."[98] However, he does specifically point out that "the direct and voluntary killing of an innocent human being is always gravely immoral."[99] Later, he states that "there is evidence of a growing public opposition to the death penalty, even when such a penalty is seen as a kind of 'legitimate defense' on the part of society."[100] He further states that "modern society in fact has the means of effectively suppressing crime by rendering criminals harmless without definitively denying them the chance to reform."[101] Having stated that, the Pope begins to move the Encyclical toward the position of questioning the legitimacy of the death penalty, based upon the right of the state to execute someone as a legitimate defense against further atrocities. If the modern state has the capability for incapacitation, which would render the offender harmless to society, he questions the legitimacy of the death penalty in light of this reality.

Pope John Paul II then moves the discussion beyond the concept of "legitimate defense" by acknowledging the states' right to execute, but questioning the moral aspects of the offender's capability for reasoning within the framework of his heinous crime. He states:

> Moreover, "legitimate defense can be not only a right but a grave duty for someone responsible for another's life, the common good of the family or of the State" (*Catechism* No. 2265). Unfortunately it happens that the need to

render the aggressor incapable of causing harm sometimes involves taking his life. In this case, the fatal outcome is attributable to the aggressor whose action brought it about, even though he may not be morally responsible because of a lack of the use of reason.

All of this culminates in Section 56 of the Encyclical when the Pope finally sets forth his exhortation on the modern use of the death penalty.

This is the context in which to place the problem of the death penalty. On this matter there is a growing tendency, both in the Church and in civil society, to demand that it be applied in a very limited way or even that it be abolished completely. The problem must be viewed in the context of a system of penal justice ever more in line with human dignity and thus, in the end, with God's plan for man and society. The primary purpose of the punishment which society inflicts is "to redress the disorder caused by the offence" (CCC No. 2266). Public authority must redress the violation of personal and social rights by imposing on the offender an adequate punishment for the crime, as a condition for the offender to regain the exercise of his or her freedom. In this way authority also fulfils the purpose of defending public order and ensuring people's safety, while at the same time offering the offender an incentive and help to change his or her behavior and be rehabilitated.

It is clear that, for these purposes to be achieved, the nature and extent of the punishment must be carefully evaluated and decided upon, and ought not go to the extreme of executing the offender except in cases of absolute necessity: in other words, when it would not be possible otherwise to defend society. Today however, as a result of steady improvements in the organization of the penal system, such cases are very rare, if not practically non-existent.

In any event, the principle set forth in the new *Catechism of the Catholic Church* remains valid: "If bloodless means are sufficient to defend human lives against an aggressor and to protect public order and the safety of persons, public authority must limit itself to such means, because they better correspond to the concrete conditions of the common good and are more in conformity to the dignity of the human person."[102]

The origin of the new paragraph, inserted into the second edition of the *Catechism of the Catholic Church,* is clearly derived from the Pope's Encyclical, *Evangelium Vitae.* This specific passage has raised a number of issues and has sparked somewhat of a controversy between Catholic theologians and others (to be discussed below). Regardless, however, it has further defined the Church's social standing on the death penalty.

One last source from which American Catholics may draw an understanding of the Catholic social teaching on the death penalty is from the United States Conference of Catholic Bishops.[103] Throughout the twentieth century, and especially in the latter half, the Conference of Catholic Bishops has become more active in publishing statements and documents that further Catholic social teachings for Americans. In regard to the death penalty, the Bishops' first statement, declaring their opposition to the death penalty, came in a one-line statement in 1974.[104] The president of the Catholic Conference of Bishops at the time, Archbishop Joseph Bernardin, called for a consistent ethic of life in Catholic social teaching, and he argued that the death penalty, as applied, did not meet this consistency. Of course, it should be noted that Archbishop Bernardin was speaking at a time when the death penalty had become a contentious issue in American politics, and a moratorium was imposed by the United States Supreme Court because of the "unusual" way in which it was being implemented.

The first full statement regarding the death penalty by the Conference came in 1980, with their "Statement on Capital Punishment." Coming in the wake of the *Gregg* decision and the first several executions since the death penalty was reinstated by the Supreme Court, the Bishops attempted to spell out their "commitment to the value and dignity of human life."[105] They stated that the three purposes of punishment were retribution, deterrence, and reform. They argued that the death penalty, as implemented, did not accomplish any of these in that it did not achieve retribution in a Christian sense by restoring order, it did not deter future murders, and it did not allow for the reform of the offender executed. They explained that abolition of the death penalty would help break the cycle of violence, it would reinforce the dignity of life, it would affirm that God is the Lord of life, and that abolition would be more Christ-like in action. The Bishops then cited the secular problems with the death penalty as further evidence that it should be abolished in America. In their conclusions, however, they conceded that "many citizens may believe that capital punishment should be maintained as an integral part of our society's response to the evils of crime, nor is this position incompatible with Catholic tradition."[106] So, while calling for the abolition of capital punishment, the Bishops clearly acknowledged that the death penalty is acceptable under Catholic doctrine.

While the Bishops would reiterate the consistency of life ethic and the call for abolition of capital punishment in other documents (e.g., *Confronting the Culture of Violence,* 1994; *Living the Gospel of Life,* 1998), it was their "Good Friday Appeal to End the Death Penalty" that would reignite the issue among Catholics. The U.S. Catholic Conference issued their statement on April 2, 1999, on Good Friday, the day Jesus Christ was executed, to bring new attention to their call for abolition. In this statement, they not only called upon their past statements regarding the death penalty, but this time they had the support of the *Catechism of the Catholic Church* and the Pope's Encyclical, *Evangelium Vitae.* The Bishops explained that

> We oppose capital punishment not just for what it does to those guilty of horrible crimes but for what it does to all of us as a society. Increasing reliance on the death penalty diminishes all of us and is a sign of growing disrespect for

human life. We cannot overcome crime by simply executing criminals, nor can we restore the lives of the innocent by ending the lives of those convicted for their murders. The death penalty offers the tragic illusion that we can defend life by taking life.[107]

This time the Catholic Bishops did not mention that the death penalty was in keeping with Catholic tradition, but rather, they urged all Catholics to work toward its abolition. They would renew this call in a special section in the statement on *Responsibility, Rehabilitation, and Restoration* (2000), which provided a more comprehensive view of the Catholic perspective on crime and criminal justice.

In March of 2005, the Bishops launched their renewed "Catholic Campaign to end the Use of the Death Penalty," and in December of that year, the twenty-fifth anniversary of their first statement on the death penalty, the Bishops released their most comprehensive statement to date titled *A Culture of Life and the Penalty of Death*.[108] They definitively state that the United States should forgo the use of the death penalty, and they list four specific justifications: (1) the sanction of death, when it is not necessary to protect society, violates respect for human life and dignity, (2) state-sanctioned killing in our names diminishes us all, (3) its application is deeply flawed and can be irreversibly wrong, is prone to errors, and is biased by factors such as race, the quality of legal representation, and where the crime was committed, and (4) we have other ways to punish criminals and protect society.[109]

Catholic Debate over the Death Penalty

While most people are familiar with the secular debate regarding the death penalty, many are not as familiar with the debate within the Catholic Church. The debate is largely centered on the insertion of the language from Pope John Paul II's Encyclical, *Evangelium Vitae*, into the second edition of the *Catechism of the Catholic Church*. An Encyclical from the Pope carries a lot of weight within the Catholic Church for defining Church doctrine, but the *Catechism* has come to be seen as the key defining publication second only to the Bible. Therefore, the Pope's language that "as a result of steady improvements in the organization of the penal system, such cases are very rare, if not practically non-existent" (CCC No. 2267) has raised a number of questions regarding the traditional teachings of the Catholic Church regarding the death penalty. Has the tradition been dismissed, or has it simply evolved? Is the Church inherently pro- or anti-death penalty? If it is now against the death penalty, what is the rationale?

Although there have been a number of articles written on this topic, it is perhaps an article by Cardinal Avery Dulles in the journal *First Things*, that has really sparked the Catholic debate over this issue.[110] In his article titled, "Catholicism & Capital Punishment," Cardinal Dulles detailed the scripture and traditions of the Catholic Church to demonstrate that, historically, the Church has reserved the right of the state to execute serious offenders for their crimes. He then, like others have, delineated four reasons for punishment: rehabilitation, defense against the criminal, deterrence, and retribution. He also cites four reasons that the death penalty would be an inappropriate punishment: the convict may be innocent, executions contribute to violence, it cheapens the value of life, and that it is incompatible with the teachings of Jesus Christ. Cardinal Dulles argues the first objection is a serious one and should not be taken lightly. The second highlights the fact that the state should not be seeking revenge, but that often the motivations may resemble those of the Roman Empire. The third is based upon Cardinal Bernardin's call for a "consistent ethic of life," but he notes that many Catholics who are against abortion and euthanasia are also pro-death penalty. Finally, Cardinal Dulles cites that the last argument is biblically faulty. Thus, he concludes,

> The four objections are therefore of different weight. The first of them, dealing with miscarriages of justice, is relatively strong; the second and third, dealing with vindictiveness and with the consistent ethic of life, have some probable force. The fourth objection, dealing with forgiveness, is relatively weak. But taken together, the four may suffice to tip the scale against the use of the death penalty.[111]

Cardinal Dulles then details that the Pope and the United States Bishops have voiced the same call, pleading for an end to the death penalty in the United States. Although neither has inherently ruled out capital punishment as an absolute, they do not believe it is justifiable as currently practiced within the United States. Yet, to address the fundamental question of whether this changes Church doctrine that has existed for over two millennium, Cardinal Dulles states he does not think it has. He explains that

> in coming to this prudential conclusion, the magisterium is not changing the doctrine of the Church. The doctrine remains what it has been: that the State, in principle, has the right to impose the death penalty on persons convicted of very serious crimes. But the classical tradition held that the State should not exercise this right when the evil effects outweigh the good effects. Thus the principle still leaves open the question whether and when the death penalty ought to be applied. The Pope and the bishops, using their prudential judgment, have concluded that in contemporary society, at least in countries like our own, the death penalty ought not to be invoked, because, on balance, it does more harm than good.[112]

He then concludes by stating, "I personally support this position."[113] What is most significant about this article is not so much the stance that Cardinal Dulles took, but the response it received which raised many of the issues regarding the Church's teachings on the death penalty.

Cardinal Dulles appears to argue that it is a combination of problematic factors that have led the Church to voice opposition against the death penalty, but not at the expense of traditional Church teaching. A number of objections have been raised regarding this position. One such objection is the change in the language from the 1566 *Roman Catechism* (the predecessor to the 1992 edition), and to some degree the 1992 *Catechism,* to the revised *Catechism* in 1997. Whereas the 1566 *Catechism* articulated the death penalty as an exception to the Fifth Commandment, and the 1992 *Catechism* stated that the death penalty was an acceptable punishment, the 1997 *Catechism* changed the language to make the death penalty not so much a "punishment" for a crime, but rather a means of collective "self-defense."[114] In other words, a society may use the death penalty to protect its citizens if no other means are available. If the death penalty is not allowed as a punishment for a crime, but only as an extension of an individual's right to self-defense, then one could argue that the Church is moving toward a change in its theology regarding capital punishment.

In addition, the language employed in the 1997 edition of the *Catechism* further signifies that the use of the death penalty as a punishment, in some cases, is no longer acceptable.[115] Remembering that, as Cardinal Dulles explained, there are four purposes of punishment: rehabilitation, defense against the criminal, deterrence, and retribution. The 1997 *Catechism* articulates that the death penalty as retribution or a deterrent to further crime are no longer acceptable justifications and suggests that rehabilitation is not given a chance if the individual is executed. Therefore, this again leaves the use of the death penalty, as a means of punishment, only being justified in cases of self-defense or for the purposes of incapacitation. And, as punishment must be public, not private, the death penalty is only justified as a means of collective defense against the criminal, if "bloodless," or rather, "non-lethal" means are not available.

Another objection that raises issue with the incorporation of the Pope's own language into the 1997 *Catechism,* from his Encyclical *Evangelium Vitae,* is in regard to the Pope's own call for a "culture of life" to become the societal norm, rather than what he sees as a "culture of death." Moving toward a restriction on the use of the death penalty would assist the Church in moving toward the "culture of life," and would help achieve what Cardinal Bernardin called for, and that is a "consistent ethic of life." Taken to extremes the objection states that this is more about what Pope John Paul II believes is right, rather than what Catholic tradition has taught. One noted Catholic, and Supreme Court Justice, did just this when he took umbrage with the Pope at a Pew Forum Conference on January 25, 2002, titled "A Call for Reckoning: Religion & the Death Penalty."[116] At this conference, Justice Scalia, speaking as a Catholic citizen and not a Justice, stated:

You will gather from what I have said that I do not agree with *Evangelium Vitae* and the New Catholic *Catechism*—or the very latest version of the new Catholic *Catechism*—that the death penalty can only be imposed to protect rather than avenge, and that since it is, in most modern societies, not necessary for the former purpose, it is wrong.[117]

Scalia went further in arguing against these Church documents when he explained:

that the statement contained in *Evangelium Vitae* . . . does not represent *ex cathedra* teaching, that is, it need not be accepted by practicing Catholics, although they must give it thoughtful and respectful consideration. Indeed, it would be remarkable to think that it was an *ex cathedra* pronouncement, that a couple of paragraphs contained in an Encyclical principally devoted not to capital punishment, but to abortion and euthanasia, were intended authoritatively to sweep aside two millennia of Christian teaching. And as for the very latest edition of the New Catholic *Catechism,* I assume that is just the phenomenon of the clerical bureaucracy saying, "Yes, boss."[118]

While strictly speaking, Justice Scalia is right, according to many theologians, including Cardinal Dulles, the Pope is not speaking *ex cathedra* (from the Chair) when issuing an Encyclical or the *Catechism,*[119] but the Second Vatican Council has pointed out in *Lumen Gentium* that "loyal submission of will and intellect must be given . . . to the authentic teaching authority of the Roman Pontiff, even when he does not speak *ex cathedra.*"[120] In other words, as Catholics, to pick and choose what we want to hear is fundamentally wrong, thus the teaching of the Pope in *Evangelium Vitae* and the revised *Catechism,* cannot be dismissed by faithful Catholics. And, since it cannot be dismissed, it must be reconciled.

Finally, one more objection has been raised, and that has to do with a more fundamental approach to the death penalty, rather than so much the changes in the *Catechism.* The argument here is based on the Catholic tradition that because the right of the state to exist is derived from God (Romans 13:1-4), the state exists to serve God's will. If the state is no longer formed to do God's work, then it merely exists to do man's work. And if the state is doing man's work and it executes someone, it is playing God.[121] In other words, a society that is based upon religious principles would recognize it is performing an earthly function to which God will be the ultimate arbiter of the person executed. If society is not based upon religious principles, then when it is executing someone it is playing God by eliminating them from society, because in a non-religious society, death is the end. Therefore, if the state does not exist to serve God, it should not be granted the right to rule over life.

The Death Penalty from a Catholic Perspective

In light of the changes to the Roman Catholic Church's teaching regarding the death penalty, what then is the Catholic perspective of the death penalty? It is perhaps easiest to explain by looking at the conclusion of two professors from Notre Dame. Charles Rice, a professor in Notre Dame's Law School, concluded that

> What is clear . . . is that if a Catholic is to be consistent with the teaching of his Church, he can no longer argue for the death penalty on the general bases of retribution, deterrence of other potential criminals, or any of the other familiar conservative or neo-conservative arguments, unless that penalty is "the only possible way of effectively defending" other lives from this criminal.[122]

Ralph McInerny, a theologian from Notre Dame, would seem to conversely state:

> no one reading the *Catechism* can ignore the reminder that the traditional teaching of the Church has acknowledged as well-founded the right and duty of legitimate public authority to exact even the death penalty in carefully defined situations.

> Some wrongly read this as the Church bidding adieu to that teaching of the Church rather than its reiteration.[123]

Despite these seeming contradictions, the current Catholic perspective really adopts both conclusions. The Catholic perspective should, at first, acknowledge that by the Bible, both Old and New Testaments, by the scholars of the Church, by Catholic tradition, and even by the Pope's exhortations in the Encyclical *Evangelium Vitae* and the revised *Catechism,* the state still has the authority to impose the death penalty. At second glance, however, it must also acknowledge that this right must be directly in support of "redressing the disorder introduced by the offense"[124] and it must be "the only possible way of effectively defending human lives against the unjust aggressor."[125] In the United States, as well as other modern societies, because we have the means to secure criminals in prison and can protect the citizenry, executions should be very rare. And, in fact, they actually are. As previously noted, it is only certain states and certain jurisdictions that have a high level of use, while most states and jurisdictions rarely use the death penalty, if at all. States like Texas, Florida, and Virginia would then be encouraged to use their right to capital punishment more in line with say, Idaho, Tennessee, or the federal government, which has executed three or fewer people since 1976. Governments that would still maintain the right to higher levels of executions, under this perspective, would be poorer third world nations that do not have the resources to hold a serious offender for life or the means to protect its citizenry. Thus, the death penalty from a Catholic perspective would reserve the right of the state to execute those who commit murder, but would at the same time advocate for a greatly diminished application of this right.

Notes

1. See Ann L. Pastore and Kathleen Maguire, eds., "Attitudes Toward the Death Penalty," Table 2.50, *Sourcebook of Criminal Justice Statistics* http://www.albany.edu/sourcebook/ [accessed November 14, 2006].

2. William G. Mayer, (1993). *The Changing American Mind: How and Why American Public Opinion Changed Between 1960 and 1988.* Ann Arbor: The University of Chicago Press; Page, Benjamin I. and Robert Y. Shapiro. (1992). *The Rational Public: Fifty Years of Trends in Americans' Policy Preferences.* Chicago: The University of Chicago Press.

3. Ann L. Pastore and Kathleen Maguire, eds., "Attitudes Toward the Death Penalty for Persons Convicted of Murder," Table 2.63, *Sourcebook of Criminal Justice Statistics* http://www.albany.edu/sourcebook/ [accessed October 9, 2003].

4. Ann L. Pastore and Kathleen Maguire, eds., "Attitudes Toward the Death Penalty for Persons Convicted of Murder," Table 2.63, *Sourcebook of Criminal Justice Statistics* http://www.albany.edu/sourcebook/ [accessed October 9, 2003].

5. James R. Kelly and Christopher Kudlac, "Pro-Life, Anti-Death Penalty?" *America: The National Catholic Weekly* 182, no. 11 (2000): 6-8.

6. Richard Hooker, *Mesopotamia: The Code of Hammurabi* http://www.wsu.edu/~dee/MESO/CODE.HTM [accessed July 2003].

7. Death Penalty Information Center, *History of the Death Penalty* http://www.deathpenaltyinfo.org/ [accessed August 2003].

8. Death Penalty Information Center, *History of the Death Penalty* http://www.deathpenaltyinfo.org/ [accessed August 2003].

9. Matthew 21:13 (*The New American Bible,* 1992-1993 edition).

10. Douglas Linder, *The Trial of Jesus* http://www.law.umkc.edu/faculty/projects/ftrials/jesus/jesus.html [accessed September 2003.

11. Mark 15:62 (*The New American Bible,* 1992-1993 edition).

12. Stuart Banner, *The Death Penalty: An American History* (Cambridge: Harvard University Press, 2002); Mark Costanzo, *Just Revenge: Costs and Consequences of the Death Penalty* (New York: St. Martin's Press, 1997); Lawrence M. Friedman, *Crime and Punishment in American History* (New York: Basic Books, 1993).

13. Stuart Banner, *The Death Penalty: An American History* (Cambridge: Harvard University Press, 2002); Mark Costanzo, *Just Revenge: Costs and Consequences of the Death Penalty* (New York: St. Martin's Press, 1997).

14. Hugo Adam Bedau, *The Death Penalty in America: Current Controversies* (New York: Oxford University Press, 1997); Mark Costanzo, *Just Revenge: Costs and Consequences of the Death Penalty* (New York: St. Martin's Press, 1997); Death Penalty Information Center, *History of the Death Penalty* http://www.deathpenaltyinfo.org/ [accessed August 2003; Matthew B. Robinson, *Justice Blind? Ideals and Realities of American Criminal Justice* (Upper Saddle River: Prentice Hall, 2002).

15. Stuart Banner, *The Death Penalty: An American History* (Cambridge: Harvard University Press, 2002).

16. Stuart Banner, *The Death Penalty: An American History* (Cambridge: Harvard University Press, 2002), 22.

17. Stuart Banner, *The Death Penalty: An American History* (Cambridge: Harvard University Press, 2002); Louis P. Masur, *Rites of Execution: Capital Punishment and the Transformation of American Culture, 1776-1865* (New York: Oxford University Press, 1989).

18. Lawrence M. Friedman, *Crime and Punishment in American History* (New York: Basic Books, 1993).

19. Stuart Banner, *The Death Penalty: An American History* (Cambridge: Harvard University Press, 2002); Hugo Adam Bedau, *The Death Penalty in America: Current Controversies* (New York: Oxford University Press, 1997); Lawrence M. Friedman, *Crime and Punishment in American History* (New York: Basic Books, 1993); Louis P. Masur, *Rites of Execution: Capital Punishment and the Transformation of American Culture, 1776-1865* (New York: Oxford University Press, 1989).

20. Stuart Banner, *The Death Penalty: An American History* (Cambridge: Harvard University Press, 2002); Hugo Adam Bedau, *The Death Penalty in America: Current Controversies* (New York: Oxford University Press, 1997); Mark Costanzo, *Just Revenge: Costs and Consequences of the Death Penalty* (New York: St. Martin's Press, 1997).

21. Stuart Banner, *The Death Penalty: An American History* (Cambridge: Harvard University Press, 2002); Mark Costanzo, *Just Revenge: Costs and Consequences of the Death Penalty* (New York: St. Martin's Press, 1997); Lawrence M. Friedman, *Crime and Punishment in American History* (New York: Basic Books, 1993).

22. Stuart Banner, *The Death Penalty: An American History* (Cambridge: Harvard University Press, 2002); Hugo Adam Bedau, *The Death Penalty in America: Current Controversies* (New York: Oxford University Press, 1997); Lawrence M. Friedman, *Crime and Punishment in American History* (New York: Basic Books, 1993).

23. Hugo Adam Bedau, *The Death Penalty in America: Current Controversies* (New York: Oxford University Press, 1997); Christopher Z. Mooney and Mei-Hsien Lee, "The Temporal Diffusion of Morality Policy: The Case of Death Penalty Legislation in the American States," in *The Public Clash of Private Values*, ed. Christopher Z. Mooney (New York: Chatham House Publishers, 2001), 170-183.

24. Hugo Adam Bedau, *The Death Penalty in America: Current Controversies* (New York: Oxford University Press, 1997); Death Penalty Information Center, *History of the Death Penalty* http://www.deathpenaltyinfo.org/ [accessed August 2003]; Christopher Z. Mooney and Mei-Hsien Lee, "The Temporal Diffusion of Morality Policy: The Case of Death Penalty Legislation in the American States," in *The Public Clash of Private Values*, ed. Christopher Z. Mooney (New York: Chatham House Publishers, 2001), 170-183.

25. Mark Costanzo, *Just Revenge: Costs and Consequences of the Death Penalty* (New York: St. Martin's Press, 1997); Death Penalty Information Center, *History of the Death Penalty* http://www.deathpenaltyinfo.org/ [accessed August 2003].

26. Death Penalty Information Center, *History of the Death Penalty* http://www.deathpenaltyinfo.org/ [accessed August 2003]; See also Hugo Adam Bedau, *The Death Penalty in America: Current Controversies* (New York: Oxford University Press, 1997).

27. Stuart Banner, *The Death Penalty: An American History* (Cambridge: Harvard University Press, 2002); Hugo Adam Bedau, *The Death Penalty in America: Current Controversies* (New York: Oxford University Press, 1997); Christopher Z. Mooney and Mei-Hsien Lee, "The Temporal Diffusion of Morality Policy: The Case of Death Penalty Legislation in the American States," in *The Public Clash of Private Values*, ed. Christopher Z. Mooney (New York: Chatham House Publishers, 2001), 170-183.

28. *U.S. v. Jackson*. (1968). 390 U.S. 570.

29. *Witherspoon v. Illinois*. (1968). 391 U.S. 510.

30. *Furman v. Georgia, Jackson v. Georgia,* and *Branch v. Texas*. (1972). 408 U.S. 238.

31. Stuart Banner, *The Death Penalty: An American History* (Cambridge: Harvard University Press, 2002).

32. *Gregg v. Georgia* (1972) was actually a series of three cases combined, which consisted of *Gregg v. Georgia* (428 U.S. 153), *Jurek v. Texas* (428 U.S. 262), and *Proffit v. Florida* (428 U.S. 242).

33. Stuart Banner, *The Death Penalty: An American History* (Cambridge: Harvard University Press, 2002); Mark Costanzo, *Just Revenge: Costs and Consequences of the Death Penalty* (New York: St. Martin's Press, 1997); Lawrence M. Friedman, *Crime and Punishment in American History* (New York: Basic Books, 1993).

34. Hugo Adam Bedau, *The Death Penalty in America: Current Controversies* (New York: Oxford University Press, 1997).

35. Death Penalty Information Center, *History of the Death Penalty* http://www.deathpenaltyinfo.org/ [accessed August 2003].

36. Hugo Adam Bedau, *The Death Penalty in America: Current Controversies* (New York: Oxford University Press, 1997).

37. Hugo Adam Bedau, *The Death Penalty in America: Current Controversies* (New York: Oxford University Press, 1997); Death Penalty Information Center, *History of the Death Penalty* http://www.deathpenaltyinfo.org/ [accessed August 2003]; Jen Joynt and Carrie Shuchart, "Mortal Justice: The Demography of the Death Penalty," *The Atlantic Monthly* (March 2003): 40-41.

38. Death Penalty Information Center, *The Death Penalty* http://www. deathpenaltyinfo.org/ [accessed August 2006].

39. Death Penalty Information Center, *The Death Penalty* http://www. deathpenaltyinfo.org/ [accessed August 2006].

40. Death Penalty Information Center, *The Death Penalty* http://www. deathpenaltyinfo.org/ [accessed August 2006].

41. Death Penalty Information Center, *The Death Penalty* http://www. deathpenaltyinfo.org/ [accessed August 2006].

42. Death Penalty Information Center, *The Death Penalty* http://www. deathpenaltyinfo.org/ [accessed August 2006].

43. Jen Joynt and Carrie Shuchart, "Mortal Justice: The Demography of the Death Penalty," *The Atlantic Monthly* (March 2003): 40-41.

44. Death Penalty Information Center, *The Death Penalty* http://www. deathpenaltyinfo.org/ [accessed August 2006].

45. Hugo Adam Bedau, *The Death Penalty in America: Current Controversies* (New York: Oxford University Press, 1997); Death Penalty Information Center, *The Death Penalty* http://www.deathpenaltyinfo.org/ [accessed August 2006].

46. Death Penalty Information Center, *The Death Penalty* http://www. deathpenaltyinfo.org/ [accessed August 2006].

47. Hugo Adam Bedau, *The Death Penalty in America: Current Controversies* (New York: Oxford University Press, 1997)

48. Death Penalty Information Center, *The Death Penalty* http://www. deathpenaltyinfo.org/ [accessed August 2006].

49. Death Penalty Information Center, *The Death Penalty* http://www. deathpenaltyinfo.org/ [accessed August 2006].

50. Death Penalty Information Center, *The Death Penalty* http://www. deathpenaltyinfo.org/ [accessed August 2006].; Jen Joynt and Carrie Shuchart, "Mortal Justice: The Demography of the Death Penalty," *The Atlantic Monthly* (March 2003): 40-41.

51. Death Penalty Information Center, *The Death Penalty* http://www. deathpenaltyinfo.org/ [accessed August 2006].

52. Death Penalty Information Center, *The Death Penalty* http://www. deathpenaltyinfo.org/ [accessed August 2006].

53. Ann L. Pastore and Kathleen Maguire, eds., "Attitudes Toward the Death Penalty for Persons Convicted of Murder," Table 2.63, *Sourcebook of Criminal Justice Statistics* http://www.albany.edu/sourcebook/ [accessed October 9, 2003].

54. Robert M. Bohm, "The Future of Capital Punishment in the United Stats," *ACJS Today* 22, no. 4 (2000): 1-6; Mark Costanzo, *Just Revenge: Costs and Consequences of the Death Penalty* (New York: St. Martin's Press, 1997); M. Sandys and E. McGarrell, "Attitudes Toward Capital Punishment: Preferences for the Penalty or Mere Acceptance?" *Journal of Research in Crime and Delinquency* 32 (1995): 191-213.

55. Mark Costanzo, *Just Revenge: Costs and Consequences of the Death Penalty* (New York: St. Martin's Press, 1997); Matthew B. Robinson, *Justice Blind? Ideals and Realities of American Criminal Justice* (Upper Saddle River: Prentice Hall, 2002); M. Sandys and E. McGarrell, "Attitudes Toward Capital Punishment: Preferences for the Penalty or Mere Acceptance?" *Journal of Research in Crime and Delinquency* 32 (1995): 191-213.

56. Robert M. Bohm, "The Future of Capital Punishment in the United Stats," *ACJS Today* 22, no. 4 (2000): 1-6; Death Penalty Information Center, *The Death Penalty* http://www.deathpenaltyinfo.org/ [accessed August 2003].

57. Death Penalty Information Center, *The Death Penalty* http://www. deathpenaltyinfo.org/ [accessed August 2006].

58. Death Penalty Information Center, *The Death Penalty* http://www. deathpenaltyinfo.org/ [accessed August 2006].

59. Matthew B. Robinson, *Justice Blind? Ideals and Realities of American Criminal Justice* (Upper Saddle River: Prentice Hall, 2002).

60. Isaac Ehrlich, "The Deterrent Effect of Capital Punishment: A Question of Life and Death," *American Economic Review* 65 (1975): 397-417.

61. William J. Bowers and Glenn Pierce, "The Illusion of Deterrence in Isaac Ehrlich's Research on Capital Punishment," *Yale Law Review* 85 (1975): 187-208; Brian Forst, "Capital Punishment and Deterrence: Conflicting Evidence," *Journal of Criminal Law and Criminology* 74 (1983): 927-942; Peter Pasell, "The Deterrent Effect of the Death Penalty: A Statistical Test," *Stanford Law Review* 28 (1975): 61-80.

62. Hugo Adam Bedau, *The Death Penalty in America: Current Controversies* (New York: Oxford University Press, 1997); Mark Costanzo, *Just Revenge: Costs and Conse-*

quences of the Death Penalty (New York: St. Martin's Press, 1997); Matthew B. Robinson, *Justice Blind? Ideals and Realities of American Criminal Justice* (Upper Saddle River: Prentice Hall, 2002); Samuel Walker, *Sense and Nonsense about Crime and Drugs: A Policy Guide,* 5th ed. (Belmont: Wadsworth Publishing, 2001).

63. Ruth D. Peterson and William C. Bailey, "Is Capital Punishment an Effective Deterrent for Murder? An Examination of the Social Science Research," in *America's Experiment with Capital Punishment: Reflections on the Past, Present, and Future of the Ultimate Penal Sanction,* eds. James R. Acker, Robert M. Bohm, and Charles S. Lanier (Durham: Carolina Academic, 1998); Matthew ·B. Robinson, *Justice Blind? Ideals and Realities of American Criminal Justice* (Upper Saddle River: Prentice Hall, 2002), 351.

64. Robert M. Bohm, "The Economic Costs of Capital Punishment," in *America's Experiment with Capital Punishment: Reflections on the Past, Present, and Future of the Ultimate Penal Sanction,* eds. James R. Acker, Robert M. Bohm, and Charles S. Lanier (Durham: Carolina Academic, 1998).

65. James W. Marquart, *The Rope, the Chain, and the Needle: Capital Punishment in Texas, 1923-1990* (Austin: University of Texas Press, 1998).

66. Avery Dulles, "Catholicism & Capital Punishment," *First Things* 112 (April 2001): 30.

67. Scott L. Johnson, "The Bible and the Death Penalty: Implications for Criminal Justice Education," *Journal of Criminal Justice Education* 11, no. 1 (Spring 2000): 22.

68. These four were Rechab and Bannah, executed by King David (2 Samuel 4:12); Joab, executed by King Solomon (1 Kings 2:34); Athaliah, executed by Jehoiada, High Priest (2 Kings 11:16); and Amon's Servant, executed by leaders of Judah (2 Kings 21:24). See Scott L. Johnson, "The Bible and the Death Penalty: Implications for Criminal Justice Education," *Journal of Criminal Justice Education* 11, no. 1 (Spring 2000): 15-33.

69. Scott L. Johnson, "The Bible and the Death Penalty: Implications for Criminal Justice Education," *Journal of Criminal Justice Education* 11, no. 1 (Spring 2000): 15-33.

70. *The New American Bible.*

71. Scott L. Johnson, "The Bible and the Death Penalty: Implications for Criminal Justice Education," *Journal of Criminal Justice Education* 11, no. 1 (Spring 2000): 18.

72. Exodus 21:22-25.

73. Footnote 21, 23ff, p. 72, *The New American Bible* (Nashville: Catholic Bible Press, 1987).

74. Scott L. Johnson, "The Bible and the Death Penalty: Implications for Criminal Justice Education," *Journal of Criminal Justice Education* 11, no. 1 (Spring 2000): 15-33.

75. Scott L. Johnson, "The Bible and the Death Penalty: Implications for Criminal Justice Education," *Journal of Criminal Justice Education* 11, no. 1 (Spring 2000): 24.

76. Mark 7:5-13; See also Matthew 15:1-12 (*The New American Bible*).

77. John 8:1-11 (*The New American Bible*).

78. Matthew 6:14-15; See also Matthew 18:21-35; Luke 6:37-38; Luke 17:3-4 (*The New American Bible*).

79. Matthew 5:38-45 (*The New American Bible*).

80. Romans 13:1-4 (*The New American Bible*).

81. H. Wayne House, "The New Testament and Moral Arguments for Capital Punishment," in *The Death Penalty in America: Current Controversies,* ed. Hugo Adam

Bedau (New York: Oxford University Press, 1997), 415-428.

82. St. Augustine, *The City of God* http://www.ccel.org/fathers/NPNF1-02/

83. Charles P. Nemeth, *Aquinas in the Courtroom: Lawyers, Judges, and Judicial Conduct* (Westport: Praeger Publishers, 2001), 81.

84. St. Thomas Aquinas, *Summa Theologica*, II - II, Question 64, A. 2, ad 1.

85. Charles P. Nemeth, *Aquinas in the Courtroom: Lawyers, Judges, and Judicial Conduct* (Westport: Praeger Publishers, 2001), 172.

86. St. Thomas Aquinas, *Commentary on the Nichomachean Ethics*, trans. C.I. Litzinger (Chicago: Henry Regnery, 1964).

87. St. Thomas Aquinas, *Commentary on the Nichomachean Ethics*, trans. C.I. Litzinger (Chicago: Henry Regnery, 1964).

88. St. Thomas Aquinas, *Summa Contra Gentiles*, trans. Vernon J. Bourke (Notre Dame: Notre Dame University Press, 1975), III-II, Chapter 140, 2.

89. St. Thomas Aquinas, *Summa Theologica*, II - II, Question 64, A. 6, ad 3.

90. St. Thomas Aquinas, *Summa Theologica*, II - II, Question 64, A. 7; See also Charles P. Nemeth, *Aquinas in the Courtroom: Lawyers, Judges, and Judicial Conduct* (Westport: Praeger Publishers, 2001).

91. St. Thomas Aquinas, *Summa Theologica*, II - II, Question 64, A. 6, ad. 3.

92. Avery Cardinal Dulles, "Catholicism & Capital Punishment," *First Things* 112 (April 2001): 31.

93. Avery Cardinal Dulles, "Catholicism & Capital Punishment," *First Things* 112 (April 2001): 31.

94. Avery Cardinal Dulles, "Catholicism & Capital Punishment," *First Things* 112 (April 2001): 31.

95. Catholic Church, *Catechism of the Catholic Church*, 2nd ed. (Washington, D.C.: United States Catholic Conference, Inc., 1997), No. 2266.

96. Catholic Church, *Catechism of the Catholic Church*, 2nd ed. (Washington, D.C.: United States Catholic Conference, Inc., 1997), No. 2267.

97. Pope John Paul II, *Evangelium Vitae* http://www.vatican.va/holy_father/john_paul_ii/encyclicals/documents/hf_jp-ii_enc_25031995_evangelium-vitae_en.html

98. Pope John Paul II, *Evangelium Vitae* http://www.vatican.va/holy_father/john_paul_ii/encyclicals/documents/hf_jp-ii_enc_25031995_evangelium-vitae_en.html Section 9.

99. Pope John Paul II, *Evangelium Vitae* http://www.vatican.va/holy_father/john_paul_ii/encyclicals/documents/hf_jp-ii_enc_25031995_evangelium-vitae_en.html Section 9.

100. Pope John Paul II, *Evangelium Vitae* http://www.vatican.va/holy_father/john_paul_ii/encyclicals/documents/hf_jp-ii_enc_25031995_evangelium-vitae_en.html Section 27.

101. Pope John Paul II, *Evangelium Vitae* http://www.vatican.va/holy_father/john_paul_ii/encyclicals/documents/hf_jp-ii_enc_25031995_evangelium-vitae_en.html Section 27.

102. Catholic Church, *Catechism of the Catholic Church*, 2nd ed. (Washington, D.C.: United States Catholic Conference, Inc., 1997), No. 2267.

103. See for instance the homepage of the United States Conference of Catholic Bishops at http://www.nccbuscc.org/

104. NCCB/USCC, *Quest for Justice: A Compendium of Statements by the Ameri-*

can Catholic Bishops on the Political and Social Order, 1966-1980 (Washington, D.C.: USCC, 1981), 221; See also J. Brian Benestad, *The Pursuit of a Just Social Order: Policy Statements of the U.S. Catholic Bishops, 1966-80* (Washington, D.C.: Ethics and Public Policy Center, 1982).

105. NCCB/USCC, *Statement on Capital Punishment: U.S. Bishops, November, 1980* (Washington, D.C.: USCC, 1980); See also Joseph M. Champlin, *Father Champlin on Contemporary Issues* (Liguori: Liguori Press, 1997), 34.

106. NCCB/USCC, *Statement on Capital Punishment: U.S. Bishops, November, 1980* (Washington, D.C.: USCC, 1980).

107. USCC, *A Good Friday Appeal to End the Death Penalty. A Statement of the Administrative Board of the U.S. Catholic Conference, April 2, 1999* (Washington, D.C.: USCC, 1999).

108. USCCB, *A Culture of Life and the Penalty of Death* (Washington, D.C.: USCC, 2005).

109. USCCB, *A Culture of Life and the Penalty of Death* (Washington, D.C.: USCC, 2005), 3.

110. Avery Cardinal Dulles, "Catholicism & Capital Punishment," *First Things* 112 (April 2001): 30-35.

111. Avery Cardinal Dulles, "Catholicism & Capital Punishment," *First Things* 112 (April 2001): 30-35.

112. Avery Cardinal Dulles, "Catholicism & Capital Punishment," *First Things* 112 (April 2001): 30-35.

113. Avery Cardinal Dulles, "Catholicism & Capital Punishment," *First Things* 112 (April 2001): 30-35.

114. E. Christian Brugger, "Cardinal Avery Dulles and His Critics: An Exchange on Capital Punishment," *First Things* 115 (August/September 2001): 7-16; Charles E. Rice, "Cardinal Avery Dulles and His Critics: An Exchange on Capital Punishment," *First Things* 115 (August/September 2001): 7-16; Kevin M. Doyle, "Cardinal Avery Dulles and His Critics: An Exchange on Capital Punishment," *First Things* 115 (August/September 2001): 7-16.

115. Avery Dulles, "Cardinal Avery Dulles and His Critics: An Exchange on Capital Punishment," *First Things* 115 (August/September 2001): 7-16; Ralph McInerny, "Cardinal Avery Dulles and His Critics: An Exchange on Capital Punishment," *First Things* 115 (August/September 2001): 7-16.

116. Pew Forum, "A Call For Reckoning: Religion and the Death Penalty," Conference held in Washington, D.C., January 25, 2002 http://pewforum.org/deathpenalty/resources; See also Antonin Scalia, "God's Justice and Ours," *First Things* 123 (May . 2002): 17-21.

117. Pew Forum, "A Call For Reckoning: Religion and the Death Penalty," Conference held in Washington, D.C., January 25, 2002 http://pewforum.org/deathpenalty/resources; See also Antonin Scalia, "God's Justice and Ours," *First Things* 123 (May . 2002): 17-21.

118. Pew Forum, "A Call For Reckoning: Religion and the Death Penalty," Conference held in Washington, D.C., January 25, 2002 http://pewforum.org/deathpenalty/resources; See also Antonin Scalia, "God's Justice and Ours," *First Things* 123 (May . 2002): 17-21.

119. Avery Dulles, "Cardinal Avery Dulles and His Critics: An Exchange on Capital

Punishment," *First Things* 115 (August/September 2001): 7-16; Avery Dulles, et al., "Antonin Scalia and His Critics: The Church, the Courts, and the Death Penalty," *First Things* 126 (October 2002): 8-18.

120. Charles Rice, "Papal Teaching Deserves 'Submission,'" *National Catholic Register,* (March 24-30, 2002): 7-10.

121. Avery Dulles, et al., "Antonin Scalia and His Critics: The Church, the Courts, and the Death Penalty," *First Things* 126 (October 2002): 8-18; Gilbert Meilaender, "Capital and Other Punishments," *First Things* 117 (November 2001): 8-10.

122. Charles E. Rice, "Cardinal Avery Dulles and His Critics: An Exchange on Capital Punishment," *First Things* 115 (August/September 2001): 7-16.

123. Ralph McInerny, "Cardinal Avery Dulles and His Critics: An Exchange on Capital Punishment," *First Things* 115 (August/September 2001): 7-16.

124. Catholic Church, *Catechism of the Catholic Church,* 2nd ed. (Washington, D.C.: United States Catholic Conference, Inc., 1997), No. 2266.

125. Catholic Church, *Catechism of the Catholic Church,* 2nd ed. (Washington, D.C.: United States Catholic Conference, Inc., 1997), No. 2267.

Chapter 8

Abortion/Euthanasia

"I have set before you life and death, the blessing and the curse. Choose life, then, that you and your descendants may live, by loving the Lord, your God, heeding his voice and holding fast to him."

- Deuteronomy 30:19-20 -

Introduction

Although the death penalty, which deals with the state's right to take the life of a convicted murderer, is generally considered an issue more central to criminal justice than abortion or euthanasia, these two issues focus on the taking of innocent life and are therefore critical to understanding a Catholic perspective on crime. Less discussed from the perspective of the secular criminal justice system, but very important from a life standpoint in the Catholic faith, are the issues of abortion and euthanasia. Each of these issues play a major role in American politics, but have little role in the duties of the American criminal justice system. While abortion is currently legal as a result of the United States Supreme Court decisions of *Roe v. Wade* (1972) and its companion case of *Doe v. Bolton* (1972), seen from a Catholic perspective, abortion is the taking of a human life and thus is murder. Therefore, a Catholic perspective on crime and justice would see abortion as a criminal act that would need to be enforced accordingly. In the case of euthanasia, which remains illegal throughout the United States except in the State of Oregon, a Catholic perspective on crime and justice would also keep the behavior criminal and enforce it accordingly. Understanding why the Catholic perspective is so strong regarding these two acts is important to understanding not only the Catholic faith, but what criminal justice from a Catholic perspective would entail.

Both the topics of abortion and euthanasia will be treated in a similar fashion in this chapter. First, there will be a discussion of each as it relates to American history, from both a social and legal perspective. Second, a review of the basic facts of each will be covered, presenting the data on the extent to which these two acts occur. The third section for each topic will discuss the

221

American public's views on the issues through the use of recent public opinion polls, as well as those that have been asked with relative frequency across time. Finally, the Catholic perspective on each of these subjects will be presented, discussing the Church's stance based on Scripture, Doctrine, and Faith. The chapter will conclude with an explanation as to why both abortion and euthanasia would be illegal under a Catholic perspective of crime and justice.

Abortion

History

Prior to the nineteenth century, abortions were neither legal nor illegal; they simply were not regulated by the criminal law. The practice was considered immoral by most due to the Judeo-Christian background of most early Americans, which is why within the practice of common law abortion was prohibited after what was known as "quickening," or the point at which the baby begins to move in the mother's womb. Summarizing the early movements of the common law in regard to abortion, Mohr explains that:

> the common law did not formally recognize the existence of a fetus in criminal cases until it had quickened. After quickening, the expulsion and destruction of a fetus without due cause was considered a crime, because the fetus itself had manifested some semblance of a separate existence: the ability to move. The crime was qualitatively different from the destruction of a human being, however, and punished less harshly. Before quickening, actions that had the effect of terminating what turned out to have been an early pregnancy was not considered criminal under the common law in effect in . . . the United States in 1800.[1]

Thus, the common law recognized the fetus after movement and regulated against abortion, but generally not prior to quickening. This practice was followed by all thirteen of the new states at the point the United States Constitution was ratified and the new federal government formed.[2]

As a result of the common law concept of abortion and Judeo-Christian values, abortions were largely driven underground and were "performed by midwives, herbalists, and rogue doctors,"[3] who either advertised their services in newspapers or through storefronts established in what would become known as "red-light districts."[4] In addition, abortion literature and devices were also sold through the mail allowing for women to perform self-induced abortions in their homes.

The first laws aimed at regulating abortion came in 1821 when Connecticut banned any abortion after "quickening."[5] New York followed suit with their own law in 1829, making all abortions illegal, to include prior to quickening, but they did enter an exception into their law legalizing those abortions that were deemed "necessary to preserve the life of such mother, or shall have been advised by two physicians to be necessary for such purpose."[6] The New York law became a model for other states that would begin adopting similar laws. A total of sixteen states adopted the New York law between 1830 and 1849.[7]

In the mid-1800s, the medical community began a movement to prevent midwives and rogue doctors from performing abortions. Physicians drew upon the fact that many saw abortion as being immoral and they aimed their justification for needed regulation as being for the health of the woman, as the midwives, herbalists, and self-abortion devices could present serious dangers to the woman's life in the performance of these abortions. However, there was also a monetary incentive for the doctors to be the only people authorized to perform abortions, thus it became a means of monopolizing the practice under the legitimate medical community. As Luker has pointed out, this largely generated a contradiction in that doctors claimed abortion to be morally wrong, but they should be the only ones who determine if an abortion should be performed and, if so, perform it.[8] Regardless, it was largely the medical community, through the growing power of the American Medical Association, that launched the movement to regulate abortion.[9]

As the concern among the medical community grew, however, awareness regarding abortions among the populace also grew. This would lead to a number of religious groups taking part in the movement from a purely moral perspective hoping to do away with abortion by encouraging lawmakers to make it illegal. As a result of both of these movements, the latter half of the nineteenth century was witness to a number of states beginning to regulate abortion. Between 1850 and 1900, an additional twenty-five states passed laws against abortion.[10] A number of these states made abortion illegal regardless, while most continued to make it illegal unless the life of the mother was threatened, and it mandated that in such cases the abortion had to be performed by a licensed physician.

In addition to state laws, the federal government also passed a law with the intent of regulating what was becoming a growing abortion industry. In 1873, Anthony Comstock proposed and Congress passed what would become known as the Comstock Act. This law made it a felony to publish, distribute, or possess "information about or devices or medications for unlawful abortions or contraception."[11] As the postal service grew, many people were capitalizing on the ease of selling items such as pornography, abortion literature, and abortion devices and medicines through the mail. Drawing upon their ability to regulate interstate commerce, Congress passed the law to target these types of mailings. While the law proposed a maximum penalty of five years at hard labor and a $2,000 fine, the law was rarely enforced due to the difficulties in investigating items in the mail due to privacy rights.

Despite the numerous laws related to abortion, either the law was continually violated or the law was not applied when abortions were discovered to have been performed. One estimate of the number of illegal abortions between 1939 and 1964 places the number at about one in every five pregnancies in America, equating to approximately one million each year.[12] As one authority on the subject in the early twentieth century explained, "I know of no other instance in which there has been so much frank and universal disregard for a criminal law."[13] Thus, as Mohr explained, the problem of abortion and the violation of the laws pertaining to the act were largely ignored, and it was not until the 1960s that the issue would again become a major national issue.

Once again, the lead-up to the 1960s debate was largely initiated by the medical community. As twentieth-century medical technology improved, the risk of performing an abortion decreased. Thus, abortions could be performed more safely and did not pose as much risk to the health of the woman during the procedure. As a result, proposals were made within the medical community to expand the circumstances under which abortions could be performed, including cases of rape or incest or when the child might be born with a physical or mental defect. In addition, there was also a movement to allow for exceptions when either the physical or mental health of the woman was threatened. The American Legal Institute proposed a model penal code in 1959 that incorporated all of these exceptions which would help to launch the abortion reform movement of the 1960s.[14] A number of organizations would sign on to the model proposed, supporting "therapeutic abortions," including the American Civil Liberties Union (1967), the American Medical Association (1967), the American Public Health Association (1968), and Planned Parenthood (1969).[15] The movement was no longer relegated to state level politics, but had moved to the national stage.

As the abortion issue spilled out onto the national stage at a time when other social issues were being challenged, it generated an issue that moved from a campaign for self-regulation by the medical community to a moral issue of the most divisive nature. The debate began to be defined in moral terms by the Roman Catholic Church under Vatican II defining abortion "as an unspeakable crime tantamount to infanticide."[16] A loose coalition of groups such as the National Organization for Women and the National Association for the Repeal of Abortion Laws (later the National Abortion Rights Action League) began defining the abortion ban as a violation of women's right to privacy over their body. This debate would find its way into state-level politics and implemented with state-level legislation. By 1973, when the decision in the Supreme Court case of *Roe v. Wade* was issued, 18 states had reformed or repealed their nineteenth-century abortion laws.[17]

Despite the fact that states were beginning to wrestle with the issue of abortion within the realm of state politics, the United States Supreme Court put an abrupt end to the issue when it put forth its decision in the case of *Roe v. Wade* (1973) and the companion case of *Doe v. Bolton* (1973).[18] The *Roe v. Wade* ruling, determined by a 7-2 vote, allowed abortions in the first trimester of a pregnancy, and the companion case of *Doe* made it permissible to have an abortion after the first trimester if the woman's health was at risk, both physically and/or mentally. In effect, the dual decisions made abortion in America legal, on-demand, throughout a woman's pregnancy.

The decision drew primarily on the issue of a woman's right to privacy as the basis for its decision. More specifically it drew upon the previous Supreme Court decision of *Griswold v. Connecticut* (1965), where the Court had invalidated a law in Connecticut that prohibited married couples the use of contraceptives.[19] As a result, it was no longer prohibited to sell contraceptives in the State of Connecticut or elsewhere to married couples. Later, the issue arose for unmarried couples, and the Supreme Court again extended the same right, based on the concept of privacy rights, allowing anyone the right to access contraceptives in the case of *Eisenstadt v. Bard* (1972).[20] In taking up the *Roe* and *Doe* cases from Texas the next year, the Supreme Court extended the right to privacy, something not explicitly provided for in the Constitution or the Bill of Rights, to the obtaining of an abortion.

Although the Supreme Court decision was believed by many to have been the final decision on abortion and that there was no longer any debate, the passage of *Roe* had the exact opposite effect. Rather than moving it through a political process based on the law, the Supreme Court decision moved abortion into the realm of moral politics, which caused people to pick sides, thus creating a highly divisive and contentious issue. As Tatalovich and Daynes explained, the "Supreme Court's landmark 1973 rulings . . . did not resolve this dispute but rather aggravated it to the point where the very fabric of democratic politics is threatened."[21] As the issue developed, there was hope from the pro-life side that the Court would overturn *Roe,* and from the pro-choice side that *Roe* would be affirmed. It was not until sixteen years later that the Supreme Court would issue another ruling so profoundly impacting the issue of abortion.

In the *Webster* (1989) decision, the United States Supreme Court upheld the constitutionality of a Missouri State Statue that prohibited public funding for programs related to abortions (e.g., abortion counseling) and public facilities (e.g., hospitals) from being used to perform abortions, except when it was deemed necessary to save the woman's life.[22] The Supreme Court's reasoning for prohibiting public funds being used to support abortion "leaves the pregnant woman with the same choices as if the state had chosen not to operate public hospitals at all."[23] As the issue was seen as limitations placed on free access to abortion, those in the pro-choice movement saw the *Webster* decision as a setback to abortion rights. Three years later, however, the Supreme Court would issue another decision that was seen as being somewhat in the pro-choice movement's favor.

In the case of *Planned Parenthood v. Casey* (1992), the U.S. Supreme Court issued a 5-4 decision that upheld a Pennsylvania law which made it mandatory for women to review material related to abortion, to have communicated to her the potential risks, and which imposed a waiting period.[24] However, when it came to the issue of spousal notification of the abortion the Court declared that a woman had a right to privacy over her body and that the states "may not give to a man the kind of dominion over his wife that parents exercise over their children."[25] In effect, the *Casey* decision reaffirmed the right to an abortion through the right to privacy that a woman has over her "bodily integrity." The case, although consisting of several minor setbacks for the pro-choice movement, was largely seen as a major victory, for it reaffirmed the overall right to abortion.

Although not directly related to abortion because the law has been very clear to delineate abortion from fetal homicide, on April 1, 2004, President Bush signed into law the Unborn Victims of Violence Act. The law became known as "Laci and Conner's Law," as Laci Peterson was murdered on Christmas Eve in 2002 while she was pregnant. She had known it was going to be a boy and had already picked out the name Conner. The crime sent shockwaves through America and raised the issue of whether or not the "fetus" was a human life and thus the murderer could be charged not only with the homicide of Laci, but with Conner as well. Twenty-five states currently recognize the "fetus" as being a life and thus can be a victim of a homicide. Another ten states recognize the "fetus" as being a life, but only at certain stages of development. When President Bush signed the Unborn Victims of Violence Act into law, the federal government came to recognize that a "fetus" could be considered the victim of a crime.

While the law has been very specific in identifying that the "fetus" can be considered a life in the case of the criminal law and thus charges brought against anyone who murders the child, it has also been very explicit that in the case of abortion, the criminal law does not apply. In other words, if the life of the "fetus" is stopped by way of an abortion, it is legal. If the life of the "fetus" is stopped by way of a homicide, in those states with such laws, it is illegal. Central to the argument in both cases, however, is whether or not the "fetus" is a life. The former argues it is not, while the latter argues definitively that it is a life. As Professor Lisa Roy has recently pointed out, the *Roe* decision is bad law because the idea "that the fetus is not a person does not work in contexts outside of abortion law."[26]

Interestingly, even the *Roe* decision, upon which the "right to abortion" is built, stated that "if this suggestion of personhood is established, the appellant's case, of course, collapses, for the fetus' right to life would then be guaranteed specifically by the Amendment."[27] It further states that even the appellant conceded to this fact on reargument, but that it was argued that "no case could be cited that holds that a fetus is a person within the meaning of the Fourteenth Amendment." Hence, if a "fetus" were to be defined as a "person," then the legal argument for abortion would collapse and *Roe* would be overturned.

The most recent foray into abortion politics has been with the passage of the Partial Birth Abortion Act of 2003. Even the name has incited a political divisiveness in that the medical procedure is known as "dilation and extraction" and "dilation and evacuation." It has come to be known as late-term abortion or partial-birth abortion by those in the pro-life movement and, for the most part, those in the general public. It is called such for in the third trimester a mother's womb is dilated, the fetal sac is then punctured and drained, and the head of the baby is then crushed, the body dismembered, and the pieces removed with forceps and suction.

The law was passed by Congress in 2003 and President Bush signed it into law on November 5, 2003. Within days, three federal judges issued injunctions which blocked the ban's enactment while it went through an appeals process. In the mean time, the State of Nebraska passed a similar law which went before the United States Supreme Court under the case of *Sternberg v. Carhart* (2000). The law was not upheld due to the fact that there was no exception in the law for allowing the procedure when it involved the health of the mother. Ultimately, the New York judges ruled against the right of Congress to ignore the health of the woman exception mandated by the Supreme Court in *National Abortion Federation v. Ashcroft* (2004), and two other cases, one in California (*Planned Parenthood v. Ashcroft* (2004)) and one in Nebraska (*Carhart v. Ashcroft* (2004)), which reached similar conclusions. The issue was once again brought up in additional cases which were then appealed to the United States Supreme Court.

The two cases, both involving the new U.S. Attorney General Alberto Gonzales, were *Gonzalez v. Carhart* and *Gonzalez v. Planned Parenthood.* In their 5-4 decision, issued on April 18, 2007, the United States Supreme Court upheld the 2003 federal Partial Birth Abortion Act. Justice Kennedy, the swing vote and the author of the majority opinion, wrote that the ban "expresses respect for the dignity of human life" and that "the government may use its voice and its regulatory authority to show its profound respect for the life within the woman."[28] The decision was seen as a victory on the pro-life side, and a slippery slope toward further regulations to do away with abortion on the pro-choice side.

Data

Although abortions have assuredly occurred with a high frequency through the years, the legalization of abortion by *Roe* has assuredly expanded the numbers of abortion in the United States since the 1973 decision. According to the Alan Guttmacher Institute (AGI), a research affiliate of Planned Parenthood, there have been over 48 million abortions in America since 1973.[29] The Center for Disease Control (CDC) estimates that there have been approximately 40 million abortions in America since 1973.[30] The reason for the disparity in numbers is the method by which abortions are counted. The AGI's figures are based on surveys of actual abortion clinics, private doctor's offices, and hospitals, which then compile the figures annually. The CDC figures are based on reports furnished by the 50 state health departments, as well as New York City and Washington, D.C., which the CDC then simply compiles to report its annual figures. It should also be mentioned that in many given years, a number of states have failed to provide their annual figures to the CDC, leaving the estimated number of abortions short. For instance, in the 1998-1999 totals, Alaska, California, New Hampshire, and Oklahoma were not counted, greatly reducing the number of abortions reported for that year. Therefore, on an annual basis, the CDC typically under-reports when compared to the AGI figures. In addition, it should be noted that the AGI admits that its figures are most likely short of the actual annual number due to under-reporting, and they estimate the annual average of under-reporting at three percent or 1.1 million abortions a year.[31]

According to the AGI figures, in 1973, the year abortion became legal, there were 744,600 abortions performed. The following year, 1974, that number jumped to 898,600, and then exceeded one million in 1975. By 1977, the figure had reached 1.3 million, by 1980, 1.5 million, and it peaked in 1990 with 1.6 million abortions. The number of abortions since 1990 has continued to decline by most estimates, falling back to exactly 1.5 million in 1993, 1.4 million in 1994, and 1.3 million by 1995. Finally, by 2002, the number had fallen to 1.2 million abortions each year in the United States, and this is where it is estimated to have remained. Hence the overall picture of abortions in the United States have shown a dramatic rise in the 1970s after abortion became legal, a leveling off in the 1980s, and a slow decline in the 1990s and into the twenty-first century.

When looking more in-depth at the data provided by the AGI, they report that half of all pregnancies of American women are unintended and that four in 10 of these end in abortion. In addition, approximately half of American women have experienced an unintended pregnancy, and at current rates more than one-third (35 percent) will have had an abortion by age 45. The AGI data also shows that nine in 10 abortions occur in the first 12 weeks of pregnancy. While AGI has acknowledged that the overall unintended pregnancy rates have stagnated over the past decade, they also report that unintended pregnancy increased by 29 percent among poor women while decreasing 20 percent among higher-income women in the early twenty-first century. More specifically, looking at the demographics of those women who obtain an abortion, the AGI reports that 56 percent of women having abortions are in their 20s; 61 percent have one or more children; 67 percent have never married; 57 percent are economically disadvantaged; 88 percent live in a metropolitan area; and 78 percent report a religious affiliation.[32]

Turning to the in-depth information regarding the CDC data, one report looked at the year for which the most recent data was available, 2002, and reported that 854,122 abortions were performed that year.[33] Again, when compared to the 1.2 million abortions reported by the AGI for the same year, despite several states not reporting (including California and Alaska), it still raises questions as to the vast difference between the two sets of figures. Despite this disparity, when looking at the demographics of those obtaining abortions in the CDC report, there are similar findings. The CDC reports that the highest percentages of reported abortions were for unmarried women (82 percent), who were white (55 percent), and less than 25 years of age (51 percent). The majority of abortions were performed in the woman's state of residence (91 percent) with 9 percent traveling out of state to obtain an abortion. The majority of women (40 percent) had no previous live births, but 27 percent had one, and 20 percent of the women had two previous live births. The majority of abortions were performed at less than 13 weeks (88 percent), with 4.1 percent being performed between 16-20 weeks and 1.4 percent at greater than 21 weeks gestation. Although most of the women obtaining abortions are 18 or older, 4,198 girls under the age of 15 received an abortion in 2002. In addition, the number of abortions for girls age 15 was 7,550. Aged 16 was 13,984, and those aged 17 was 20,899.

Public Opinion

As previously stated, the legalization of abortion by the United States Supreme Court in the case of *Roe v. Wade* (1973) did little to settle the legal dispute over abortion and, in fact, exacerbated the issue, making it one of the most divisive issues in modern times. How Americans have come to see the abortion issue is not so simple. While many public opinion polls simply ask if one favors abortion or not, Americans' opinions related to if and when abortion should be legal are not so simple. In fact, understanding where Americans stand on abortion is important to understanding the debate itself. Although public opinion polls related to abortion often conflict due to both timing and wording of the questions, they do begin to present an overall picture of Americans' views on abortion; hence they are important to review.

A consistent question, asked by the Gallup Poll organization, since abortion became legal is "do you think abortions should be legal under any circumstances, legal only under certain circumstances, or illegal in all circumstances?"[34] Since the question was first asked in 1975, the figures have been largely consistent over time. For instance, in 1975, 21 percent of the sample stated that abortion should always be legal and 22 percent stated it should never be legal. In 2005, thirty years later, 23 percent of that sample said it should always be legal and 22 percent said it should never be legal. The majority, in both the 1975 and 2005 public opinion polls said that it should be legal under certain circumstances with responses of 54 percent and 53 percent respectively. These figures demonstrate that most Americans believe that abortion should not be totally legal or totally illegal, but rather it should be legal in certain circumstances. What those circumstances are, are not specified.

Another example of the vagueness of many of these polls comes from the Higher Education Research Institute which has also asked its own version of the abortion questions since 1977. The question is asked annually of college freshmen and it is simply, "should abortion be legal."[35] Those responding in the affirmative have remained consistent over time. In 1977, 55 percent of males and 55 percent of females reported it should be legal for a total of 55 percent answering in the affirmative. In 2005, the response rate of males was 55 percent, females 54 percent, and the total average being 55 percent. Although the total response rates in the affirmative did rise in the 1980s by as much as 10 percentage points, by the 1990s they had dropped back to the mid-fifty percentage points. Yet, like the Gallup poll, the question does not fully address the issue of what is meant by legal. Legal all the time, regardless, or legal in certain circumstances. These types of questions simply raise more questions about Americans views (and college freshmen views) on abortion.

A recent Zogby poll in 2004 expanded the types of questions that the survey respondents were asked.[36] For instance, respondents were asked if they considered themselves pro-life or pro-choice and 49 percent reported they were pro-life, while 45 percent reported they were pro-choice. When asked if abortion should not be permitted after the fetal heartbeat has begun, by combining those who responded strongly agree and somewhat agree, 61 percent agreed with the statement. When combining those that strongly disagreed and somewhat disagreed, 34 percent disagreed with the statement. When the statement was changed to fetal brainwaves being detected, 65 percent agreed that abortions should not be performed and 28 percent disagreed. When asked if they felt that abortions should be paid for with tax dollars, 74 percent disagreed and 22 percent agreed with that statement.

Turning to the specifics of when respondents felt that abortion should be legal or illegal, the questions were more nuanced then other public opinion questions. Respondents reporting that abortion should never be legal was 18 percent, while those reporting it should only be legal when the life of the mother was in danger was 15 percent, and an additional 23 percent reported in should be legal in the case of rape or incest. Totaling the figures for abortion never being legal or legal only in certain circumstances amounts to 56 percent of the sample. Those reporting that abortion should always be legal in the first trimester was 25 percent with only 4 percent reporting within the first six months. Those reporting that abortion should be legal at any time during a woman's pregnancy was 13 percent. Thus combining those that answered legal at some point in the pregnancy for any reason totaled to 42 percent of the sample. The overall picture, then, is that most Americans want severe restrictions placed upon abortion, and that it should only be used in the extreme cases of rape, incest, or when the life of the mother is endangered.

Turning to the young, 18-29 year olds, who are most likely to advocate abortion, the Zogby poll found that a total of 60 percent of the sample wanted severe restrictions placed on abortion. The percentage of 18-29 year olds reporting that abortion should never be legal was 26 percent, much higher than the 18 percent of total respondents to the survey.

According to an in-depth report by the Gallup Poll, over the thirty years since the landmark decision of *Roe v. Wade* (1973), the overall consensus is that Americans believe abortion should be limited to the first trimester and only in those cases involving the life of the woman, rape, or incest.[37] Although many Americans believe that this is in fact the case, that *Roe* did limit abortion to the first trimester, the reality is that *Roe's* companion case *Doe,* allows for abortion after the first trimester when the woman's physical or mental health is jeopardized. So, while *Doe* allows for abortions in the second and third trimester, the majority of Americans want abortion outlawed during these two stages, and it should always be outlawed in the case of lifestyle choices (e.g., financial reasons, mother doesn't want a second or third child, etc.). Finally, the Gallup Poll found that the majority of Americas were against late-term abortions or more specifically what has become known as partial-birth abortions.

The Gallup Poll survey questions related to abortion also highlights the division in America between the pro-life and pro-choice sides. They found that 50 percent of respondents who identified themselves as pro-choice believed that abortion should be legal in all cases, with only 4 percent of those identifying themselves as pro-life agreeing with the statement, whereas 31 percent of those identifying themselves as pro-life believed that abortion should be illegal in all cases, and 3 percent of those reporting to be pro-choice agreed.

The report also looks at other issues related to abortion, such as informed consent, parental consent, and waiting periods.[38] The survey finds that 86 percent of Americans do support the practice of informed consent, where doctors are required to tell their patients about the impact of an abortion on a woman, both mentally and physically, and that there are alternatives to abortions. In addition, 70 percent of Americans support a requirement that husbands be notified if the woman decides to have an abortion. In regard to parental notification, the percentage of those favoring those under 18 years of age being required to notify their parents of an impending abortion ranges from 69 percent to 82 percent; on average it tends to be approximately 75 percent of respondents. Another 75 percent of respondents also advocated a twenty-four-hour waiting period for women to have abortions. Finally, the study found that a majority of Americans were against partial birth abortion, with 77 percent favoring a total ban of the procedure.

Another telling aspect of Americans' nuanced views of abortion shows in under what circumstances they would allow or would want abortion to remain legal.[39] In the case of rape or incest, 79 percent of those responding to the survey favored keeping abortion legal. When asked if for the mental health of the woman, the percentage favoring legal abortion dropped to 64 percent. When positing that the baby would be mentally impaired, 53 percent favored abortion, and when physically impaired, 51 percent favored abortion. As more social reasons were asked, the numbers began to drop off even further. For instance, if it would force a teenager to drop out of school, only 42 percent favored abortion. When the woman could not afford the baby or that the woman did not want more children, 39 percent favored abortion. When the question posited a couple not wanting to marry because of the pregnancy, only 35 percent favored abortion. Finally, when it came to simply fertility selection, only 29 percent favored abortion, and when the reasoning for an abortion was that the baby would interfere with the woman's career, only 25 percent still favored abortion.

Catholic Views

The Catholic view on abortion is in actuality related to the Catholic view on life. Catholics believe that we are made by God and in His image. Life is a continual process upon which God has command, for God knows us before we are conceived. Therefore, from even before the point of conception, but in the very least at the point of conception, human life is sacred. It must be respected and nurtured, from conception, through development in the womb, and then from birth until death. It is this specific right that all humans have, for as the *Catechism of the Catholic Church* explains, "human life must be respected and protected absolutely from the moment of conception" and that "from the first moment of his existence, a human being must be recognized as having the rights of a person—among which is the inviolable right of every innocent being to life."[40] This last phrase communicates very directly the perspective of the Catholic Church in how it would perceive abortion under the criminal law. As it is an inviolable right, laws must be made to protect against such violations of the law, and, hence, abortion would be illegal.

In order to further explore the Catholic Church's views on abortion, it is important to draw upon the rich heritage provided in Scripture, Church writings, as well as those presented by the U.S. Catholic Bishops. In fact, when discussing the inviolability related to the right to life for every human being, the *Catechism* quotes several passages from Scripture. One that highlights the understanding that we are all created by God is found in Jeremiah 1:5 (as well as Job 10:8-12 and Psalms 22:10-11), "before I formed you in the womb I knew you, and before you were born I consecrated you."[41] Although Scripture does relay the belief that life is sacred, there are often situations in the Bible where life is taken. The same can be said for abortion, for there are many times in the Bible where abortion is clearly conveyed as being immoral and wrong, but there are some incidents where abortion is seen as the "lesser of two evils." As William Kurz explains, "those like myself who argue that the Bible (or at least the "biblical world view") never permits direct abortion for any reasons or in any circumstances generally use natural law reasoning to supplement and reinforce their biblical principles and arguments."[42] As a result, strict interpretation of the Bible may create situations where some may conclude that abortion may be acceptable under certain circumstances, but under Catholic teaching, a rich history of Catholic traditions, theology, and philosophical ethical considerations present the view that abortion is always immoral.

According to Kurz, "the bedrock passage for prolife appropriation of Scripture is *Genesis* 1:26-27."[43] This passage in Genesis states, "then God said, 'Let us make man in our image, after our likeness; and let them have dominion over the fish of the sea, and over the birds of the air, and over all the earth, and over every creeping thing that creeps upon the earth.' So God created man in his own image, in the image of God he created him; male and female he created them."[44] The key aspect of this passage is that it is the completion of the creation story, after creating the universe, earth, and all the creatures on earth, God creates man. And in doing so, creates him to be in his own image. As Pope John Paul II explained in his encyclical, *Theology of the Body*, this is critical for our humanity, specifically masculine or feminine, is based upon God's blessing, and it is essential to our being in God's image.[45] Thus, man and woman are given a special place on earth and told further in Genesis to "be fruitful and multiply, and fill the earth and subdue it."

According to Kurz,[46] the key to the creation of man by God is that while God created man to have "dominion" over the earth, God did not make man and woman gods unto themselves, but rather he remained the one and only God. This means that man must still be obedient to God and obey his authority and not supercede that authority. The later commandment of "thou shalt not kill," expressly denotes what is beyond man's authority, such as abortion. This is because God places a high value and dignity upon the human life that He created. This can be seen in the desire by God that man "be fruitful and multiply," and conversely in the biblical punishment of being "barren" or sterile, which was seen as a curse.[47] Still further, the explicit prohibitions against idolatry and homosexual intercourse highlight the importance of life to God, for in neither of these acts can life spring forth.

As the *Catechism* highlights the passage that God knows us before we are conceived, Kurz argues that this is representative of the "biblical conviction that God has a plan and vocation or mission for humans, even before they are born."[48] He highlights the passage found in the *Catechism* (Jeremiah 1:5) and notes that the verse is echoed by Paul in Galatians (1:15) when Paul writes, "but when he who had set me apart before I was born . . . ." Thus, God knowing each human prior to conception and having a plan for each child, would not want that child aborted, because he or she is destined to life.

Kurz uses a syllogism to convey the biblical view on abortion by arguing the major premise related to life, the minor premise based on early biblical understanding of life, and the conclusion that abortion would be biblically prohibited. He explains the major premise as being "Scripture absolutely prohibits shedding innocent human blood (i.e., killing innocent human beings)."[49] The minor premise is that "the biblical world view, gleaned from both Old Testament and New Testament, but certainly by the time of the New Testament, regards the prenatal baby in the womb as an innocent human being."[50] This leads to the conclusion that "abortion (as shedding innocent human blood) would be absolutely prohibited."[51] Kurz explains further that "the species 'abortion' fits under the genus 'shedding innocent human blood,'" and is therefore "absolutely forbidden."[52]

While understanding a Scriptural perspective on abortion is important, also important within the Catholic faith are the traditions and teaching that have been built over time by the Church. According to the *Catechism* "since the First Century the Church has affirmed the moral evil of every procured abortion" and that "this teaching has not changed and remains unchangeable."[53] It states that a direct and purposeful abortion, whether the abortion was the means to something or and end unto itself, is "gravely contrary to the moral law."[54] Citing some of the early writings of the Church, the *Catechism* offers evidence that this has always been the teaching of the Catholic Church. One example comes from the *Didache,* the teachings of the Apostles written toward the end of the first century, which states, "you shall not kill the embryo by abortion and shall not cause the newborn to perish."[55] The Catholic Church's stance on abortion has remained unchanged throughout its history, and its stance has been reaffirmed in a number of recent writings, including *Gaudium et Spes.*

In 1965, published under the promulgation of the Vatican II council, *Gaudium et Spes* was a restatement of the social teachings of the Catholic Church, placed within the context of the modern day. *Gaudium* asserted that the social conditions created by man must ensure that three things are always safeguarded, and they are the dignity of the human person, the common good, and the unity of all mankind. Asserting its understanding of life as related to the dignity of the human person, the Church explained that "God, the Lord of life, has entrusted to men the noble mission of safeguarding life, and men must carry it out in a manner worthy of themselves."[56] Further, *Gaudium et Spes* stated that "life must be protected with the utmost care from the moment of conception: abortion and infanticide are abominable crimes." Although *Gaudium* was not specifically addressing the issue of abortion, taken in its larger context it demands that in order for human life to be dignified and respected, it cannot be taken. Rather, it must be safeguarded and protected, even when life is just beginning at the point of conception.

Pope John Paul II makes this same point in his book *Crossing the Threshold of Hope* when he explains that "for man, the right to life is the fundamental right."[57] He argues that modern-day culture has begun to deny that right and has attempted to make it an "uncomfortable right," one which people become uncomfortable in defending because it goes against the grain of popular culture. Yet, Pope John Paul II argued that to deny the right to life is to deny the existence of the very person himself. Still further, he argued that the existence of laws that allow abortion is one of the greatest abominations of this right to existence. The Pope explained:

> The legalization of the termination of pregnancy is none other than the authorization given to an adult, with the approval of an established law, to take the lives of children yet unborn and thus incapable of defending themselves. It is difficult to imagine a more unjust situation, and it is very difficult to speak of obsession in a matter such as this, where we are dealing with a fundamental imperative of every good conscience—the defense of the right to life of an innocent and defenseless human being.[58]

The Pope continues further by dealing with one of the common arguments for abortion and that is the woman's right of choice, to choose whether or not to have an abortion. The Pope frames the question in the same manner as the consistent teachings of the Catholic Church has presented the issue over time, and that is the "woman should not have the right to choose between giving life or taking it away from the unborn child." As the Pope explained, "anyone can see that the alternative here is only apparent . . . it is not possible to speak of the right to choose when a clear moral evil is involved, when what is at stake is the commandment *do not kill!*"[59] Still further, the Pope deals with the often desired exception to the total prohibition against abortion, such as in the case of rape or incest. However, the Pope points out that in the case of both cited circumstances the infant is not the aggressor; the perpetrator is the aggressor. Thus, even under the hypothesis of legitimate defense "a child conceived in its mother's womb is never an unjust aggressor; it is a defenseless being that is waiting to be welcomed and helped."[60] Thus, there can be no exception or moral justification for the act of abortion from a theological or ethical stance, as in all cases it is the killing of a defenseless life.

The year following the publication of his book, Pope John Paul II released his encyclical letter, *Evangelium Vitae*, "The Gospel of Life."[61] In this encyclical, the Pope discusses the value and inviolability of human life, as he explains that "human life is sacred because from its beginning it involves the creative action of God and it remains forever in a special relationship with the Creator."[62] The Pope proceeds to establish a very definitive defense of life, not just as related to the issue of abortion, but as it relates to all human life. The Pope explains that "nothing and no one can in any way permit the killing of an innocent human being, whether a fetus or an embryo, an infant or an adult, an old person, or one suffering from an incurable disease, or a person who is dying."[63] Definitively, the Pope states that abortion is always wrong, and he says so when he later states that, "I declare that direct abortion, that is, abortion willed as an end or as a means, always constitutes a grave moral disorder, since it is the deliberate killing of an innocent human being."[64] The encyclical, once again drawing upon the consistent teachings of the Catholic Church across time, is very clear: abortion is always wrong.

While the prohibitions against abortion are clearly laid out by the Catholic Church, and have remained so for nearly two thousand years, it is important to understand how the Church reacts to the commission of such an act. In terms of the Church itself, the canonical penalty, the penalty imposed by the Church itself, is excommunication. In fact, the Church teaches that a person who purposefully obtains an abortion or performs the abortion is excommunicated in *latae sententiae* which means "by the very commission of the offense." To be excommunicated, means to be outside of the church, and the person can no longer participate or be part of the faithful. In the 1917 Canon there were thirty offenses that would lead to *latae sententiae* excommunication, but in the 1983 Canon the number was reduced to only seven. Abortion remains one of the seven. Hence, abortion is considered a serious violation within Church law.

The Catholic Church also sees the act of abortion as a violation of human life and, within the realm of civil society, a violation of civil and criminal law. The publication by the Congregation for the Doctrine of the Faith, *Donum Vitae,* addresses this specific issue and is quoted in the *Catechism* at length. It summarizes why abortion is considered a criminal act and why the Church believes that it should be legislated against. It states:

> The inalienable rights of the person must be recognized and respected by civil society and the political authority. These human rights depend neither on single individuals nor on parents; nor do they represent a concession made by society and the state; they belong to human nature and are inherent in the person by virtue of the creative act from which the person took his origin. Among such fundamental rights one should mention in this regard every human being's right to life and physical integrity from the moment of conception until death.[65]

> The moment a positive law deprives a category of human beings of the protection which civil legislation ought to accord them, the state is denying the equality of all before the law. When the state does not place its power at the service of the rights of each citizen, and in particular of the more vulnerable, the very foundation of a state based on law are undermined . . . As a consequence of the respect and protection which must be ensured for the unborn child from the moment of conception, the law must provide appropriate penal sanctions for every deliberate violation of the child's rights.[66]

It is clear then, that drawing from Scripture, tradition, and the teachings of the Catholic Church, abortion is always immoral and an act against not only God, but all of humanity. As the protection and safeguarding of human life is critical to the relationship among a civil and political society, abortion, the taking of a life, is considered immoral. As a result, it must be legislated against, made a criminal act, and appropriate penal sanctions laid accordingly. Therefore, when developing a conceptual understanding of criminal justice from a Catholic perspective, abortion would be illegal with no exceptions. The law would recognize this within the criminal and civil codes, and the criminal justice system would be responsible for enforcing the law.

Euthanasia

The term euthanasia means the consensual assistance in the taking of another's life. It is delineated as being separate from murder because it is willing, and it is separated from suicide as there is another person involved, beyond the person attempting to take their own life. Recently in America there has been much discussion of assisted-suicide, where one person assists another in taking their own life, and physician-assisted suicide, where a licensed medical doctor assists an individual in the taking of their life. The Church has further defined euthanasia as "active euthanasia" and "assisted suicide." Active euthanasia is defined as being when "a doctor or medical staff person administers a lethal dose of medication with the intention of killing the patient."[67] Assisted suicide is defined as being where "a doctor or medical staff person prescribes a lethal amount of medication with the intent of helping a person commit suicide," but that "the patient then takes the dose or turns the switch."[68] It is to this latter means that Dr. Jack Kevorkian gained his fame by assisting people in the commission of their suicide by providing them the means, then allowing them to commit suicide on their own. In this manner, he argued that he was not killing the individual, they were in effect committing suicide, and therefore, he was not ethically culpable. Despite the ethical chicanery, the Catholic Church is very clear that both types of euthanasia are ethically immoral.

In discussing euthanasia the Church has also found it important to delineate between the level of care afforded to a sick or dying individual. Pope Pius XII, in the 1950s, was the first to begin delineating the circumstances revolving around euthanasia. Drawing upon the teaching of the respect of human dignity, he distinguished between ordinary and extraordinary treatments. He explained that under certain circumstances, when treatments were "extraordinary," they might be withdrawn and still be licit.[69] This concept was reaffirmed by the Congregation for the Doctrine of the Faith in its *Declaration on Euthanasia* as well as Pope John Paul II's *Evagenlium Vitae,* "The Gospel of Life." In more recent writings, the terms have shifted from "ordinary" and "extraordinary" to "proportionate" and "disproportionate," denoting a more medical perspective, rather than a moral one.[70]

Proportionate means are defined as "medical treatments that offer a reasonable hope of benefit and do not involve an excessive burden."[71] Disproportionate means are defined as "medical treatments that either does not offer a reasonable hope of benefit or imposes an excessive burden."[72] The difference may be found in the use of devices intended to keep a person alive such as the breathing machine and a feeding tube. Although individuals may be placed on life support machines that breathe for them, if there is no possible means of curing the individual (e.g., it is not a temporary solution to the medical problem), it is not euthanasia to disconnect the machine, even if that means the individual would die. The breathing machine is not natural and not a requirement. In the case of the feeding tube, however, food and water are natural and not an excessive burden. The removal of a feeding tube would amount to the denial of something natural and necessary for life, and hence it would be considered a disproportionate means.

History

Richard S. Myers paints a legal history of euthanasia that conveys it as a relatively modern phenomenon, only coming about over the past two decades.[73] Prior to the 1990s, the acts of suicide, assisted-suicide, and physician-assisted suicide were all criminal behaviors, and had been largely undisputed throughout American history. He argues that the abortion case of *Planned Parenthood v. Casey* (1992) (previously discussed) opened the legal door to granting the "right" to euthanasia as that case stated that "at the heart of liberty is the right to define one's own concept of existence, of meaning, of the universe, and of the mystery of life."[74] He then explained that in the early 1990s, there were several challenges to the laws that banned assisted suicides, and they cited the language in the *Casey* case. These cases were circulating in the States of Washington and New York, and they challenged the law as existing only because of religious convictions, and they argued that they did not provide equal protection under the law. Eventually the cases of *Washington v. Glucksberg* and *Vacco v. Quill* (1997) were heard by the United States Supreme Court, and the court rejected the constitutional challenge of the laws that banned assisted suicide. The court rejected all of the lower courts' rationales for allowing assisted suicide.

In a number of states, the issue of allowing assisted suicides moved from the judiciary and into the legislature. A number of states, including Maine, Hawaii, and Michigan, passed legislation that would put the issue to the voters, allowing them to decide whether or not they would overturn the long existing bans. In all of these states, the citizens voted against the removal of the ban, some by a wide margin (Michigan with 71 percent) and some by a narrow margin (Maine with 51 percent).[75] So, then the question begs as to how Oregon became the only state in the nation that allows assisted suicides.

According to the Oregon Department of Human Services, the initiative to allow assisted suicides arose in the early 1990s, and an initiative, The Oregon Death with Dignity Act (DWDA), was put before the populace in November of 1994. The initiative passed, narrowly, with 51 percent in favor of allowing assisted suicides. Immediately, a legal injunction was placed on the initiative, which was challenged for several years. Eventually the Ninth Circuit Court lifted the injunction on October 27, 1997. The next month, a measure was again placed before the citizens of Oregon asking them to repeal the Death with Dignity Act. The voters overwhelmingly rejected the measure, and thus the initiative was retained and implemented. There have been additional legal challenges, such as the one by the U.S. Attorney General John Ashcroft, which attempted to prohibit doctors from prescribing the drugs used in the assisted suicides, but these have been to no avail in the Ninth Circuit Court, and the U.S. Supreme Court has only heard one appeal, in 2005, which affirmed the lower court's decision. Hence, since 1998, in the State of Oregon, physician assisted suicide has been legal.

Data

There is little data kept on euthanasia in the United States, so it is difficult to ascertain the actual annual number that die in this manner. According to the National Institute for Mental Health, approximately 30,000 people die each year by suicide, but it is difficult to know how many of these may have been through either assistance or physician-assistance.[76] In addition, it has been found that 2.2 million deaths occur annually in American hospitals, and it is estimated that 1.5 million of these die from an explicit decision to withdraw or withhold some form of treatment.[77] Yet, again, it is difficult to ascertain how many of these fall into the ordinary/proportionate or extraordinary/disproportionate means. The only accurate data that can be provided comes from the State of Oregon which has had legalized euthanasia since 1998.

According to a recent report regarding Oregon's "end-of-life care" cases, there have been a total of 292 cases where a patient died after ingesting a lethal dose of medication from 1998 through 2006.[78] That is approximately 33 cases annually over the nine year period. There tended to be slightly more males (54 percent) than females (46 percent) committing assisted suicide, and the majority tended to be aged 60 or older with a median age of 70. However, there were 3 cases of those between 18 and 34 committing this act. An overwhelming majority tended to be white (97 percent), married (46 percent), and with a college education (41 percent). The underlying illness tended to be some form of cancer, and most were enrolled in Hospice. The primary reasons for ending their lives consisted of multiple responses with the justifications of "losing autonomy," "less able to engage in activities making life enjoyable," and "loss of dignity" being the most cited reasons. Most of the patients committed assisted-suicide at home using either a lethal dose of Secobarbital or Pentobarbital. In the majority of the cases some type of provider other than a doctor was present (53 percent), in some the prescribing physician was present (29 percent), and in a small percentage there were no providers (18 percent). The most serious complication reported was regurgitation of the medicine (6 percent) and one percent had to call for emergency medical service.

Public Opinion

Public opinion surveys related to the issue of physician-assisted suicide became common in the mid to late 1990s as the issue came to the forefront of media attention with Dr. Jack Kevorkian, the legislative activities of several states to legalize assisted-suicide, and the U.S. Supreme Court becoming involved in a physician-assisted suicide case. In 1996, a Gallup Poll survey asked respondents, "when a person has a disease that cannot be cured and is living in severe pain, do you think doctors should or should not be allowed by law to assist the patient to commit suicide if the patient requests it?" Approximately half (52 percent) of the respondents answered that it should be allowed, while the other half either felt it should not be allowed (42 percent) or they had no opinion (6 percent). As the debate became more prevalent in the late 1990s, the percentage of Americans voicing acceptance of physician-assisted suicide began to slowly rise to 58 percent in January of 1997 and 57 percent in June of that same year. In 1998, it moved to 59 percent, in 1999 to 61 percent, and by 2001 the percentage answering that it should be allowed peaked at 68 percent. As the issue left the forefront of American politics, replaced with issues such as terrorism and the war in Iraq, the percentage voicing acceptance began to fall with 62 percent voicing acceptance in 2003 and 58 percent in 2005.

Catholic Views

Like the Catholic teaching on abortion, that it is always wrong and immoral regardless of the circumstances, the same can be said for euthanasia. Dating back to some of the earliest Church scholars, suicide and assisted suicide was seen as immoral. For instance, St. Augustine wrote that "it is never licit to kill another: even if he should wish it, indeed if he request it, hanging between life and death . . . nor is it licit even when a sick person is no longer able to live."[79] In modern times, the Church has had to make a strong assertion of the immorality of assisted-suicide, especially physician-assisted suicide, as more affluent countries have come to assert the necessity of granting people the right to end their life.

In order to understand the Church's teaching on euthanasia, it is important to understand the Church's stance on suicide. The *Catechism of the Catholic Church* teaches that "we are stewards, not owners, of the life God has entrusted us" and thus "it is not ours to dispose of."[80] It states further that suicide "contradicts the natural inclination of the human being to preserve and perpetuate his life."[81] Moreover, not only is "it gravely contrary to the just love of self," it is also "contrary to the love for the living God."[82] Thus, if committing suicide is immoral and always wrong, then assisting someone in the commission of the act of suicide can never be right.

Addressing more specifically the act of euthanasia, the *Catechism* argues that "those whose lives are diminished or weakened deserve special respect" and that those who are sick or handicapped "should be helped to lead lives as normal as possible."[83] The *Catechism* then explains that "whatever its motives and means, direct euthanasia consists in putting an end to the lives of handicapped, sick, or dying persons" and then definitively states that "it is morally unacceptable."[84] The *Catechism* then becomes more detailed in explaining the moral imperative as it relates to euthanasia. It states:

> Thus an act or omission which, of itself or by intention, causes death in order to eliminate suffering constitutes a murder gravely contrary to the dignity of the human person and to the respect due to the living God, his creator. The error of judgment into which one can fall in good faith does not change the nature of this murderous act, which must always be forbidden and excluded.[85]

The Church then deals with those circumstances as they relate to the medical profession and the circumstances under which not providing care amounts to euthanasia. The *Catechism* explains:

> Discontinuing medical procedures that are burdensome, dangerous, extraordinary, or disproportionate to the expected outcomes can be legitimate; it is the refusal of 'over-zealous' treatment. Here one does not will to cause death; one's inability to impede it is merely accepted. The decisions should be made by the patient if he is competent and able or, if not, by those legally entitled to act for the patient, whose reasonable will and legitimate interests must always be respected.[86]

Continuing with this line of discussion, the *Catechism* further states:

> Even if death is thought imminent, the ordinary care owed to a sick person cannot be legitimately interrupted. The use of painkillers to alleviate the sufferings of the dying, even at the risk of shortening their days, can be morally in conformity with human dignity if death is not willed as either an end or a means, but only foreseen and tolerated as inevitable. Palliative care is a special form of disinterested charity. As such it should be encouraged.[87]

The U.S. Catholic Bishops in their publication of the *United States Catholic Catechism for Adults,* is more direct in its conveyance of the morality of euthanasia, perhaps because the recent debate over physician-assisted suicide that came to the forefront of American politics in the late 1990s. The U.S. Bishops argue that "the emergence of physician-assisted suicide, popularized by the right-to-die movement, seeks to legalize what is an immoral act." More directly, the *U.S. Catechism* states that "intentional euthanasia, sometimes called mercy killing, is murder."[88] Thus, the U.S. Conference of Catholic Bishops conveys most succinctly the Catholic perspective on euthanasia, that like abortion, regardless of the circumstances, assisted-suicide is always immoral, it is always wrong, and it should be defined legally as murder.

Conclusion

America currently allows abortion and is making overtures to allowing euthanasia. Although the United States Supreme Court recently held against the use of partial-birth abortions and a number of states have maintained their support for the illegality of assisted suicides, the fact is that abortions across America, and euthanasia at least in the State of Oregon, still occur. From a Catholic perspective of crime and criminal justice, these instances of legality are unacceptable, and a complete ban should be put in place and enforced to the extent that the criminal justice system is able to enforce these laws. From a Catholic perspective of criminal justice, these two acts would be illegal based on the dignity and sacredness of human life. As a "fetus," the baby growing inside the mother's womb is a human life given by God as a gift. The act of an abortion amounts to murder and thus should be illegal in the laws of mankind and treated as the crime it is. The same holds true for euthanasia, for as God formed the person and gave him or her life, it is only natural that God be the one that takes the life back and that the laws of mankind protect the human dignity of the individual by not allowing another to assist in their death. Making those who suffer as comfortable as humanly possible and preserving life, within the ordinary/proportionate framework, is the role of doctors, nurses, and all mankind.

It can be clearly said that any law which tries to legitimize the direct killing of any human being, especially defenseless infants in the womb, through abortion or euthanasia, are in complete opposition to the immutable right to life that is afforded to every individual. By allowing for this type of murder under the law, they deny the equality of everyone before the law, as they discriminate against certain groups, such as the old, the feeble, or the unborn. Thus, any laws that authorize and promote abortion or euthanasia are not only opposed to the good of the individual, they are opposed to the common good of all mankind. In sum, they lack legitimacy.

It is recognized that not all Catholics adhere to the beliefs of the Church, despite the defense of a consistent ethic of life as found in Scripture, Doctrine, and Faith. One reason often cited is because the act is legal it therefore must be legitimate. Despite their legality, they still lack legitimacy, and those adhering to the Catholic faith should not allow its legality to be equated to legitimacy. Catholics are thus called to conscientiously object to the law and reject the legality of abortion.

Perhaps the best means of summarizing the problems with the "legality" of abortion and euthanasia can be found in the words of Cardinal Ratzinger, now Pope Benedict XVI:

242

A state which arrogates to itself the prerogative of defining which human beings are or are not the subject of rights and which consequently grants to some the power to violate others' fundamental right to life, contradicts the democratic ideal to which it continues to appeal and undermines the very foundation on which it is built. By allowing the rights of the weakest to be violated, the state allows the law of force to prevail over the force of law. One sees, then, that the idea of absolute tolerance of freedom of choice for some destroys the very foundation of a just life together. The separation of politics from any natural content of right, which is the inalienable patrimony of everyone's moral conscience, deprives social life of its ethical substance and leaves it defenseless before the will of the strongest.[89]

Notes

1. James C. Mohr, *Abortion in America: The Origins and Evolution of National Policy, 1800-1900* (New York: Oxford University Press, 1978), 3.

2. Ronald J. Rychlak, "Abortion, Thinking Americans, and Judicial Politics," *Life and Learning XIV: Proceedings of the Fourteenth University Faculty for Life Conference* (Washington, D.C.: University Faculty for Life, 2005), 77-112.

3. Robert F. Meier and Gilbert Geis, *Criminal Justice and Moral Issues* (Los Angeles: Roxbury Publishing Company, 2006), 146.

4. Barbara Katz Rothman, *Recreating Motherhood: Ideology and Technology in a Patriarchal Society* (New York: Norton, 1989).

5. Raymond Tatalovich, *The Politics of Abortion in the United States and Canada: A Comparative Study* (Armonk, NY: M.E. Sharpe, 1997).

6. Lawrence Lader, *Abortion* (Indianapolis, IN: Bobbs-Merrill, 1966), 87.

7. Raymond Tatalovich, *The Politics of Abortion in the United States and Canada: A Comparative Study* (Armonk, NY: M.E. Sharpe, 1997).

8. Kristin Luker, *Abortion and the Politics of Motherhood* (Berkeley, CA: University of California Press, 1984).

9. Ronald Dworkin, *Life's Dominion: An Argument About Abortion, Euthanasia, and Individual Freedom* (New York: Knopf, 1993); Christopher Z. Mooney and Mei-Hsien Lee, "Legislating Morality in the American States: The Case of Pre-Roe Abortion Regulation Reform," *American Journal of Political Science* 39, no.3 (1995): 599-627.

10. Raymond Tatalovich, *The Politics of Abortion in the United States and Canada: A Comparative Study* (Armonk, NY: M.E. Sharpe, 1997).

11. Willard M. Oliver and James F. Hilgenberg, Jr., *A History of Crime and Criminal Justice in America* (Boston: Allyn & Bacon, 2006); Ronald J. Rychlak, "Abortion, Thinking Americans, and Judicial Politics," *Life and Learning XIV: Proceedings of the Fourteenth University Faculty for Life Conference* (Washington, D.C.: University Faculty for Life, 2005), 77-112.

12. Jerome E. Bates and Edward S. Zawadzki, *Criminal Abortions: A Study in Medical Sociology* (Springfield, IL: Thomas, 1964).

13. Frederick J. Taussig, *Abortions, Spontaneous and Induced: Medical and Social Aspects* (St. Louis, MO: V. Mosby, 1936), 422.

Chapter Eight

14. Christopher Z. Mooney and Mei-Hsien Lee, "Legislating Morality in the American States: The Case of Pre-Roe Abortion Regulation Reform," *American Journal of Political Science* 39, no.3 (1995): 599-627.

15. Donald T. Critchlow, *Intended Consequences: Birth Control, Abortion, and the Federal Government in Modern America* (New York: Oxford University Press, 1999).

16. Donald T. Critchlow, *Intended Consequences: Birth Control, Abortion, and the Federal Government in Modern America* (New York: Oxford University Press, 1999).

17. Christopher Z. Mooney and Mei-Hsien Lee, "Legislating Morality in the American States: The Case of Pre-Roe Abortion Regulation Reform," *American Journal of Political Science* 39, no.3 (1995): 599-627.

18. *Roe v. Wade.* (1973). 410 U.S. 413.

19. *Griswold v. Connecticut.* (1965). 381 U.S. 479.

20. *Eisenstadt v. Bard.* (1972). 405 U.S. 438.

21. Raymond Tatalovich and Byron W. Daynes, "The Trauma of Abortion Politics," *Commonweal* 108 (1981): 644.

22. *Webster v. Reproductive Health Services.* (1989). 492 U.S. 490.

23. *Webster v. Reproductive Health Services.* (1989). 492 U.S. 490.

24. *Planned Parenthood of Southeastern Pennsylvania v. Casey.* (1989). 505 U.S. 833.

25. *Planned Parenthood of Southeastern Pennsylvania v. Casey.* (1989). 505 U.S. 833.

26. Ronald J. Rychlak, "Abortion, Thinking Americans, and Judicial Politics," *Life and Learning XIV: Proceedings of the Fourteenth University Faculty for Life Conference* (Washington, D.C.: University Faculty for Life, 2005), 91.

27. *Roe v. Wade.* (1973). 410 U.S. 413.

28. *Gonzalez v. Carhart* (2007) and *Gonzalez v. Planned Parenthood* (2007). 05-380 and 05-1382.

29. Alan Guttmacher Institute, "Abortion," http://www.guttmacher.org/sections/abortion.php [accessed June 1, 2007].

30. Lilo T. Strauss, Joy Herndon, Jeani Chang, Wilda Y. Parker, Sonjya V. Bowens, and Cynthia J. Berg, "Abortion Surveillance—United States, 2002," *Centers for Disease Control, Morbidity and Mortality Weekly Report.* http://www.cdc.gov/mmwr/preview/mmwrhtml/ss5407a1.htm [accessed June 1, 2007].

31. National Right to Life. (2007). "Abortion in the United States: Statistics and Trends." Available on-line at http://www.nrlc.org/abortion/facts/abortionstats.html Downloaded June 1, 2007.

32. Alan Guttmacher Institute, "Abortion," http://www.guttmacher.org/sections/abortion.php [accessed June 1, 2007].

33. Lilo T. Strauss, Joy Herndon, Jeani Chang, Wilda Y. Parker, Sonjya V. Bowens, and Cynthia J. Berg, "Abortion Surveillance—United States, 2002," *Centers for Disease Control, Morbidity and Mortality Weekly Report.* http://www.cdc.gov/mmwr/preview/mmwrhtml/ss5407a1.htm [accessed June 1, 2007].

34. Sourcebook of Criminal Justice Statistics, "Table 2.1 - Attitudes Toward the Legality of Abortion," http://www.sourcebook.org [accessed June 1, 2007].

35. Sourcebook of Criminal Justice Statistics, "Table 2.91 - College Freshmen Reporting that Abortion Should be Legal," http://www.sourcebook.org [accessed June 1, 2007].

36. National Right to Life, "Zogby International Abortion Poll," http://www.nrlc.org. [accessed June 1, 2007].

37. Lydia Saad, "Special Report: Public Opinion About Abortion—An In-Depth Review," *Gallup Poll Special Reports* http://www.gallup.org [accessed September 30, 2004].

38. Lydia Saad, "Special Report: Public Opinion About Abortion—An In-Depth Review," *Gallup Poll Special Reports* http://www.gallup.org [accessed September 30, 2004].

39. Lydia Saad, "Special Report: Public Opinion About Abortion—An In-Depth Review," *Gallup Poll Special Reports* http://www.gallup.org [accessed September 30, 2004].

40. Catholic Church, *Catechism of the Catholic Church,* 2nd ed. (Washington, D.C.: U.S. Catholic Conference, 1997), 2270.

41. Catholic Church, *Catechism of the Catholic Church,* 2nd ed. (Washington, D.C.: U.S. Catholic Conference, 1997), 2270; *New American Bible* (Washington, D.C.: U.S. Conference of Catholic Bishops, 1987).

42. William S. Kurz, "Catholic Appropriation of Biblical Perspectives Regarding Abortion," in *Life and Learning XII: Proceedings of the Twelfth University Faculty for Life Conference,* ed. J. W. Koterski (Washington, D.C.: University Faculty for Life, 2002), 241.

43. William S. Kurz, "Catholic Appropriation of Biblical Perspectives Regarding Abortion," in *Life and Learning XII: Proceedings of the Twelfth University Faculty for Life Conference,* ed. J. W. Koterski (Washington, D.C.: University Faculty for Life, 2002).

44. *New American Bible.*

45. Pope John Paul II, *Theology of the Body* (Vatican: Roman Catholic Church, 1984).

46. William S. Kurz, "Catholic Appropriation of Biblical Perspectives Regarding Abortion," in *Life and Learning XII: Proceedings of the Twelfth University Faculty for Life Conference,* ed. J. W. Koterski (Washington, D.C.: University Faculty for Life, 2002).

47. See for instance Matthew 19:12 and Luke 1:7,13, 25.

48. William S. Kurz, "Catholic Appropriation of Biblical Perspectives Regarding Abortion," in *Life and Learning XII: Proceedings of the Twelfth University Faculty for Life Conference,* ed. J. W. Koterski (Washington, D.C.: University Faculty for Life, 2002), 247.

49. William S. Kurz, "Catholic Appropriation of Biblical Perspectives Regarding Abortion," in *Life and Learning XII: Proceedings of the Twelfth University Faculty for Life Conference,* ed. J. W. Koterski (Washington, D.C.: University Faculty for Life, 2002), 248.

50. William S. Kurz, "Catholic Appropriation of Biblical Perspectives Regarding Abortion," in *Life and Learning XII: Proceedings of the Twelfth University Faculty for Life Conference,* ed. J. W. Koterski (Washington, D.C.: University Faculty for Life, 2002), 248.

51. William S. Kurz, "Catholic Appropriation of Biblical Perspectives Regarding Abortion," in *Life and Learning XII: Proceedings of the Twelfth University Faculty for Life Conference,* ed. J. W. Koterski (Washington, D.C.: University Faculty for Life,

2002), 248.

52. William S. Kurz, "Catholic Appropriation of Biblical Perspectives Regarding Abortion," in *Life and Learning XII: Proceedings of the Twelfth University Faculty for Life Conference,* ed. J. W. Koterski (Washington, D.C.: University Faculty for Life, 2002), 248.

53. Catholic Church, *Catechism of the Catholic Church,* 2nd ed. (Washington, D.C.: United States Catholic Conference, 1997), 2271.

54. Catholic Church, *Catechism of the Catholic Church,* 2nd ed. (Washington, D.C.: United States Catholic Conference, 1997), 2271.

55. Catholic Church, *Catechism of the Catholic Church,* 2nd ed. (Washington, D.C.: United States Catholic Conference, 1997), 2271.

56. Catholic Church, *Gaudium et Spes* (1965), 51, 3.

57. Pope John Paul II, *Crossing the Threshold of Hope* (New York: Alfred A. Knopf, 1994), 204.

58. Pope John Paul II, *Crossing the Threshold of Hope* (New York: Alfred A. Knopf, 1994), 205.

59. Pope John Paul II, *Crossing the Threshold of Hope* (New York: Alfred A. Knopf, 1994), 205. Note: emphasis in original.

60. Pope John Paul II, *Crossing the Threshold of Hope* (New York: Alfred A. Knopf, 1994), 206.

61. Pope John Paul II, *The Gospel of Life: On the Value and Inviolability of Human Life: An Encyclical Letter* (Washington, D.C.: U.S. Conference of Catholic Bishops, 1995).

62. Pope John Paul II, *The Gospel of Life: On the Value and Inviolability of Human Life: An Encyclical Letter* (Washington, D.C.: U.S. Conference of Catholic Bishops, 1995), 94.

63. Pope John Paul II, *The Gospel of Life: On the Value and Inviolability of Human Life: An Encyclical Letter* (Washington, D.C.: U.S. Conference of Catholic Bishops, 1995), 102.

64. Pope John Paul II, *The Gospel of Life: On the Value and Inviolability of Human Life: An Encyclical Letter* (Washington, D.C.: U.S. Conference of Catholic Bishops, 1995), 112.

65. Congregation for the Doctrine of the Faith, *Donum Vitae* III., Catholic Church, *Catechism of the Catholic Church,* 2nd ed. (Washington, D.C.: United States Catholic Conference, 1997), 2273.

66. Congregation for the Doctrine of the Faith, *Donum Vitae* III., Catholic Church, *Catechism of the Catholic Church,* 2nd ed. (Washington, D.C.: United States Catholic Conference, 1997), 2273.

67. Wilton D. Gregory, "Catholic Update: Why the Church Opposes Assisted Suicide" (Cincinnati: St. Anthony Messenger Press, 1997), 3.

68. Wilton D. Gregory, "Catholic Update: Why the Church Opposes Assisted Suicide" (Cincinnati: St. Anthony Messenger Press, 1997), 3.

69. Pope Pius XII, "The Prolongation of Life," *The Pope Speaks* 4, no. 4 (1958): 395-396.

70. Edmund D. Pellegrino, "Decision at the End of Life: The Use and Abuse of the Concept of Futility," *Life and Learning X: Proceedings of the Tenth University Faculty for Life Conference* (Washington, D.C.: University Faculty for Life, 2002), 85-110.

71. Wilton D. Gregory, "Catholic Update: Why the Church Opposes Assisted Suicide" (Cincinnati: St. Anthony Messenger Press, 1997), 3.

72. Wilton D. Gregory, "Catholic Update: Why the Church Opposes Assisted Suicide" (Cincinnati: St. Anthony Messenger Press, 1997), 3.

73. Richard S. Myers, "Physician-Assisted Suicide and Euthanasia: A Current Legal Perspective," *Life and Learning XI: Proceedings of the Eleventh University Faculty for Life Conference* (Washington, D.C.: University Faculty for Life, 2002), 3-27.

74. *Planned Parenthood v. Casey* (1992) as cited in Richard S. Myers, "Physician-Assisted Suicide and Euthanasia: A Current Legal Perspective," *Life and Learning XI: Proceedings of the Eleventh University Faculty for Life Conference* (Washington, D.C.: University Faculty for Life, 2002), 3-27.

75. Richard S. Myers, "Physician-Assisted Suicide and Euthanasia: A Current Legal Perspective," *Life and Learning XI: Proceedings of the Eleventh University Faculty for Life Conference* (Washington, D.C.: University Faculty for Life, 2002), 3-27.

76. National Institute for Mental Health, *Suicide in the United States* http://www.nimh.nih.gov/publicat/harmsway.cfm [accessed June 12, 2007].

77. Edmund D. Pellegrino, "Decision at the End of Life: The Use and Abuse of the Concept of Futility," *Life and Learning X: Proceedings of the Tenth University Faculty for Life Conference* (Washington, D.C.: University Faculty for Life, 2002), 85-110.

78. Oregon Department of Human Services, *Death with Dignity Act Annual Report* http://oregon.gov/DHS/ph/pas/ar-index.shtml [accessed June 12, 2007].

79. As quoted in Jack Wintz, "Catholic Update: The Gospel of Life" (Cincinnati: St. Anthony Messenger Press, 1995), 4.

80. Catholic Church, *Catechism of the Catholic Church*, 2nd ed. (Washington, D.C.: United States Catholic Conference, 1997), 2280.

81. Catholic Church, *Catechism of the Catholic Church*, 2nd ed. (Washington, D.C.: United States Catholic Conference, 1997), 2281.

82. Catholic Church, *Catechism of the Catholic Church*, 2nd ed. (Washington, D.C.: United States Catholic Conference, 1997), 2281.

83. Catholic Church, *Catechism of the Catholic Church*, 2nd ed. (Washington, D.C.: United States Catholic Conference, 1997), 2276.

84. Catholic Church, *Catechism of the Catholic Church*, 2nd ed. (Washington, D.C.: United States Catholic Conference, 1997), 2277.

85. Catholic Church, *Catechism of the Catholic Church*, 2nd ed. (Washington, D.C.: United States Catholic Conference, 1997), 2277.

86. Catholic Church, *Catechism of the Catholic Church*, 2nd ed. (Washington, D.C.: United States Catholic Conference, 1997), 2278.

87. Catholic Church, *Catechism of the Catholic Church*, 2nd ed. (Washington, D.C.: United States Catholic Conference, 1997), 2279.

88. U.S. Conference of Catholic Bishops, *United States Catholic Catechism for Adults* (Washington, D.C.: U.S. Conference of Catholic Bishops, 2006), 393.

89. Cardinal Joseph Ratzinger, "Doctrinal Document on Threats to Life Proposed," *Origins* 20 (1991): 755-757.

Chapter 9

Victimless Crimes

"Turn from evil, and do good; seek peace, and follow after it. The Lord has eyes for the just, and ears for their cry. The Lord confronts the evildoers, to destroy remembrance of them from the earth. When the just cry out, the Lord hears them, and from all their distress he rescues them."

- Psalm 34:16-18 -

Introduction

The Catholic perspective of crime and justice is clear in how it would respond to the serious issues of both abortion and euthanasia. It would take a stance against these acts as being not only crimes against the individuals, but crimes against society as well, thus making them criminal behaviors. There are a number of other types of crimes that must be addressed in American society that have come to be referred to as "victimless crimes." Unlike crimes such as murder, rape, and robbery, which are committed by a perpetrator against an unwilling victim, and clearly a violation of humanity and hence criminal, victimless crimes are those behaviors where both adults are willing participants in the behavior, but the behavior is considered immoral. America used to have fairly stringent laws against these behaviors, largely built up during the 1800s and carried well into the twentieth century. However, over the past fifty years, there has been a slow erosion of the laws, either by way of legislative acts or court decisions, a lessening in public perception of these behaviors as crimes, and a reduction in the enforcement of these laws.

Perhaps the most commonly cited and most pervasive of the so-called victimless crimes is illegal drug use. Drugs have become a pervasive problem in the United States, as well as many parts of the world, and it is often argued that drugs should be legalized as the party engaging in the illicit drug use does so of their own free will, and that most drug users do no harm to others. Another categorization of victimless crimes centers on the issue of sexual relations and includes such behaviors as pornography, prostitution, and adultery. Each of these is considered to be victimless crimes because, as long as committed by adults,

249

these types of behaviors are generally consensual between the two parties. Finally, one other example of victimless crimes is gambling. Often derided by many religious groups, gambling has flourished in the United States over the past fifty years.

All of these behaviors have a sordid history in terms of American law and American law enforcement. Public opinion related to each of these behaviors tends to be highly nuanced. The actual amount of crime related to each of these varies in America based upon time, space, the law, and public concern, creating what is today a patchwork quilt of conflicting ideas of when each is legal or illegal and whether or not it is enforced. Despite the lack of clarity on the part of the American legal system, the Catholic Church, through faith, scripture, and doctrine, is very clear in regard to each of these behaviors, and after an exploration of each, one can discern the Catholic perspective of justice as it relates to each of these victimless crimes.

"Victimless Crimes"

In the academic community, a term that became popular in the 1960s was that of "victimless crimes" to describe behaviors that were considered immoral, but engaged by consenting adults. The term was first used by Edwin Schur in a 1965 publication titled, *Crimes Without Victims*.[1] A debate quickly ensued as to whether or not there were in fact victims of the so-called "victimless crimes." While a general consensus developed that there were victims outside of the consenting adults, such as third parties (e.g., the children of prostitutes, the families of gamblers, women who fell victim to pornographic-induced rapists, etc.), the question centered on whether the consenting adults were victims. In addition, the notion that society is harmed was also debated as the notion that society could be harmed by consenting adults seemed tangential to the acts themselves. Still further, many argued that simply because of their moral grounding, these behaviors should not be regulated by the law, regardless of how sinful or morally reprehensible they may have been.

The issue of the criminalization of deviant behavior has been addressed by a number of early scholars, ranging from such philosophers as Aristotle and St. Thomas Aquinas, to more modern scholars of criminology such as Cesare Beccaria. It was perhaps the early sociologists Edwin Sutherland and Donald Cressey who said it best when they explained that:

> Laws have accumulated because the mores have been weak and inconsistent; and because the laws have not had the support of the mores they have been relatively inefficient as a means of control. When the mores are inadequate, laws are unnecessary; when the mores are inadequate, the laws are ineffective.[2]

In other words, when the laws are ineffective these morality issues become an issue for government to address. Hence morality policy becomes the purview of government.

Morality policy has been defined by Christopher Z. Mooney as consisting of primarily a debate over first principles.[3] First principles are those core beliefs that are rooted in people, based upon religion, morality, and their personal ethics. These first principles are immutable and largely unchangeable. If a person were to change their first principles it would have to be preceded by a major upheaval of their religion, morals, and ethical framework, something that rarely occurs. As a result, when people respond to moral issues, they often do so through debate over the issue and by formation of advocacy coalitions. These groups then "portray the issues as one of morality or sin and use moral arguments in its policy advocacy."[4] What is then demanded is that government pass laws to enforce the morals. Herein lies the major issue: Which group's morals does the legislature enact?

It has been said that in a homogenous society where most people tend to share the same values, first principles do not play out into debates and advocacy coalitions for the mere fact that everyone agrees and has the same first principles. There is no need for government to get involved in the policy issue as there is no issue. In short, there exists no political controversy.

In a heterogenous society, however, where people have vastly different views, there are no shared basic values, and first principles become a source of political and social controversy. In fact, when debate ensues over a moral issue, codification often becomes the solution. At this point, because the basic values are so entrenched, a virtual battle ensues regarding which perspective will be codified. To make prostitution legal or illegal? To legalize marijuana or keep it illegal? To legalize pornography or make it illegal? These become the issues of contention, and the law becomes the battleground upon which morality and values play out. For as Mooney explains:

> These values define not only who each individual is and his or her place in society, but also society itself. If these values change, then society changes. Nothing is certain anymore. It is as if Newton's third law of motion was suddenly repealed.[5]

This is why a certain grounding in morality or an ethical framework in which morality can be understood is important for developing an understanding of what should be codified and why. While it is acknowledged that there are many ethical frameworks available and that many would reach vastly different conclusions, the Catholic Church recognizes its moral and ethical framework as coming from God and Jesus Christ. Thus, it is important to understand that any codification of morality by the government, from a Catholic perspective, would originate from the Holy Scriptures and the teaching of the Catholic Church. This is the framework in which the question of "victimless crimes" would be assessed

251

and codification proposed, passed, implemented, and enforced.

Although there are many perspectives found in Catholic doctrine upon which moral laws would be based, operating from the perspective of that which forms the basis of the political community, namely the family, is the best place to start. The *Catechism of the Catholic Church* emphasizes the role of family in society as being the "original cell of social life."[6] Among a number of things that the *Catechism* explains the political community has a duty to honor the family and to assist them is in "the protection of security and health, especially with respect to dangers like drugs, pornography, alcoholism, etc."[7]

The purpose of the law is to protect society and to enforce the moral law. As many of these behaviors inflict harm on not only individuals, but the family and society as a whole, they must be legislated against and enforced. A decent society has not only the duty, but the right to regulate these types of behaviors. However, one of the problems that have been noted by a number of individuals is that America has entered a sort of malaise. The Pontifical Council on the Family has noted that when it comes to drugs, people have entered a malaise in their attempt to downplay the seriousness of drugs and drug addiction. Former Senator Patrick Moynihan in his famous piece tried to explain that America was defining deviancy downward, that behaviors that once were considered immoral and clearly illegal are coming to be seen as acceptable.[8] Even many scholars in the academic fields have made this same argument. One example is James Q. Wilson who argued that "many Americans worry that the moral order that once held the nation together has come unraveled," and that "despite freedom and prosperity—or worse, perhaps because of freedom and prosperity—a crucial part of the moral order, a sense of personal responsibility, has withered under the attack of personal self-indulgence."[9] Government, then, is needed to enforce the moral order.

Perhaps the best argument for this position comes from Patrick Devlin, a British judge, in his book *The Enforcement of Morals*. In this book, which presents a defense for why government must enforce morality within the law, Devlin writes:

> Societies disintegrate from within more frequently than they are broken up by external pressure. There is disintegration when no common morality is observed and history shows that the loosening of social bonds is often the first stage of disintegration, so that society is justified in taking the same steps to preserve a moral code as it does to preserve its governmental and other institutions.[10]

One issue that is almost certainly raised whenever the topic of immorality, or vice, is raised is the issue of tolerance. Many people in today's society tend to point out that whenever someone is against a particular behavior, such as illegal drugs, homosexuality, or prostitution, they are intolerant. What is associated with this intolerance is the notion that they are immoral or wrong for being intolerant of such behaviors. Yet, the tolerance of vice is not virtuous because tolerance is neither a vice nor a virtue. Tolerance can be used for both good and evil. One could be tolerant in the early American South of slavery, something which would have been seen as perfectly acceptable at the time, but something we see today as having been clearly evil. One could also be tolerant of children's table manners, which is certainly not a vice (although it is debatable as to whether it would be considered virtuous). Since tolerance can be both good and evil it has no moral basis, thus tolerance should never be considered a moral virtue.

Recognizing that government has the right and duty to legislate morality and that the Catholic faith brings an ethical framework of morality to the policy table, it is possible to look at the so-called victimless crimes to understand how a Catholic perspective would apply the law and justice.

Types of Victimless Crimes

Drugs

Drugs, or more exactly defined as the problem of drug abuse and addiction, have largely been an extant problem throughout history, whether it has been the use of alcohol or various opiate drug elixirs sold for their medicinal value. Today is no different, and drugs are pervasive in our society and readily available. According to the World Health Organization, drug addiction is defined as:

> state of periodic or chronic intoxication produced by the repeated consumption of a drug (natural or synthetic) which produces the following characteristics: 1) an overpowering desire or compulsion to continue taking the drug and to obtain it by any means; 2) a tendency to increase the dosage, showing body tolerance; 3) a psychic and generally a physical dependence on the effects of the drug; and 4) the creation of an individual and social problem.[11]

In order to understand the complexities of the drug problem in America, it is important to look at the public's perceptions regarding drug abuse, the extent to which the criminal justice system deals with those addicted to drugs, and the impact the system is having on drugs in America.

In 1972, Nixon declared the first war on drugs which consisted of a number of policies ranging from border interdiction to drug treatment of addicted veterans returning from Vietnam. The war on drugs would be resurrected under the Reagan administration and heavily advanced by his Vice-President, George Bush, when he assumed the Executive office in 1989. Looking at public opinion polls related to how well people feel the nation is making progress in coping with the problem of illegal drugs, the response rates have remained flat despite the efforts of these two declared wars on drugs. In 1972, only three percent of respondents felt that America was making much progress, while 32 percent felt that America had made some progress.[12] An additional 20 percent felt that we had stood still. Moreover, 21 percent stated we had lost some ground, and another 20 percent felt that America had lost much ground. After two wars on drugs and an effort that continues today to combat the problem of drugs, Americans responding to the same question have barely moved in their responses. In 2005, only two percent voice that we had made much progress, while 31 percent stated that we had made some progress. The biggest change came in those who said that America has stood still, moving from 20 percent to 30 percent. Twenty-three percent said that we had lost some ground, and 13 percent felt that we had lost much ground. The years in-between witnessed little fluctuation.

Another question that has been asked by the Roper Center for Public Opinion research has focused on respondents' beliefs that too little is being spent on the problem of dealing with drug addiction.[13] In 1973, as Nixon's war on drugs began, 65 percent of Americans felt that too little was spent. By 1978, that percentage had dropped to 55 percent. During the Reagan and Bush years in office, when drugs became a major public policy, the numbers increased with 1988 and 1989 witnessing 71 percent of Americans voicing their opinion that too little was spent on dealing with drug addiction. That percentage has since dropped once again and was back to the mid-fifty percentage points by 2000 with 57 percent voicing this response in 2002. It also does not appear to matter what sex, race, age, education, income, occupation, region, religion, or political affiliation one has, the majority tend to believe that too little is spent on the issue of drugs.[14] The concern of Americans seems to be relatively split with rises in concern when it becomes the focus of American public policy.

When it comes to specifically asking about reversing course and legalizing drugs, most Americans do not advocate this position. When asked in a Roper public opinion poll if marijuana should be legalized, the majority of Americans say that it should not.[15] There have been some fluctuations in the response to these questions over time as they follow a similar pattern to the earlier question. In 1976, 69 percent of Americans felt that marijuana should not be legalized, increasing to 76 percent in 1983, and 81 percent in 1987. In the 1990s, the response rate would again fall, to 72 percent in 1994, 66 percent in 1998, and 60 percent in 2002. Even high school seniors, a group that one would think might be more open to the use of drugs, are pretty adamant that they disapprove of the behavior.[16] Seventy-eight percent of the class of 2003 stated that it was wrong to smoke marijuana regularly, and 53 percent stated it was wrong to try it once or twice. In addition, 85 percent stated it was wrong to try LSD, 89 percent said it was wrong to try cocaine, and 94 percent said it was wrong to try heroin. However, it should be noted that the same class stated that it was fairly easy or very easy to obtain marijuana (87 percent), cocaine (43 percent), and heroin (27.9 percent), demonstrating that while most are against it, most can readily obtain the illegal drugs in our society.

Turning, then, to the actual use of drugs in the United States, it is difficult to obtain an actual figure of drug use, for there is no direct method of collecting this type of data. One means is by asking people about their drug use, but many probably do not answer truthfully, either overinflating (to brag) or underinflating (to hide) their actual usage. Another means is looking at emergency room episodes related to drug abuse to obtain a better understanding of the wide-spread use and abuse of illegal drugs. And finally, there are arrest data kept under the FBI's Uniform Crime Reports Part II offenses. Taken together they present at least some understanding of the pervasiveness of drugs in America.

When asked if they had used any illicit drug in their lifetime, 46 percent of the entire sample taken in 2003 reported that they had used an illicit drug at some point in their life.[17] Extrapolating from that figure, based on a population in the United States of 300 million, that would mean that approximately 125 million Americans have tried some form of illegal drug in their lifetime. The most-used drug was marijuana with 40.6 percent of the respondents saying they had at least tried marijuana once. When marijuana was removed, when asked if they had used any other drug at least once, 29.9 percent of the respondents answered in the affirmative. When looking at the breakdown by specific drugs, 14 percent reported using cocaine, 14 percent using a hallucinogen, and 20 percent reported using a psychotherapeutic drug, not for medical purposes.

In looking at the drug abuse-related emergency department episodes, according to the U.S. Department of Health and Human Services, there were 670,307 emergency visits by those experiencing some form of complication from taking illegal drugs. That figures to a rate of 261 visits for every 100,000 population in the United States. The number of visits was largely split between males (355,155) and females (308,098). The majority tended to be white (372,727) with Blacks reporting the second most frequent visits (142,974). Most of the emergency room visits came from people 35 or older (318,799), followed by those 26 to 34 (145,806) and 18 to 25 (140,475). The primary reason that the individuals took the drug was because of their dependence on the drug (239,653), attempting suicide (189,198), or seeking a psychic effect from the drug (132,711). The primary reason for the emergency room visit was because of an overdose (239,653), followed by an unexpected reaction (131,315), and seeking detoxification (103,674). The disposition for most of the emergency room visits was either they were treated and released (319,378) or they were admitted to hospital (331,240).

It should be noted that many of the emergency room visits for drug abuse do not necessarily get turned over to the police, so the figures tend to be low in regard to the number of drug users. Also, most drug users do not end up in the hospital. And still further, it is also a pretty safe assumption that most drug users do not get arrested. That said, according to the FBI's Uniform Crime Reports for 2002, a staggering 1,103,017 people were arrested for some type of drug abuse violation that year.[18] The majority of those arrested tended to be male (81 percent), rather than female (18 percent). Most of the arrests tend to be for possession of the drug (80 percent), while the rest are for sale and/or manufacturing of the illegal drug (20 percent). In addition, most of the arrests are for either marijuana (45 percent) or heroin (30 percent), with 20 percent for other drugs (including cocaine) and a few for synthetic drugs (4 percent).

Although over one million are arrested each year for drug violations, and nearly 3/4 of a million people end up in the emergency room, neither of these methods of responding to drug abuse deal with the actual problem which is drug addiction. The issue here is providing some form of drug treatment to the drug addict, whether it be methadone maintenance for the severe heroin addict, the use of a therapeutic community, or some form of outpatient drug-free program. In more recent years, many offenders are diverted to drug courts where treatment becomes the first course of action in order to avoid traditional prosecution; drug treatment becomes a condition of the addict's probation.

The benefit to drug treatment, as one study has found, is a reduction in cost. The study estimated that the treatment of a drug offender costs approximately $2,941, while the savings to society is estimated at $9,177, due to the reduction in crimes, arrests, prosecutions, and imprisonment of drug offenders.[19] One of the problems, however, has been a very limited number of drug treatment facilities available in the United States. According to the United States Department of Health and Human Services, in 2005 there were a reported 13,371 facilities.[20] However, it is estimated that over 900,000 people are enrolled annually into these treatment centers and that roughly three to four times more are in need of treatment.[21] A large portion of those needing drug treatment also tend to be in prison where they do not receive the drug treatment they need.

Perhaps the most important question, and the least understood answer, is whether or not treatment actually works. It is an important question, because if drug treatment did not work, then the only alternative would, in fact, be imprisonment. Yet, if it does work, then one would wonder why it isn't advocated more. Conventional wisdom seems to suggest that drug treatment does not work. Research does not inherently agree with this statement, but the research related to the effectiveness of drug treatment is largely mixed. At first glance, nearly all types of drug treatment methods appear to be effective in that they do have the ability to break the drug abuser's addiction.[22] There are a number of qualifications, however, to these positive indicators. First, many of the drug treatment programs are self-selecting. This also applies to drug courts. Many programs and most drug courts simply look for indicators of potential success among drug addicts and enter those individuals into drug treatment, excluding the less hopeful cases from treatment. Second, once entered into the programs, there is a high drop-out rate, which is typically not factored into the ability to treat, as the individual did not receive the full treatment program. Third, those who do come off of their addiction, where the drug treatment is considered a success, often later return to drugs and/or criminal behavior. Finally, it should be noted that just because the drug offender is treated and free of drugs, does not mean that the individual no longer commits crimes; hence criminality is not necessarily reduced from drug treatment. The ultimate factor for successfully dealing with both problems appears to be personal commitment to end both addiction and criminal behavior. Absent that commitment, drug treatment is far less successful. Yet, that does not mean that just because addicts are not necessarily willing participants that society should give up on them and resort to criminal punishment in order to deal with the drug problem in America. Nor does it mean that legalization of drugs would solve these problems either. While it may eliminate the direct criminal violations of drug abuse, it certainly has the potential to raise the number of crimes associated with drug addiction, and it will most definitely increase the need for treatment, counseling, and rehabilitation, just as the legalization of such behaviors as gambling and alcohol have witnessed. Thus, drug abuse is a highly complex problem. It is one needing a strong ethical framework by which to focus policy direction. This is what the Catholic faith can provide, as it is pretty evident in its stance against drugs.

The *Catechism of the Catholic Church* is very direct in its argument against the use of illicit drugs. It states its reasoning is based on the fact that "the use of drugs inflicts very grave damage on human health and their life," and that because of this, "their use, except on strictly therapeutic grounds, is a grave offense."[23] The Church explains that the "clandestine production of and trafficking in drugs are scandalous practices" and "they constitute direct co-operation in evil, since they encourage people to practices gravely contrary to the moral law."[24] It is very clear, then, to understand where a Catholic perspective of crime and justice would fall when it comes to illicit drugs. If the practice is gravely contrary to the moral law, then the criminal law should continue to legislate against any illicit and non-therapeutic use, and the laws should be enforced. This is not to say, however, that the Church advocates that all drug users be imprisoned, rather they advocate the use of drug treatment and rehabilitation as the proper means of dealing with drug abuse.

The Pontifical Council for the Family, in their report titled *From Despair to Hope: Family and Drug Addiction,* explains that we must not lose sight that "the human person, unique and unrepeatable, with his or her own interior life and specific personality, is really at the center of the problem of drug dependence."[25] In a later publication by the council they explain that "it is not drugs that are in question, but the human, psychological and existential issues implicit in this kind of behavior."[26] The Council argued that drug use was symptomatic of a "malaise." They explain that drug addiction does not just happen or appear out of the blue, but rather results from some human need, often in adolescence. This need is both psychological and social, but once the drug is administered, it also becomes a physiological need. Most important, however, is what Pope John Paul II pointed out, and that is "a correspondence has to be recognized between the deadly pathology caused by drug abuse and a pathology of the spirit which leads a person to flee from self and to seek illusory pleasures, in an escape from reality, to the point that the meaning of personal existence is totally lost."[27]

In light of this, the Pontifical Council on the Family argued that there are a number of social restraints that have created the need, especially among adolescents, to turn to drugs. They argue that children grow up too fast today, are often left to their own devices too early, and that they lack the adult support and role models to develop their ability to mature. Absent parents and a culture and marketplace that work against the proper development of children creates a situation where children seek out the support of their friends. These other children, often poor in spirit themselves, turn to drugs as a means of seeking out something which they have lost and influence others along the way. As a result, the use of drugs often develops into physical addictions that further exacerbate the problem. The policy answer by many is to simply legalize some of the "soft" drugs, such as marijuana, but the Church is explicitly opposed to that idea.

As the Pontifical Council explained, the rationale to legalizing some drugs is to have the opposite effect of what currently exists. Many argue that if it were legal, children would be less likely to engage in the behavior. And if it were legal it would of course not be illegal and therefore it would be "normal." The problem, as the council highlights, is that it would also be considered by many to be "moral," for the mere fact that it would be "normalized" through the law. More specifically, they argue, "it is not the product that is thereby legalized, but rather the reasons leading to the consumption of the product that are justified."[28] Thus, all of the societal ills that lead to drug addiction would become rational and acceptable were drugs to be legalized. In the end, society would still have to deal with the education, treatment and rehabilitation of those addicted to drugs, despite their legality, as it must deal with those addicted to alcohol, gambling, and other such vices.

The answer to the drug problem is not legalization. On this the Church is clear. Left still with the pervasive problem of drugs in society today, the issue is how governments should respond to the problem. As the Council explains:

> In view of these problems, the primary duty of the state is to safeguard the common good. This requires it to protect the rights, stability and unity of the family. By destroying a young person, drugs destroy the family, both the family of the present and that of the future. Should this vital and primordial cell of society be threatened, society as a whole will suffer.[29]

Therefore, it is clear that illicit drugs must remain illegal and that the laws must be enforced in order for the state to ensure the common good for all the people. Society, they argue, must combat all drugs and all states should adopt a "consistent and courageous stance on drugs."[30] This is not to say, however, that society must lose sight of the fact that those arrested and convicted of drug abuse are human. While society must enforce the laws against illicit drugs, it must at the same time balance out the reality that those addicted to drugs, those arrested for drug abuse, and those convicted of related crimes, are human beings who need help. Thus, punishment through imprisonment alone is clearly not the right response to the human being at the center of the drug addiction.

The United States Conference of Catholic Bishops in their publication *Responsibility, Rehabilitation, and Restoration,* emphasized under their policy directions section that the criminal justice system must make a serious commitment in confronting the pervasive role of drug addiction in crime. They argued that "far too many people are in prison primarily because of addiction" and that "locking up addicts without proper treatment and then returning them to the streets perpetuates a cycle of behavior that benefits neither the offender nor society."[31] They recommend that:

> Persons suffering from chemical dependency should have access to the treatment that could free them and their families from the slavery of addiction, and free the rest of us from the crimes they commit to support this addiction. This effort will require adequate federal, state, and local resources for prevention and treatment for substance abusers. Not providing these resources now will cost far more in the long run. Substance abusers should not have to be behind bars in order to receive treatment for their addictive behavior.[32]

The Bishops also turn to an explanation that in order to address the societal ills of drug abuse, America must also address the underlying problems or "root causes" as they are generally referred to in the criminological literature. These include, according to the Bishops, such problems as "lack of employment, poverty, inadequate education, family disintegration, lack of purpose and meaning, poor housing, and powerlessness and greed."[33] They argue that these factors create an environment where people either resort to the illegal drug market to make money or they use drugs as a means of escape from these conditions. In either case, the Bishops state emphatically that this is unacceptable.

One solution the Bishops advocate for those that are arrested for drug crimes is to divert them from the criminal courts. In particular, they cite the growing trend of using Drug Courts as a better means of dealing with the drug abuser. Drug Courts are special courts that deal more broadly with the offender, by not only focusing on the crime committed, but on the drug abuse. Generally, Drug Courts divert individuals from the justice system by placing them into treatment and rehabilitation programs.

Another solution has simply been a closer embracing of one's Catholic faith, for it has been found through several research studies that those people that embrace their faith are less likely to abuse alcohol or illegal drugs.[34] One study from the National Center on Addiction and Substance Abuse at Columbia University found that adults who never attended religious services were more than five times likelier to have used illegal drugs and that adults who considered religion unimportant were found to be four times more likely to take illicit drugs. In terms of teenagers, the study found that those who never attended worship were twice as likely to drink and smoke, and that those who considered religion unimportant were four times more likely to use marijuana and seven times more likely to use other illicit drugs. Drug use, as Pope John Paul II pointed out, truly does seem to be a pathology of the spirit.

Pornography

According to the *Dictionary of Criminal Justice,* pornography is largely an ambiguous term that is closely identified with obscenity in that it refers "to the portrayal of particular sexual acts or excessive violence in sex."[35] The pornography industry in the United States has developed into a billion-dollar-a-year industry from one that was largely driven underground for most of American history. The change was brought about in the 1950s in a United States Supreme Court case, *Roth v. Alberts* (1957) where the Court ruled that laws forbidding obscenity are, in fact, constitutional. The issue rises in what is considered to be obscenity. Supreme Court Justice Potter Stewart, alluding to the varying attempts to define it, stated in the Supreme Court case of *Jacobellis v. Ohio* (1964) that "perhaps I could never succeed in intelligibly [defining obscenity], but I know it when I see it."

In order to assist in the definition, the *Roth* case generated a three-part test. The first step was to determine if the dominant theme of the material attempted to appeal to a prurient interest in sex. If so, then the second part of the test was to determine if the material could be said to be patently offensive in that it is an affront to contemporary community standards. The final part of the three-part test was to determine if the material had no redeeming social value. Another case, *Miller v. California* (1973) determined that the community standards must be locally determined, not nationally, and they need not be utterly without social redeeming value, but need only be lacking in value. In other words, if they had some literary, artistic, political or scientific value, then they would not be considered an obscenity and hence, not pornography. This specific Supreme Court decision would find its guidelines written into federal and state statutes as the main means of dealing with pornography. Yet, neither the legislation nor the Supreme Court's three-pronged test have resolved the problem identified by Potter, and that is how to adequately define it so that when someone was to see obscene material they could readily classify it as pornography.

The one thing that is clear is state and local governments do have the right, according to the Supreme Court's rulings, to pass legislation against obscenity, and the laws would not be ruled unconstitutional. The problem, however, perhaps lies in the fact that this is a very decentralized method of generating policy and one in which the ability to define the criminal behavior is difficult to place into law. But not, as Stewart said, to identify it when one sees it. Hence, laws against pornography have largely been ignored and unenforced, allowing for pornography to flourish in the United States, largely unchecked. Although the

U.S. mail, international carriers, and other forms of commerce transportation have expanded the availability of pornography to Americans, it is the Internet that has become the largest purveyor of pornography in the United States.

It is difficult to assess the actual amount of pornography in the United States because, as previously said, some of the pornography is considered legal, and hence there are no criminal statistics. Data from various sources within the porn industry itself have alleged that the distribution and sales of pornography have continued to escalate over the past thirty years and amounts to between one billion and ten billion dollars each year.[36] In addition, the Internet has caused a strong proliferation of pornographic material, and most estimates (although many again by the porn industry itself) is that internet sales of pornography have skyrocketed as well. Pornography is now largely available in the United States in not only specialty stores, but mainstream commercial stores and video rental stores. It is available online through such carriers as Yahoo! and AOL. And it is available in many hotels and motels across the country.

In terms of criminal behavior and criminal violations regarding pornography, the primary violation stems from the problem of child pornography. The F.B.I. has increased its focus on these violations over the past decade and has concentrated much of its resources into investigating child pornography online through its cyber division. In 2005, 38 percent of the cyber divisions investigations centered on child pornography. This is largely because of an increase in the number of cases that have been developed because of the proliferation of the Internet and the amount of child pornography on the Internet. According to the F.B.I. statistics, there has been a 2,026 percent increase in cases opened, an 856 percent increase in indictments, a 2,325 percent increase in arrests, and a 1,312 percent increase in convictions and pretrial diversions. It is very clear that pornography has become a growing problem in the United States, one that has been given somewhat of a free license due to the Supreme Court's ambivalent decision about regulating the industry and because of the proliferation and availability of the Internet. However, if the regulation of the industry can be reined in through the deeming of pornography as obscenity, how has public opinion shifted regarding pornography over the past two decades?

According to the Roper Center for Public Opinion Research, the proliferation of pornography seems to have had a lessening of the public's standard, rather than a hardening of the public's stance against pornography. The Roper poll has asked the following question across time: "which of these statements comes closest to your feelings about pornography laws: there should be laws against the distribution of pornography whatever the age; there should be laws against the distribution of pornography to persons under 18; or there should be no laws forbidding the distribution of pornography."[37] In 2002, the most recently available poll, Roper found that 38 percent of Americans wanted laws regardless of age, while 56 percent wanted laws for those under age 18. Another five percent wanted no laws forbidding distribution. In comparison, the 1988 poll found that

43 percent wanted regulation regardless of age, 50 percent based on under age 18, and again, five percent wanted laws forbidding the distribution. The trend has been a lessening of regulating at all ages, but an increase in regard to regulating to those under age 18.

Interestingly enough, when looking at the data overall, it tends to hide the characteristics of those who want pornography regulated regardless of age. So, while the national average in 2002 was for 40 percent of the people calling for regulation at whatever age, only 26 percent of the males responding wanted such restrictions, while 49 percent of women wanted these restrictions. Whites tended to want more restrictions (41 percent) than Blacks (31 percent), and those over 50 years of age wanted more restrictions (54 percent) than those 18 to 20 (16 percent). Education seemed to be a strong indicator, as it has been argued that education has a liberalizing effect. Only 36 percent of those with a college degree wanted pornography regulated regardless of age, while 51 percent of those with less than a high school degree wanted such regulation. Those in clerical/support occupations had a higher response rate to regulation regardless of age (45 percent), with those in farming and agriculture having the lowest response rate (25 percent). Those living in the west wanted more regulation (44 percent) while those in the northeast wanted the least (34 percent). Those who identified themselves as Protestant and Republican had the highest call for regulation (43 percent), while those who identified themselves as either having no religion (18 percent) or Jewish (4 percent), and either Democrat or Independent had the lowest call (38 percent). Finally, it should be noted that 38 percent of those identifying themselves as Catholic wanted regulation at whatever age, with 58 percent of Catholics wanting it regulated for those under 18, and four percent of Catholics stating that there should be no laws forbidding the distribution. In sum, Catholics would appear to have no different response than the general public, despite Catholic teachings on the subject.

Turning to the those teachings, the *Catechism of the Catholic Church* explains that pornography "consists in removing real or simulated sexual acts from the intimacy of the partners, in order to display them deliberately to third parties."[38] The Church states definitively that this is immoral as "it offends against chastity because it perverts the conjugal act" which is "the intimate giving of spouses to each other."[39] The *Catechism* explains that the resulting effect is a "grave injury to the dignity of its participants (actors, vendors, the public), since each one becomes an object of base pleasure and illicit profits for others."[40] This is why the Bishops of the United States have so succinctly stated that "pornography assaults the dignity of women and contributes to violence against them."[41]

In sum, the Church explains that pornography "immerses all who are involved in the illusion of a fantasy world," thus it is deemed a "grave offense."[42] So, when it comes to regulating the pornographic industry and the distribution of its materials, the Church argues that "civil authorities should prevent the production and distribution of pornographic materials."[43] A Catholic perspective of crime and criminal justice would move to legislate against the production and distribution of pornography in the United States and set the punishment in accordance with the crime, but also encourage the counseling and treatment of those who are addicted to these illicit images.

Prostitution

According to the *Dictionary of Criminal Justice,* prostitution is defined as "offering or agreeing to engage in, or engaging in, a sex act with another in return for a fee."[44] Every state has a law regarding prostitution. Most, like California, tend to define the violation as consisting of anyone "who solicits or who engages in any act of prostitution (including) lewd acts between persons for money or other considerations."[45] There are, however, two states that have left the decision regarding the legalization of prostitution to their respective counties, and they are Arizona and Nevada. No county in Arizona has voted for its legalization, while only two counties in Nevada have allowed for its legalization, meaning that other than two counties, everywhere else in the United States, prostitution remains illegal.

Data is maintained by the Federal Bureau of Investigation regarding prostitution and commercialized vice under what is known as their "Part II" offenses. According to the 2002 data, there were a total of 58,756 arrests for prostitution with 20,127 (34.3 percent) being males and 38,631 (65.7) being females. Typically these arrests consist of female prostitutes and their male customers, typically referred to as the "johns." While there are male prostitutes who typically provide their services to other males, the percentage of these arrested tend to be very small.

Like pornography, the Catholic Church is adamantly against prostitution in any form as it is degrading to not only the individuals involved but to humanity as well. The Church draws largely on Scripture for its stance against prostitution as the Bible has always been explicit in its condemnation of the practice. For instance, Chapter 7 of the Book of Proverbs is clearly discussing the topic of prostitutes and states emphatically that "her house is made up of ways to the nether world, leading down into the chambers of death."[46] Still further, it was expressly against biblical law for fathers to turn their daughters into prostitutes or "else the land will become corrupt and full of lewdness" (Leviticus 19:29), and it was against the law to have a prostitute among the Israelite women, as well as the men (Deuteronomy 23:18). The typical punishment for the women was execution, often by stoning to death.

In the New Testament, there are several references to prostitutes, but none greater than the story of the woman caught in adultery.[47] The Scribes and Pharisees brought a woman to Jesus who had been caught in adultery and made her stand in the middle of them. They said to Jesus, "Teacher, this woman was caught in the act of committing adultery. Now in the law, Moses commanded us to stone such women. So, what do you say?" As John teaches, the Scribes and Pharisees were clearly testing Jesus, trying to corner him into saying the prostitute should not be stoned and that the law is wrong, thus committing a crime against God. Jesus ignored them and drew symbols in the sand with his finger. The Scribes and Pharisees persisted and continued to press for an answer. Jesus stood up abruptly and stated, "Let the one among you who is without sin be the first to throw a stone at her." He then bent back down and continued his drawings in the sand. Eventually, each in turn left, until there was only Jesus and the accused prostitute left. Jesus then stood up and asked the woman, "Where are they? Has no one condemned you?" The prostitute answered, "No one, sir." And Jesus then replied, "Neither do I condemn you. Go and from now on do not sin any more."

Although much has been made about this passage from a number of points, such as the fact that the man caught in the act with the woman was dismissed or the fact that the prostitute by many has been identified as Mary Magdalene, the key to the passage regarding prostitution is that Jesus did not refute the law. In other words, he never said that the law was unjust or unlawful, nor for that matter the sentence, but he was much more lenient by challenging the accusers as to their purity, and hence their standing to be accusers. Thus, it is safe to say that even Jesus did not overturn or change the biblical law that prostitution was a crime, but readily identified it as a sin in keeping with Mosaic Law.

In today's terms, the *Catechism of the Catholic Church,* makes the point that prostitution "does injury to the dignity of the person who engages in it, reducing the person to an instrument of sexual pleasure."[48] This loss of dignity occurs clearly on the part of the prostitute for she is not only engaging in adultery, but engaging in it for a profit. As sexual intercourse is limited to married couples in keeping with Catholic doctrine, then the act of prostitution is always immoral. The *Catechism* also expressly states that "the one who pays [for the prostitute] sins gravely against himself: he violates the chastity to which his Baptism pledged him and defiles his body, the temple of the Holy Spirit."[49] Again, as it is clearly an act of adultery, the male paying for the prostitute sins not only against himself, but the woman and humanity. This is why the Catholic Church sees prostitution as a social scourge and explains that "it is always gravely sinful to engage in."[50] Recognizing that much of the basis for identifying prostitution as a sin is linked with adultery, it is important to discuss this topic and how it would be dealt with from a Catholic perspective of crime and justice.

Adultery

Adultery is defined by the *Dictionary of Criminal Justice* as "voluntary sexual intercourse between a married person and a partner other than his or her spouse."[51] Adultery has consistently been a crime throughout the Judeo-Christian world based on the sixth commandment: "You shall not commit adultery." In the United States, adultery was seen as immoral, a sin, and hence a crime. Every state had a statute making adultery a criminal act, although it was rarely enforced. Many of the early American settlements adopted the sixth commandment as codified law, such as the Puritans, and the sentence, like in the biblical world, was often execution. Despite the severity of the punishments, they were rarely carried out, and the ultimate punishment would typically be some form of shaming.[52]

As time has gone by though, adultery has been seen as less and less of a crime by the American populace. In addition, the commission of the crime, typically committed behind closed doors, has largely been unenforceable due to privacy protections. In fact, it is these very privacy protections that have seen a number of laws related to adultery abolished. For instance, sodomy, prior to the 1960s, was illegal in all fifty states. Between 1960 and 2003, 35 states abolished their sodomy laws.[53] Then, in 2003, based on previous Supreme Court decisions that granted citizens a right to privacy, the Supreme Court ruled that sodomy laws are unconstitutional (*Lawrence v. Texas* (2003)). While adultery still remains on the books as a criminal violation and is grounds for civil divorce in all states, it is rarely enforced. In fact, the only place in which it is enforced, though not necessarily on a routine basis, is in the United States military under the Uniform Code of Military Justice.

In order to understand the Catholic Church stance on adultery, one must first understand their understanding of society being ordered and based on the smallest unit, that of the family. The family is defined through the sacrament of marriage, which is ordered between a man and a woman. Once a man and a woman enter into matrimony it is rightly ordered that they engage in conjugal love, but that this conjugal love is strictly limited to the man and the woman who are married. As the *Catechism* explains, "marriage bonds between baptized persons are sanctified by the sacrament," that "in marriage the physical intimacy of the spouses becomes a sign and pledge of spiritual communion," and that "sexuality is ordered to the conjugal love of man and woman."[54] More directly, the Church teaches that "sexuality, by means of which man and woman give themselves to one another through the acts which are proper and exclusive to spouses, is not something simply biological, but concerns the innermost being of the human person as such" and "it is realized in a truly human way only if it is an integral part of the love by which a man and woman commit themselves totally to one another until death."[55]

Anything outside of marriage is considered a sin and goes against the fidelity of the marriage. Anything outside of the love of man and woman is also considered immoral. And any such conjugal relationship before marriage is also considered immoral as it violates the future fidelity to one's spouse. Thus, adultery refers to marital infidelity. As the *Catechism* explains, "when two partners, of whom at least one is married to another party, have sexual relations—even transient ones—they commit adultery."[56] It further states that "Christ condemns even adultery of mere desire" and that "the sixth commandment and the New Testament forbid adultery absolutely."[57]

The reason for the absolute sinfulness of adultery is because it is an injustice. The person who commits adultery fails in their commitment to their spouse. As the *Catechism* explains, "he does injury to the sign of the covenant which the marriage bond is, transgresses the rights of the other spouse, and undermines the institution of marriage by breaking the contract on which it is based."[58] As this contract is a contract before God, and not merely limited to the civil contract that most societies order, it is a mortal sin.

As the sacrament of marriage is very explicit as to what it entails, a number of other sins, beyond adultery, are based on violations of the covenant between a man and a woman. Premarital sex, polygamy, incest, free unions, masturbation, homosexuality, pornography, prostitution, and divorce are all forms of violations of marital fidelity and are against the teachings of the Catholic Church.[59] It is this reason that all of these types of behaviors are considered sinful and would be legislated against and enforced from a Catholic perspective of crime and justice.

Gambling

Gambling is defined by the *Dictionary of Criminal Justice* as "staking or wagering of money or anything of value on a game of chance or an uncertain event."[60] In early America, gambling was not regulated and there were only sporadic laws related to gambling being illegal.[61] As the 1800s ensued and Victorian principles began to take hold, states began making gambling an illegal activity. By the turn of the twentieth century, gambling was predominately illegal throughout the United States, although it was haphazardly enforced. As the twentieth century progressed, various states began to reverse course once again. In 1931, Nevada became the first state in the twentieth century to legalize gambling. This would be followed by the extensive growth of Las Vegas in the 1950s, generally attributed to the mafia. The first state to adopt a state-sponsored lottery was New Hampshire, in 1963. In 1977, the State of North Dakota legalized bingo, and then in 1981 blackjack gambling in locations outside of casinos such as restaurants and bars. In 1978, Atlantic City, New Jersey, would become the Las Vegas equivalent on the east coast. In 1988, a federal law allowed for Native Americans to be allowed to run casinos on their reservations. In 1991, the first Riverboat Gambling Casino since the late 1800s began operation out of Davenport, Iowa. In each of these cases, the legalization of gambling in one state would typically see the adoption of the same type of gambling in other states. Gambling has become very common in the United States.

There are currently only two states that do not allow gambling, and they are Utah and Hawaii. Almost every other state either has a state-run lottery or has some form of legalized lottery. Over twenty states allow for some type of casino gambling, although most tend to have strong restrictions regarding their location. A sure sign of the growth of gambling is found in the fact that in 1974 it was estimated that Americans spent $17 billion on gambling.[62] That figure increased to $330 billion in 1992, $550 billion in 1995, and over $750 billion a year by the twenty-first century. The FBI estimates that more than $50 billion dollars is wagered each year on illegal gambling, and under its Part II offenses it reports there were 7,525 arrests for illegal gambling in 2002.[63] The majority of illegal gamblers tend to be men, who make up 90 percent of the arrests.

Gambling is a somewhat broad term, for it entails a number of different types of betting. According to Meier and Geis there are six forms of gambling: "1) casino-style gambling, including the proliferation of gambling sites on Native-American reservations; 2) betting on horse and dog races, both at track and at off-track sites; 3) lotteries; 4) internet gambling; 5) wagering on athletic events; and 6) betting on numbers."[64]

The Catholic Church has always faced some criticism for the fact that it "allows" gambling. It is not uncommon to find a number of churches at various functions, bazaars, and events engaging in the game of bingo, which in effect, is a game of chance. While many Christian religions are adamant that any game of chance is against Christ's teachings, the Roman Catholic Church argues that "games of chance (card games, etc.) or wagers are not in themselves contrary to justice."[65] In other words, not all "gambling," as broadly defined, is against the Church's teachings. Bingo played at Church functions to raise money for charity or simply purchasing a lottery ticket at the local convenience store does not amount to an act that goes against justice, nor is it necessarily sinful.

The *Catechism*, however, does express that they do "become morally unacceptable when they deprive someone of what is necessary to provide for his needs and those of others" and when "the passion for gambling risks becoming an enslavement."[66] In other words, when a person engages in these types of behaviors at the expense of money that is needed to live on or they deprive their family members of the necessary means of living, then the behavior has crossed over to one of sin and would therefore be against justice. The best example is the strong relationship between gambling and predatory crime, where many of those who are addicted to gambling prey upon other people through both personal assaults and property theft in order to fund their habit.[67] Still further, the Church teaches that even if the gambling is deemed strictly for charity, such as a bingo fundraiser, if the individual becomes obsessed with the game and they begin to gamble money that would deprive them or others, it would be considered a sin.

Conclusion

A Catholic perspective of the so-called "victimless crimes" should be relatively clear in that they consider none of these behaviors to be truly victimless. The victim is either the individual participants or society as a whole. In either case, there is harm and, hence, a crime has been committed. The Catholic Church takes a strong stance against the scourge of drugs that has come to envelop American society, and unless for medicinal purposes, no drugs would be legal. Yet, when harm has occurred, the traditional response of punishment by way of imprisonment is not the route the Catholic faith would advocate. Rather, for those solely arrested for drug violations, it is clear the Church would advocate drug treatment and counseling over imprisonment. As the Bishops in the United States have explained, "locking up addicts without proper treatment and then returning them to the streets perpetuates a cycle of behavior that benefits neither the offender nor society."[68] When a crime has occurred in association with drug abuse, the Church appears to advocate that the addiction be treated while at the same time the individual is held responsible for their criminal behavior.

In terms of the sexual categories of victimless crimes, which include pornography, prostitution, and adultery, the Church is very clear: these behaviors are a sin, immoral, and should be criminalized. As the foundation of society is the family, it is the family unit that is most important for protecting society. Within the family unit, the Church teaches that the basis of the family is a man and woman entering into the sacrament of holy matrimony. It is for this relationship and the ability to procreate that sexual relations exist. Within this relationship, sexual relations are perfectly normal, healthy, and encouraged. Outside of marriage, sexual relations are immoral and go against the teachings of faith, Scripture, and the Church. Therefore, any behavior such as pornography, prostitution, or adultery, moves sexual relations outside of the intimate relationship of a married man and woman, and hence it is immoral and society should criminalize such immoral behavior. While it is recognized that the "enforceability" of this crime is limited, due to privacy protections, it does not change the fact that the behaviors are harmful and destructive to society, and thus should be legislated against.

Finally, and perhaps most difficultly, is understanding the perspective of the Church in regard to gambling. While innocent games of chance are not considered immoral, when the individual deprives his or herself or others of basic means of living and becomes addicted to gambling, it crosses over into immorality. How to legislate in regard to gambling is a tenuous proposition. Even if only allowing for charitable games of chance to be played, when individuals become addicted to even these games, it crosses the realm of immorality. The Catholic Conference of Illinois addressed this problem in 1999 and argued that individuals should first do their own assessment of their enslavement to gambling. That said, they argued that one aspect that should be analyzed is the morality of depending upon state-sponsored gambling as a means of raising funds for the state, and that the advertising of gambling should be regulated so as not to be misleading or deceptively enticing.[69] Finally, they argue that the Church itself should consider its impact on individuals and society when it engages in charitable gambling. While the Catholic perspective on gambling is less clear than the other so-called victimless crimes, it does provide some moral considerations for dealing with this particular public policy issue.

Notes

1. Edwin Schur, *Crimes Without Victims: Deviant Behavior and Public Policy* (Englewood Cliffs, NJ: Prentice Hall, 1965).

2. Edwin Sutherland and Donald Cressey, *Principles of Criminology*, 6th ed. (Philadelphia: J.B. Lippincott Co., 1960), 11.

3. Christopher Z. Mooney, *The Public Clash of Private Values* (New York: Seven Brdiges Press, LLC., 2001).

4. Donald P. Haider-Markel and Kenneth J. Meier, "The Politics of Gay and Lesbian Rights: Expanding the Scope of the Conflict," *The Journal of Politics* 58 (1996): 332-350.

5. Christopher Z. Mooney, *The Public Clash of Private Values* (New York: Seven Brdiges Press, LLC., 2001), 4.

6. Catholic Church, *Catechism of the Catholic Church,* 2nd ed. (Washington, D.C.: United States Conference of Catholic Bishops, 1997), 2207.

7. Catholic Church, *Catechism of the Catholic Church,* 2nd ed. (Washington, D.C.: United States Conference of Catholic Bishops, 1997), 2211.

8. Patrick Moynihan, "Defining Deviancy Down: How We've Become Accustomed to Alarming Levels of Crime and Destructive Behavior," *The American Scholar* (Winter 1993).

9. James Q. Wilson, *Moral Judgment: Does the Abuse Excuse Threaten Our Legal System?* (New York: Basic Books, 1997), 11.

10. Patrick Devlin, *The Enforcement of Morals* (London: Oxford University Press, 1965), 13.

11. As cited in George E. Rush, *The Dictionary of Criminal Justice,* 5th ed. (Guilford, CT: Dushkin/McGraw Hill, 2000), 115-116.

12. Sourcebook of Criminal Justice Statistics, Table 2.44, "Respondent's Perceptions of the Nation's Progress in Coping with Illegal Drugs" http://www.albany.edu/sourcebook/

13. Sourcebook of Criminal Justice Statistics, Table 2.41, "Respondent's Perceptions of the Nation's Progress in Coping with Illegal Drugs" http://www.albany.edu/sourcebook/

14. Sourcebook of Criminal Justice Statistics, Table 2.43, "Attitudes Toward the Level of Spending to Deal with Drug Addiction" http://www.albany.edu/sourcebook/

15. Sourcebook of Criminal Justice Statistics, Table 2.68, "Attitudes Toward Legalization of the Use of Marijuana" http://www.albany.edu/sourcebook/

16. Sourcebook of Criminal Justice Statistics, Table 2.85, "High School Seniors Disapproving of Drug Use, Alcohol Use, and Cigarette Smoking" http://www.albany.edu/sourcebook/

17. Sourcebook of Criminal Justice Statistics, Table 3.86, "Estimated Prevalence of Drug Use During Lifetime" http://www.albany.edu/sourcebook/

18. Federal Bureau of Investigation, *Uniform Crime Reports* (Washington, D.C.: U.S. Government Printing Office, 2003).

19. Office of National Drug Control Policy, *Drug Treatment in the CJ System*

(Washington, D.C.: U.S. GPO, 2001).

20. Sourcebook of Criminal Justice Statistics, Table 6.62, "Drug and Alcoholism Treatment Facilities" http://www.albany.edu/sourcebook/

21. Samuel Walker, *Sense and Nonsense About Crime and Drugs,* 6th ed. (Belmont, CA: Thomson Higher Education, 2006).

22. See for instance the review article M. Douglas Aglin and Yin-Ing Hser, "Treatment of Drug Abuse," *Drugs and Crime,* eds. Tonry and Wilson (Chicago, IL: University of Chicago Press, 1990).

23. Catholic Church, *Catechism of the Catholic Church,* 2nd ed. (Washington, D.C.: United States Conference of Catholic Bishops, 1997), 2291.

24. Catholic Church, *Catechism of the Catholic Church,* 2nd ed. (Washington, D.C.: United States Conference of Catholic Bishops, 1997), 2291.

25. Pontifical Council for the Family, *From Despair to Hope: Family and Drug Addiction* (Libereria Editrice Vaticana, 1992), 6.

26. Pontifical Council for the Family, "Should Drugs Be Legalized?" *The Pope Speaks: The Church Documents Bimonthly* 42, no. 4 (1997): 215.

27. Pope John Paul II, "Message of the Holy Father to Dr. Giorgio Giacomella, Undersecretary-General, Executive Director of the United National International Drug Control Program on the Occasion of the International Day Against Drug Abuse and Illicit Trafficking," *L'Osservatore Romano,* (June 26, 1996): 4.

28. Pontifical Council for the Family, "Should Drugs Be Legalized?" *The Pope Speaks: The Church Documents Bimonthly* 42, no. 4 (1997): 216.

29. Pontifical Council for the Family, "Should Drugs Be Legalized?" *The Pope Speaks: The Church Documents Bimonthly* 42, no. 4 (1997): 217.

30. Pontifical Council for the Family, "Should Drugs Be Legalized?" *The Pope Speaks: The Church Documents Bimonthly* 42, no. 4 (1997): 217.

31. U.S. Conference of Catholic Bishops, *Responsibility, Rehabilitation, and Restoration: A Catholic Perspective on Crime and Criminal Justice* (Washington, D.C.: U.S. Conference of Catholic Bishops, 2000), 41-42.

32. U.S. Conference of Catholic Bishops, *Responsibility, Rehabilitation, and Restoration: A Catholic Perspective on Crime and Criminal Justice* (Washington, D.C.: U.S. Conference of Catholic Bishops, 2000), 42.

33. U.S. Conference of Catholic Bishops, *Responsibility, Rehabilitation, and Restoration: A Catholic Perspective on Crime and Criminal Justice* (Washington, D.C.: U.S. Conference of Catholic Bishops, 2000), 42.

34. National Catholic Register, "Religious People Less Addiction-Prone, Study Finds," *National Catholic Register* (December 2-8, 2001): 2.

35. George E. Rush, *The Dictionary of Criminal Justice,* 5th ed. (Guilford, CT: Dushkin/McGraw Hill, 2000), 257.

36. See for example the PBS show *Frontline's* interview with Dennis McAlpine, http://www.pbs.org/wgbh/pages/frontline/shows/porn/interviews/mcalpine.html

37. See Sourcebook of Criminal Justice Statistics, Table 2.97, "Attitudes Toward Laws Regulating the Distribution of Pornography" http://www.albany.edu/sourcebook/

38. Catholic Church, *Catechism of the Catholic Church,* 2nd ed. (Washington, D.C.: United States Conference of Catholic Bishops, 1997), 2354.

39. Catholic Church, *Catechism of the Catholic Church,* 2nd ed. (Washington, D.C.: United States Conference of Catholic Bishops, 1997), 2354.

40. Catholic Church, *Catechism of the Catholic Church,* 2nd ed. (Washington, D.C.: United States Conference of Catholic Bishops, 1997), 2354.

41. U.S. Catholic Bishops, *Confronting a Culture of Violence: A Catholic Framework for Action* (Washington, D.C.: U.S. Catholic Bishops, 1994), 2.

42. Catholic Church, *Catechism of the Catholic Church,* 2nd ed. (Washington, D.C.: United States Conference of Catholic Bishops, 1997), 2354.

43. Catholic Church, *Catechism of the Catholic Church,* 2nd ed. (Washington, D.C.: United States Conference of Catholic Bishops, 1997), 2354.

44. George E. Rush, *The Dictionary of Criminal Justice,* 5th ed. (Guilford, CT: Dushkin/McGraw Hill, 2000), 272.

45. George E. Rush, *The Dictionary of Criminal Justice,* 5th ed. (Guilford, CT: Dushkin/McGraw Hill, 2000), 272.

46. Proverbs 7:27 (*The New American Bible*).

47. John 8: 1-11 (*The New American Bible*).

48. Catholic Church, *Catechism of the Catholic Church,* 2nd ed. (Washington, D.C.: United States Conference of Catholic Bishops, 1997), 2355.

49. Catholic Church, *Catechism of the Catholic Church,* 2nd ed. (Washington, D.C.: United States Conference of Catholic Bishops, 1997), 2355.

50. Catholic Church, *Catechism of the Catholic Church,* 2nd ed. (Washington, D.C.: United States Conference of Catholic Bishops, 1997), 2355.

51. George E. Rush, *The Dictionary of Criminal Justice,* 5th ed. (Guilford, CT: Dushkin/McGraw Hill, 2000), 7.

52. Willard M. Oliver and James F. Hilgenberg, Jr., *A History of Crime and Criminal Justice in America* (Boston: Allyn & Bacon Publishers, 2005).

53. Samuel Walker, *Sense and Nonsense About Crime and Drugs,* 6th ed. (Belmont, CA: Thomson Higher Education, 2006).

54. Catholic Church, *Catechism of the Catholic Church,* 2nd ed. (Washington, D.C.: United States Conference of Catholic Bishops, 1997), 2360.

55. Catholic Church, *Catechism of the Catholic Church,* 2nd ed. (Washington, D.C.: United States Conference of Catholic Bishops, 1997), 2361.

56. Catholic Church, *Catechism of the Catholic Church,* 2nd ed. (Washington, D.C.: United States Conference of Catholic Bishops, 1997), 2380.

57. Catholic Church, *Catechism of the Catholic Church,* 2nd ed. (Washington, D.C.: United States Conference of Catholic Bishops, 1997), 2380.

58. Catholic Church, *Catechism of the Catholic Church,* 2nd ed. (Washington, D.C.: United States Conference of Catholic Bishops, 1997), 2381.

59. Catholic Church, *Catechism of the Catholic Church,* 2nd ed. (Washington, D.C.: United States Conference of Catholic Bishops, 1997), 2351-2355, 2357-2359, and 2380-2391.

60. George E. Rush, *The Dictionary of Criminal Justice,* 5th ed. (Guilford, CT: Dushkin/McGraw Hill, 2000), 151.

61. Ronald M. Pavalko, *Risky Business: America's Fascination with Gambling* (Belmont, CA: Wadsworth/Thomson Learning, 2000).

62. George E. Rush, *The Dictionary of Criminal Justice,* 5th ed. (Guilford, CT: Dushkin/McGraw Hill, 2000), 151.

63. Federal Bureau of Investigation, *Uniform Crime Reports.* (Washington, D.C.: U.S. Government Printing Office, 2003).

64. Robert F. Meier and Gilbert Geis, *Criminal Justice and Moral Issues* (Los Angeles: Roxbury Publishing Company, 2006), 209.

65. Catholic Church, *Catechism of the Catholic Church,* 2nd ed. (Washington, D.C.: United States Conference of Catholic Bishops, 1997), 2413.

66. Catholic Church, *Catechism of the Catholic Church,* 2nd ed. (Washington, D.C.: United States Conference of Catholic Bishops, 1997), 2413.

67. Earl L. Grinios, *Gambling in America: Costs and Benefits* (New York: Cambridge University Press, 2004); John D. Rosecrance, *Gambling Without Guilt: The Legitimization of an American Pastime* (Pacific Grove, CA: Brooks/Cole, 1988).

68. U.S. Conference of Catholic Bishops, *Responsibility, Rehabilitation, and Restoration: A Catholic Perspective on Crime and Criminal Justice* (Washington, D.C.: U.S. Conference of Catholic Bishops, 2000), 42.

69. Catholic Conference of Illinois, *A Catholic Perspective on Gambling in Illinois* (Springfield, IL: Catholic Conference of Illinois, 1999). Available on-line at http://www.catholicconferenceofillinois.org/bins/site/ftp/Gambling%20Statement.pdf.

Index

About the Author

Willard M. Oliver is an associate professor of criminal justice at Sam Houston State University, Huntsville, Texas. He is the author of several books including *Community-Oriented Policing: A Systemic Approach to Policing, 4th Edition* (2008) and *Community Policing: Classical Readings* (2000). He is also the author of numerous peer-reviewed journal articles. His research interests include policing, crime policy, and criminal justice history. He serves as a Lector for St. Thomas Catholic Church in Huntsville, Texas.